THE ROUTLEDGE COMPANION TO HISTORICAL STUDIES

THE ROUTLEDGE COMPANION TO HISTORICAL STUDIES

Alun Munslow

London and New York

First published 2000
by Routledge
11 New Fetter Lane, London EC4P 4EE

Simultaneously published in the USA and Canada
by Routledge
29 West 35th Street, New York, NY 10001

Routledge is an imprint of the Taylor & Francis Group

Typeset in Galliard by Routledge
Printed and bound in Great Britain by St Edmundsbury Press, Bury St Edmunds, Suffolk.

British Library Cataloguing in Publication Data
A catalogue record for this book is available from the British Library

Library of Congress Cataloging in Publication Data
Munslow, Alun
The Routledge companion to historical studies/Alun Munslow.
p. cm.
Includes bibliographical references (p.) and index.
1. Historiography–History–20th century.
2. History–Philosophy.
I. Title.
D13.M47 1999
907′ .2–dc21 99–27243

ISBN 0–415–18494–0 (hbk)
ISBN 0–415–18495–9 (pbk)

Dedicated to my Parents
Beatrice Munslow
(15.9.1922 – 13.3.1999)
and
Samuel Wallace Munslow
(18.11.1924 – 3.11.1997)

CONTENTS

AUTHOR'S INTRODUCTION ix

LIST OF ENTRIES xiii

History today: critical perspectives 1
Entries A–Z 21

BIBLIOGRAPHY 235

INDEX 263

AUTHOR'S INTRODUCTION

Rethinking history

In one important respect at least, this is no different from any other history book in that it is written from a particular perspective. That perspective is the result of my experience and understanding of the post-empiricist challenge to history. As a history student in the late 1960s I was immersed in the then vogue for the social sciences, as social history became the constructionist successor to reconstructionist political and economic history. Then, in my final year as a postgraduate student, in 1973, the American historian Hayden White published his book *Metahistory*. Although its rethinking of the impact of the literary composition of history was not recognised until the early 1980s it is now viewed as signalling history's linguistic turn. But that decade also witnessed the emergence of cultural and women's history resulting from developments in European philosophy as well as cultural and linguistic theory. Although I was hardly aware of it at that time, the basic model of history that had been established and popularised as the direct result of the Enlightenment and its empiricist and positivist social science thinking, and of which social history had been but the latest manifestation, was being radically challenged.

With these developments in mind I have tried to provide a short, convenient and yet critical introduction to the keywords, concepts and issues central to the rethinking of history that has taken place since the early 1970s. In my experience the major practical obstacle to understanding the contemporary challenge(s) to the standard model of historical study is the need for students of history to acquaint themselves with intellectual developments in other humanities disciplines. To understand the challenge to history requires a knowledge not only of the accepted basics of conventional historical explanation and method, but also the ideas of key philosophers, theorists and practitioners of history, and be aware of ideas in cultural and critical theory, literature and linguistics. This *Companion* is intended to introduce and contribute to this rethinking about history.

While this rethinking in 'doing history' has been most obvious in the development of cultural and women's history, it has entailed a far more fundamental reassessment of how we come to know things about the past. The result has been to ask serious questions about the discipline's empirical foundations, the nature and functioning of evidence, the role of the historian and his/her use of social theory, the significance of narrative as a form or mode of explanation, and the more radical post-empiricist idea that history is as much an invention of the past as a discovery of it. This has also raised other questions about objectivity and truth in historical study, the methodology required to guarantee them, and the impact of the form of representation in which its conclusions are described.

This rethinking of history focuses on two competing claims. The modernist claim is that 'proper' history's boundaries are those of the limits of its procedures for objectively understanding the evidence and creating truthful interpretations, and the postmodernist counter-claim that the frontiers of history can be expanded by moving beyond the empirical to fully explore the logic that it is the culturally situated historian who, in his/her composition of the history text, is producing an invented narrative form of knowledge. It is the implications of these claims that this *Companion* addresses.

The *Companion*

The entries are ordered alphabetically and to ease cross-reference all are written in **bold** when they are first cross-referenced in other entries. Thus, in the entry on the 'linguistic turn', you will find references to Richard **Rorty**, **historical explanation**, **objectivity** and **truth**, all of which are entries in their own right. In addition to a full bibliography each entry has recommended readings. A substantial index is also provided. By the fact of their selection and their definitions the entries are intended to demonstrate my assumptions and conclusions about the disputed nature of history today. My judgements reflect how I perceive the post-empiricist challenge to conventional thinking about the past. In the entry on 'evidence', for example, I acknowledge how the 'rules of evidence' are conventionally regarded as necessarily based on the assumption that **empiricism** constitutes history's basic procedure. My position, however, offers an alternative perspective. As an epistemological sceptic of a post-empiricist kind, I am prompted to ask if the 'rules of evidence' ought not to be viewed as a choice rather than a given around which there cannot be disagreement. In other words, empiricism is an option, not a prerequisite to history. I have also provided an introductory chapter, called 'History today: critical perspectives', in which I have tried to set out the state of the discipline as it appears to me at the present time. This commentary chapter, which is also cross-referenced, may be read before, during or after consulting any of the entries. While it is not, of course, necessary to read this chapter at all, it does offer the overall rationale for the *Companion* and explains more fully my particular perspective on how to rethink history in light of the post-empiricist challenge.

[illegible]

LIST OF ENTRIES

A

A priori/a posteriori
Author

B

Barthes, Roland

C

Carr, E.H.
Causation
Class
Colligation
Collingwood, R.G.
Concepts in history
Constructionist history
Continental philosophy
Covering laws
Croce, Benedetto
Cultural history

D

Deconstructionist history
Derrida, Jacques
Discourse

E

Elton, Geoffrey
Empiricism
Emplotment

Enlightenment, The
Episteme
Epistemology
Event
Evidence

F

Facts
Form and content
Foucault, Michel

H

Hegel, G.W.F.
Hermeneutics
Historical explanation
Historical imagination
Historicism
Historiography

I

Inference
Intentionality

K

Kant, Immanuel

L

Liberal humanism
Linguistic turn

M

Metanarrative
Metaphysics
Modernism

N

Narrative
Nietzsche, Friedrich

O

Objectivity
Ontology

P

Positivism
Postmodernism

R

Reality/realistic effect
Reconstructionist history
Relativism
Rorty, Richard

S

Structuralism

T

Teleology
Trope/figuration
Truth

V

Vico, Giambattista

W

White, Hayden
Women's history

HISTORY TODAY

CRITICAL PERSPECTIVES

The empirical foundation: realist history

Modernism, as the product of the seventeenth- and eighteenth-century **Enlightenment**, produced the dominance of certain ways of thinking about how we create knowledge. **Postmodernism** in the late twentieth century has directly questioned those ways of thinking. The two central modernist avenues to knowledge are sceptical **empiricism** and **positivism**, both of which directly influenced the creation of history as a discipline. Empiricism, defined as the observation of the **evidence** of our senses and the **inference** of its meaning, is the prerequisite to positivism defined as the experimental derivation of the laws that govern the sensible world (the world known through the senses). Modernist or 'proper' history bases its claims to legitimacy as a discipline by discovering the meaning to the pattern of past reality: a meaning that is enduring and that can be described faithfully by the suitably distanced historian. The historian is equipped, therefore, to faithfully recover that which is gone. The historian's cultural significance resides in his/her ability to know the meaning of the past. Without this, so modernist history thinking claims, we are condemned to live in a perpetual present, an everlasting now without a sense of who we are and having abandoned the lives of those people who came before us. It is this claim of needing to know the past as it actually was, in order to know ourselves, that has been challenged through the post-empiricist revolution in history thinking. The challenge to modernist history has been to deprivilege its thinking as *the* way to knowing about our changing selves over time, and that our empirically derived knowledge of the past is an indispensable feature of our lives.

For modernist – unlike postmodernist – history, the written representation of empiricism's discoveries is an issue less significant than the verification and comparison of the evidence. In other words reality or the content of the past determines the form of history in the shape of the historical **narrative** (see FORM AND CONTENT). This determinist and reductive empiricist priority of content over form was clearly expressed throughout the Enlightenment. Take the example of the Scottish philosopher and historian (of the common-sense school) Adam Ferguson (1723–1816) and his influential entry on History in the Second Edition to the *Encyclopaedia Britannica*

(1780). Ferguson's view of history was emblematic of his age. He viewed history as the account of **facts** arranged in the true order in which they actually took place, together with their **causation** and effects. This definition stated what was, for Ferguson, the 'natural' desire to know the past and, by maintaining the distance between observer and observed, to impartially and objectively represent such domesticated knowledge in the language of the **discourse** of history (see OBJECTIVITY).

Ferguson, in his modernist desire to exercise control over that which is 'out there', was, like his friend the sceptical empiricist philosopher David Hume, self-reflexive enough to realise that he had to organise his knowledge conceptually before (re-)presenting it as history (see CONCEPTS IN HISTORY). This process of conceptually organising the past I shall henceforth refer to as 'the-past-as-history'. As I think Ferguson realised, 'the past' and 'history' are not the same. Ferguson understood that there was a paradox or inconsistency/contradiction in modernist thinking and it was the existence of the objective and yet engaged historian. This discrepancy, that historians write history but can be objective (see HISTORIOGRAPHY), is unavoidable in modernist thought because one of the key features of Enlightenment-inspired modernism is the eighteenth-century bourgeois **liberal humanism** that places the rational, purposive and undivided thinking self at the centre of all things – the intentional and centred subject, 'Man', 'the self', 'I' (see INTENTIONALITY). The 'I' was also taken to be, as convenience dictated, 'reality' or 'the evidence'.

The autonomy inscribed in this ideology of the 'I' or the 'evidence' gave birth to many dualisms that still ground much Western analytical thinking, in addition to the inconsistency of the separation of the self/subject from the other/object, but also the conscious from the unconscious, fact from fiction, **truth** from invention, world from word, signifier from signified, real from the unreal, and presence from non-presence. In the eighteenth century the philosophy of liberal humanism, as the ideology of mercantile and eventually market industrial capitalism, self-interestedly promoted the notion of the white, masculine and preferably middle-class, eurocentric, freedom-loving, self-conscious, knowing subject who could exercise sovereignty over himself, his environment, his future, and his past (the masculine self, for example, exercising authority over the feminine other) (see WOMEN'S HISTORY). Central to the ideology of the 'I' is its belief in its own universality. The inconsistency is that the centred knowing subject, as the originator of and authority for knowledge, can still be capable of separating him ('I') or itself ('evidence') from the process of knowledge creation. The aim of this bourgeois ideological manoeuvre was to establish credentials for the argument that this is *the* natural, unalterable and universal process for knowing while it was actually fixing as immutable certain preferred or assumed social, economic and cultural conditions for that knowing.

For Ferguson **historical explanation**, although it must begin with direct reference to the known **event**, the need for conceptualisation as well as its description, required history to be subject to the control of the historian. Ferguson recognised that as a result each historian would, in all likelihood, describe the past differently. But while, as he said, one historian may choose to build it around the names of statesmen and warriors, another scholars and men of letters, this was still a matter of content rather than form. Avoiding the implications of the modernist inconsistency was easily done, in fact, by insisting that factualism and its written representation were synonymous. Sceptical though he was about his evidence and its ability to reveal reality to him, Ferguson believed the language of historical facts was quite adequate to convey meaning through the pen of the knowing subject. Ferguson believed that if his historical narrative fell short of an absolute reflection of reality it had more to do with the shortcomings of the evidence and the historian's inference, than his powers of representation. Empirical procedures thus avoided the relativist implications of the modernist inconsistency (see RELATIVISM). The implication of this has been singularly important: namely that objectivity and truthful knowledge of reality can be achieved by the honest historian, as revealed in the parallel or continuity/conformity between his/her explanation and the shape of the narrative. The match between explanation and the language of description should be as high as possible. The tighter that connection, the better the history.

As with all modernist disciplines, therefore, history possesses a **metaphysics** that comprises a coherent structure of inquiry into being and reality through the knowing subject (in this case the historian). The architecture of history's metaphysics is that its content (the study, through the evidence, of change over time) dictates a way of thinking about past reality and existence, that which philosophers refer to as its **ontology**. In turn, how modernist-inspired historians are able to conceptualise or categorise their knowledge of it is referred to as its **epistemology**. The techniques deployed to go about acquiring this knowledge constitutes the methodology or procedures of historical explanation. Ontologically modernist history holds that we can know, through the universal-centred knowing subject, the reality of the-past-as-history. This translates in turn into the epistemology of empiricism, positivism and inference. This is modernist history's epistemological turn.

Ferguson chose to believe that empiricism and positivism, as the key features of the metaphysics of 'proper' history, were founded on a particular set of assumptions. Upholding its truth-acquiring self-belief 'proper (i.e. modernist) history' depends on four assumptions: first, that there is a past reality that is intrinsically knowable by the knowing subject through the discovery of its structural principles; second, historical truth is found in the referential correspondence of the historians' facts to that structural reality, as derived through the conceptual procedure of inference; third, language is up to the job of written representation; and fourth, from these prior beliefs one absolutely basic law of human behaviour becomes evident: by knowing things about the real past we can reasonably conclude, as liberal humanists, that individuals act rationally and possess purposive agent intentionality. These four assumptions directly dictate the procedures of modernist historical explanation. These procedures can be seen in the methodology of hypothesis-testing, the **colligation** and verification of the evidence, and the eventual determination of meaning through the establishment of causation. The conclusions inferred from this process of empiricism tempered by conceptualisation can then be offered in the form of truthful and justified historical descriptions.

This thinking derives from that of the German philosopher Immanuel **Kant** (1724–1804) who argued it is only when the knowing subject strikes the right balance between concept and fact will he/she know the truth about reality. Accordingly, modernist historical procedures are founded specifically on the process philosophers refer to as abductive inference. Abduction is the imaginative derivation of meaning from a limited range of evidence. This process has three necessary steps: first, the outline of hypothetical but potentially explanatory concepts; second, the colligation or organisation of the facts through each concept in turn; finally, the verification of the most plausible/probable explanation by yet further reference to evidence and concept. The aim of this process is to find the pattern in what may seem at first blush to be disordered events. This process thus effects a convincing and meaningful explanation. This seeking out of probable connections is literally reasoning after the event. We should be quite clear here: the metaphysics of modernist history consists of an ontology of subject-centred knowable reality, accompanied by a dedicated epistemology and methodology of explanation that requires the separation of the discovery of meaning from writing it up as history (see HISTORIOGRAPHY).

The empiricist method of historical explanation, being explanation after the event, requires that historians distinguish between a priori and a posteriori forms of explanation (see A PRIORI/A POSTERIORI). A posteriori explanations derive knowledge from the evidence through the three-step abductive inference process. Additionally, a posteriori thinking invokes Kant's belief that, because reality is independent of historians and their representations of it, history can know the truth of reality without reference to a known or desired outcome (see TELEOLOGY). Such teleological explanations are to be avoided, not because they necessarily preclude the truthful explanation of the intentions of people in the past, but because such explanations have tended to be open to the charge of wish-fulfilment on the part of those historians who are trying to discover history's inner directedness. To avoid this, the 'proper' modernist historian views historical knowledge as being created by factual inference and ordered and classified by the rational mind of the knowing subject rather than through a priori or propositional logic, the truth of which may be determined either by a known outcome, that is driven teleologically, or more unusually without reference to factual reality at all.

It should be clear by now that modernist historical methodology is an evidence-based empirical and a posteriori study, the aim of which is to generate a truthful and objective historical explanation founded upon the discovery of the relationship between causation and its effects. It suggests its means of operation is a practical, pragmatic and constrained positivism in the application of only the most well-attested theories of behaviour, or **covering laws**, which allow historians to explain individual human actions essentially as one would events in the natural world by acknowledging their regularity of occurrence (see POSITIVISM). Individual events are often explained as examples of a commonly occurring category (of events); that is, there is a pattern to be discovered in apparently disordered events. Not surprisingly, given the strength of the appeal of liberal humanism, the most common cause of patterned behaviour in modernist human experience is agent intentionality as explained according to the (liberal humanist) ontology of rational action.

In the last quarter of the twentieth century, self-reflexive modernist thinking, or call it postmodern rethinking if you prefer, suggests there is no longer a consensus about the ontological nature of existence and, therefore, the epistemology of history. History's procedures for the derivation of meaning are no longer universally accepted. Not all historians share the same measurement as to what it is that constitutes history (Hunt 1998). It is this uncertainty that has defined what are the three main approaches to history today, **reconstructionist history**, **constructionist history** and **deconstructionist history** (Munslow 1997a). Reconstructionists, like the British historians Geoffrey **Elton** and Arthur Marwick, and the Americans Jack Hexter and Gertrude Himmelfarb, are thin on the ground these days because they profess to believe that a genuine knowledge of empirical reality is achievable (Elton 1967, 1991; Hexter 1972; Marwick 1989 [1970]; Himmelfarb 1989). Knowledge of empirical past reality is obtained, so they argue, through a restrained abductive inference that is soberly referential, shrewdly anti-theoretical (because concepts usually beg questions of the evidence), and non-judgemental. Its empirical procedures deliberately detach questions of knowledge (epistemology) from being (ontology), keeping knowing and being separate – the modernist inconsistency. This foundational thinking makes the centred knowing subject the only route to objective historical knowledge. The intentions of people long dead can be known by this method (and it must be perceived as a (the?) method rather than an ontologically situated epistemology) because people in the past were just like us – rational, purposive and knowing creatures. Without any discernible embarrassment reconstructionism accepts, as a gift from nature, a liberal humanist rationality translated into the epistemological gap, which is claimed does and must exist between the knowing subject and the object of knowledge.

One of the more obvious, if not cheap, ploys of postmodernist historians has been to attack the easy target of reconstructionist history. The fact that not many historians today admit to being active or consenting reconstructionists has blunted the postmodernist message. While historians still seek the evidence to a knowable past, most claim not to be doing it in the manner of a knowing subject intent on discovering *the* meaning of an event. Few historians fall into the trap of viewing the past and history as one in the same. Instead the majority assert they are practical or critical realists who know the implications of the modernist inconsistency, and they are also aware of the constraints imposed by history's textualism in both its documentary raw materials, as well as their own processed secondary writings. However, the mainstream contend that neither the modernist contradiction nor history's textualist basis means it is impossible to do proper history that, these days, must be a version or subspecies of constructionist history.

Constructionist history comes with a vast range of subjects and a medley of complex theoretical models. The relevance of constructionist or mainstream history lies in its truth value, which is demonstrated by its conceptually informed empiricism and the correspondence theory of knowledge (Thompson 1963, 1978; Tosh 1991; Appleby *et al.* 1994; Kirk 1995; Callinicos 1995; Windschuttle 1995; Evans 1997a; Bunzl 1997; Iggers 1997; Snooks 1998; McCullagh 1998; Warren 1998; Zagorin 1999). The constructionist historian, unlike his/her reconstructionist cousin, does not just cut and paste evidence with a minimum of conceptual glue. In his late 1970s attack on what he saw as the pernicious effects of what was a **structuralism** out of control in the work of French Marxist Louis Althusser, the British social historian E.P. Thompson summarised and set the standard for Anglo-American constructionist historians with a modified, liberal humanist-inspired, and materialist correspondence theory of history. In defending his (self-proclaimed humanist) version of Marxist history as a continuous dialogue between theory and empiricism as *the* way to recover the real (rather than the empirically impoverished structuralism of Althusser), Thompson renewed his vows to the belief in the knowing subject and rational action theory.

The post-empiricist challenge to Thompsonian constructionism has subsequently and primarily rested on questioning the intellectual assumption of referentiality and representationalism. What is claimed to be novel in this challenge can, in fact, be read in the work of a number of historians and philosophers of history stretching back to the Neapolitan philosopher Giambattista **Vico** (1668–1744) and re-emerging in the work of the Italian historian and historiographer Benedetto **Croce** (1866–1952), the British philosopher-archaeologist-historian R.G. **Collingwood** (1889–1943) and the British historian of the Soviet Union and successful part-time philosopher of history E.H. **Carr** (1892–1982). Each in their own way questioned the representationalist correspondence theory of knowledge that supports all four assumptions of proper historians. These critics confronted the claim that documentary sources are knowable because, in spite of their patent textuality and rhetorically compositional character, they possess a transparency of meaning

(Bunzl 1997; Poster 1997; Munslow 1997b). Both reconstructionists and constructionists read the documents, therefore, for the reality they reflect intending to re-present their meaning in a linguistically unambiguous historical text. What I have called the deconstructionist rendering of history disputes the possibility of this written representational correspondence between the word and the world. In other words, deconstructionist historians are rethinking modernist history's priority of content over form that results from the distinction of the ontological and the epistemological but, and this is most important, they are not offering this reversal as an alternative better and more truthful process. When modernist historians ask how else can we know the reality of the past, that is, its truth, except through the priority of its content, deconstructionist historians respond that it is not a matter of 'how else' because there is no single privileged route to it.

This reorientation has produced the so-called **linguistic turn** that has moved historical explanation to a discussion about the part played by language in producing and shaping historical meaning: what the American philosopher Richard **Rorty** (1931–) calls 'making true' (Rorty 1991: 4; Rorty 1992 [1967]). The issue is about the extent to which truth, objectivity and justified descriptions are feasible once we reverse the priority of empirical content (the past) over its form (the-past-as-history). Just how can we grasp the meaning of events through the representational form of the historical narrative? This raises what Hayden **White** (1928–) referred to in his 1973 book *Metahistory* as the poetics of history. By this he means an alternative to the conventional constructionist or practical realist theories or concepts of history customarily deployed to squeeze out the truth of the past. White is, for example, particularly antagonistic to Marxian history's assumption that in the evidence it has discovered *the* truth of the past that it can then successfully reveal as *the* narrative of historical materialism (White 1995).

The alarming result of rethinking the priority of content over form, of the past over history, is the collapse of what have hitherto been regarded as the partitions between history, fiction, perspective and ideology. The linguistic or narrativist turn has revitalised the relativist and/or anti-representational implications of the modernist inconsistency/contradiction. By placing form before content it means that what is also highly significant in creating a sense of the past are the ways in which historians organise, configure and prefigure it. The important issue becomes *how* we constitute those informing concepts, classifications, theories, arguments and categories that we use to order and explain historical evidence and generate meaning from it. Doing history in the post-empiricist age requires turning to the epistemological or explanatory power of our narratives that, in turn, means re-examining the ontological-epistemological relationship.

The postmodern reversal: the real end of history or the end of realist history?

Recent variants of constructionist history, like the New Cultural History and post-feminist gender history, have grown not only as the result of the deliberate acts of the historian behaving like a highly self-conscious **author**, purposefully borrowing ideas and concepts from other disciplines (like anthropology, sociology and philosophy), but also as a result of the wider intellectual movement of post-structuralism that emerged from literary theory in the 1970s (Hunt 1989). This has become the vanguard of the post-empiricist rethinking of history by accepting the full implications of seeing *both* the past and the-past-as-history as knowable only through the model of narrative discourse. Rethinking history as a discourse through which meaning is created rather than discovered stresses the cultural processes of knowledge creation and organisation, rather than simply seeing knowledge as some kind of discoverable given that is capable of a truth-insightful naturalistic representation. This is an alternative view that sees history as a truth-making, rather than a truth-finding, discourse. As such, history is conceived of as producing subjectivity. Such a rethinking of history, as critics like Keith Jenkins and Frank Ankersmit argue, confronts the determining knowing subject with the situation that it is not he/she (in the shape of the liberal humanist) who is the privileged origin of meaning, but that other equally or even more important forces are at work (Jenkins 1991, 1995, 1997, 1999; Ankersmit 1994). In effect it is not the past or the evidence that originates history defined as a truth-duplicating process; instead all we have is a non-privileged cultural discourse I call the-past-as-history. We can not 'get back' to a situation before the-past-as-history began to view the naturally occurring past. The question is, then, what is the nature of the discursive and culturally determined character of the-past-as-history? It is revealed, I suggest, in the implications of the postmodern reversal of content and form.

This reversal, that rather than the existence of a knowable past reality there is nothing but the-past-as-history, is derived from the work of European cultural historians and philosophers of history like Benedetto Croce, Jacques **Derrida** (b. 1930) and Michel **Foucault** (1926–84) (D.D. Roberts 1995). Jacques Derrida, heavily indebted to the German founding father of the idealist strand of **continental philosophy**, the philosopher Friedrich **Nietzsche** (1844–1900), rejects Anglo-Western analytical philosophy's preoccupation with the knowing subject, and its translation, as he describes it, in the power of presence in its explanations. According to Derrida this presence reveals itself in the precedence given to speech (content) over writing (form). This misleads us into believing that (the presence of) the speaker is evidence for the fixed origin of, among other things, author and agent intentionality and meaning, and that there must be a given or fixed connection between the signifier (the word) and the signified (the world) so we can legitimately believe in empirically derived essential meanings/truth of the referent. What I have called deconstructionist history does not stop at challenging the correspondence theory of knowledge and its corollary the representational theory of perception, therefore, but following Derrida, the ontological belief that knowledge emerges from the intentional, centred individual and objective knowing subject.

The deconstructionist rethinking of the conditions and procedures for generating historical explanations is under obligation to the tradition of continental philosophy and a revised **hermeneutics** (the study of the nature of interpretation), which questions that the truth of external reality is waiting to be 'discovered' and is not the result of the human mind or its facilities for perception. Much of Derrida's deconstructive criticism hinges not, therefore, on just rejecting the idea that our understanding of reality is not dependent on its description, but also the whole range of assumptions and preconceptions upon which modernist history is built: rational propositional logic, the correspondence theory of knowledge, empiricism, the contextualisation of evidence, representationalism, the truthful statement, inference, and social theory constructionism.

One reason for the unpopularity of deconstructionist history hitherto (apart from the fact it doubts objective truth will emerge through the empirical process of prising open what is assumed to be a knowable past) has been the necessity to grasp some (fairly basic it has to be said) philosophy. In order to make an informed judgement on post-empiricist history, historians ought to become acquainted with the consequences of continental philosophy's divergence from the analytical tradition. This really began with the rethinking by G.W.F. **Hegel** (1770–1831) of Kant's epistemology or theory of knowledge. In opposing Kant, Hegel noted the historical situatedness, or what Nietzsche would later call the perspectivism of knowledge, specifically that the self, as the knowing subject, is not natural or universal, is not a given, but is a construction of time, place, discourse and ideology. This suggests that while an observer may not choose to doubt the existence of reality, its true meaning can not be known or represented absolutely or, in fact, anywhere near the level of certainty that empiricism imagines flows from the contact between the word and the world.

Indeed, it can not be other if we accept that the autonomous subject (that believes this) is itself a creation of a particular ideology and/or set of cultural practices (that demands this belief). It follows that, ontologically speaking, Kant's transcendent reason must be subject to a greater or lesser degree of relativism – to time, location, ideas, material circumstance, teleology, personal ambition, gender, race, language use, and so forth. So knowledge of the past becomes, at the very least, relative not only to the evidence or to the reasonable correspondence of word and world but also its composition as a narrative that exists within the larger discourse of the cultural practice I have called the-past-as-history. For Hegel the self-conscious knowing subject and the object of his/her attention must be ontologically related because they exist within the same cultural ground, discourse or practice. The modernist contradiction and much of the intellectual trappings of modernist thinking are swept away if we choose to view the knowing subject as no longer privileged, as itself determined rather than determining, and if we accept that knowing (as a self-conscious act) plays a crucial part in our understanding of being (Mensch 1997).

This Hegelian and Nietzschean idealism divided into several related domains of criticism in the twentieth century, notably a revised hermeneutics and a voguish post-structuralism. Hermeneutics defined as the process of textual interpretation was offered in a revised form by German philosopher Martin Heidegger who suggested we grasp the meaning of texts by virtue of our being in the world. Rethinking the ontological-epistemological relationship is particularly evident in the post-structuralist work of Derrida and Foucault. As a direct consequence of their doubts over the knowing subject, both rejected the possibility of a mirror-like picturing of external reality by the interpreter and the fixing of what Derrida described as the transcendental signified or ultimate meaning. They conclude that history, like all forms of cultural knowledge, is primarily about the uses of power and ideology, as well as the failure of representation. Whatever history is, it is not a culturally neutral depiction of past reality. Once historians come to terms with the full implications of this, history becomes the-past-as-history. History starts out as an empty signifier but does not remain so for very long. It is filled with the meanings and definitions we want. It is not a naturally occurring given.

The debates between representationalist and anti-representationalist philosophers that began in the early twentieth century with the likes of Ludwig Wittgenstein (in his later phase), Martin Heidegger and John Dewey, and developed more recently with Donald Davidson, W.V. Quine, David Dummett, Wilfred Sellars and Richard Rorty, have never had much impact on practising historians. Apart from the empiricist suspicion that dabbling in speculative philosophy is ultimately dangerous to the health, it is the metaphysics of its four assumptions that demand it must be in touch with the truth defined as correspondence to reality. Although this full-strength epistemological absolutism is cut by sceptical empiricism, there is still no modernist alternative to truth defined as correspondence to reality.

Deconstructionists, however, do not demand such a metaphysics. Truth is not just an empirical phenomenon. They would say you only have to look at mainstream constructionist history to see that. Not sharing either modernist ontology (the knowing subject) or epistemology (that places content before form), deconstructionist or post-empiricist historians do not think the fissure between truth and its demonstration is resolvable by empiricism alone. Instead they resort to ethical decision-making; that is, historical meaning flows from what it is good or socially responsible to believe *about* the evidence of the past, rather than discover its *true* moral content. To discover the meaning of the Holocaust or to correct the prejudice of masculinist modernist epistemology is not just dependent on facts, but on the belief that they are wrong in a moral sense. Facts are an integral part of the ethical and cultural landscape. Those who derive and deploy them do so with moral claims in mind. Reconstructionist, constructionist and deconstructionist approaches to history are ethical as much as epistemological positions. Beyond the simple factual or truth-conditional statement, historical truth is ethically situated, culturally dependent, and rhetorically created. Historical truth should, perhaps, be defined pragmatically as a term of commendation rather than as signifying an epistemology that can access the intrinsic meaning of nature (Rorty 1991: 21–34;

Rethinking History: The Journal of Theory and Practice 1998, Special Issue, 2(3)).

Before the advent of the postmodernist intellectual movements of hermeneutics, post-structuralism and post-empirical deconstructionism, there was, therefore, little reflection on truth beyond its correspondence definition. It fell primarily to Hayden White to point out that history can not fathom the intrinsic nature of the past because it is a rendered knowledge that creates its own reality through its composition and construction as a contemporary or historicist text (see HISTORICISM). The past thus influences history; it does not determine it. Post-structuralism, which rejects the modernist idea of the existence of deep structures that organise the world, and that makes knowledge of the real possible, specifically addresses how we use language, how language uses us and, most significantly, language's inadequacy as a mirror of reality (Rorty 1979). For writing the-past-as-history post-structuralism raises, therefore, the issue of how figuration and rhetoric directly determine the power of the narrative to create meaning.

The cultural, gendered and ideological positioning of language, as focused through the self of the historian (traditionally the white, male, eurocentric, and bourgeois centred knowing subject) are constraints that inference and the referential truth-conditional statement can not side-step. History, like all cultural discourses, is an inherently and intensely relativist activity. The cold water of the post-empiricist reversal may be seen in how deconstructionists, and increasingly constructionists, reject the belief that history, through its claim to representational authority, must correspond to *the* objectively knowable past. This is not, as some scare-mongering realists still like to suggest, to deny the factualism of the past (Warren 1998; Zagorin 1999). Denying factualism results in the monstrosity of Holocaust denial and propaganda versions of the-past-as-history. The deconstructionist historical consciousness is concerned instead with the relativism that exists in the process of creating the meanings of the-past-as-history precisely because it is a cultural practice, a discourse subject to other discourses. Deconstructionist history is not anti-factual but is intent on exploring how the meaning(s) of facts are constituted through their organisation. Consequently it welcomes the ever more widespread acknowledgement of the (rather mundane?) observation that it has never been the past that has produced varieties of history like those of **class**, or **cultural history**, or women's history. Instead it should be openly acknowledged that it is historians who author those histories as (very often) ethical ways of balancing or countering the prejudices of the modernist male and individualist history of which they disapprove – as ways of commending the truth of the-past-as-history as a moral as much as an epistemological act.

Because it expresses the idea of the end of realist history rather than the real end of history, it is the question of narrative that is at the heart of the reversal. The deconstructive or Nietzschean-inspired incredulity about the epistemological basis of realist history has meant confronting the narrative form of historical writing and the array of **metanarrative** questions this entails. Do we live our lives as narratives, do historians re-tell *the* narrative of past events, or do historians invent *a* narrative in order to impose a conceptual sense of order on the sublime character of what once was and is now irrevocably gone (Danto 1965; White 1987; Mink 1978; Jenkins 1991; Ankersmit 1994)? Other metanarrative issues focus on the fiction–reality polarity. The insecurity of the modernist notion that all historical texts must not only reference external reality but be knowable as such prompts the question of whether historians should *primarily* address the cultural and language use forms in which history is written and conceived? Should historians rethink their evidence, not as the privileged centre of knowledge, but as *one* site of knowledge among *many*? The traces of the past can not give exclusive historical knowledge, only an impression of pastness.

In other words, why not challenge the epistemological straitjacket of the priority of empirical content over narrative form? As both Nietzsche and later Derrida argued, the best reason for this post-empirical reversal is that knowledge of the real is understood through its metaphoric character (D.D. Roberts 1995; Mensch 1997). The assumption that our knowledge of the real past flows from the reciprocity of the concept and the empirical is nothing more than what the French cultural commentator Roland **Barthes** (1915–80) memorably called the reality effect of figurative language (Barthes 1957, 1967, 1977 and 1988) (see REALITY/REALISTIC EFFECT; TROPE/FIGURATION). Because it is a second-hand narrative knowledge, Barthes concluded (in contradiction to the conclusion of Ferguson and all subsequent sceptical empiricists) that history is epistemologically little different in its imaginary narration from novels or plays. The consequence is that history, precisely because of its preconfigured narrative form, can never be more than a referential illusion (Bann 1984). This is famously and spectacularly seen in the way the vast bulk of historical narratives – even self-reflexive constructionist history – almost invariably omit the historian as author, the 'I', in favour of the 'real' source of historical knowledge, the evidence. This procedure, claims Barthes, is intended to sustain the distinction of knower and known (built on the modernist inconsistency) in order to retain history's claim to empiricist objectivity and its truth-knowing status.

At this point deconstructionist historians submit that sceptical-empiricism can not escape (in addition to the problematic status of its referentiality) the pre-figurative character of narrative. The historical narrative is never able to evade its prefiguration be it through the rhetorical use of language, the deployment of rational action theory as a historical argument, or any other kind of political, ethical, gendered, post-colonial, feminist, post-feminist, or whatever personal preference of the historian. Deconstructionists insist it is not enough for historians to note history's constraints as a cultural discourse while at the same time invoking, as an escape clause, the belief that its empirical and inferential procedures will preclude untruthful interpretations. Deconstructionists hold that history's priorities should be ontological, anti-epistemological and rhetorical. Rethinking the nature of history in this way not only reverses history's metaphysical status, but will not allow that history has been radicalised when all we have done is maybe tweak its methods or import yet another bright theoretical idea from anthropology or sociology.

Post-empiricist history recognises, therefore, that history is a literary performance. It is first and foremost a deliberate and calculated written act on the part of the historian rather than a neutral reflection or correspondence. Modernist history's claim to a mirror-like referentiality in its narratives (*the* narrative of the historian (form) reflects *the* narrative in the past (content)), and hence its capacity to discover the truth, can not be sustained because of its status as an authored version of the past. Post-empiricist history is thus the historian's impression of pastness. The way in which the historian comes to terms with the loss of the unreconstructable what once was. In creating and acknowledging such an impressionistic process, and in recognising the parallel existence of the historian, history itself becomes the other, the 'alterior' (a mix of alternative and other). It can not be identical to reality for it is an absence of, or an alternative to, reality. It can no longer conform to empirical definitions of truth. Historical truth is henceforth beyond the simply referential.

Historical truth, defined as that which people commend as being good within a defined community at a particular time, is a view much associated with the American philosopher Richard Rorty. Denying he is a relativist, Rorty insists he is an anti-representationalist whose aim is to highlight the historicist nature of knowledge in the humanities and social sciences. When Rorty claims historical knowledge and the assumptions that underpin it are historicist, he means that every historical epoch or **episteme** possesses its own peculiar (rather than manifesting transcendent) measures through which it resolves what was, and is, truthful knowledge. The definition of historical truth for me is that, while a historical statement possesses referentiality, its meaning is the product of its linguistic composition as well as the discursive structure of the epoch in which it was produced. The concept of the episteme is central to post-empiricist criticism in that it alerts us not only that all historical periods organise the acquisition and utilisation of knowledge according to differing criteria and for distinct purposes, but, as Michel Foucault suggests, that the criteria for knowledge creation invariably revolve around the social distribution of power. Historians do tend to use 'the facts' to create their own meanings. If they did not then would history be much less revisionist (re-visionist) than it is?

The episteme signifies the interconnections that exist between all the separate discourses (for example those of science, medicine, philosophy, literature or history) that together generate those ontological and epistemological assumptions that mediate the power structures upon which they are built. The nature of the episteme reveals itself through the figurative and narrative structure of human thought. It is the troping process, or the way in which, say, the meaning of the Nazi-engineered Holocaust is created through the human capacity to recognise and articulate difference, which gives each episteme its peculiar cultural and epistemological signature. Like the historical agents whose lives they reconstruct/construct/deconstruct, no historian can escape from his/her own epoch. As a result all written history is inflected by the textualised epistemic gravity well that conditions the historian's existence (ontology) and production of the-past-as-history (epistemology and methodology). It is being captured in time, space, culture and language that precludes genuine knowing but, most importantly, true meaning. Can any amount of referentiality avoid that?

As both Foucault and the leading philosopher of the linguistic turn Hayden White suggest, historians are epochal as well as textual creatures and as such will prefigure the historical field accordingly. Historians will, therefore, be influenced by the ontological and epistemological assumptions of the present. These assumptions, like the four that are foundational to modernist history, are established and made manifest as the historian brings his/her narrative, conceptual and ethical explanatory strategies to bear on the content of the past. This is done through the activity of the **historical imagination** in the initial process of troping or using figurative language to distinguish meaning. The historical imagination next composes the historical narrative through the deliberate sequencing of events to effect an explanation; what modernists would think of as finding the pattern, but what for deconstructionists is the imaginative process of **emplotment**. In the judgement of those persuaded by Vico, Nietzsche, Foucault and White, how we emplot the-past-as-history is, unavoidably, a mediation of the episteme in which we exist. The history we write is, therefore, an engagement with our own age.

It is the function of the historical imagination not just to establish connections between the documents, but also couple the past, the present and the future. The historical imagination, working through the troping process of analogy and difference, creates (as opposed to discovers) causal links in the form of metaphorical descriptions. Metaphor, as Donald Davidson and Richard Rorty suggest, is as much a cognitive and epistemological process as is empirical referentiality (Rorty 1991: 163). Indeed perhaps more so as empiricism is misunderstood by those historians who choose to believe that the observation of the document stimulates knowledge, which means the document must have conveyed that knowledge. A simple but devastating error. What you see is not what you get. Following Vico, Nietzsche and Foucault, Hayden White suggests how each age secures and applies its evidence-based knowledge by it being fixed in a culturally provided figurative language. White's major contribution to post-empiricist thinking is his suggestion that historians interpret the cultural history of any period by reference to its dominant tropic prefiguration, while bearing in mind the epistemic signature of their own epoch (Munslow 1992). It is this self-consciousness on the part of the historian that makes the-past-as-history self-reflexive and revisionist.

With this in mind Foucault suggested historians should consult the historical archive in order to establish the precise nature of that aggregate of discourses (particularly in Foucault's case the disciplines of history and medicine) that established and developed what passed for knowledge within different historical epistemes or eras. Foucault has advised historians to investigate the linguistic and narrative bases that, when taken together, create rather than correspond to, or represent, the world of real things. In other words historians should relinquish the quest for *the* original meaning of events in favour of locating the culturally determined discursive practices, both then and now, that provide the form in which linguistically based knowledge has been created. Hence the notion that meaning in history can not be only factual but must be discursive. Not accepting this allows room for the specious argument that knowing that an event occurred in a certain way equates with 'the truth' of that event.

It certainly seemed reasonable to the British historian R.G. Collingwood, that the inference of meaning in history is ultimately a projection of what is first imagined as a figurative relationship. Empiricism alone, Collingwood suggests, can not provide the necessary connections. But Collingwood, ultimately a realist, drew back from what in later years has become the post-empiricist and Foucaultian tropic or poetic end result to his line of thought. Collingwood argued that metaphor is the mechanism that enables the historian to create the correct mental picture of things as they actually occurred. Collingwood, however, missed the point understood later by Foucault and White, that history is about the textualised rendition and exploration of cultural power. This failure to rethink history, or think the unthinkable, that facts and truth do not necessarily correspond, has lead mainstream historians to share the conclusion of the philosopher of history William B. Gallie, when he defined history as getting at *the* story based on the evidence (Gallie 1964).

The big question, so forcefully put by Hayden White, is does the-past-as-history correspond with *the* story that exists in the evidence? How can *a* historian's narrative discover *the* real narrative (the modernist homology of the empirical and the descriptive)? White, while believing in the past at the factual level and our capacity to represent it with some accuracy, maintains that, nevertheless, historians do not discover *the* story. Instead we invent emplotments to explain the facts (some to 'find the truth') because we prefigure the past as a history of a particular kind. The stories we impose on the past are done so for reasons that are contemporary cultural, linguistic, conceptual, discursive, ideological – for reasons that are epistemic. Historians always have an end in mind. The nature of our present existence demands it (even if it is that particular cultural demand that they get *the* truth). History, for White, is always written teleologically through its prefiguration. In other words, choices are made about how the-past-as-history is composed and configured, because of wished-for ends; for some it may be the need to discover the truth, while for others it is the wish to establish and promote a variety of intellectual, gender, ethical, cultural, economic or social programmes.

By assuming a different set of conditions to those of modernism exist today, deconstructionist historians insist the metaphysics of history will be different. If we do exist in a condition of being and knowing that is postmodern, encompassing an ontological uncertainty about knowable reality, then a decentred subject, who is a subject of his/her material, cultural, ideological and linguistic situations, will no longer invest much time or effort in the natural referential correspondence of the historians' facts to reality through inference. He/she will, moreover, not accept language as being up to the job of direct representation, and may well find him/herself agreeing that the liberal humanist assumption of purposive agent intentionality is little more than a male, middle-class, heterosexual, ideological fiction that has served its time.

Conclusion

Deconstructive or post-empiricist history is most clearly manifest in its anti-modernist assumption that 'proper' history is overdue for a rethinking of its metaphysical status. Writing the-past-as-history is not only about epistemology, nor less about procedures. Post-empiricist history is an ontological issue. The historian is an author in a particular state of existence not an impersonal observer outside time and place. What is the point of pretending it is not me creating the-past-as-history? Relatedly, because I have a moral sense that some things are wrong and others right, an important element of post-empiricist history is that I do not expect my evidence to direct me to objectivised knowledge, that the facts will contain *the* ethically correct answer.

Post-empiricist history is for me an authored story constructed out of evidence, argumentation, language, culture and my ethical choices. My history is historicist and epistemic, which makes it a contemporary emancipatory cultural practice that does not depend on the desperate modernist insistence that empirical reality will equate with truth. Moral argument does just as well when I want to believe things about the past. It is not necessary, in other words, that in order to know or believe things about the past I must solely depend on its documentary traces as the only vessels for truth (if I seek that) or meaning (which I presume I will always want). Instead, historical study can escape the suffocation induced by seeing evidence as the be-all and end-all of history by being open to non-conventional modes of historical representation. History can be experimental in its form and wider in what it chooses to call historical knowledge. We can learn, as Hayden White suggests, by exploring the content of the form.

For me the-past-as-history is a cultural history that is an overtly critical discourse. It is anti-representational in that it questions a sceptical empiricism paraded as the only game in town. My history collapses knowledge and representation, and representation and being, and enjoys the permeable relationship of past factualism and the present. It critiques conventional concepts of materialist-inspired cause, effect and inference, emphasising instead the ideas of the historian, his/her ideology and perception, and how language and description create meanings. To recognise that we are textualised creatures widens and deepens the range of the historical project – it has already – moving historians into new areas of identity construction, embodiment, cultural appropriation, liminality, the 'other', but above all thinking about how we construct the-past-as-history out of our ontological and epistemological principles.

Much in our thinking about history has thus changed in the past quarter-century. Few historians today are unaware of the invented nature of their work. Few would try to deny that they are creatures locked in the cages of time and language, or that they can or want to shake off ideological preferences, or that they do not have gender, race, sexual, class and cultural predispositions and affiliations. Most historians today are also aware that they construct narratives under the impress of language, tropes, preferred arguments and emplotments that are plausible because they resonate epistemically. But the bulk of the historical mainstream are still reluctant to let go of the modernist wreckage and accept that we can not know the true meaning of the past. They continue, therefore, to endorse the idea that we can have a direct and essentially unmediated access to past reality. In the turn from epistemology to language I would suggest, however, that historians no longer need to read documents as Adam Ferguson did solely and exclusively as referents, and do not need to assume there is knowable truth locked within them.

A

A PRIORI/A POSTERIORI

The distinction between a priori and a posteriori thinking derives from the debate over what can be known by pure reason alone. A proposition, object or a concept (see CONCEPTS IN HISTORY) is known as a priori if its content is determined true or false without reference to experience (see TRUTH). Such a judgement is based on deductive inferential reasoning (see INFERENCE) from abstract general premises (what philosophers call deductive-nomological knowledge). Philosophically speaking, apriorism maintains that our minds can acquire knowledge separately of experience through logic, intuition, ingrained ideas or mental capacities. The term a priori is distinguished from a posteriori, which is the acquisition of knowledge by means of the senses and inductive/abductive inference from **evidence**. Such knowledge does not entail the necessary, universal and truthful outcomes of apriorism. A posteriori thinking, therefore, produces judgements that have an empirical origin (see EMPIRICISM). The a priori is assumed to be independent of the experience that the a posteriori presupposes.

Immanuel **Kant** argued a priori thinking established truths through the mental categories that organise experience. This was the central aim of his *Critique of Pure Reason*, namely the establishment of the intuitions and concepts through which we understand the world: time, space, cause, number, substance, etc. Kant's basic argument is that the concepts and categories we use must be attached to our experience, and in applying the concepts we can make objective statements (see OBJECTIVITY). This Kantian or rationalist position is important to historians because of its **epistemology**; that is, the acceptance that some knowledge of the evidence a posteriori is a necessary prerequisite to establishing the concepts involved in an a priori proposition. As Kant said, the attempt to extract from an arbitrary idea the existence of an object corresponding to it is an unnatural procedure. Historians since the **Enlightenment** have taken this to mean that empiricism precedes rationality, hence the foundational claim that historical knowledge begins with inductive/abductive inference though be it processed by the rational mind. Thus it is that most historians argue from the (essentially anti-rationalist position) that all knowledge is ultimately obtained from experience and so, by definition, historical knowledge is derived a posteriori.

The truth of an a priori proposition can, therefore, be conceived and understood by reason alone, but the unpredictable truth of an a posteriori proposition can only be found by reference to a matter of fact. For example, the sum 47 + 45 = 92 is known a priori, whereas the statement 'the American labour propagandist Henry D. Lloyd was married to Jenny Bross' is known a posteriori. The truth of the addition sum is known logically (deduction) whereas the truth of the statement can only be justified empirically by the observation and verification of evidence. When historians say they rely primarily on a posteriori propositions for truthful knowledge they reference history's raw materials (people, events, actions and social processes). It is in the nature of these raw materials to demand inference that is inductive/abductive rather than deductive.

Like most people historians tend to stretch the Kantian notion of the a priori into a world-view. They find the implicit meaning of certain empirical observations become part of their own psychological a priori. My re-definition is very much in line with Friedrich **Nietzsche**'s position that a priori categories considered as foundational concepts do not have absolute or universal validity because they are ultimately the products of personal, cultural and ideological perspective. Historians come to possess what some see as the rational apriorism of, for example, class, race, gender, nationalism, or whatever. These empirically based and 'rationally justified' conceptual filters form the mental grid through which methodologies are constructed and interpretations are made.

This mental or propositional grid thus 'explains' the appearances found in the evidence. Reconstructionist historians (see RECONSTRUCTIONIST HISTORY) do tend to deny that this grid of metaphysical (see METAPHYSICS) categories prefigures their methods by arguing empiricism is the natural method of history and their interpretations are confirmed through judicious hypothesis-testing. Although they will admit that a priori or necessary truths exist they deny such truths can give us the full picture of what really happened in the past. The reason for this is that the past is presumed to be contingent and while rational agent **intentionality** is of central importance in historical explanation, actions and events are not primarily determined by human logic or, for that matter, any other single cause (see CAUSATION). What to some may look like a priori categories (like the assumption of rational agent intentionality) reconstructionists consider to be justified and truthful a posteriori interpretative statements founded on research in the archive.

Clearly, experience of the archive is relevant in moulding the psychological a priori. According to reconstructionist and constructionist historical thinking (see CONSTRUCTIONIST HISTORY) historians need the evidence to acquire the appropriate concepts. For example, when considering the nineteenth-century 'Condition of England' question most historians deploy a hierarchy of concepts like 'class', 'the city', 'pauperism' and 'crime'. Under the concept of class might be subsumed other concepts like alienation. The evidence suggests, however (i.e. the process of inference), that certain concepts like 'poverty' are inappropriate, as the consensus among British social historians holds 'poverty' was a concept not known to agents at the time and that, therefore, could not have affected their actions. 'Poverty' does not exist in the evidence. The rationale for this sophisticated empiricism is provided by the British nineteenth-century liberal and empiricist philosopher John Stuart Mill's claim that the only historical truths are empirical and founded on observation and perception (i.e. known a posteriori).

What we have then is the synthesised a priori widely found in history thinking. As the products of a self-reflexive **modernism**, historians do not deny reason has a role in what they do. But they are careful to say reason is dependent on the evidence of experience. History thinking requires observation of the evidence followed by limited generalisation that then loops back to empirical justification and that, after a number of loops, produces objective knowing. The problem with this is, of course, that historians have to accept this process offers no proof, only exemplification and plausibility. In this they accept the British empiricist philosopher John Locke's belief that there are areas of knowledge that are, at best, only likely to be true – and history is one of them.

In none of the foregoing have I made mention of either the role of the **historical imagination** or the importance of language and culture in establishing truthful a priori or a posteriori knowledge. It is through our imagination we come to terms with both our psychological a priori, the scepticism that a sophisticated empiricism demands, and the presentism of the here and now. What I am suggesting is that there are linguistic determinants and cultural processes that serve to collapse the distinction of knower and known, and that influence the way we bring together our concepts and the evidence.

The history thus produced testifies to the historian's a priori belief that the evidence was necessarily connected in some way. As I have argued, this is central to the mechanism whereby historians come to hold certain core convictions about the past. It is possible to consider the structure of **narrative** as a priori and that historians order their perceptions of the evidence through narrative's pre-packed figurative codes. This encodation is worked into the historical narrative according to the nature of our metaphoric prefiguration – allocating meaning to events through similarity and resemblance, contiguity and difference, and cause and effect. It is only a brief step from this troping process (see TROPE/FIGURATION) to making moral judgements in and about history, and taking up ideological positions about what constitutes dominance and subordinance in society. Even if all the individual sentence statements in a historical narrative are deemed to be true a priori or a posteriori, the narrative structure imagined and brought into existence by the historian is a performative and organisational act that sequences and patterns knowledge without being knowledge itself. Figuration and narrative interpretation, as the basis of historical telling, mediates both a priori and a posteriori knowledge.

Further reading

Bonjour, L. (1985)
Danto, A. (1965)
Kant, I. (1933 [1781])
Moser, P.K. (1987)
Priest, S. (1990)
Putnam, H. (1983)
Quine, W.V. (1963)

AUTHOR

How far is the-past-as-history an act of discovery by the historian? Since René Descartes, Immanuel **Kant**, John Locke, the **Enlightenment** and the advent of **liberal humanism**, Western society has reaped the benefits of its investment in **epistemology** (its theory of knowledge) with historical knowledge being found in the data (see EVIDENCE) as guided by the general inferential rules (see INFERENCE) as understood and applied by the knowing subject (in this case the historian). The Enlightenment favoured and promoted the Cartesian subject – the rational knowing subject, the self, the self-fashioning 'man', the subject as the centre of knowledge, unfettered, unified, stable, intending, timeless, causal, the controller of culture, the creator and source of meaning, and the autonomous author (of texts). This figure was predicated on the independent existence of mental categories of knowing that reflected reality, and a transparent language *through* which all forms of reality including the historical could be perceived, represented and made familiar. The model for history that this mind-set contrived held sway until the twentieth-century structuralist revolution (see STRUCTURALISM). Such a model assumed, common-sensically, that history tells the **truth** as understood by the discrete empirical subject, the historian (see EMPIRICISM). Jacques **Derrida** described the subject as the transcendental signified. In the case of the historian, his/her methods are taken to demonstrate objectively his/her hypothesis, thus creating truthful interpretations that provide the well-spring of the history text's definitive meaning and explanation. The past gives us the evidence and the historian deploys reason and inference to make sense of it. The historian is not where the past begins, but where it ends.

In this conventional model the historian-as-autonomous-author-of-history-texts supplies the epistemology through which he/she knows the past and makes it meaningful. The inevitable subjectivity that accompanies authorship is not a problem for the modernist historian because it can be overcome through the strict application of empirical method, which makes for truthful interpretations. The historical genre of biography, for example, is expected to conform to the principles of the method, but standards are different for degraded types of history like the historical novel or the autobiography. But most historians will admit (albeit reluctantly in some cases) that it is not actually possible to compare and contrast the interpretation of the historian (as statements of fact) with the real past as it happened. This remains the case despite the detailed use of the referential paraphernalia that is meant to suggest otherwise. The effect of what can, upon occasion, be a massive empiricist overkill in the footnotes is to obliterate the problem of limited inference and indirect knowledge that permits only of weak **historical explanation**. Nevertheless, empiricist common-sense urges the historian to get on with his/her immersion in the archive as the only way to objectivity. It is with this tactic that empiricism avoids confronting its liberal humanist **ontology** (its state of being), as well as its epistemological, and methodological assumptions.

Empiricist assumptions and referential paraphernalia apart, it is possible that the historian is far more like an author than the proper history of the conventional model is usually willing to admit. The historian-as-author is someone who will manifestly identify with the object of study and who may make conscious interventionist choices about the past, effectively resisting empiricism's objectivist lures. What I am suggesting is that it may be necessary to take another look at the historian-as-author's powers of signification. This should encourage a closer focus on what it really means to talk of the historian as an interpreter, and this should lead to rethinking the nature of his/her subjectivity and his/her connection with the past through his/her history writing.

The shift in recent years away from the model of the historian-as-observer to historian-as-participant (who 'reads' texts within various contexts and then writes about them) has been accompanied by what is for many historians a worrying scepticism in colleagues about that which constitutes historical truth, and how we can tell it in an intertextual world. This, it turns out, is far more than a crisis of methodology. Developments in the wake of structuralism, **postmodernism** and **continental philosophy** have challenged the Enlightenment ideal of the steadfast knowing subject and the goal of unclouded representation. Until the postmodern critique this ground was the firm foundation for the multiple pillars of Western philosophy: objectivism, representation, truth, factualism, reference, realism, the subject–object binary, all of which were ideally located in the figure of the disinterested modernist historian (a.k.a. the knowing subject) (see OBJECTIVITY; TRUTH; FACTS; REALITY/REALISTIC EFFECT). According to at least one leading commentator, the first principle of the postmodern moment is a refocusing on history – about questions of representation and stories told (and untold) with a Will to Power that unavoidably places the knowing and objective subject (a.k.a. the historian) under a question mark (Marshall 1992: 10, 25).

While this challenge is being mounted historians remain mildly embarrassed. The reason is because we know the grubby practicalities of our work makes history, though perceived as a legitimate epistemology, fall far short of the Enlightenment ideal. Historians can not avoid the fact that they are writing *about* the past. It is hard, therefore, to defend the notion that the past flows *through* us like low-voltage electric current that is not in any way obstructed or short-circuited by its medium. History, as the only access we have to the past, is a second-order epistemology. It has no direct contact with reality. Primary evidence so called is still entirely removed from its referents (all evidence refers to other evidence). I suppose the irony is that in a *real* sense history is dependent for its meaning upon the skills of the historian-as-author and the authoring process for the creation of the reality-effect through its form (see FORM AND CONTENT). There is, therefore, an unexpungeable subjectivity in the creation of historical knowledge because the historian is the organiser of the-past-as-history. The evidence of the past is selected, rejected, shaped and formed through inference, theory, trope, argument, style, **narrative**, moral situation, the extant **historiography** (present and past traditions of inquiry and interpretation), and empathy with the object of study (see INFERENCE; TROPE/FIGURATION). Objective historical knowledge demands a platform above and outside history. But historians know such a platform does not exist. It is the historian who authors the connection between event, narrative, understanding, meaning and interpretation.

The historian is thus heavily dependent upon his/her organisational and authorial skills with the data – most particularly his/her narrative capacities. Because truth does not emerge from any known historical methodology, we are thrown back on to the individual historian's attempt to persuade the reader through his/her narrative construction as well as the judicious use of the evidence. The historical narrative is thereby an act of **historical imagination**, of will, of design, of desire, of form, and of content although many still insist they are demonstrating (a residual modernist belief in) objective knowing. This tension between form and content may well be unresolvable. The Enlightenment assertion that every rational and knowing subject possesses the power to command and reconstruct reality (from the archive) is faced with the collapse of meaning and representation as proclaimed by Michel **Foucault** and Roland **Barthes** in their joint avowal of the death of the subject/author.

It might be helpful to consider the paradox that underpins history as a discipline specifically in connection with the functioning of the historian. Let us revisit the modernist model of history. History is a corpus of thought and material made coherent by its methodology, its shared topics of interest (its objects of study), and its practitioners (the historians). In this model there is a lack of parity between method, that which is known (object), and the knower (historian/knowing subject). The object of study comes first, the method second, and the historian last. The paradox (the modernist paradox) surfaces quickly in this model because the end product – historical knowledge (the interpretative narrative of the-past-as-history) – is always associated with the historian. The historian is named and becomes the referent for the interpretation because it is he/she who has *discovered* the truthful interpretation. The model insists that the historian, in discovering the past, is above and beyond history, is somehow divorced from the whole process. The past unfolds itself. But yet the historian is, as we know, authorial and is the creator of the text in which he/she reveals the truthful interpretation, explains it, argues for it, and displays the evidence he/she has chosen that supports his/her argument. Here is the paradox. The historian has a double consciousness: he/she is both separate and involved, is the witness to the past, yet also must be a participant in it because he/she authors it as written history as a discourse on the past (see STRUCTURALISM).

The paradox is never resolved but is coped with by viewing the historian not as an author (creative, interventionist) but as a historian (separate, outside the text, beyond the past; who discovers the truthful interpretation). In 'The discourse of history' (1967) Roland Barthes points to history's investment in the correspondence theory of knowledge and the factualism and objectivism this produces and that necessitates the elision of the historian as an authorial voice. When Foucault described the death of the author he could have been speaking about the way in which the modernist historian removes him/herself from the project, not as a knowing subject, but as the fabricator of knowledge. In this way the historian is complicit in the pretence of allowing 'the past' to use him/her as its vessel or mouthpiece – so the past speaks for itself. It is this confederacy that disguises the paradox of history.

Modernist history thereby denied the characterisation of the historian-as-author long before postmodernism. But the aim was not to de-centre the historian-as-author as a knowing subject in order to reveal his/her cultural situatedness, or how language constructs his/her identity, or the lack of control he/she has over the meanings of the text, but rather to demonstrate his/her separation from the present (ideology, society, politics, text) – to make him/her *ahistorical*. This *ahistoricality* is evident in the distinctive caste of historical narrative. It is the-past-as-history not the historian-as-author that narrates events. In history there is no 'you', 'me', or 'I'. The past exists in the form of an auto-narrative. This is the modernist aim to blot out history as an authored discourse. Why is this done? It is done to perform the (liberal humanist ideological?) function of containing and repressing the connection between the subject and language. In this way the historical narrative is caught in the snare (as has been pointed out on numerous occasions) of the nineteenth-century realist novel whereby the reader is expected to consume the truthful narrative as a coherent reflection of reality. In the same way the historian smoothes out the contradictions in the past usually by acknowledging them (a.k.a. the **historical explanation**), and then offering a resolution (a.k.a. the historical interpretation).

Constructed by the realist historical narrative the reader is called or hailed by the historical narrative – ideologically interpellated as French cultural critic Louis Althusser describes it – in such a way that he/she recognises him/herself as another knowing subject. He/she thus accepts as natural the existence of the liberal humanist knowing subject. He/she shares what is taken to be a natural situation of knowing. Historical knowing is not, however, natural. Liberal humanist knowing is not the only way. But it is in its appeal to empiricism that history obscures its liberal humanist constructedness. Unfortunately, if the knowing subject (as the subject of ideology and his/her cultural situatedness) is crumbling, fragmented, dispersed, constantly constructed and reconstructed by **discourse** and in a language that is out of control, that subject can not fulfil the traditional conception of proper empirical history, and it may end up simply making the paradox in history more stark – a method and object that together are assumed to give access to reality, and the historian-as-author who creates the-past-as-history; what Michel de Certeau has called its closed discourse (de Certeau 1988 [1975]: 21).

If the reader elects to view the historical narrative not as a reflection of the past, but as a construct of an author who is subject to many cultural and linguistic tides – that is refuses interpellation – then the historical narrative becomes open to a deconstruction (see DECONSTRUCTIONIST HISTORY) (of that which is already constructed), and the process of its production can be examined. The deconstructive aim is first to find the unity of the work, its drive toward explanatory closure and how it goes about dispelling ignorance. Next, the deconstructive reader will try to locate the contradictions in the text and the literary devices that reveal where the text escapes its realist captivity and its meaning becomes plural or fictive. The deconstructive assumption is that the text is always too slippery for the historian-as-author to control. So, the deconstructive reader asks, among other things, what is its ascendant trope, what are its underlying arguments (inference and causal analysis), what is the nature of its ideological positioning (moral and ethical appeals), is there a dominant **emplotment**, who or what constitutes the 'hero' and how is the evidence of the hero's life marshalled within the available emplotment or contemporary mythic motifs, and what does the selection of sources reveal about the explanation and the aims of the historian-as-author?

To deconstruct the history text requires breaking another confederacy, the unstated modernist complicity between the historian and the reader whereby the historian is offering truth to the reader. By viewing the historian as an author who is not only the constructor of the-past-as-history, but who is also him/herself constructed in language, it is possible to see that it is not the past that speaks through the historian, but the text, language and culture. From a postmodern perspective (see POSTMODERNISM) we are never outside the universe of discourse. We can never escape to a place that is extra-discursive. If we could then we would be able to affirm the basis upon which the knowing subject is built – the modernist conviction that individual consciousness is the fount of knowledge, meaning and understanding. Our postmodern condition demands, however, that as we recognise the historian-as-author, at the same time we de-centre him/her as a transcendental signified.

The obvious question then is if the historian is aware of all this how does he/she do history? Does he/she author something we can call postmodern history? Well, it may be that the historian-as-author who is no longer weighed down by the modernist sense of the-past-as-history, will opt for experimentation, will intervene in or impose him/herself on history. Precisely how these history experiments can be undertaken is the point of the experiment so I can not prejudge. But, if pressed, I would suggest experimenting with authorial intrusion, exploring the death of the author (de-centring the subject in some way), mixing the fictional and factualist forms, offering alternative versions of the 'same' story, and so on. This idea of experimentation in history is not a particularly new idea of course. Linda Hutcheon described it over ten years ago as 'historiographic metafiction' (Hutcheon 1988: 87–101). Historians can exercise a choice: they can elect to write about the past as if they had discovered it as it actually happened, but the historian-as-author is equally free to adopt any post-empiricist position he/she chooses.

He/she may favour disrupting the text so the reader is given the opportunity to take what they want from the narrative. The reader is no longer forced to accept it as an enclosed, finished, modernist job-lot. The point is, even when the historical narrative claims to leave the question open, the material has been presented in a fashion that presumes there is no other way to do it. Rather than this take-it-or-leave-it attitude that results from empiricism, realism, factualism (i.e. no choice), the reader may be invited to fill in the spaces left by the playful historian-as-author. Would it be too arch for me to suggest the historian-as-author might list all the references known to them on a particular historical object, write a thousand-word interpretation, then suggest the reader go and read the sources and make up their own mind (history as bibliography)? This assumes that the deconstructive reader will 'play' their part. If they do not, of course, it rather negates the point of the game. No doubt the modernist practical realist historian will say if the historian plays like this then he/she is not doing history.

Well, it is likely it would not be modernist, truth-fulfilling history. It would be history that minimally asks who is writing it and why, who is reading it and why, and how many kinds of stories can be told about the same event(s). The historian-as-author would thus be inviting the reader to engage in creating the-past-as-history rather than having it disclosed to them (i.e. exhibited, imparted, divulged, published). As a comfort to the modernist historian I feel obliged to say that none of this means throwing out the moral baby with the empiricist bath-water. Creating or authoring the past does not mean fictionalising events, people or processes and being amoral or nihilistic to boot. But what it does mean is decontrolling the project by not offering history as if it were the result of an act of objective discovery, and thereby closing down the options for the reader to participate in, and make up his/her own mind.

There is no ready-made reading list for the idea of the historian-as-author. You will have to consult a variety of texts dealing with the self, the subject, the author, and the postmodern critique of history. My recommendations are below.

Further reading

Althusser, L. (1971)
Barthes, R. (1977)
—— (1974)
Burke, S. (1992)
de Certeau, M. (1988 [1975])
Derrida, J. (1978)
Dreyfus, H.L. and Rabinow, P. (1983)
Hutcheon, L. (1988)
Marshall, B.K. (1992)
Porter, R. (1997)
Smith, P. (1988)

B

BARTHES, ROLAND (1915–80)

Roland Barthes was one of the leading French literary theorists and cultural critics of the mid-twentieth century. His reputation generally rests on his work in semiotics and the popularisation among the wider academic community of the principles of **structuralism**. His interest to historians, however, centres on his examination of the relationship between language, literature and the historical narrative. Barthes commented on the *naïveté* of the distinction made between history and (history) writing (*écriture*). Because the historical narrative conforms to a set of literary/narrative codes that give it its form, he argued it is not readily separated from its content or its historicity, that is, its frame(s) of reference (conceptual, ideological, social, cultural) (see FORM AND CONTENT). In his text *Writing Degree Zero* (1967) he argued much wasted effort was put by historians into imagining a style of writing that was assumed and intended to be devoid of all language constraints, and that presumed that the word and the world can be viewed as separate domains. For Barthes literature is language and form its product. Content does not generate form. When form and content are, however, deliberately (and erroneously) conflated, history appears to be the natural product of the evidence. The object of this empiricist (see EMPIRICISM) exercise, claims Barthes, is to deny that myth and ideology exist in written history.

By distinguishing between *histoire* in which events apparently narrate themselves, and *discourse* which is self-consciously authorial, in his essay 'The discourse of history' (1967) Barthes objects to history's reliance on the correspondence theory of knowledge that generates historical facts, producing along the way, the 'reality effect' of 'objective' history. As Stephen Bann has said, the rhetorical analysis of historical narrative ' … cannot grant to history, a priori, the mythic status which differentiates it from fiction' (Bann 1981: 5).

Barthes's analysis of narrative in 'The discourse' denies history the status of a distinct **epistemology**. History, he notes, is usually:

> justified by the principles of 'rational' exposition [but] ... does this form of narration really differ, in some specific trait, in some indubitably distinctive feature, from imaginary narration, as we find it in the epic, the novel, and the drama?
>
> (Barthes in Bann 1981: 7)

Barthes reminds historians that their work resides in the translation of the past into a narrative of historical interpretation, and their common deployment of the minutiae of events, the deliberate control exercised over temporality (compressing, re-winding and fast-forwarding time in the narrative), and the elision of the historian-as-author (denying the performative aspect of writing history), all work to produce the perception of realism as though there were a direct hold on the referent from where, as he says:

> history seems to be telling itself all on its own. This feature ... corresponds in effect to the type of historical discourse labelled as 'objective' (in which the historian never intervenes). ... On the level of discourse, objectivity ... thus appears as a particular form of ... referential illusion, since in this case the historian is claiming to allow the referent to speak all on its own.
>
> (Barthes in Bann 1981: 11)

Barthes points out this projected correspondence between ordinary language, the evidence, and historical **truth** is also found in realist novels that similarly appear objective because they too have overpowered the signs of the 'I'. Barthes maintains, therefore, that historians thus deploy the real to play the epistemological trick of disengaging historians from the history production process in order to demonstrate unalloyed access to the reality of the past whereby history signals objectivity. Barthes's point is that the historian intentionally mystifies history by collapsing the signified with the referent to create a signifier–referent correspondence. Barthes summarises this by claiming in objective history the 'real' is never more than an unformulated signified, hiding behind the all-powerful referent. This constitutes history's 'realistic effect' (Barthes in Bann 1981: 17). This is akin to Michel **Foucault**'s notion that discourses are perspectives that generate truth effects. This is not anti-referentialism, rather the identification of referentialism's limits as a form of representation (see Richard RORTY).

Further reading

Bann, S. (1983)
—— (1981)
Barthes, R. (1988)

—— (1986)
—— (1984 [1967])
—— (1983)
—— (1981 [1967])
—— (1977)
—— (1975)
—— (1974)
—— (1972)
—— (1967)
—— (1957)
Burke, S. (1992)
Calvet, L.-J. (1994)
Culler, J. (1983)
Payne, M. (1997)
Sontag, S. (1982)
White, H. (1984)
Wiseman, M.B. (1989)

C

CARR, E.H. (1892–1982)

Edward Hallett Carr was recognised as a distinguished historian of Russian and Soviet history. However, he is often, if not better remembered, for his ideas on the character of history in his book *What is History?*, first published in 1961. These were regarded initially, and still are in some quarters, as dangerously relativist. The divisions over history as an **epistemology** (theory of knowledge) is nowhere better demonstrated than in the conflicting opinions held on Carr's views on history, or the way his legacy can readily be appropriated by all sides, proper and postmodern (see POSTMODERNISM). Until Keith Jenkins's reappraisal of Carr's philosophy of history, Carr had been seen, almost universally among historians, as standing for a distinctively relativist, if not indeed a sceptical, conception of the functioning of the historian (Jenkins 1995).

Explaining Carr's 'radicalism' the philosopher of history Michael Stanford has argued that Carr 'insisted that the historian cannot divorce himself from the outlook and interests of his age [*sic*]' (Stanford 1994: 86). Stanford also quotes Carr's own claim that the historian 'is part of history' with a particular 'angle of vision over the past' (Stanford 1994: 86). As Stanford points out, Carr's 'first answer ... to the question "What is History?" ' is that it is a dialogue between the historian and his/her facts, generating an unending debate between the present and the past. The British historian John Tosh also weighs in with his judgement that Carr's arrogant thinking, by placing the historian at the centre of the history project, merely strengthens the hands of the epistemological sceptics (Tosh 1991: 148).

These examples do not seem to me worrying for historians because they do not represent a case of epistemological radicalism. My concerns about Stanford and Tosh's doubts are, of course, the product of my intellectual situatedness as a writer about the past. Today, with our sense of the frailties and failures of representationalism, referentialism, and inductive **inference**, more and more history writing is based on the assumption that we can know nothing genuinely truthful about the reality of the past beyond the single sentence-length statement. It is quite wrong, in my view, to suggest that Carr views history as the fabrication of the historian. Rather, what has happened is that our contemporary conditions of existence have created a much deeper uncertainty about the nature of knowledge creation and its (mis-)uses in the humanities.

It follows, a growing number of historians believe, that we do not 'discover' (the 'truthful?' 'actual?' 'real?' 'certain?') patterns in apparently contingent events because, instead, we unavoidably impose our own hierarchies of significance on them (this is what we believe/want to see/read in the past) (see EVENT). I do not think many historians today are naïve realists. Few accept this/here is a given meaning in the **evidence**. While we may all agree at the event level that something happened at a particular time and place in the past, its significance (its meaning as we narrate it) can only be provided by the historian (see NARRATIVE). The meaning is not immanent in the event itself. Moreover, the challenge to the distinction of fact (see FACTS) and fiction as we configure our historical narratives, and further acknowledgements of the cognitive power of rhetoric, style and trope (metaphors are arguments and explanations), provide not only a formal challenge to traditional empiricism, but forces us to acknowledge that as historians we are making moral choices as we describe past reality (see TROPE/FIGURATION).

Does all this add up to a more fundamental criticism of historical knowing than imagined in *What is History?* by Carr? I think so. If this is what historical relativism means today, I believe it provides a much larger agenda for the contemporary historian than Carr's acknowledgement that the historian is in a dialogue with the facts, or that sources only become evidence when used by the historian. As Jenkins has pointed out, Carr ultimately accepts the epistemological model of historical explanation as the definitive mode for generating historical understanding and meaning (Jenkins 1995: 1–6, 43–63). This fundamentally devalues the currency of what Carr has to say, as it does of all reconstructionist empiricists who follow his lead. This judgement is not, as you would imagine, widely shared by them. For illustration, in misunderstanding the nature of 'semiotics – the postmodern?' as he querulously describes it, the historian of Latin America Alan Knight has claimed that Carr remains significant today precisely because of his warning a generation ago to historians to 'interrogate documents and to display a due scepticism as regards their writer's motives' (Knight 1997: 747). To maintain, as Knight does, that Carr is in some way pre-empting the postmodern challenge to historical knowing is unhelpful to those who wish to establish Carr's position in *What is History?*.

Carr, for example, tried to fix the status of evidence with his objections to what he understood to be the logic of R.G. **Collingwood**'s sceptical position. Collingwood's logic could, claims Carr, lead to the dangerous idea that this/here is no certainty or intrinsicality in historical meaning – this/here are only (what I would call) the discourses of historians – a situation that Carr refers to as 'total scepticism' – a situation where history ends up as 'something spun out of the human brain' and that leads to the dangerous conclusion that this/here can be no 'objective historical truth' (Carr 1987 [1961]: 26) (see DISCOURSE; OBJECTIVITY; TRUTH). Carr explicitly rejects Friedrich **Nietzsche**'s notion that (historical?) truth is effectively defined by fitness for purpose. The basis for Carr's opinion was his belief in the power of empiricism to deliver the truth, whether it fits or not (Carr 1987 [1961]: 27). Historians ultimately serve the evidence, not vice versa. This guiding precept thus excludes the possibility that 'one interpretation is as good as another' even when we can not (as we can not in writing history) guarantee 'objective or truthful interpretation'.

For all his epistemological conservatism, Carr wished to reinforce the notion that he was a radical. As he said in the preface to the 1987 Second Edition of *What is History?*, 'in recent years I have increasingly come to see myself, and to be seen, as an intellectual dissident' (Carr 1987 [1961]: 6). But his contribution actually lies in the way in which he failed to be an epistemological radical. In the manner of his return to the Cartesian and foundationalist fold lies the importance of *What is History?*. The book's distinction is its rejection of epistemological scepticism.

The *idée fixe* of mainstream historians today is that history is an inferential and interpretative process that can achieve truth through objectivism, that is, getting the story straight (from the evidence). The unresolved paradox in this is the legacy of *What is History?*. I assume a good number of historians recommend Carr to their students as the starting point of methodological and philosophical sophistication in order to vouchsafe the ultimate priority of factualism, objectivism over the dialogic historian. This is why *What is History?*, for the majority of historians, is something of a bulwark against post-constructive and post-empirical history. For others it is a walk on the epistemological wild side.

Further reading

Carr, E.H. (1987 [1961])
—— (1958–64)
—— (1950–3)
Jenkins, K. (1995)
Jones, C. (1998)

CAUSATION

This is one of the most important metaphysical issues historians come across (see METAPHYSICS). Its importance is, oddly, reflected by the fact that most professional historians tend to avoid talking about the nature of causation. Generally speaking causal relations exist between events (see EVENT): if event

A occurs then event B occurs, and it can be reasonably demonstrated that event A explains the subsequent (temporally sequential) occurrence of event B. The central question for most historians is how to explain the determining nature of the relationship. The fact that the debate on the nature of causality remains potent among philosophers of history (if not its practitioners) is evidenced by Benedetto **Croce**'s and R.G. **Collingwood**'s questioning of if causality is really a part of what it is that historians do. Both Croce and Collingwood suggested that all history is the history of thought and while this does not mean causation is wholly redundant in history, it does imply the really important object is to find the thought behind the action (see INTENTIONALITY). This means the event itself is secondary to a prior form of knowledge that is ideational, that is of, relating to, or produced by ideas in the mind of the historian and the agent (Collingwood 1994 [1946]: 214–15) (see A PRIORI/A POSTERIORI). Re-enacting thoughts behind actions and events is thus one way to address causation. Another is that of the **covering laws** as proposed by Carl Hempel whereby historians subsume actions/events under general laws that explain particular groups of actions/events. Causation has thus divided the philosophers into at least two camps: idealists and positivists. The debate still exists today in the work of idealist philosophers of history like William H. Dray and Alan Donagan, and positivists Patrick Gardiner and more recently Clayton Roberts.

In determining causal relations the historian is caught in the perennial bind of what appears to be, and what is. The Scottish sceptical empiricist philosopher David Hume argued that in judging the nature of a causal relationship all we have to go on are our perceptions of the pattern(s) of connection (see EMPIRICISM). We can not know, through observation, the *real* nature of determining forces. By consulting the evidence and under the influence of appropriate social theory historians do, however, believe this problem can be overcome, thus making understanding causal connections the central feature of **historical explanation**. As such, historical explanation demands that historians discover the *real* causes of the events and processes found in the past through inference.

What has become the conventional view of causal analysis was summarised by the British historian E.H. **Carr**, who argued that the relation of the historian to causes is the same as that to **facts**:

> The causes determine his interpretation of the historical process, and his interpretation determines his selection and marshalling of the causes. The hierarchy of causes, the relative significance of one cause or set of causes or of another, is the essence of interpretation.
>
> (Carr 1987 [1961]: 103)

Hence, as Carr claims, the study of history is a (circular) study of causes (and facts). Carr's recommendation to the historian when faced with events and the need to explain them is first to assign several possible causes, then establish a hierarchy that implies a pattern of relationships between the facts as events. Once the historian distinguishes underlying as well as more immediate causes he/she is well on the path to an interpretation that can then be cast as a historical **narrative**.

Carr alerts us to the problem all historians face, which is understanding the role of necessity in cause and effect. For the main part historians reject the philosopher David Hume's scepticism about not being able to know real causes, preferring to seek out those forces that necessitate subsequent events. This is sometimes (and confusingly) referred to as sufficient causality. Such a posture is demanded by the empiricist and realist thrust of most conventional **reconstructionist history** and **constructionist history**. The empiricist theory of causation recognises its enormously complex nature, but it is founded four-square on the presumed existence of objectively derived and knowable 'facts', only through which can we find causes. Take the question of what caused the assassination of Abraham Lincoln. A full explanation of why it occurred involves the historian recognising that Lincoln wanted to visit Ford's Theatre to relax with his wife (agent intentionality?); that, given Lincoln's anti-slavery stance, some Americans would hold a grudge (human nature, a covering law, or historical determination of some kind?); and that hand-guns can kill people (the mechanistic physics of nature?). Any of these 'facts' could be regarded as the primary cause of Lincoln's assassination. Or any from another list.

A cause is sufficient, therefore, if the effect always follows that cause (being shot at point blank range is sufficient to kill you). Sufficient cause is usually distinguished from necessary cause. A cause is necessary if its effect would otherwise have been absent (the assassin had not been in the theatre). Most historical explanations thus depend on sorting out what are necessary and what are sufficient causes, and what hierarchy exists among what may turn out to be chains of causes? Also what of the counter-factual situation – what if Lincoln had not had an anti-slavery stance? The complexity of causation is further evidenced by the reversal of Friedrich **Nietzsche**, that to grasp the nature of causality (or rather to reject it altogether) the effect is primary in the search for cause. In a larger sense the future always determines the past because it determines our apprehension of the present – the future is the place where we locate our goal-making desires and the past is the material for their realisation. This orientation suggests why history is written much like fiction. It is because historical narrative has the power to complicate cause and effect. Causes do not have to be offered sequentially, indeed they are often described in the historian's narrative as a problem in need of a solution – behind the effect a prior fact lurks that 'explains the situation'. So it is that in history causes are often given as effects in search of an interpretational explanation (see TELEOLOGY).

In the physical or natural sciences deductive inference has generally held sway. In science, causation is a matter of observation of regular occurrences, hypothesis framing, and then empirical testing (experimentation) with the express aim of generating covering laws. Truth emerges through the correspondence theory of knowledge. In the literary or human sciences we are less able to see behind the appearances of (historical and usually textualised) phenomena. Tailor-made for most conventional historians, however, is the realist-inspired explanation of causality provided by the philosopher C. Behan McCullagh. Working from the assumption that the aim of causal theory is to distinguish those aspects of causes that explain what are causes and what are not, McCullagh confirms the definition offered in the first paragraph of this entry, but adds the gloss that a cause 'is an event which produces a conjunction of something that has a tendency to produce an effect of the kind which occurred in certain circumstances, and [in] the presence of . . . triggering circumstances' – probabilities plus a combination of necessary and sufficient causes (McCullagh 1998: 179).

But the decisions involved in such a realist process of causal analysis are almost entirely based on the assumptions held by the historian. His/her presentist and teleological assumptions concern the forces he/she believes influence people, processes and events like free agency, intentionality, motivational psychology, and various determinisms such as geography, gender, ideology, ethics, materiality, culture and race. The teleological assumptions held by the historian (the future conceived in the present determines the past) influences the form in which causal questions are put. Because of his/her prior consideration of the historical field, the questions he/she frames about causality take a particular shape. In asking why did this happen or what if something else had happened so would the same effect be found, the historian is not only predetermining meaning (to a greater or lesser) extent by the form in which he/she casts the problem, but he/she is also working teleologically within his/her own selection and arrangement of the evidence.

Causal analysis is undertaken, therefore, according to a set of pre-formed ideas about what is most likely to be the meaning of one set of events occurring after another. The decision to fix meaning through a particular causal connection will be based, in large part, on the historian's preference for a particular interpretative outcome rather than *the* one found objectively in the evidence. Facts, fairly obviously, do not just turn up and certainly do not carry within themselves predetermined meanings. In the end much depends on the type of historian you are and what answers you give to questions like 'How did the world work in the past?' (or, for that matter, does in the present), 'What are your ontological beliefs?', and 'What methodology do you intend to apply to give effect to them?' Do you believe in agent intentionality, or the materialist theory of history, or the power of complex social structures to flatten out historical change? Just what mechanism do you believe shapes change over time either generally or in specific instances?

The nature of causation can be usefully explored, therefore, by looking at it from the other end of the process – from how and why we deploy our theories of causality. As we know, the assumptions and desires of the historian are eventually cast in a narrative form of explanation. How does the construction of our narrative influence our causal explanation? Only the crudest of reconstructionist historians (see RECONSTRUCTIONIST HISTORY) believe that if their interpretational historical narrative is written with direct reference to the **evidence**, then its structure or pattern will correspond to the causal structure of the past. Slightly more sophisticated reconstructionists and probably all constructionist historians (see CONSTRUCTIONIST HISTORY) realise causation, when translated into narrative, is a far more complex process than the simple notion of the narrative defined as 'this happened, then that'. Narrative does not require nor entail *the* cause be followed by *the* effect. From the politically liberal perspective of those who believe in agent intentionality, narrative represents people's decisions as choices, and events as particular responses rather than effects. Narrative is explanatory for politically directed liberal historians because they reject a deterministic causality that they believe to be associated with ideological positions of which they disapprove. The reverse also applies of course.

We should be clear that the complexity of causation can not be easily divorced from questions of narrative explanation, not least because narrative itself has an ambiguous status among historians. Some philosophers of history, like William Gallie, believe narrative is *the* essence of history because there is a strong epistemological connection between evidence and explanation via causality as translated into the narrative form (see FORM AND CONTENT). Other historians like John Tosh speak for the constructionist mainstream in finding narrative to be a relatively weak method for explaining the past if it is simply a causal description of 'this happened, then that' (Tosh 1991: 116–18).

The ambiguity of narrative seems, therefore, to have something to do with the individual historian's attitude to the authority of empiricism as a way of knowing and its ability to establish and explain causal connections (see EPISTEMOLOGY). Historians like Hayden **White** claim the narrative, as an explanation of causal connectivity, is imposed precisely because it is prefigured by the historian. White criticises as naïve any rustic empiricist evidence–causation–narrative symmetry. As he says the idea that the causes 'for events (necessary if not sufficient) or reasons (conscious or unconscious) for events' taking place as they in fact did [and which] are set forth in the narrative in the form of the story it tells' fails to recognise the variety of narratives that can be told and that themselves prefigure the type of causal connections to be made (White 1987: 41). White endorses the argument that the historian brings to the evidence beliefs in all manner of things that affect their thinking about how history 'works' as an epistemology. It is White's particular contribution to the argument to point out that, because history is a literary artefact, historians make causal links as part of their overall constitution and prefiguration of the historical field through the exercise of their **historical imagination** and employment of trope, **emplotment**, argument, ideological preference and philosophical orientation (see TROPE/FIGURATION).

All this suggests that causation is a central but, like so much else in history these days, an open question. The strong advocate of constructionist social science history Christopher Lloyd argues any ambivalence about causation among historians may be the fault of philosophers because of their lack of agreement about the nature of causal explanation (Lloyd 1993: 50–1). From Lloyd's perspective, causal explanation is necessarily bound up with hypothesis testing and model-making, and without that historians can not offer convincing explanations. As Lloyd puts it, the need for historians today is to establish causal connections between complex social structures, and that demands the construction 'of the problems and objects for enquiry [which] takes place within theories [that are] responsive to empirical findings that they help to uncover and interpret' (Lloyd 1993: 51). Like Patrick Gardiner, Lloyd seems to be saying empiricism alone is never enough; it has to be theoretically informed and, by implication, that the form in which the causal analysis is cast is of secondary significance.

But there is little doubt that in recent years the interest in history has moved increasingly from an absorption with causation and social science explanation, to the form in which historians deploy their stories. The search for the Holy Grail of Real Causes is now discredited as an example of (what it always was?) bad metaphysics (Gardiner 1961 [1951]: 110). It seems clear that it is the contribution of Hayden White that has prompted this shift in focus to the analysis of history as a discourse, rather than simply as a trade in empirical data organised via the free market of social theory. History is seen more and more as being constituted through the poetic, ideological and ethical decisions of the historian, but most importantly there is the growing acceptance that the empirical foundation is not a sheet anchor that guarantees contact with the real past. Historians now often begin their work thinking about the kind of narrative they wish to generate as much as the evidentially secure and true statements they endeavour to make.

Michel **Foucault**, for example, offers his own version of causality and its role in the creation of historical knowledge. He argues that as a linguistically determined perspective, historical knowledge can not distinguish between what philosophers of history think and practitioners do. It is only when history is busy examining its philosophy, and where its knowledge comes from (and how it is used), that we can confront anew issues like causation and the nature of change over time. Through his deployment of the **episteme**, the term he uses to refer to how a culture co-ordinates knowledge within a historical period, he has radically challenged the conventional notion of causality. His paradigm of four epistemes holds that historical epochs do not grow organically out of each other, but instead unexpectedly emerge homologously to fill in the epistemological spaces suddenly vacated by other conditions of knowledge creation. Foucaultian causality does not exist in the modernist (see MODERNISM) sense of evolving historically, but rather issues forth structurally as a discursive formation (see DISCOURSE).

It is important in thinking about causality to grasp the significance of the present debate on the nature of history: that the challenge to the empiricist paradigm assumes our descriptions of historical events are at best only representations because there is no direct way to acquire first-hand historical knowledge. Moreover, historians should admit the consequences of the overlapping character of historical event and historical interpretation, in that the historical text is an inter-text touched and chastened by the social and political structures of the age that produced it (see HISTORICISM). This seems to suggest that causality will always remain uncertain. Uncertain because of the way it can only point to what *appears* to be, because of its inferentially construed nature, and because of the vast array of assumptions and prefigurations the historian brings to bear. These qualifications undermine the reconstructionist and constructionist foundational commitment to an accurately discernible reality 'out there', and the belief that we can adequately justify causal explanation through empirical testing.

Further reading

Carr, E.H. (1987 [1961])
Collingwood, R.G. (1994 [1946])
Croce, B. (1970 [1927])
—— (1968 [1917])
—— (1964 [1913])
—— (1923)
Donagan, A. (1959)
Dowe, P. (1992)
Dray, W.H. (1957)
Gardiner, P. (1961 [1951])
—— (1959)
Hempel, C.G. (1965)
—— (1942)
Lloyd, C. (1993)
McCullagh, C.B. (1998)
Munslow, A. (1997a)
Roberts, C. (1996)
Tosh, J. (1991)
White, H. (1996)
—— (1987)

CLASS

Class is a substantive concept (see CONCEPTS IN HISTORY) that historians deploy to organise the-past-as-history. Two basic questions must be asked of class as they are asked of all the concepts that historians use. First the epistemological (see EPISTEMOLOGY): as a way of knowing why does a particular historian prefer one concept over another to explain the-past-as-history? Second the ontological (see ONTOLOGY): how influential on the choice is the historian's present state of existence (see HISTORICISM)? It seems to me that the concepts we use are as much the result of a conscious choice about the form of the history we wish to write (a choice that may be ideological, and in the case of class usually it is) and the particular position on the anti-realist/realist spectrum that the individual historian occupies, as they are derived from the evidence (see FORM AND CONTENT).

According to the leftist cultural materialist historian and literary critic Raymond Williams, class as a modern historical term emerged in English history in the period 1770 to 1840, growing out of the social experiences of the industrial revolution and urbanisation: effectively redefining class from the earlier sense of estates, ranks or orders to one of an emergent social system based on changed material structures. As Williams's exercise demonstrates, distinguishing the senses in which the term class was used in that period is regarded as an important function of the historian with, it is argued, the utility of the concept dependent upon the source(s). But – I suggest – does it not also depend upon the historian's attitude toward the nature of representationalism and reality, as well as his/her personal and ideological predispositions? Just as Williams may perceive class through his own epistemological and ontological assumptions, so an American historian reading Alexander Hamilton's Federalist essay number 35 might elect to infer in a particular way the relationship of class to an anti-Federalist position based upon his/her understanding of linguistic usage in the late 1780s (see INFERENCE). Equally, his/her personal preferences for a particular representational relationship between class and federalism can not be overlooked. The historian may find the meaning sought in the concept he/she invents.

The work of the historian is bounded by many constraints. But two are particularly important here: inferentialism (the notion that reality generates concepts) and representationalism (that the concepts thus generated represent reality). These boundaries, while permitting the defence of empiricism, also allow that concepts presuppose language use and social practice(s). Without this acknowledgement how else can we explain the huge variety of uses and meanings squeezed out of the concept of class? Every use of class illustrates the links between **evidence**, the historian's position on representation and reality, and their conceptual organisation of content through form. For example, in the **historiography** of class the reductionism so beloved of economistic Marxists has been modified often and vigorously by, for instance, Lenin's reformulation through the vanguard of the proletariat, by Antonio Gramsci's re-casting in the shape of hegemony and the organic intellectual, by E.P. Thompson's emphasis upon the younger (and less reductionist) Marx, by Gareth Stedman Jones's anti-representationalist recognition of the languages of class, through to Patrick Joyce's narratives of class. Few historians doubt that certain well-attested events occurred, but the particular class model invoked by a historian is much more the consequence of their attitude toward the knowability of reality and their belief in their capacity to represent it.

Patrick Joyce, for instance, in his analysis of class in England points to the evidence of how class was constituted as part of a **discourse** rather than as a single unalloyed fact. He claims the Reform Bill of 1832 became justified as the 'representation' of the burgeoning middle class who viewed themselves 'as an objective social fact (a facticity it has ever since retained, such is the power of this nineteenth century discourse over us)' (Joyce 1995: 323). So powerful did this facticity become in the hands of certain historians that

Joyce maintains the lineage of the middle class has been imagined to go back to the Middle Ages. In other words, how historians use their concepts directly structures their disposition of history. Joyce's intellectually marginalised position among British nineteenth-century social historians stems from his anti-representationalist *and* anti-inferentialist assumptions that class is not intrinsic to the past, but is largely the historian's **narrative** imposition upon a pre-existing social discourse. Following the work of Gareth Stedman Jones and others, Joyce views the middle class as the discursive construction of nineteenth-century political liberals rather than the brute experience of class relations as generated by the harsh realities of the industrial city.

I would suggest historians who deploy class (or for that matter any foundational or realist concept) constantly demonstrate what pragmatic and anti-realist philosophers like John Dewey, Charles S. Peirce, W.V. Quine, Wilfred Sellars, and, more lately, the anti-representationalist Richard **Rorty** have argued, that the logical empiricist distinction between what is granted to the evidence by the mind of the historian is a social convenience rather than an epistemological necessity. Concepts like class, because of their centrality to much historical explanation, have to be confronted epistemologically by asking can historians rely on either representationalism or inference to derive truth value? In spite of being thought of otherwise, concepts like class are not representations of reality, and neither are they indisputable inferences – they are only guides to further thinking within the discourse of history.

The response of the practical realist defenders of concepts like class is to suggest to the deconstructionist historian (see DECONSTRUCTIONIST HISTORY) that all concepts, words, standards and values in history unavoidably coexist and react with the other material structures and social experiences of the past. Historical understanding is far more complex than the assumption of anti-representationalism and anti-realism will allow. This debate is unlikely to be resolved given the gulf in the assumptions of the linguistic turners and those practical realist historians who believe in conceptually knowable and objective social experience – or as one of America's leading historians of class Harvey J. Kaye might insist, thinking historically by seeing the reality.

Listed below under further reading are useful introductions to the nature of class as a historical concept and that (usually and perhaps unintentionally on the part of the author) also tell us much about attitudes toward reality and representation.

Further reading

Belchem, J. and Kirk, N. (1997)
Brody, D. (1979)
Jones, G. S. (1983)
Joyce, P. (1995)
—— (1994)
Kaye, H.J. (1995)

Kiernan, V.G. (1988)
Kirk, N. (1987)
Marable, M. (1995)
Rothenburg, P.S. (1998)

COLLIGATION

Many historians have a view of inductive **inference** that holds that any concepts (see CONCEPTS IN HISTORY) used to navigate the past are determined by observed **facts**. Most historians possess, therefore, an empiricist explanation for the formation of their concepts (see EMPIRICISM). When historians conceptualise a structure or pattern to the events (see EVENT) in the past it is generally assumed, if correct inferential methods have been deployed, to be an objective discovery (see OBJECTIVITY). The question is, however, are these *real* structures or patterns, or are they deformed as they are filtered through the mind of the historian? Indeed, are they ultimately just imposed by the historian? Colligation describes this process of discovering–imposing new explanatory patterns on the past.

The philosopher of history W.H. Walsh brought the idea of colligation to the attention of historians, based on the Kantian-inspired thinking of the British nineteenth-century philosopher-scientist William Whewell (1794–1866) (see KANT). Following Whewell, Walsh argued colligation was what was distinctive in historical methodology. He claimed it was the basic means to explain an event by tracking its primary connections to other events within their shared historical context. So the nineteenth-century Irish migration to Argentina can be explained as part of the earlier Catholic links between Ireland, Spain and her South American colonies. The connecting link lies in the complexities of the Irish diaspora. It is assumed by Walsh that what creates these links are purposive actions by individuals at the time (see INTENTIONALITY), and we as historians understand by examining, in this instance, the diasporic context (Walsh 1984 [1967]).

Colligation as a mechanism of **historical explanation** raises several issues. Not least is the role of the historian's concepts in the process of induction and the creation of **constructionist history**. There is, as many students over the years have noted with resigned regret, a constant process of revisioning going on in history. This revisioning occurs according to newly discovered facts and to new ways of presenting, organising and representing them (as well as re-presenting all the old ones!). It may be helpful here to think of historical explanation as the narration of observed effects in terms of a proposed hypothetical cause (see TELEOLOGY). Every so often a fresh conceptual or hypothetical organisation of the facts takes place in order to represent (and re-present) their **causation** afresh. The new conceptualisation (of causation) then connects the facts together in a new narrative description. To make history, the refreshed colligation process has to link events plausibly, touching as many evidential bases as possible. This is usually summarised as inference to the best explanation (McCullagh 1998).

Although inference to the best explanation is an imprecise way of producing history, historians are generally sure about what constitutes the best explanation because they hold to a crucial 'common-sense' belief. Historians do not worry too much about the theory-ladenness of their words and concepts. Except when concepts are being deliberately re-defined, common-sense dictates that concepts are empirically well-understood. Most historical facts are described presupposing a shared and generally accepted **truth** about them. Thus 'containment' as a term describing American foreign policy is used as a common-sense empiricist concept the definition of which all historians agree upon. Unfortunately, this is never the case. All uses of words and concepts are fluid and observed facts are no guarantor of meaning. The line between reality and invention is constantly crossed. Nevertheless, the colligation of facts by means of a concept as explanation remains a pivot of historical explanation (see INFERENCE). Colligation requires the historian to seek out *the* pattern in the past – determinedly with knitted brow – colligating hitherto disjointed and incongruous past events into meaningful historical sentences.

Further reading

McCullagh, C.B. (1998)
Roberts, C. (1996)
Walsh, W.H. (1984 [1967])
Whewell, W. (1967a [3 vols 1837])
—— (1967b [2 vols 1840])

COLLINGWOOD, R.G. (1889–1943)

R.G. Collingwood was one of the most influential twentieth-century philosophers of history. He believed history was a justifiable and objective **epistemology** (way of knowing and organising knowledge). History was not, however, totally indebted to the rationalist legacy of the **Enlightenment**, nor did it ultimately depend upon the scientific or covering-law model (see COVERING LAWS). But most significantly he placed the historian at the heart of the historical enterprise (see A PRIORI/A POSTERIORI; CONTINENTAL PHILOSOPHY; Benedetto CROCE; HERMENEUTICS; INFERENCE; OBJECTIVITY; POSITIVISM; Giambattista VICO; Hayden WHITE). For Collingwood the key question in history was how did people in the past derive the meaning of their lives? His answer was to equate meaning with agent **intentionality**. From this assumption, that to seek the meaning of the past we must infer its purpose, he launched his two big ideas: first, that the interrogative historian must empathise with past experience by rethinking past thoughts in the present, and second, the means for this was his/her particular vision of the **historical imagination**. Collingwood accepted what might today be regarded as a postmodern idea (see POSTMODERNISM): that the historian must be self-reflexive enough to grasp his/her own wants, wishes and purposes as well as those of the historical agent.

Although Collingwood's historical method presupposes a narrow historicist (see HISTORICISM) philosophy that centres upon the actions and intentionality of individual historical agents, to explain such intentionality historians must begin with self-knowledge. By this Collingwood meant knowledge about human nature and the human mind: how human beings universally act and think. This suggests the primary concerns of the historian are above the simple level of the empirical (see EMPIRICISM). For Collingwood the right way 'of investigating mind is by the methods of history' and 'history is what the science of human nature professed to be' (Collingwood 1994 [1946]: 209). What this meant, for what he called the plain method of history, was that the historian should look at both the outside and inside of events (see EVENT). The historian can not look for **causation** in isolation from the thoughts that gave rise to the agent's actions that precipitated events. The only way to do this is through empathy: by rethinking past thoughts in the historian's own mind within the fullest possible knowledge of period and context. Only then can the historian accurately decode the words that expressed those thoughts. Because all history 'is the history of thought' Collingwood concludes that when the historian knows the facts he/she knows why they happened – the facts have their purpose embedded in them (Collingwood 1994 [1946]: 215).

Taken at face value this *verstehen* approach (internal understanding rather than objective observation) is asking rather a lot of the historian – to rethink and re-experience thoughts and actions in the past. Not only was it asking a lot, for historians like E.H. Carr it was a step too far in the direction of an idealism (and continental philosophy) that jeopardised objectivity. How can the historian be self-conscious and historicist? In this case aware of, but divorced from, the present. To be fair, what Collingwood is actually doing, I think, is suggesting historians should try to get inside the heads of people in the past to contemplate what they probably thought, and discover which thoughts prompted their actions (inasmuch as they can be judged by the available **evidence**). In doing this Collingwood rejected what he called scissors-and-paste history whereby historians just collate the testimonies of sources (Collingwood 1994 [1946]: 257–61). Collingwood is thus offering historians a methodology that is dependent upon a particular vision of the powers of the historian's imagination: the power to rethink and re-experience *imaginatively.*

As I have explained it Collingwood did not favour any picture of history that placed a primary emphasis on examining only the outside of the event: empiricism to the exclusion of the thought of the agent. Essential to entering the thoughts in the mind of the agent is to grasp the way in which they imagined their present and future. The interrogative historian thus engages or meshes imaginations with that of the historical agent, and is then better equipped to think as they did with their own anticipations in mind (see TELEOLOGY). Collingwood, although no idealist, was always conscious of the idealist risks of his method. So, while he insisted that the guiding principle of all historical activity was the self-justifying historical imagination, its form was always to be constrained by its content (see FORM AND CONTENT) (Collingwood 1994 [1946]: 249). Keeping the historian's imagination on a short leash was assured by three simple rules: the imagined past must be localised in space and time; it must be consistent with itself; and it must be bound by the evidence. Having said this, Collingwood's empiricist leash was always strained by his emphasis on the role of the historian in the here and now. It was the historian, after all, who provided an 'innate idea with detailed content' that could only be assured by using the present as the model for the past. As he said every present 'has a past of its own, and any imaginative reconstruction of the past aims at reconstructing the past of this present, the present in which the act of imagination is going on, as here and now perceived' (Collingwood 1994 [1946]: 247). By this method the historian is tethered to the reality of the past while acknowledging the effects of the here and now.

There are clearly problems with this vision of how the historian works, especially that thinking in the present can somehow not affect what the content of the past means (a point Collingwood acknowledged in his 1940 *An Essay on Metaphysics*), or the difficulties with the fashioning of an imaginative insight of purposive action into a **narrative**, or how rethinking the past can resolve the problems associated with language use and chains of significatory meaning. Nevertheless, the fact that he was loyal to a narrow conception of empirically verifiable and objectively knowable human action, intentionality and causation, while emphasising the role of the historian, has made his perspective lastingly influential for all but the most sectarian of reconstructionist or radical of deconstructionist historians (see DECONSTRUCTIONIST HISTORY).

Further reading

Ankersmit, F.R. (1994)
Carr, E.H. (1987 [1961])
Collingwood, R.G. (1994 [1946])
—— (1940)
Donagan, A. (1962)
Dray, W.H. (1995)
—— (1989)
—— (1980)
Gardiner, P. (1961 [1951])
Jenkins, K. (1995)
Mink, L. (1969)

CONCEPTS IN HISTORY

Thinking about the use of concepts in history points to the ontological (concerned with our general state of being/existence; see ONTOLOGY) and epistemological (concerned with the theory of knowledge; see EPISTEMOLOGY) distinctions between the three main kinds of historians: common-sense or reconstructionist realists (see RECONSTRUCTIONIST HISTORY); mainstream constructionists (see CONSTRUCTIONIST HISTORY); and postist or anti-realist sceptics (see DECONSTRUCTIONIST HISTORY; POSTMODERNISM; RELATIVISM). For the first two groups history is generally adequate to the task of explaining the past because it is by the method of relating **empiricism** (the **evidence** of experience) and concept (its analytic organisation) that reliable and justified historical knowledge can be represented and demonstrated. For postist anti-representationalist sceptics this is problematic because they view historical knowledge as a linguistic and cultural creation and history, therefore, as a secondary epistemology (see EMPLOTMENT; NARRATIVE). They would tend to chime with the postist views of British social historian Patrick Joyce, that history is indistinguishable from its textual representations and the conceptual and ideological forces that construct them (Joyce 1991: 208). The question is 'Why do historians choose to adopt certain concepts and why do so many believe they offer access to the **truth** of the past?'

To philosophers concepts are the essential constituents of thought, the categories through which we apprehend reality (see Immanuel KANT), summoned up to explain the nature of being and knowing. They can be applied to mental images, graphic representations, the senses, objects, events (see EVENT), words, as well as ordering our rational processes. Mention concepts to most historians, however, and they will likely think of the guiding principles that emerge out of the past to make sense of its incoherent nature. Among the most obvious examples are race, gender, class, nationalism, and imperialism. Given what is a restricted notion of concept (restricted to the epistemological realm of knowing) the questions most often asked about the conceptual choices made by historians are those of an epistemological kind: Why is this historian adopting concepts that produce a feminist/gendered epistemology while another deploys concepts that generate race, nationalist, imperialist or class epistemologies? But in asking such questions there is a tendency to forget the broader philosophical definition, which suggests that conceptualisation in history stretches beyond the organisation of content. It moves into the ontological realm of the creation of form as well (see FORM AND CONTENT).

If indeed concepts are the instruments through which we give the past its form (the-past-as-history), then it is important that we acknowledge our dependence upon the conditions of knowledge in which we work. By conditions of knowledge I mean the epistemic state of affairs in the disciplines adjacent to history and upon which historians regularly call for their ideas, theories of society, philosophies of history and concepts (see HISTORICAL IMAGINATION; HISTORICISM; EPISTEME; MODERNISM; POSITIVISM). Historians have no fixed object. Historians study a process not an object: change over time. For the post-empiricist historian this absence at the centre of history is necessarily filled by the present conceptual state of the historian's mind as mediated by his/her present ontological situation. The question postists then ask is to what extent the historian believes he/she can escape his/her ontological situation (his/her present existence) to locate the truth of the past through his/her conceptualisation derived from the evidence?

Unlike philosophers, who validate their concepts through logic and a priori mechanisms historians have to infer (see INFERENCE) the truth of their propositions and statements in the crucible of the evidence a posteriori, or after the fact (see A PRIORI/A POSTERIORI). In seeing themselves as yo-yoing between evidence and explanation historians run the risk of creating a rather naïve science, where the investigation and verification of facts can all too easily become the be-all and end-all of the process. When this happens it is usually because the propositional and here-and-now nature of the conceptualisation exercise has been forgotten. Historians who claim their concepts arise from the evidence, then, forget that they borrow concepts from disciplines in the here and now. The point is made by the European cultural historian Carl E. Schorske (1998: 220–1). According to Schorske not only are our raw materials second-hand – the rags and remnants of evidence – but so are the concepts we use to process them, bought in from other disciplines. Like all second-hand dealers we historians do our best to make the trade look good by polishing pre-owned concepts so they will appear attractive and marketable.

This points to the most significant consequence of this second-hand trade, the tendency to use concepts as a way of giving evidence a plausible meaning, to invest historical interpretations with a persuasive conviction. What I mean by this is that historians very rarely try to prove the truth of the concepts they have borrowed, assuming instead they must be appropriate because they come from the specialist discipline that deals with the area of evidence they happen to be addressing and, what is more, they appear to 'fit' the **facts**. If a historian is seeking to explain the connection between slavery and the political structures of the United States in the first half of the nineteenth century, he/she may well feel satisfied in borrowing selectively from the wide variety of race or class models readily available off the sociology or politics shelves. It is quite easy in all this to lose sight of two things: the teleological or future-anticipating nature of our second-hand concepts (presumably there is a reason for buying in someone else's vision of the future to apply to the past?), and that they, and propositions, are not analogous to objects or facts (in spite of the good 'fit') (see TELEOLOGY).

The sophisticated constructionist historian does have some inkling of these problems of course, realising that concepts are not mental bridges that link the word (the written or speech act) and the world (references to reality). Instead of being the mental representations of events/actions/ processes in the past, concepts stretch to *how* we imagine the form in which we cast history. Generally speaking, most historians feel they have no choice but to work on the prior principle of concepts embodying referents (the word, the object and its meaning) because otherwise they would not be doing history but philosophy instead or, what might be even worse, the philosophy of history (see REALITY/REALISTIC EFFECT). Reconstructionist historians are much less exercised by these worries, maintaining that concepts are accurate enough descriptions of reality when they are properly thought out. To ensure the quality of history, therefore, the only concepts that can be used are those that exist independently and immanently in the real past and that thereby constitute its discoverable causal principles (see CAUSATION). For the reconstructionist historian there are no unresolvable ontological or epistemological questions here.

This thinking is the foundation for the reconstructionist claim that historical knowledge is capable of being objectively discovered through the rationally justifiable process of inference from the evidence (see OBJECTIVITY). This inferential process demonstrates the natural existence of the concepts inspired by the evidence, so there is very little problem with conceptual relativism. Contrary to the post-empiricist sceptic's (anti-realist) view, proper historians do not make the past. Historians only create descriptions that the real past may fit (or may not as the case may be). Without a real past there is nothing from which to derive concepts, and nothing to which to re-apply them. It is then up to the historian's skill with the evidence to establish their accuracy and explanatory power. Reconstructionist historians equate the past with reality, and treat it accordingly.

The post-empiricist (or conceptual relativist) does not view history in the same way as the empiricist, that is, as past reality. The problem of knowing the past is not, as the empiricist historian assumes, the same as the problem of knowing reality. While most post-empiricist historians accept the past existed at the basic level of the single descriptive statement, and that we can presuppose reality in our everyday lives because we have immediately verifiable sense experience of it (and postists in their daily lives ignore the extreme scepticist arguments against *really* knowing through experience), we can not make the same assumption for the past. History is not like that: it is not ontologically objective and, therefore, independent of our formalised representation or conceptualisation of it (i.e. content knowable, and form given). Every application of a social theory, or a concept in the pursuit of history, is a destabilisation of the past. Every conceptualisation and every appeal to laws of human behaviour are interventions. The post-empiricist assumption is that, in effect, the past existed but not independently of the historian's mind, which is unavoidably implicated in fashioning that which seemed to have happened. Historians are not ontologically detached bystanders but are, through our organising concepts, active participants in making knowledge of the past – not what it once was, but what it is now.

Further reading

Callinicos, A. (1995)
Gardenfors, P. (1997)
Joyce, P. (1991)

Neisser, U. (1981)
Peacocke, C. (1992)
Schorske, C.E. (1998)
Searle, J.R. (1995)
Smith, E.E. and Medin, D.L. (1981)
Weitz, M. (1988)

CONSTRUCTIONIST HISTORY

Constructionist history describes a range of approaches to the past by historians from the sophisticated practical realist to the post-empiricist methodological and epistemological spectrum (see EPISTEMOLOGY; METAPHYSICS). The term, although it designates a wide variety of orientations to the study of the past, as a generalisation all constructionist types of history share the belief that history results from a conceptual dialogue between the historian and the past. Not even the most unreconstructed of reconstructionist historians (see RECONSTRUCTIONIST HISTORY) denies that he/she must be active in seeking meaning in the past. As the British historian-philosopher R.G. **Collingwood** put it, no historian just scissors-and-pastes **evidence** (Collingwood 1994 [1946]: 33, 257–82). Central to constructionist history, as an act of intervention by the historian, is the way its **truth** is cast as history via the process of conceptualising the evidence (see CONCEPTS IN HISTORY).

For most practical realist historians the judicious application of social, political or economic concepts (e.g. race, gender, nationalism, class) is a prerequisite to understanding the structures that shaped the lives, the decisions, and the actions of people in the past. Historians generally do not view this intervention as producing history that could be regarded as wholly or even primarily fabricated. The kind of interventionism suggested by this vision is inspired by a sophisticated and self-conscious, yet fundamentally empiricist (see EMPIRICISM), methodology (see COLLIGATION). Regardless of the assumptions they make about the nature of the past, realists view concepts, categories, and tools of analysis (native to history or borrowed from other disciplines) as the servants of the evidence.

A somewhat more sceptical view of history as a construct holds that it can only offer a highly mediated and indirect access to the past because, as R.G. Collingwood suggested, it deals only with its traces. His position assumes that our knowledge of the past is the result of the historian's imaginative and constructive engagement with the evidence (see HISTORICAL IMAGINATION). Although Collingwood doubted that empiricism can provide a distanced platform for knowing, his scepticism was moderated by the belief that, while we exist in the here and now, our powers of inference are flawed, and our language is uncertain, historical methodology will ultimately offer us reasonable grounds for knowing (see INFERENCE; NARRATIVE) (Collingwood 1994 [1946]: 319).

Both Collingwoodian sceptics and practical realists, therefore, ultimately remain firmly realist – their historical constructionism is directed to reconstructing the past as it most probably was. For various kinds of non-realists, however, the term 'constructionist' as a modifier of 'history' is redundant. History is, from the post-empiricist perspective, clearly the construction of the historian and the language they use, or that uses them in the narratives they create. Every application of a social theory, or a concept in the pursuit of history, is a destabilisation of the past. Every conceptualisation and every appeal to laws of human behaviour are impositions or arrangements of the past by the historian. From the perspective of language as a localised, unfixed and polyvalent medium of communication, history is only ever constructed, and its meanings are situational and historicised. It follows that we access the past through concepts created in language and that can only do their work of **historical explanation** through our narratives.

Constructionism can refer to social theory-invoking general laws of historical explanation, as in the French *Annalistes*' attempt at total explanations, or to the sociologically inspired work of individual historians like Robert Darnton and Marshal Sahlins. It can also be taken to mean the modernisation theories of W.W. Rostow and C.E. Black, or the Marxist and neo-Marxist materialist school represented in the work of Eugene Genovese, Christopher Hill, Herbert Gutman, Eric Hobsbawm and E.P. Thompson. It can designate the anthropological or sociological history of Clifford Geertz and Anthony Giddens. Constructionist history emerged from the empiricist mainstream in the nineteenth century thanks to Marx, Comte and Weber. This was not because they or historians in general doubted the modernist belief in the existence of factual knowledge as discovered in the evidence, but because of the naïve empiricist claim that it was feasible to have justified historical interpretations based on observable evidence alone, with the historian standing outside history, outside ideology, outside pre-existing cultural narratives, and outside organising concepts.

Further developments in **continental philosophy** in the twentieth century resulted in the so-called **linguistic turn** away from empiricist epistemology toward the recognition of the role of language and discourse in creating historical understanding. What became seen as the dangerous incursion of postmodernist thought into the mainstream of history was noted by the British historian Lawrence Stone in a 1979 article, 'The revival of narrative', in which he detected the end of one form of constructionist or social theory history, with a return to an earlier kind of narrative history (see POSTMODERNISM). In a later article, 'History and post-modernism', Stone argued history was, by the early 1990s, in danger of losing sight of its foundationalist narrative empiricism because of the argument that there is no reality outside language. Here Stone located the latest form of constructionism – the linguistic turn to a rhetorical constructionism based on the notion that language constitutes meaning in the social world, and the object of historical study is always created by the historian (Stone 1979, 1991; Fay, Pomper and Vann 1998).

The implication is clear, that our access to the past is always textualised – the text as source, as the historian's written interpretation, and as meaning and knowledge. Stone rejected the consequence of, as he saw it, this form of extreme rhetorical constructionism, that history is only about the relationships existing between texts, with real life being squeezed out. More sanguine has been the view of the French historian Roger Chartier, who has argued that all historical texts are best viewed as the result of a construction on the part of the historian forming *a* representation of the past, not its reality. For Hayden **White** also, history is unavoidably a literary construction created out of tropes, figuration (see TROPE/FIGURATION), emplotments (see EMPLOTMENT) and ideology. Constructionist history, therefore, may be best considered as a self-conscious description of the variety of ways available to understand the past, ways that recognise the epistemological, methodological and narrativist impositions made by professional historians.

Further reading

Bann, S. (1984)
Bunzl, M. (1997)
Callinicos, A. (1995)
Chartier, R. (1997)
Collingwood, R.G. (1994 [1946])
Geertz, C. (1983)
—— (1973)
Giddens, A. (1976)
Goldstein, L. (1976)
LaCapra, D. and Kaplan, S.L. (1982)
Munslow, A. (1997a)
Sahlins, M. (1989)
—— (1985)
—— (1981)
Scott, J.W. (1989)
—— (1988)
Stone, L. (1992)
—— (1991)
—— (1979)

CONTINENTAL PHILOSOPHY

The fact that historians are now, as never before, actively rethinking the temper, theory, purposes and conditions of historical knowledge is evidence of the direct challenge to analytical philosophy – the tradition upon which the Anglo-American processes of historical analysis and **hermeneutics** are built – of continental philosophy. To understand the nature of the challenge we need to be mindful of what it is that is being challenged.

The principles underpinning two millennia of Western historical inquiry have culminated in the traditions of analytical philosophy, namely, all that flows from the Platonic/realist understanding of meaning, **truth** and knowledge. In the Platonist universe genuine knowledge of the object 'out there' is waiting to be 'discovered' and is not the product of the mechanism(s) deployed for the inquiry (language, psychology of perception, etc.). This means reality (the world) is independent of **discourse** (the word), and genuine knowledge must be ahistorical – perspectivally neutral. From these basics a variety of **Enlightenment**-inspired interlinked foundational concepts (see CONCEPTS IN HISTORY) have developed that have, in large part, informed historical thinking and methodology: propositional logic and coherent argumentation, the correspondence theory of truth, **empiricism**, the contextualisation of **evidence**, referentiality, representationalism, factualism (see FACTS), truth-conditions for historical descriptions, **inference**, and social theory constructionism. These principles are normally couched as dualities – the separations of knower and known, observer and observed, history and fiction, history and historian, and truth and value.

So what is the nature of the critique of continental philosophy? While the questions of truth and knowing are as elemental to it as they are to analytical philosophy, the continental tradition begins to differ in its thinking with G.W.F. **Hegel**'s reconceptualisation of Immanuel **Kant**'s theory of knowledge. Unlike Kant, Hegel accepted the historical situatedness of reason and knowledge. (Kant's categories are in themselves historical creations.) Knowledge, reason and truth can not escape the gravitational pull of the world. The perspectivism that emerges with Hegel is confirmed given that the individual knowing subject also exists within a proscribed time and place (see the ENLIGHTENMENT). The fact that the individual knowing subject is the product of his/her conditions of existence means that, although reality exists, it can not be wholly independent of his/her representations of it. So, with Hegel we move from the ahistorical to the conditional, from the individual (as the source of knowledge) to cultural processes. Modifying Kant's transcendent rationality means knowledge must be, to a greater or lesser extent, subjective and/or contingent.

This means the historian (like everyone else who is trying to gain 'genuine knowledge') is a part of the reality being examined. For Hegel this suggests the subject (possessing consciousness) and the object (external reality) are ontologically connected – part of a chain of being (see ONTOLOGY). Because our categories of analysis and methodologies, like ourselves, are culture-bound there is no way to break free of class, race, gender, ideology, etc. For Friedrich **Nietzsche** neither the world of 'what is' nor 'what seems' can offer a measure by which to judge the truth claims of genuine knowledge. Eventually, Nietzsche argued, certain knowledges are regarded as truthful just because their genealogy is so remote. This suggests truth is perspectival – a cultural practice that generates a **reality/realistic effect**, rather than a separate and genuinely knowable reality.

The nineteenth-century basis to continental philosophy provided by Hegel and Nietzsche has branched in the twentieth century into several related spheres associated with a number of key thinkers: phenomenology

(Edmund Husserl (1859–1938), Martin Heidegger (1889–1976) and Jean-Paul Sartre (1905–80)); hermeneutics (Hans Georg Gadamer (1900–) and Paul Ricoeur 1913–)); post-structuralism (Michel **Foucault** (1926–84), Roland **Barthes** (1915–80), Jean-François Lyotard (1924–) and Jacques **Derrida** (1930–)); and critical theory (Jürgen Habermas (1929–), Theodor Adorno (1903–69), Max Horkheimer (1895–1971) and Louis Althusser (1918–90)). Phenomenology, as a theory of knowledge, and directed by its founder Edmund Husserl, takes up the notion of perspective and ways of knowing as problems of perception and consciousness (what we only genuinely know is our a priori consciousness: see A PRIORI/A POSTERIORI). Hermeneutics, as the art of textual and (post-Wilhelm Dilthey) cultural interpretation, is indebted especially to Martin Heidegger who, for example, examined the subjective aspect of knowing through his attempt to understand nature of the being of the interpreter of texts (Dasein). Heidegger's phenomenology is hermeneutic in that being is not viewed as an a priori/transcendental access to reality, for our being is prefigurative. We are pre-programmed to understand the meaning of texts by our being in the world (interpretation thus reveals our being beyond the texts). Heidegger's pupil, Gadamer, also explored the period, place and conceptual boundaries of the subject's 'horizon' of knowledge, and that truth arises in the dialogue between knower and known, and the document and the interpreter (each possessing different horizons) that occurs at a particular time and in a certain place.

Rethinking these connections is most clearly demonstrated in the work of the post-structuralists Michel Foucault and Jacques Derrida, with their joint (Nietzschean-inspired) questioning of the fixity of truth-conditions, the transparency of representation, and the transcendental signified: all producing forms of knowledge that are tied to power, ideology, space and time, rather than corresponding to a knowable and discourse-independent reality. Critical theory is largely indebted to the so-called Frankfurt School of German philosophy and sociology founded by (among others) Max Horkheimer in 1923, and his belief that social theory can only be relatively independent of context. This means social critics, sociologists, philosophers and historians must evaluate the origins of their explanations (be self-reflexive) rather than accept them as the products of independent and value-free methodologies of knowledge discovery.

For historians the impact of continental philosophy has been most obvious in the postmodern (see POSTMODERNISM) challenge to history's foundational tenets, although the term 'postmodern history' is probably misleading. As my comments indicate, the philosophical origin of much that is described as postmodern actually began in the nineteenth century with Hegel, and especially with Nietzsche's critique of the Enlightenment conceptualisation of language and being. Much that we call postmodern history is, in effect, continental philosophy's critique of its own modernist (post-Hegelian) founding principles. There is nothing, for example, novel or postmodern in Nietzsche's deconstruction of causality (the effect is primary in the search for cause) (see CAUSATION).

The properties or features we associate with postmodern history, but which are the product of continental philosophy, include many new questions and a willingness to accept fresh orientations to the study of the past: a questioning of epistemological certainty (see EPISTEMOLOGY), placing a question mark over inference, assuming an anti-representationalist position, being open to teleological explanation (the past viewed as future flight) (see TELEOLOGY), accepting that there is no knowable reality (there are only discourses), viewing history as truth-effect rather than truth, presuming we do not *discover* patterns in contingent events but instead impose them because that is how we want to emplot (see EMPLOTMENT) or organise the past, rethinking the facile distinction of fact and fiction, welcoming the ideological self-reflexivity of the author-historian by rejecting grand **narrative**/totalising or foundationalist concepts of explanation (e.g. class did not exist in the past until historians borrowed it from sociologists as a concept), reconceiving historical truth as existing at the local here-and-now level, noting that narrative closure is not essential to writing the past, granting there are no historical facts (apart from simple consensual statements), acknowledging that metaphors are deployed as historical explanations (see HISTORICAL EXPLANATION), confirming that history is always about moral choices (not assuming there *must* be a given meaning in the evidence, and what it *must* suggest according to a transcendent ethic), and exploring the possibilities in the relationship of **form and content** in historical explanation. This is a list that could be extended depending on what you choose to borrow from the continental philosophy tradition.

Further reading

Appleby, J. *et al.* (1996)
Baynes, K., Bohman, J. and McCarthy, T. (1987)
Bernstein, R. (1983)
Kearney, R. and Rainwater, M. (1996)
Lechte, J. (1994)
Roberts, D.D. (1995)
Stromberg, R.N. (1994)

COVERING LAWS

As a form of **historical explanation** the covering-law model assumes history to be an empirical (see EMPIRICISM) undertaking, the **facts**, events (see EVENT) and processes of which can be explained according to the conditions that govern their probable, regular or law-like occurrence. So, although individual events can not be explained as individual events, they can be taken as examples of a particular category of occurrences determined according to conditioning explanatory laws. The philosopher of history and science Carl

Hempel suggested historians invoke covering laws all the time to account for human behaviour (Hempel 1942). Conventionally taken to be opposed to this law-seeking constructionist (see CONSTRUCTIONIST HISTORY) approach to historical explanation is that of the sophisticated hermeneutic (see HERMENEUTICS) or interpretative tradition represented by the British philosopher and historian R.G. **Collingwood** (and subsequently others like William H. Dray, Alan Donagan and G.H. von Wright) as well as in the work of a variety of reconstructionist (see RECONSTRUCTIONIST HISTORY) historians and philosophers (like G.R. **Elton**, Arthur Marwick, Jack Hexter, Gertrude Himmelfarb, C. Behan McCullagh, Michael Stanford, Chris Lorenz and Perez Zagorin).

However, according to the anti-realist philosopher of history Frank Ankersmit, there is less to this division than meets the eye, because both orientations are essentially inferential and constructionist, and their respective practitioners believe history can explain what really happened in the past (see INFERENCE). Hempel's short article on 'The function of general laws in history' published in 1942 loosed a wave of positivist-inspired (see POSITIVISM) constructionist **empiricism** that suggested history could work according to general laws, which themselves could be determined by the deduction of the meaning of the event (the *explanandum*) from statements consisting of the general law and antecedent conditions (the *explanans*). Hempel understood, however, that historians do not work in such a strictly deductive manner instead producing what he called 'explanation sketches' that, after the cultivation of the **evidence**, would yield – in all probability – the relevant laws of human behaviour from which the likely causes and meaning of events and processes could be inferred (see CAUSATION; COLLIGATION). This covering-law model was, in effect, a watered-down version of what philosophers call deductive-nomological thinking, whereby events can be explained by a set of initial conditions plus the application of a general law, so the event described *must* follow given the premises undergirding it.

As Ankersmit points out, conservative reconstructionist historians have generally rejected the full-strength Hempelian covering-law model (with the same assurance as they have rejected the sceptical idealism of Collingwood). They regard it as quite unnecessary to their analysis of the sources or their constitution of unique historical facts and events, because it is unavoidably deductive and, therefore, an inappropriate form of historical thinking. The issue between constructionist advocates of such a model (like Karl Popper, Patrick Gardiner, Ernest Nagel and Clayton Roberts) and extreme reconstructionist doubters (see above list) is whether the subject matter of history – accounting for agent **intentionality** – is amenable to such explanation.

Ankersmit argues the attempt has been made to locate a dilute form of the covering-law model based on inductive inference, as a compromise between the extremist models of sceptical empiricist reconstructionism and history-as-science (a compromise promoted of late by Clayton Roberts). The compromise derives from the wish, prevalent among mainstream constructionist historians (see CONSTRUCTIONIST HISTORY), to defend as objective and truth-conditional (see TRUTH) their preferred methodology that is – unsurprisingly – founded on the inductive inference (i.e. derivation) of agent intentionality (see OBJECTIVITY). It follows that laws or theories of behaviour are only at best suggestive of likely causes for events – explanations to the best fit. Indeed, it can be argued that historians happily enjoy a theory-free existence in the sense that no covering law and no large-scale theory can explain what historians are actually interested in – the immediately needful, and rational (or occasionally irrational for 'good' reasons) intentions of people in the past. Neither are historians concerned with projections about the future (see TELEOLOGY). Most are pleased to indulge in exploring large-scale social and institutional structures while accepting that such imaginative speculations do not permit the absolute prediction of individual intentionality or action. For Ankersmit this suggests both approaches have moved toward a convergence in their joint attempts to domesticate the past and promote the idea that the historian's referential language can mirror it faithfully. Premised like this the majority of historians continue to believe history is an interpretative yet factualist act of agent intentional discovery and, it follows, the discipline is a distinctive truth-seeking **epistemology**.

It is at this point the deconstructionist historian (see DECONSTRUCTIONIST HISTORY) will submit that neither approach can effectively resolve the central problem of **form and content**, namely, that, while history may wish/claim to be about getting closer to the real truth of the past (its content), it is actually never able to escape from the language or concepts (see CONCEPTS IN HISTORY) used to describe it (the form of the past that is the-past-as-history). As Ankersmit suggests, the covering-law model can not encompass both a knowable agent intentionality and fully control the historian's language as a mirror of reality, that is, bridge the gap between knowing and telling, and history and **historiograph**y (see Hayden WHITE; LINGUISTIC TURN; Richard RORTY). The same criticism would, of course, also be levelled at mainstream Collingwoodian-type interpretative history.

Further reading

Ankersmit, F.R. (1994)
Donagan, A. (1962)
Dray, W.H. (1957)
Hempel, C.G. (1942)
Lorenz, C. (1998)
Murphey, M.G. (1986)
Nagel, E. (1961)
Popper, K. (1962 [1945])
Roberts, C. (1996)
Snooks, G.D. (1998)
Stanford, M. (1994)
von Wright, G.H. (1971)
Zagorin, P. (1999)

CROCE, BENEDETTO (1866–1952)

A one-time Marxist and positivist, the Italian philosopher Benedetto Croce became increasingly attracted to idealism (what he called his philosophy of the spirit), **historicism**, and the study of the connections between literature, the aesthetic (art), philosophy and history (see POSITIVISM). Croce is an important philosopher of history because of his rejection of the basic tenets of positivism and **metaphysics**, his response to the ideas of Giambattista **Vico**, Immanuel **Kant**, G.W.F. **Hegel**, Friedrich **Nietzsche** and Karl Marx, his views on history as an art form, and because of his influence on philosophers of history like R.G. **Collingwood**, Martin Heidegger, Hans-Georg Gadamer, Richard **Rorty**, Jacques **Derrida** and Hayden **White**. Croce's ultimate contribution to the study of the-past-as-history was what he called 'absolute historicism' or doing history in a twentieth-century world that is never fully formed, where there are few if any certainties, and all that is solid eventually melts into air. Hence it is that knowledge can not be scientific because such knowledge depends on nature being in virtually all respects finished, completed, knowable and explicable.

In trying to compromise the rational and the aesthetic Croce maintained (in a materialist and realist fashion) that the historical event is the wellhead of philosophy and, under Hegel's influence, the study of history is essential to understanding meaning (see EVENT). But his philosophy of history was also heavily influenced by his idea that the aesthetic, built upon his notion of the (lyrical) intuition, exists prior to representation and to rely solely on common-sense **empiricism** tells only half the story. For Croce **facts** only come into existence when they have been imaginatively created by the historian from the thoughts of the historical agent (see the ENLIGHTENMENT; HISTORICAL IMAGINATION; CONCEPTS IN HISTORY). Croce, in his appeal to the idealist connection of being and consciousness, tried then to resolve the problem of historical knowing in a world without dependable empirical foundations.

Croce believed that art, produced through intuition, is a pre-conceptual (non-scientific) **epistemology** (a way of knowing) holding that works of art are pure forms of knowledge precisely because they are non-material and intuitively created. Knowing exists not just in science alone but in the image produced by intuition of which it is the expression. Artists have intuitions and (because they are artists) they have the capacity to express them clearly and so create understanding. The material form (see FORM AND CONTENT) given to the expression – located in the technique of representation – is central to the process of understanding what there is in the real world. The expression (the form) of that which is intuited can have, so Croce chose to believe, a transcendental aspect so it encompasses the universal human spirit. This can be found only in great art, literature and history. His notion of the origin of intuition has a certain parallel with Vico's conception of the first or metaphoric stage human beings create – the fantastic age of gods and myth (*fantasia*).

What does it mean if history is viewed as an art form? It means at least two things: first, that the intuitive a priori creates the-past-as-history through the mind of the historian rather than the correspondence theory of knowledge; and second, that history (and art) represent the unique and the individual. Although Croce believed (in a realist sense) that our historical knowledge of the event was the basis of all understanding, the origin of historical knowledge itself (the meaning of the event constituted as facts and then as truthful interpretations) must emerge from the historian's power to imagine or intuitively think out the meaning of the single object of study. The historian intuits the meaning of the object by predicating its meaning (see A PRIORI/A POSTERIORI; INFERENCE; HISTORICAL IMAGINATION; REALITY/REALISTIC EFFECT; RELATIVISM). As described thus far this is not that different from what most orthodox constructionist historians (see CONSTRUCTIONIST HISTORY) do. Their perception and inference from the **evidence** is organised by concepts/theory as expressed in language. While not accepting the full anti-correspondence implications of history as an art form, this can be of some comfort to empiricists everywhere. As the realist philosopher of history Patrick Gardiner says, in summary of Croce's position and borrowing heavily from Kant, intuitions without concepts are blind (Gardiner 1961 [1951]: 42). Gardiner is not intending, of course, to vindicate Croce's idealism, but rather his own positivism by stressing Croce's realist side.

But where Croce differs from the constructionist historical mainstream is when he talks about what makes history an independent programme of knowledge. This is the historian's power to envision and contemplate the thing done, at the expense of placing the unique factual event under a general explanation (generalisation), systems of thought, social theory, or abstract covering law (see COVERING LAWS). Indeed, Croce has severe idealist-inspired doubts about the very concept of **causation** (see COLLIGATION). Linking facts together by seeking the causal connections between them seems wrong to Croce because it means that historians must be working from a false principle, that we have the empiricist capacity to discover the First Cause when all we actually have is an infinite regression of causes. From the perspective of a realist Croce appears to be demanding here that without an absolute knowledge of why something happened we can not be sure it did happen. While a fuller reading of Croce would dispel that impression the question remains, how can the historian obtain any degree of certainty? For Croce the only hope of gaining historical **truth** is to rethink, as R.G. **Collingwood** later also insisted, the thoughts that gave rise to it.

This idealist (sceptical anti-science) view of history is reinforced by Croce's insistence that history is the **narrative** representation of the facts via linguistically embedded concepts as construed and conceived by the historian. This suggests a break, not just with categorising and generalising about events as a scientist would, but also means doubting the referentiality of the correspondence theory of knowledge. This confirms for Croce the need for historians to intuit (infer?) the meaning of the past by mentally reliving it. For Croce rethinking the unique event seems to bear out the peculiar nature of historical thinking that characterises history *sui generis* (unique to itself).

Croce places himself in the situation of trying to maintain history as a legitimate discipline, defined by its access to past reality, while at the same time arguing for the central role of the historian in creating historical knowledge. Although Croce begins with history, his idealism places the historian at the centre of the process of doing history. This leads to Croce's most famous opinion that all history is contemporary because, as he says, the past vibrates in the here and now, within the evaluative historian's mind. As the American philosopher of history David Roberts says, Croce's vision of history offers a way of coming to terms with both knowing and doing in a post-metaphysical (see METAPHYSICS) world (D.D. Roberts 1995: 82).

This conception of history has made Croce unpopular with the mainstream of orthodox realist historians, who prefer to believe in knowable reality because they are sensibly sceptical about what the evidence can tell them. In spite of Croce's wish to find out the truth of the past, critics like positivist Patrick Gardiner are largely dismissive of Croce, along with fellow idealists like Michael Oakeshott and R.G. Collingwood, because of their contention that history must begin with the thoughts of historians (Gardiner 1961 [1951]: 31). The reconstructionist historian Geoffrey **Elton** views Croce (and Collingwood, who is also irredeemably lost) as the very worst of historians – he (they) were utterly wrong, he said, to place the historian at the centre of the historical reconstruction (Elton 1991: 43) (see RECONSTRUCTIONIST HISTORY). The British reconstructionist social historian Arthur Marwick has delighted in suggesting that Croce (whom he lumps in with Hegel) meant little to him as a historian because of the **relativism** that was Croce's legacy (Marwick 1989 [1970]: 8, 79). While these realists have little time for Croce's variety of history, his pursuit of historical truth through the intuitive historian remains some kind of balance to the hard-hat empiricism of reconstructionist history and the 'probable' history of constructionism (see CONSTRUCTIONIST HISTORY).

Further reading

Brown, M.E. (1966)
Collingwood, R.G. (1994 [1946])
Croce, B. (1970 [1927])
—— (1968 [1917])
—— (1964 [1913])
—— (1923)
Elton, G. (1991)
Gardiner, P. (1961 [1951])
Marwick, A. (1989 [1970])
Moss, M.E. (1987)
Roberts, D.D. (1995)
—— (1987)

Struckmeyer, O.K. (1978)
Wellek, R. (1981)

CULTURAL HISTORY

Before we can define cultural history we must define culture. I take culture to encompass three main features of lived experience as understood in the West; the first and second are the aesthetic/intellectual, and the social (see the ENLIGHTENMENT; MODERNISM). First, by the aesthetic/intellectual dimension I mean cultural development in respect of thinking about and producing the scientific and academic disciplines of history, art, literature, political ideas and philosophy. Included here are the intellectual processes and practices whereby society reflects upon its past self, the present and the future, and how it invests its intellectual and social life with meaning (see EPISTEMOLOGY; ONTOLOGY). By the social features of culture I mean those cultural practices that are understood through lived experience. As historians we should not forget that such historical understanding is organised by the concepts (see CONCEPTS IN HISTORY) our intellect provides to make sense of our experience – in this example we may utilise **class**, race and gender (see WOMEN'S HISTORY). The upshot is that we choose to view intellectual and social life over-determining each other. The third feature in my definition of culture is the representation of these first two elements – how we re-present or mediate our intellectual and social life, and create meaning. This is the textual or signifying dimension to culture. This feature is, I would suggest, dependent upon the other two in respect of how society understands, problematises and organises cultural practice(s) as cultural representation (see FORM AND CONTENT).

It is the exploration of these three defining and inter-related features of culture that is both the subject matter of cultural history and which influences our thinking about its form. Questions of form can not be ignored because cultural history is itself a cultural practice differentiated by its modes of representation. The varieties of cultural history evidence the extent to which they are the products of the professional and discipline consensus of historians, as well as actual historical circumstance. Just as history itself emerged as an eighteenth- and nineteenth-century modernist project, with the intention of domesticating and giving useful meaning to the past, so the long crisis of modernity since the end of the eighteenth century (the intellectual crisis of ontology (being) and epistemology (knowing)) produced history's various forms as responses to the events (intellectual, social, political and material) of that long crisis.

However, almost as soon as the German empiricist historian Leopold von Ranke (1795–1886) had begun to impose his classic objectivist epistemology, with its priority of content over form on the emergent discipline of history, an early social history burgeoned under the influence of the influential Swiss-born historian Jacob Burckhardt (1818–97) (see EMPIRICISM).

In his *The Civilization of the Renaissance in Italy*, first published in 1860, Burckhardt established what, according to the theorist of cultural history Peter Burke, were to become several of the central concerns of later cultural history (Burke 1997). In the book Burckhardt addressed the intellectual, social and representational aspects of the Renaissance cultural history of Italy. He described the role of the individual within an emergent national polity, the role of history as a nationalist force, the growth of the academic disciplines, the role of biography, the relationships between men and women, and various aspects of popular culture including costume and fashion, festivals, social etiquette, domestic life and home management, music, education, religion and superstition, and poetry and language, which he saw as a subject of 'daily and pressing importance' (Burckhardt 1990: 240).

In the early part of the twentieth century the rise of the masses into political life, the increasing impact of science and technology, the consequences of a hugely unbalanced wealth creation, the arrival of total war, and the intellectual promise of the social sciences, combined to produce the century's dominant form of historical study – social (and to a lesser extent economic) history. Widening historical study in this way did not at first create doubts about the empiricist nature of the exercise. Indeed, while both Burckhardt and his successor as the pre-eminent 'cultural historian' Johan Huizinga (1872–1945) stressed the empathic approach to the study of the past, the advent of the social sciences (and the application of statistics to history – cliometrics) seemed to reinforce the historian's capacity for telling the truth about the past as it actually happened (see R.G. COLLINGWOOD; OBJECTIVITY). But it was the total-history approach (covering all aspects of culture) of the *Annales* school in France that transmuted social history into cultural history – the present highly complex study of the inter-relationships of the three aspects of social life noted above.

The rise of cultural history in the second half of the twentieth century has been very much the result of the influence of contemporary events in the USA and Western Europe on the lives of historians. The clashes of race, class and gender in an age of rapid technological growth and imperial and internal de-colonisation, has meant that the historian's own lived experience of social and material life, as well as the post-empiricist intellectual debates of the past twenty years, have constituted the character of today's cultural history (see LINGUISTIC TURN; RELATIVISM; TRUTH). The contemporary material and intellectual crisis of modernity has been, therefore, the context for the emergence of cultural history in its manifestations as historical analysis and cultural practice. All this means is that cultural history today is the prime intellectual site for competing visions of what constitutes history and the study of the past.

Cultural history is now the focal point for many different (sometimes converging, sometimes diverging) developments within historical studies. Because of the nature of cultural history (covering all aspects of past intellectual and social life and their representation), as well as experiencing the impact of the intellectual developments of the postmodern (see

POSTMODERNISM) and deconstructionist revolution (see DECONSTRUCTIONIST HISTORY), the cultural historian has to be continuously self-reflexive in his/her thinking about how to do history. The medley of theories, concepts, approaches, philosophical positions, metahistorical perspectives and forms, as well as the new ranges of topics, evidences and sources now available have meant an explosion of epistemological and methodological choices for the cultural historian. What epistemological choice to make is often the most difficult. Today, historians can elect to accept or challenge the very idea of history as a licit discipline, by occupying any position on a continuum that stretches from naïve reconstructionist empiricism, via a bewildering variety of social theorising and historical constructionism (see CONSTRUCTIONIST HISTORY), through to (any one of several forms of) post-empiricism. However, while the linkages between history and the discipline of anthropology, but also psychology, archaeology, sociology, philosophy, critical theory and literature, have occupied ever increasing numbers of historians, the common currency of these disciplines – the investigation of cultural change and formation, and the role of the intellectual in its understanding and representation – remains. So, whichever epistemological and/or methodological orientation is preferred, the topics of culture continue to be central.

When she wrote ten years ago, Lynn Hunt argued that 'the anthropological model' then reigned supreme in cultural history (Hunt 1989: 11); she was quoting the work of Clifford Geertz with his 'Thick description: Toward an interpretive theory of culture', and 'Deep play: Notes on the Balinese cockfight', in *The Interpretation of Cultures* and *Local Knowledge: Further Essays in Interpretative Anthropology* as the most visible contributions then made to the field (Geertz 1973: 3–31, 412–54 and 1983). According to Hunt there are also other 'models' for cultural history quoting the 'anti-historical' work of Michel **Foucault**, the cultural materialism of E.P. Thompson and Natalie Zemon Davis in their explorations of *mentalités*, and Hayden **White** and Dominick LaCapra in their deconstruction of historical narrative. However, according to the cultural historian Peter Burke, the undoubted indebtedness of cultural history to anthropology has not yet replaced the mid-nineteenth-century modernist conception of Burckhardt or Huizinga (Burke 1997). For Burke, however, cultural history is less defined by its methods and approaches than the variety of its contents. Taking a somewhat contrary position, the French cultural historian Roger Chartier argues the annexation by cultural historians of other 'fields of study, techniques, or standards of scientific objectivity' (especially in the evaluation of the *histoire des mentalités*) tends to suggest the continuing social scientific credentials of cultural history, while at the same time he acknowledges the contemporary debates on the objective existence of social structures and the subjectivity of their representations (the illusions of the historian's discourse?) (Chartier 1988: 3–6). These differing views of Hunt, Burke and Chartier typify today's debates on what constitutes the appropriate epistemology, methodology and content of cultural history.

However, the epistemological and/or methodological as well as the evidential and/or topic choices made by cultural historians (form as well as content decisions) means all three elemental features constituting the study of past cultural life are usually recognised (to a greater or lesser extent) in all works of cultural history. On a bibliographical note it would be impossible to list here all the significant works of cultural history. What ought to be said, and the cultural historian Peter Burke said it recently in his book *Varieties of Cultural History* (1997), while historians have adapted and adopted many different and sophisticated models and explanatory theories, the heritage of Jacob Burckhardt and Johan Huizinga can still be seen in the topics addressed.

Further reading

Burke, P. (1997)
—— (1993)
—— (1991)
Chartier, R. (1988)
—— (1987)
Darnton, R. (1986)
—— (1980)
Geertz, C. (1983)
—— (1973)
Ginzburg, C. (1982)
Goodman, J. (1997)
Hunt, L. (1989)
Maza, S. (1996)
Munslow, A. (1992)
Pittock, J.H. and Wear, A. (1991)
Poster, M. (1997)
Thomas, K. (1978)
White, H. (1978)
—— (1974)

D

DECONSTRUCTIONIST HISTORY

A term used to designate the application of several postmodern approaches to the study of the past, particularly those associated with a variety of historians including Michel **Foucault**, Hayden **White**, Keith Jenkins and F.R. Ankersmit, and cultural theorists like Jacques **Derrida**. One of the basic philosophical assumptions of the Cartesian-inspired **Enlightenment** was that genuine knowledge is possible through the processes of logic and rational thought all made accessible through a neutral, passive and stable system of language that operated beyond the object of description. Such a metaphysical realist position enables us to deduce the realities beneath the misleading world of appearances and sensual data (see METAPHYSICS). But philosophical developments later in the eighteenth, nineteenth and twentieth centuries have undermined this belief in the nature of knowing and the power of language to represent the real world accurately. While some historians may still have a certain sympathy for foundationalism, in spite of the **linguistic turn**, more and more have taken its implications into account in their work.

F.R. Ankersmit provides, I think, an appropriate short introduction to the issue of deconstructionist history. He begins with the comment that 'postmodernism's aim ... is to pull the carpet out from under the feet of science and modernism ... [and] ... the best illustration of the postmodernist thesis is ... provided by historical writing' (Ankersmit 1994: 167–8). What Ankersmit goes on to argue is that historical interpretations exist only in relation to each other (there is no original meaning that **hermeneutics**, the art of interpretation, can uncover). This means their identity is determined by their relationship to other texts. Just as significantly, the historical interpretation exists only in language that suggests to Ankersmit, as it does to Hayden White, that the traditional distinction between language and reality loses its meaning. Language can not be the mirror of nature, for it is directly implicated in the reality depicted. Language (written down history) and the past become one. So historians are led to talk about the past as if they were making statements about reality, rather than participating the construction of that reality through their interpretative historical narratives (see NARRATIVE). To use the language of feminism or **class** is, therefore, to constitute a preferred reality. Avoiding this 'mistake' has been a traditional aim of historians. But this aim is now always honoured in the breach. For Ankersmit, this makes the historical narrative an essentially postmodernist (see POSTMODERNISM) undertaking. Thinking about the implications of the conflation of language and reality is at the forefront of deconstructionist history. To understand in more detail what a deconstructionist history entails it is necessary to establish the intellectual derivation of deconstructionism as a sceptical philosophical tendency.

Deconstruction, at its most general level, refers to the interrogation of those discourses (see DISCOURSE) through which human beings attempt to engage with the real world. The deconstructionist objective is to establish how such discourses, like the discourse of history, can achieve or fail to achieve the objective of truthful knowing. Deconstruction as a process of investigative thought should be important to historians, as Ankersmit points out, because it questions our traditional disciplinary investment in the concept of referential language upon which we found our belief that we can more or less accurately and truthfully interpret the world of the past as an entity separate from ourselves. The idea of a representational language that permits both the separation and the correspondence of word and world has long been scrutinised by philosophers ranging from Scottish sceptical empiricist David Hume, transcendental idealist Immanuel **Kant**, and perspectivalist Friedrich **Nietzsche** in the eighteenth and nineteenth centuries, Ferdinand de Saussure, Benedetto **Croce** and Martin Heidegger in the earlier part of this century, to Hans-Georg Gadamer, Paul Ricoeur, Michel Foucault, Richard **Rorty**, Hayden White and Jacques Derrida more recently. The debate between Hume and Kant on the nature of knowledge and the distinction between appearance and reality, while it is central to all later philosophical developments, is of particular significance here, because Nietzsche's reading of the debate led him in a direction that was to have enormous implications for the emergence of deconstructionist history.

David Hume (1711–76) believed it was impossible to have any definitive or all-encompassing knowledge of the real world. This is a fundamental scepticism that most historians today would probably endorse in some degree. For Hume all our knowledge is proscribed, and can never be total. Our knowledge is limited by our current experience (for historians this is the range of sources from which we create facts) and, moreover, this situation can not be ameliorated by any convincing appeal to deductive reasoning (see A PRIORI/A POSTERIORI). Such reasoning can not, in and of itself, establish historical knowledge. Not even when taken together can experience and reason provide either unequivocal knowledge of the real world in terms of telling us what actually happened, or permit us to determine what it really meant (see INFERENCE). Historians can not, for example, establish causal connections irrefutably. We know the Second World War occurred, and we have evidence of the events that prompted the post-Second World War US foreign policy of containment. But historians can not establish a certain causal connection between such events. By Hume's reasoning all we have is a sequence – world war and cold war. The nature of cause and effect in this example can not be established through either observation or deductive logic.

As is well-known, Immanuel Kant tried to overcome this problem of sceptical empiricism by producing what has been called a representationalist model of philosophy (Critchley 1996: 27). Kant argued that the human mind possessed innate a priori categories (meaning mental categories like space, time and causality existing independently of experience) that allow us to order our experience. The important consequence of this thinking for historians is that, like everyone else, we are capable of discovering the truth of the world at least to the extent that it appears to us, if not the world as it actually is. Kant's distinction between perception and experience translates today into the distinction of the form of experience from its content (see FORM AND CONTENT). Kant argued the form of our experience we know a priori, the content always a posteriori (according to the evidence of experience). For Kant, objective knowledge is possible because our subjective categories correspond with reality. To have the fullest possible knowledge of reality, of course, we use both form and content. As post-Kantians we can not, therefore, accept a foundationalist empiricism. Nevertheless, the question of reality versus appearance remains. How can we determine which of our mental categories correspond to reality and which to its appearance?

Friedrich Nietzsche, while accepting we have a priori categories, challenged Kant by arguing such categories can not have any universalist or transcendental validity, because they do not correspond with reality. Indeed, categories and concepts are only ever interpretations, and they are arbitrarily determined by our cultural situatedness, perspective, ideology and power relationships (personal, gender, class, race, disciplinary). So far as the deconstructionist historian is concerned Nietzsche's contribution is important because this directly challenges the nature of the very concepts in which not only philosophy states its problems, but all interpretational disciplines, especially history. Nietzsche refuses absolute meaning in concepts and language. For Nietzsche, **truth** can not be known because of the blanket of figurative discourse that is thrown over reality. The metaphoric nature of language means reality and, therefore, truth, is not directly accessible. It is only by denying this that philosophers can claim unmediated access to reality and to truth. This is a double whammy for historians. It means there are no disinterested historians because no historical concepts can lay a claim to correspondence, and no historical method can overcome the inherent relativism of language use.

Nietzsche's perspectivism – that we interpret rather than know – was paralleled by Ferdinand de Saussure (1857–1913) as the structuralist (see STRUCTURALISM) insight. Saussure's crucial argument was to de-couple the word and the world by pointing out (in Nietzschean fashion) the arbitrary nature of the sign – the culturally determined signifier–signified relationship. Saussure made the assumption that meaning in language emerges through the mechanism of difference (as binary opposition). Language does not mirror nature but is a socially constructed medium that can only confound the common-sense idea of object and its (neutral) description. Saussure broke the natural correspondence or link between representation and referentiality (see NARRATIVE; OBJECTIVITY). The Kantian response to this – one usually deployed by 'proper' historians – is that the reader possesses a culturally attuned narrative competence that permits conventional understanding of what the text means based on cultural expectation and context, as well as the usually accepted rules of syntax and grammar.

However, the arbitrary nature of the sign is important for deconstructionist philosophy, because it endorses the rejection of the notion of a foundational and universalist (transcendental) knowing signifier. For Roland **Barthes**, for example, language is subject to a second-order or hidden metalanguage that suggests an infinite regression of meaning. We can never scrape back the layers of meaning to arrive at the original. The implications of this line of argument make most 'proper' historians somewhat queasy. This thinking de-privileges history as a form of knowledge by removing certainty in language and also, therefore, in history's interpretational narratives. Such thinking forms the basis of the critique of Western philosophy of Jacques Derrida. He maintains that philosophers (in particular), but historians as well, have continued to claim epistemological authority only by deliberately ignoring the unstable and resistant character of language. Although there are distinct differences between their approaches, Foucault also displayed a similar preoccupation with the link between the word and the world. The failure to find origins meant that the past only exists as written history, and is never finished, never tidied up. As the philosopher-historian David Roberts has it, there is nothing but history (D.D. Roberts 1995).

Derrida pursues this with reference to the tropic, figurative and metaphoric device he finds used in the discourse of philosophy (see TROPE/FIGURATION). Influenced by Nietzsche's preoccupation with the obfuscatory effects of figurative language, it occurs to Derrida that all texts are hermeneutically unrecoverable (incapable of interpretation back to their original meaning) (see HERMENEUTICS). One implication of this for the study of the past is that historians ought to become more linguistically and narratologically self-reflexive. We should start, perhaps, by recognising that the effacement of the question of language and narrative (and by implication the erasure of the historian as narrator) means that the conception of history as a natural, legitimate, honest, debunking and truthful narrative shield against liars and the morally depraved is rather more effect than reality.

Derrida is not saying reality is textual, rather that everything is language and reality can not be nailed down through it. So, appearance, reality, language, history and representation (metaphor) merge together.

It is, of course, Hayden White who has most famously insisted on a deconstructive approach to history with his now famous return to the issue of form and content. Returning to this Kantian preoccupation, White insists form is more important to the history production process than is usually accepted. For most 'proper' historians the vast majority of the work they do is in the archive, with the historical narrative still assumed to be a convenient receptacle for the results of painstaking research, and which will, with sufficient care, reveal *the* true story discovered in the sources. The deconstructionist historian objects, arguing that the historical narrative is far more central to the process, at least to the extent of placing form and content on an equal footing. History, instead of being seen solely as a practical method for accessing the truth of the past, ought to be viewed as a literary genre possessing distinctive philosophical objectives.

Deconstructionist historians do not claim that because there is no one absolute way of regarding the real world, then one way must be as good as another. Rather they are suggesting one particular view ought not to be privileged over another: in effect the correspondence theory of knowledge over the textual. There is a substantial debate between a deconstructionist perspective and, for example, a thoroughgoing social science constructionist (see CONSTRUCTIONIST HISTORY) 'real-world' approach like that of Marxist historians. The debate centres on whether or not all frameworks are perspectival. Perhaps we ought not be too surprised at the emergence of the deconstructive vision of history given the epistemologically sceptical heritage of the Enlightenment, and the contemporary profusion of models, hypotheses, figurative styles and idioms, topics, concepts, categories, arguments and materials. The interplay of reconstructionist intent and constructionist consequence suggests that history can never be grounded solely in the past, but unavoidably exists in the present, in the presence of the historian, and is effectively proscribed by the seemingly perennial problem of appearance, reality and representation.

Further reading

Ankersmit, F.R. (1994)
— (1983)
Caputo, J.D. (1997)
Culler, J. (1982)
Derrida. J. (1978)
— (1976)
Eagleton, T. (1983)
Ellis, J.M. (1989)
Foucault, M. (1972)
Jenkins, K. (1997)
Kearney, R. and Rainwater, M. (1996)
Megill, A. (1985)

Munslow, A. (1997a)
Norris, C. (1990)
—— (1987)
—— (1982)
Putnam, H. (1992)
Ricoeur, P. (1984, 1985)
—— (1981)
Roberts, D.D. (1995)

DERRIDA, JACQUES (1930–)

Born and raised in Algeria, Derrida trained in Paris in the 1950s as a philosopher, coming under the intellectual influence of the founder of phenomenology Edmund Husserl (1859–1938). Derrida was also influenced by Friedrich **Nietzsche** and Martin Heidegger (1889–1976). Derrida first came to prominence with his translation of Husserl's *The Origin of Geometry* (1962), but the works for which he is best known were published in the late 1960s and early 1970s (especially his *Of Grammatology*, 1967; English translation 1976) in which he single-handedly established the philosophy of deconstruction. Deconstruction is benchmarked by Heidegger's challenge to the representative theory of perception and the correspondence theory of knowledge/**truth** also heavily dependent upon Nietzsche's insistence on the indeterminacy of language. Following Heidegger, Derrida challenges the Western philosophical preoccupation with the present in its explanations (rejecting Heidegger's early acceptance of the transcendental signified). Derrida's preoccupation is with the traditional Western hierarchy of speech taking precedence over writing (phonocentrism). According to Derrida this idea mistakenly assumes that the speaker provides a privileged or fixed origin for meaning (see AUTHOR; INTENTIONALITY). Put another way, there is no fixity in the relationship of signifier and signified, so no certain or transparent meaning is achievable.

The doubtful thinking that generates this phonocentrism (that speech is the true voice of ideas (*logos*)) implies that writing is an inferior surrogate for speech. Moreover, in writing the speaker's designs and meanings, no longer present, are inclined to be betrayed as language takes over and figuration creates and subverts meaning (see TROPE/FIGURATION). So, the ascendancy of the voice (*logocentrism*) becomes firm and unchanging, and for Derrida this constitutes a dubious Western philosophical habit. In Derrida's critique of texts this means as we read texts – unless we self-consciously deconstruct them – we will be compliant in locating a specious centre of truthful meaning. In practice doing this produces quite misleading 'truths', usually in the shape of everyday oppositions like subject and object, masculine and feminine, real and unreal. What we ought to recognise instead is that our understanding of texts is produced by the difference between signifiers (the meaning of the sign is always there *and* absent – under erasure), so that what texts 'mean' is nothing more than a continuous process of deferral, with the reader playing as important a function in deriving meaning as the author. In effect the knowing subject has disappeared (see the ENLIGHTENMENT; STRUCTURALISM).

For as long as the historical **narrative** is felt to be an accurate transcription of the past (and narrative's unpredictable nature is suppressed, domesticated or ignored), so **empiricism** will remain predominant in the **metaphysics** of history. The real presence of the past will thus continue to exert its primacy in history as it exists in the narrative. Among the consequences of Derrida's basic assumption that there is no transcendental signifier is the doubt inevitably cast on empiricism, **facts**, **inference**, **truth**, **objectivity** and knowable historical reality. If there is no absolute point of origin for meaning in the shape of author intentionality or the referentiality of the evidence beyond the text, then texts can only be evaluated for their possibilities of meaning within themselves. We should not be misled here: Derrida does not doubt referentiality *per se*, only knowable original meanings. All the historian has are endlessly deferred and undecidable and undecipherable meanings. One of the advantages of this perspective is that it allows historians to radically play with the form of what they write (see FORM AND CONTENT). For Derrida writing is the condition for the creation of history, and so history becomes an effect of writing. This is depressing news for empiricists, because it means Derrida's neo-Kantian idealism (abandoning **epistemology**?) carries the 'cost' of never being able to reach definitive answers through the evidence as to what the past *really* means. There can be no closure in history because we can not pin down the past for what it actually was.

Further reading

Bennington, G. (1993)
Burke, S. (1992)
Derrida, J. (1982)
—— (1979)
—— (1978)
—— (1976)
Ellis, J.M. (1989)
Gasché, R. (1986)
Megill, A. (1985)
Norris, C. (1987)
—— (1982)
Sallis, J. (1987)
Sturrock, J. (1979)

DISCOURSE

Historians generally have not made much of the notion of discourse, although the concept possesses a very broad usage among many humanities-orientated disciplines including critical theory, linguistics, sociology, philosophy and social psychology (Mills 1997: 1–3). The few historians who have addressed the nature of discourse have found it central to what historians do.

The philosopher of history Michael Stanford defines the term in talking about 'history as discourse' to demarcate it from other types of history like history as knowledge, history as action, or **event**, relic, theory, or history as sequence. Stanford's definition of history as discourse refers to the **narrative** (or non-narrative) means for the conveyance of that knowledge derived about the past that we call history (Stanford 1994: 79–108). History is a discourse but, lest there be confusion, this does not mean that history is generated by its discursive form rather than its content (see FORM AND CONTENT). In other words history is a discourse of **empiricism**. Historical knowledge is obtained, for Stanford, by the appropriate use of established investigative mechanisms: the critical and comparative study of the **evidence**, double-checking the inferences drawn about it (see INFERENCE), establishing causal connections (see CAUSATION), and withal a clear understanding of the constraints of cultural relativism and language use. Historical meaning is thus generated as an interpretation, which in its turn is accurately described (getting the story straight). In other words, history as discourse does not emerge from the historiographical, the writings of historians (see HISTORIOGRAPHY).

What this means, I think, is that while most historians willingly accept that an understanding of the event can not be wholly separated from their account of it, the discourse of historians is secondary to research, inference of meaning, and explanation through establishing causal connections (see CAUSATION; COLLIGATION; FACTS; OBJECTIVITY; TRUTH). By this logic history, defined as an empirical discourse, can only be constructed as a complex series of statements about a knowable object. To make sense of such evidential statements (to infer their original authorial meaning) historians require an extensive knowledge of the evidence and the historical context(s) to which the evidence refers (see AUTHOR; INTENTIONALITY). In other words, the historian's inferred meaning will be expected to equate to *the* meaning of *the* author, that is, understanding *the* story as related in the text.

History, defined as an empirical discourse, requires that we acknowledge the role of historical description, but it means not forgetting that history and narrative must remain separate. Traditionally understood, history is a way of producing knowledge according to recognised rules of investigation, while narrative is not cognitive in the same way. However, following the arguments of Emile Benveniste, the French philosopher-historian Michel de Certeau notes the peculiarity in the relationship between history and description, what he calls 'a strange situation, at once critical and fictive' and that the 'gap separating reality from discourse' will never be filled (de Certeau 1988 [1975]: 8–9). For de Certeau, unlike Stanford, historiography constitutes the discourse of historians as we try to represent events in referential texts. As he says, at the end of the history process the discourse of the historian is a fiction witnessed in the story that is told as a performance, as he says, as a 'a staging of the past' (de Certeau 1988 [1975]: 9).

De Certeau's grounds for these assertions are now the pretty well-known ones of the cultural relativism of the historian, his/her moral position, the social theory he/she imposes, and the nature of the composition process that takes the historian from practice to text (*écriture*) (de Certeau 1988 [1975]: 56–113). Writing is not, therefore, just an objectivist investigative method but is an aesthetic cultural practice involving the author of the evidence, the author of the history and the eventual consumer as reader (and we might also add the manuscript referees, the copy editor and the publishing editor).

The unavoidable modernist paradox is that while historical discourse claims to provide a truthful content (based on the rules of evidence) it has to do it in the form of a knowing narrative (see MODERNISM). But, when historians put finger to keyboard to write, there is what de Certeau calls a 'metaphorical slippage': a shift or transposition from one genre to another, from the genre of the event and the factual to a literary form (de Certeau 1988 [1975]: 93–4). The discourse of the historian de Certeau describes as a 'laminated text', a historiographical discourse constructed 'as a knowledge of the other' usually found in the processes of reference, citation and direct quotation. This lamination also requires the effacement of the 'I' in the interpretative text, the use of the event and fact as hooks on which to hang the configured or emplotted narrative (the kind of story invented by the historian), and the creation thereby of the 'realistic illusion' (collapsing the link between signifier and referent) (de Certeau 1988 [1975]: 94–5) (see Roland BARTHES; EMPLOTMENT; RELATIVISM; REALITY/REALISTIC EFFECT). It is through these processes we can gain an understanding of the social/cultural/ideological metalanguage of historical discourse, so we accept the fact that writing history is itself an act that imposes a quite different (another?) set of rules and constraints on our understanding of the past. Like other discourses history is authored within a social context that is directly affected by other discourses and practices. It is a relativist undertaking that suggests history as a discourse is not a mirror on the past.

Further reading

Bann, S. (1983)
Barthes, R. (1986)
Berkhofer, R.F. (1995)
Dant, T. (1991)
Foucault, M. (1970)
Munslow, A. (1992)
Pecheux, M. (1982)
White, H. (1998)
—— (1992)
—— (1987)
—— (1978)
Young, R. (1981)

E

ELTON, GEOFFREY (1921–94)

The Library of Congress catalogue has forty-four entries for Geoffrey Elton, which is testament to the productivity of one of Britain's most famous historians (in large part the result of his popular textbook writing). Born in Germany and arriving in England after studying in Czechoslovakia and escaping from the Nazis, his main contributions fell within the Early Modern period, notably politics and society under the Tudors. An important part of his standing was, however, derived from his forthright defence of **reconstructionist history** (notably political history). Elton endorsed a common-sense conception of the referentiality of the past while sturdily repudiating a priori (see A PRIORI/A POSTERIORI) deductive **inference** (see CONCEPTS IN HISTORY). Theory of virtually any kind was anathema to Elton, who was among the most outspoken promoters of the modernist 'craftsman' vision of historical study, arguing history was about reconstructing the choices and actions of people in the past (see INTENTIONALITY; MODERNISM). By objectively serving the sources (see EVIDENCE), we can thereby judiciously reconstruct the past to get at its **truth** (see OBJECTIVITY).

Elton promoted this vision in a number of important defences, but notably in three books: *The Practice of History* (1967); his debate with social scientist and cliometrician William Fogel in *Which Road to the Past?* (1983); and *Return to Essentials: Some Reflections on the Present State of Historical Study* (1991). In the last he argued the most important aspect of the work of the historian was the rational and impartial empirical investigation of the documents of human choices within their context (see EMPIRICISM). By these means history would be both accurate and insulated against social theory and ideological **relativism**.

Importing the historian into the process of writing history was, for Elton, a fundamental mistake, a point he made very clear when he took E.H. **Carr** to task for committing (what Elton misconstrued as) some of these sins in the latter's philosophy of history. Elton used his attack on Carr to vigorously rebut and jettison the big idea of R.G. **Collingwood** that writing history necessitates an empathic re-enactment in the historian's mind of the thoughts of historical agents that gave rise to past actions and events (see EVENT). Such a dangerous procedure could pull down the barricades of rationalism that stand guard against the dangers of ideology and presentism (see HISTORICISM). As he said in *Return to Essentials*, and he had feminist historians in mind at the time, this 'corruption' was probably the result not of perniciousness, but rather 'bigoted idleness' (Elton 1991: 67–8). Despite his tone and personal attacks, Elton did, of course, address a key problem that history faces: is it a cultural artefact or the objective pursuit of truth?

The central weakness in Elton's position emerges in his unwillingness to engage in what he dismissed as scullery philosophy. For Elton, firm as he was in his belief in *the* historical method of inductive inference, history is first, last and always about the study of evidence. It is this that makes history both epistemologically independent and capable of reconstructing the past as it actually happened, and without any imposition from the historian. To fall from the historian's professional standards is to abdicate 'the task of telling about the past to the untrained and largely ignorant – to the writers of fiction, avowed or disguised, to the makers of films, to the journalists and speculators of the pen' (Elton 1991: 70). Elton's message was that historians can represent reality objectively, and to doubt that means accepting we can not explain anything at all.

Further reading

Elton, G. (1991 [1955])
—— (1991)
—— (1990 [1958])
—— (1986)
—— (1983)
—— (1973)
—— (1972)
—— (1970)
—— (1968)
—— (1967)
—— (1966)
—— (1960)
—— (1953)
Jenkins, K. (1995)
Kenyon, J. (1983)
Roberts, G. (1998)

EMPIRICISM

Empiricism is knowledge acquisition through the use of the senses as we observe and experience life, or through statements or arguments demonstrated to be true. Developing in parallel with scepticism in the Anglo-

American tradition of writing history, empiricism has been the methodological foundation of both **reconstructionist history** and **constructionist history**, with its insistence on the corollary of the objective observation of the reality to be discovered 'out there' (see OBJECTIVITY). Empiricism assumes what we as historians can know about the past is what it tells us through the available **evidence**. This means we must observe the evidence of our senses without passion or self-interest, without imposition or question-begging. The past is, therefore, a 'given' and historians discover its meaning through the priority of sense over intellect, content before form (see FORM AND CONTENT). It follows our capacity for **historical explanation** must remain tightly controlled as we extract the meaning found in the evidence.

This immediately sets off the alarm bells of sceptics who ask how it is that all we can ever know is what our senses tell us directly? Surely our ideas have to represent the (assumed?) external past world? Sceptical empiricism (of the common-sense George Berkeley and David Hume varieties) became locked into this dilemma, attempting to resolve it by claiming that, in fact, all we can know about the (past) real world is what our ideas represent to us. But thought, surely, provides us with the categories with which to evaluate and organise sensory data? It is the special contribution of Immanuel **Kant** to historical understanding that he explored the need for this mental addition to the empirical process – his famous categorical imperative.

The problem usually encountered by empiricism, then, is that thought does not simply emerge from experience, but actually provides us with concepts or mental categories that we utilise to organise and make sense of our experience. This inevitably leads to the relativist inquiry, 'How can we truly know the reality "out there" given that our observations may well be only constructions of our mind, intuition, or our existence influencing us? How can we prove anything objectively?' Ludwig Wittgenstein (following Kant) pointed out that since sensory data (our evidence) exists only when we comprehend it in our mind we can not be certain as to its true nature or, for that matter, that other people comprehend it in the same way as ourselves. This is, presumably, the source of the perennial problem of competing historical interpretations: historians do not 'read' or 'see' the evidence in the same way.

Most historians today accept a middle position that rejects extreme empiricism (a.k.a. rationalism) maintaining that we observe but we also mentally process information deploying a priori (see A PRIORI/A POSTERIORI) knowledge and categories of analysis as appropriate and helpful. Empiricism can, of course, take the form of a denial of a priori knowledge. Today most historians do not accept that history can be known through an exact correspondence of knowing (see EPISTEMOLOGY) and being (see ONTOLOGY). Most historians these days regard themselves as sophisticated empiricists who judge the reality of the past by a measure of understanding based upon sense-data as filtered through the grid of mental structures pre-existing in our minds. In practice this means the organising concept precedes consideration of the evidence in the shape of a hypothesis to be confirmed or refuted. Few historians today would defend a crude sceptical empiricist position. It is often claimed that such sophistication has resulted in, for example, a feminist empiricism that holds that history (as knowledge) has to be purged of its (usually unconscious) masculinist biases. However, as philosopher-historians like Keith Jenkins and Frank Ankersmit point out, empiricism does not necessarily resolve the word–world translation problem, that is, the evidence of the past is always pre-packaged within stories or narratives (see NARRATIVE), so knowable reality is ultimately about the deconstruction (see DECONSTRUCTIONIST HISTORY) of those stories. Strictly speaking, of course, empiricism is about sensory input in the here and now, whereas history, being a second-hand trade, is not. There is, therefore, a case to be made for history not being primarily an empirical discipline at all.

Further reading

Appleby, J., *et al.* (1994)
Berlin, I. (1997)
Bonjour, L. (1985)
Dowe, P. (1992)
Elton, G. (1991 [1955])
Jenkins, K. (1991)
Nelson, L.H. (1990)
Priest, S. (1990)
Sellars, W. (1997 [1956])
Topolski, J. (1991)
Zagorin, P. (1999)
Zammito, J.H. (1998)

EMPLOTMENT

Building on Immanuel **Kant**'s notion of emplotment as a category of knowing, and specifically the work of literary critic Northrop Frye, Hayden **White** claims history is the literary artefact that results from the historian's shaping and imposing of a **narrative** on the past. This suggests historical knowledge and understanding are acquired not exclusively as an empiricist research enterprise, but are rather generated by the nature of representation and the aesthetic decisions of the historian (see EMPIRICISM). When viewed from this perspective, our knowledge of the past becomes, to an important degree, the product of the form of the cultural practice we call history (see FORM AND CONTENT). White maintains, therefore, that any model of the historical consciousness ought, therefore, to recognise the complex arrangement of prefiguration (tropes) and associated levels of explanation of which emplotment is one, along with argument/social theory, and ideological preferencing, in addition to the scrutiny of the **evidence** (see TROPE/FIGURATION). While the precise nature of their connection is not clear, White argues it is the tropes that possess the power to determine and configure the other levels of **historical explanation**.

When we place events (see EVENT) in a particular order ('this happened, then that') we are emplotting their sequence. We shape the historical narrative by invoking evidence and causality blending them together to constitute a plausible and truthful explanation (see CAUSATION; COLLIGATION; TRUTH). In doing this we usually fail to acknowledge the functioning of our (Western) culture's main forms of emplotment – romance, tragedy, comedy, satire. That failure permits us to argue that we have discovered *the* referential connection between the narrative and the evidence. Referentiality allows us to find *the* story of the events (see EVENT). For White, however, stories are not lived, but told. As he says historical situations are not *inherently* tragic, comic or romantic, and 'All the historian needs to do to transform a tragic into a comic situation is to shift his point of view or change the scope of his perceptions' (White 1978: 85). This is a step too far for most empiricists, especially as White goes on to suggest that it is down to the historian to match a favoured plot structure with a chosen set of historical events upon which he/she wishes to confer a particular meaning.

The type of emplotment that the historian chooses is determined by the power of the hero of the plot over her, his or its environment. A romance, for example, would be identified by the power of the historical agent/hero as ultimately superior to circumstances, questing with ultimate success, seeking and achieving redemption or transcendence. Satire is the opposite in that the agent/hero is a subject of their context, destined to a history of adversity and rejection. In tragedic emplotments the hero strives to beat the odds and fails, eventually being thwarted by fate or their own fatal personality flaws. The end result is usually death (actual or metaphoric). In a comedic emplotment there is progress and the hope of at least a temporary victory over circumstance through the operation of reconciliation. At the closure of comedic narratives festivities tend to celebrate the connection and consensus achieved with others by the hero (White 1973b: 7–11).

It would be wrong to see what is a radical modification of the correspondence theory of knowledge – with narrative (form) having priority over the evidence (content) – as allowing historians an absolute freedom to choose any trope–emplotment–argument–ideological arrangement they want, and which they can then impose on the evidence. Evidence does exist, and the **facts** built on it are constructed as individual referential statements. Clearly events did or did not happen, and single descriptive statements may be regarded as accurate or inaccurate in degrees. But facts are only ever events under description, and they only become meaningful when we emplot them within a constructed narrative. The truth of historical research, as expressed in single referential statements, may be demonstrated only inasmuch as they correspond to other statements with the same referent saying the same things about it. This correspondence of internal consistency does not mean the historian's imposed narrative interpretation is necessarily truthful (or false) in relation to reality. Narrative interpretations can only signify the past. They can not correspond to it. White is not alone in arguing that history is as much about writing as archival research. Philosophers of history Louis Mink and William B. Gallie have both observed the historian's narrative does not depend solely on factualism to work, but it also depends on a narrative containing a pattern of events, arguments and ethical positions that the reader can understand, and with which they can empathise (Mink 1978; Gallie 1964).

So, when historians try to explain the facts of any set of events the issue becomes: 'How are the facts to be described giving priority to one way of explaining them over another?' Establishing that priority is part of the emplotment procedure and it usually demands ideological, social theory and/or cultural decisions (see CONCEPTS IN HISTORY). In the majority of cases events can be emplotted in a number of different ways in order to furnish those events with different meanings. The input of the historian, therefore, resides both in the archive, and in his/her ability to develop the figurative character of his/her fabricated narrative as a mode of explanation. The facts, once created out of the evidence, must be constituted again as part of a narrative structure. It is a structure, however, written in anticipation of a preferred outcome (see TELEOLOGY). There are always purposes for history.

Further reading

Berkhofer, R.F. (1995)
Callinicos, A. (1995)
Carr, D. (1986a)
Frye, N. (1957)
Gallie, W.B. (1964)
Mink, L. (1978)
Munslow, A. (1992)
Vann, R.T. (1998)
White, H. (1992)
—— (1973b)

ENLIGHTENMENT, THE

A widespread intellectual, cultural and technological/scientific movement usually regarded as the origin of the Modern Era (see EPISTEME; MODERNISM). Beginning in the early seventeenth century in England (with Francis Bacon, John Locke and Thomas Hobbes) and France (with René Descartes), and ending at the close of the eighteenth in France and Germany (with Voltaire, Denis Diderot, Immanuel **Kant** and G.H. Lessing), but found throughout Europe, thought was characterised, in a time of great technological and scientific change, by an acceptance of new ideas like **positivism**, experimentation in science, and the close observation of natural phenomena with reason and rationality promoting explanation through the knowing subject (see LIBERAL HUMANISM). Other new ideas emerged concerning government through contract rather than force (based on the emerging doctrine of liberalism, with its central tenets of popular sovereignty and equality of opportunity), and a new conception of the market-place as a rational economic mechanism. The Enlightenment must also be acknowledged for its influence over the **form and content** of history. As a historical period characterised by the acquisition and organisation of knowledge in particular ways, its epistemological legacy had a direct bearing on how we, in subsequent periods, have understood the historical project itself (see EPISTEMOLOGY; ONTOLOGY).

The Enlightenment, as a description, is usually taken to signify the contrast with the superstitious irrationality that is presumed to have been the cultural and intellectual signature of the Middle Ages. The period is often regarded as the seed plot of several of the basic principles (see META-NARRATIVE) of modernism: namely, reason is the motor and measure of historical change; humanity (man) is capable of progress; all men (if not women) are by their faculty for reason created equal and should, therefore, enjoy equality before the law while exercising tolerance to minorities (reason ruling passion); the sovereignty of 'We, the people'; and the protection of individual rights against the tyranny of undue force. It is sometimes claimed that the ideals that engineered the French and American Revolutions represent these principles in civic practice. The American Declaration of Independence and the US Constitution are often viewed as key documents of the Enlightenment because they are held to embody these principles. The political consequence of the Enlightenment is evidenced in the growth of the doctrine of liberalism (rational political choice), with its chief economic consequence in the free market (rational economic choice).

Its impact on history is in the very creation of history as a discipline founded on the belief it could, and should, become the record of progress and human perfectibility. Perhaps inevitably Enlightenment rationalist thought eventually turned in on itself, questioning its own central tenets. While this self-assessment has been most notable in our own present (or postmodern age: see POSTMODERNISM), the reaction(s) to the Enlightenment project became a central feature of the nineteenth and early twentieth centuries. In the nineteenth century a number of thinkers began to question the assumptions that underpinned the Enlightenment as the disastrous effects of free-market industrialisation and nationalism became clearer – both processes and movements unleashed as a consequence of the Enlightenment frame of mind. The notion of automatic progress was attacked by Karl Marx as merely the ideological construction of the emergent bourgeoisie, while Friedrich **Nietzsche** rejected wholesale the belief that the real world could ever be adequately represented in an unmediated mirror-like fashion. The corollary was to doubt objectivity and science-inspired rationality. Modernism – the offspring of the Enlightenment – was radically transmuted at the close of the nineteenth century into an often violent anti-modernism, especially in the literary and artistic worlds, producing surrealism and Dadaism in art, shifts in literature from author to text to reader, and the confronting and challenge to history conceptualised as the distanced and objective reconstruction of the past (see

CONSTRUCTIONIST HISTORY; DECONSTRUCTIONIST HISTORY; RECONSTRUCTIONIST HISTORY).

Further reading

Appleby, J. *et al.* (1996)
Gay, P. (1966–9)
Kramnick, I. (1995)
Mensch, J.R. (1997)
O'Brien, K. (1997)

EPISTEME

Michel **Foucault** uses the term to designate how a culture acquires and organises knowledge in a given historical period (see EMPIRICISM; EPISTEMOLOGY; ONTOLOGY). The episteme connects all the separate discourses (see DISCOURSE) (religious, scientific, historical, medical, etc.) into a more or less coherent structure of thought founded on a set of shared assumptions about how such knowledge is obtained and deployed. These shared assumptions are elaborated and fixed through the troping process (see TROPE/FIGURATION), which takes place at the deep level of the human consciousness, and which is basic to the emplotments (see EMPLOTMENT) historians generate. Foucault maintains knowledge is generated through the human faculty or sense of difference and/or resemblance that all human beings possess. In *The Archaeology of Knowledge* (1972) Foucault offers the following definition

> something like a world-view, a slice of history common to all branches of knowledge, which imposes on each one the same norms and postulates, a general stage of reason, a certain structure of thought that the men of a particular period cannot escape – a great body of legislation written once and for all by some anonymous hand.
>
> (Foucault 1972: 191)

The notion of the episteme is not new having been previously elaborated by the Italian philosopher Giambattista **Vico** in the eighteenth century. In fact Foucault's definition makes it sound very similar to the concept of the *Zeitgeist* or spirit of the age. He constructs his notion of the episteme on the same premise that fired Vico – that we can only have any degree of certainty about that which we have ourselves created. Knowledge and history emerge from our own social constructions – in this instance Foucault is offering to us the epistemic basis of historical experience. Knowledge has thus been organised within each of the four distinctive historical epistemes that Foucault maintains existed from the sixteenth to the twentieth centuries: Renaissance, Classical, Modern/Anthropological and Postmodern.

Foucault assumes the four epistemes did not grow organically out of each other. Instead they spontaneously appeared in parallel, filling in the spaces suddenly vacated by competing varieties of knowledge creation. In this fashion we see an archipelago of branches of knowledge constituting epistemes rather than a peninsula linked by bridges of causality – as seen in other forms of knowledge like **class**, industrialisation processes, frontier experiences, catastrophic famines, scientific discoveries, individuals bent on world domination, information revolutions, or whatever else is taken to link historical epochs. In the language of **structuralism** Foucauldian history does not evolve, but is best understood as a discursive structure.

The first episteme, from the Middle Ages to the late sixteenth century (the Renaissance), characterises knowledge according to the dominant cultural/linguistic or narrative protocol of resemblance or similitude. In the second episteme, from the seventeenth to the eighteenth centuries (the Classical), knowledge was generated according to the linguistic protocol of the representation of differentness. The epistemological breaks between epistemes thus provided the space for the third episteme (the Modern or Anthropological), from the end of the eighteenth century through to the early twentieth, and which was preoccupied with Man ('I', the 'self') as the subject and object of reality. This preoccupation is, for Foucault, best understood through the invention of the knowing subject and the discipline of history. History's modernist definition requires the understanding of social change by tracing origins and development as cast in the trope of differential succession by the knowing subject (a.k.a. the historian).

In this fashion Foucault perceives the Modern episteme as creating a basic epistemological paradox for humanity: man as the product of his lived social experience, and also the constitutor of knowledge. This invention created the predominant nineteenth and twentieth century conception of history as a realist epistemology, a conception that is seen now for what it is, as a vestigial remain of a previous epoch preserved by **reconstructionist history**. It is the intellectual space in which this crisis of modernist history exists that suggests to many historians the existence of the fourth episteme. For the post-empiricist historian the assumptions and/or attitudes that characterise each age are located in language (metaphors of similarity or difference), and they are displayed in the narratives (see NARRATIVE) that prefigure access to the 'reality' supposedly found in the **evidence**.

Further reading

Bernauer, J. and Keenan, T. (1988)
Forum (1993)
Munslow, A. (1992)
Noiriel, G. (1994)
White, H. (1974)
—— (1973a)

EPISTEMOLOGY

Epistemology is the branch of philosophy that addresses the nature, theory and foundations of knowledge, its conditions, limits and possibilities. Historians, as the creatures of the modernist (Cartesian or **Enlightenment**) revolution, have tended to stick with a particular vision of what history is, derived from a certain kind of analytical philosophy (this is often un-thought out as most historians are not actively engaged by philosophy of any sort). When it is articulated it usually takes the following form: historical knowledge is ultimately discovered through the (highly complex and) rationally justifiable process of the evidence-based inductive method (see CAUSATION; COLLIGATION; CONCEPTS IN HISTORY; EMPIRICISM; EVENT; FACTS; INFERENCE; INTENTIONALITY; OBJECTIVITY; TRUTH).

As practical realists, most historians would also accept that, while this process will help distinguish knowledge from belief, it can not, through either a priori thinking, or model-making, or a posteriori empiricism (see A PRIORI/A POSTERIORI), offer an error-free and unambiguous correspondence between the evidence and the given meaning it is assumed to possess. The reasons for this are, of course, well-understood, namely, we have no direct contact with the past and historical explanation depends on the interpretation of the evidence that must be selected (subjectivity enters the process at this point), or it may be that the evidence we have is misleading, or then again our inferences may be faulty, or we may misconceive the appropriate social theory (see COVERING LAWS; POSITIVISM) we think is suggested by the evidence, or we can not establish all the necessary truth-conditions that will make even our singular statements fully reliable.

For most historians a compromise is advisable – but it is necessarily one that leans toward a realist position, that historical statements, if we stick to tried and tested methods of historical scholarship, will pretty much match our mind-independent observation of the evidence – so we derive knowledge through criteria that are usually cast in terms of arguments to the best explanation. To justify our historical knowledge means bringing our object (historical event, process, action) within a circle of explanatory propositions. This is normal inductive inference, and it will permit, so realist historians anticipate, the constitution of truthful statements about the past (in the sense of discovering the most likely meaning in the evidence of the past). Empiricism (evidence of experience) and logic (reason) together will iron out most of the problems encountered by most historians, most of the time.

For post-empiricist historians epistemology is about the extent to which, and precisely how, historical knowledge is prefigured and composed (for example, a feminist epistemology is knowledge for whom?). For epistemologically sceptical historians (not necessarily the same as anti-realist historians) it is not only (or even?) a matter of asking if there is anything in historical method that can generate reliable and/or truthful historical statements, but what happens when our statements are incorporated into the bigger historical narrative, which itself may be the product of, and relative to, a set of even larger-scale cultural practices and intertextualities? It is a question not just about the possibility of inference up to this level, but what is there in the Western (analytical-empirical) tradition in the first place that can guarantee reliable (and ungendered?) interpretations?

Much **continental philosophy** insists that Western analytical philosophy grants no privileged access to justifiable historical knowledge, and this has prompted increasing numbers of historians to address its implications in terms of whether or not history can make a legitimate claim to being a distinct epistemology. Such a position represents a paradigm shift away from (Western) analytical philosophy in both its empiricist and logic forms. The rejection of empiricism, inference, truth-conditions, natural language, representation, proof and logic all indicate a shift to anti-realism/post-empiricism, with its associated collapse of the distinctions of **ontology** (being) and epistemology (knowing), the priority of content over form (see FORM AND CONTENT), the conflation of observer and observed, and the authorial integration of historian and history (see AUTHOR). Some, like the post-empiricist philosopher Frank Ankersmit, have declared the end of epistemology, while others like Keith Jenkins the end of history (as a modernist moment now dead and gone) (Ankersmit 1994; Jenkins 1999). Doubting the epistemological foundations of history means, therefore, there is also collateral damage to notions of **objectivity** and truth.

Further reading

Ankersmit, F.R. (1994)
Atkinson, R.F. (1978)
Audi, R. (1998)
Barthes, R. (1981 [1967])
Bevir, M. (1994)
Code, L. (1991)
Collingwood, R.G. (1994 [1946])
Cooper, D.E. (1999)
Ermarth, E.D. (1992)
Foucault, M. (1977)
—— (1972)
Hunt, L. (1998)
Jenkins, K. (1999)
Scott, J.W. (1989)
Veyne, P. (1984)
Zagorin, P. (1990)

EVENT

At first sight it may seem unproblematic defining what constitutes an event in historical analysis. An event is commonly assumed to be a singular occurrence or incident: the Charge of the Light Brigade, the assassination of Abraham Lincoln, the Cuban Missile Crisis. Usually historians define a single event as a change of situation. Such a definition distinguishes it from the bigger process(es) of which it may form a part: the Cuban Missile Crisis as an event in the cold war that effected a change, over time, in US foreign policy. For philosophers of history like C. Behan McCullagh the truth-conditions of events can be ascertained and described, so it is worthwhile (and necessary) to linger over events so as to determine their significance/triviality. While individual events may teach us relatively little in themselves, fitting them into the overall picture teaches us much (the process of **colligation**). In filling in the detail we can get close to the **truth** of what went on (see METAPHYSICS). The detail provides the boundary we walk between the important and the insignificant in the past and in the present (see Benedetto CROCE).

Without being able to determine the nature of events accurately we lose, it is claimed, both the capacity to judge moral worth and to discover *the* meaning of the past. Moreover, without the ability to construe events as real and understandable we are said to be in danger of losing touch with the reality of the past. But historians recognise that the single event also exists in the mind of the historian. The historian takes what he/she assumes to be a real event and to characterise it imagines it at a point somewhere, for example, between the unique and the commonplace or between the ineffable and explicable (see COVERING LAWS; POSITIVISM). Or he/she can conceive of the event as being capable of accurate description or lying beyond the powers of representation. This would be discomforting to those historians who believe it is vital we fix the past in (as?) history. If we can not pin down the reality of the past through the objective event, we can not escape the present, and we could end up with a history without a tangible object. This would surely mean falling prey to an inability to distinguish fact from fiction, being unable to tell history from literature, and eventually sinking in the sea of historical relativism.

Nevertheless, behind all this thinking about events, and the metaphysical reality of the past, is the ontological state of mind of the historian as manifested in his/her prefiguration of the 'this happened, then that' process (see ONTOLOGY). This **narrative** configuration is important to the characterisation of the historical event not just to demonstrate it is the real thing, but as the vehicle for telling the reader what it means. For example, for some historians the 1848 Revolution in France was not a single event but a series of interconnected events driven, to a greater or lesser extent, by an emergent yet fearful bourgeoisie and an increasingly disillusioned proletariat. For other historians it was a series of events connected through individual decisions based upon the historical agents' perceptions of their own history and desired future. This example suggests that all historians make a personal choice, selecting one of a variety of determinisms – in this instance agent psychologism or **class**.

The nature of the historian's ontological (pre-)conception of the event and its significance (the historian decides when an event drastically affects continuity and change) determines, therefore, the concepts through which the event is structured and the narrative form in which events are composed and connected (see CONCEPTS IN HISTORY; EMPLOTMENT). It follows that how events are conceptually conceived, and then arranged as narrative representations, determines the epistemological outcome, that is, what becomes a significant fact (the fall of the French government in March 1848 as part of the French Revolution of 1848?). Events do not become facts, therefore, until the historian tropes them (see TROPE/FIGURATION). That is, the historian places events under a description or a narrative proposal. It is the historian who 'realises' events as history. There are no necessary epistemological ties between events, only between events and their description in language (Ankersmit 1994: 75–161).

According to conventional historical thinking the preconception of the historian investigating the event is modified, or even rejected, when the evidence consistently does not conform to the hypothesis/theory. But this assumes the modernist precedence of the epistemological over the ontological, which is not always a well-supported assumption (see MODERNISM). The argument is regularly put that patterns, structures and, for that matter, emplotments in history are as real as the events they encompass if their truth-conditions can be established – but here again demonstrating this is not straightforward. The historian's ontological commitments quite often remain unclarified in historical writing, and this constantly pushes us up against the limits of historical representation. While events are conventionally regarded as the building bricks of history, they are themselves constructed/represented within a set of assumptions about the nature of existence, what governs it, and how we can describe it. The meaning or interpretation of events is, perhaps, ultimately determined by what strikes the historian as right or wrong in ethical terms, *and* how this can be narrativised. The historian's a priori (see A PRIORI/A POSTERIORI) is at least as significant as the range and veracity of the evidence consulted about the event (see HISTORICAL IMAGINATION). At some point all historians have to come to terms with the narrative construction of the event and the reality/meaning it is supposed to represent.

Further reading

Ankersmit, F.R. (1994)
Danto, A. (1968a)
Davidson, D. (1980)
Friedlander, S. (1992)
Jameson, F. (1984)
McCullagh, C.B. (1998)
Mandelbaum, M. (1977)
Oakeshott, M. (1983)
Quine, W.V. (1990)
—— (1969)
Sobchack, V. (1996)

EVIDENCE

The empirical method presupposes what historians know about the past begins with the evidence (see EMPIRICISM). What it is that is distinctive about the historian's intellectual training originates with the way in which the sources of the past are mined as evidence for the nature of change over time. It is usually claimed that evidence provides the bond between history and the past. Epistemologically the strength of that bond is to be found in the closest possible correspondence between events (see EVENT) and their description (see EPISTEMOLOGY). Without evidence, therefore, history would be just fiction. This is the issue. Can we write proper, or non-fictional history if we re-conceive the nature of this bond?

It is hard to underestimate the strength of the epistemological attachment to evidence held by historians. Most members of the profession would be likely to agree, for example, that it is only through a study of the evidence that the 'historical perspective' can be used to illuminate the present through historical contrast. Moreover, the skills of both analytical and creative thinking are honed by working on the evidence – gathering and sifting it, discriminating it prior to interpretation, and overcoming its deficiencies by hypothesis testing and modification. It is in the nature of things that historians only indirectly observe the past through the filter of both primary evidence (in the shape of residual traces of the textual, architectural, oral and landscape remains of the past) or secondary evidence (the history produced by historians). It is enormously difficult to establish the conditions through which a corpus of evidence can support an interpretation of its meaning. Establishing possible connections between evidence and its meaning is not enough to justify our inferences.

In spite of this, the pursuit of the justified and hence truthful interpretation remains the historian's *raison d'être*. It is normally maintained that this can be achieved through the aim *and* strategy of objectively assessing the evidence without either dangerous over-enthusiasm or deceiving self-interest (see OBJECTIVITY). The aim is to discover the meaning of the past, or get as close to it as our best efforts and procedures will allow. Our interpretation must be as closely aligned as possible to the reality disclosed by the evidence. The better this correspondence the closer we are to the **truth**. For the reconstructionist historian (see RECONSTRUCTIONIST HISTORY) history is nothing if it is not true and tenaciously held fast by the **facts**.

Historians invest much time and effort in organising and categorising primary sources according to type, period and place to judge their provenance (by comparison with other sources), and reliability (knowledge of the perspective of the author(s) of the source(s)). The aim is to discover the most likely meaning contained within the sources by drawing inferences (see INFERENCE) to the best explanation about the actions of people in the past. Historians conventionally argue that they look at the sources to gain an insight into the decisions made by purposive historical agents acting under specific circumstances of time and place.

The inference of agent **intentionality** is the result of a long process of hypothesis-testing (refining the problem to be 'answered') and a scrupulous internal criticism (interpretation of the text's content). Historians accept that working with partial and misleading evidence (we know it often signifies something other than that which the author may have intended) often makes deriving *the* explanation impossible. *The* meaning is not really given up and, despite our mining and exploration metaphors, as hard-headed sceptical empiricists we do not expect always to quarry *the* meaning from a source. But we do expect our skills in historical method to offer a good chance of discovering the *most likely* explanation – one that comes pretty close to the broad truth of the past – inference to the best explanation. The resulting 'truthful interpretation' applies until new evidence emerges that demands we revise our interpretation. All history is, therefore, provisional according to our (continuing encounter with the) evidence.

But historians today, under the influence of the postmodern (see POSTMODERNISM) post-empiricist impress, are increasingly acknowledging that despite our critical methods, we still have to compose our interpretation in the form (see FORM AND CONTENT) of a **narrative** – the written expression of our **historical imagination**. The limits to historical knowledge now become suddenly and bleakly apparent. The narrative composition itself represents the organising process, rather than merely the culminating report of findings. Indeed, the intellectual process of organising and 'seeing' connections between events and people in the evidence of the past is a continuous process that goes on as we engage with the evidence. Indeed, the tropic processing of information within the historical imagination could be considered to be anterior to the research stage (see LINGUISTIC TURN; TROPE/FIGURATION). Our present cultural milieux, along with what is presently *en vogue* among the interests of the profession, usually determines what topics in the past we want to examine and, also, what is valuable in the evidence (gender evidence rather than race evidence?).

But it is not just a matter of how the historian uses his/her (chosen) evidence (or how his/her culture uses the historian). At the far more profound level of epistemic uncertainty it may be that insisting evidence is *the* foundation to history is a flawed assumption. No matter how extensively and constantly we hedge our epistemological bets about the evidence by reiterating its capacity to mislead the unskilled, we invariably fall back on our belief in the power of inference to the best explanation as if the incantation will work magic. Instead of realising the shortcomings of our skills and the failings of the inferential method by asking where does meaning emerge between the single factual statement and the monographic interpretation, we persist with the idea that the more evidence we have and the more we refine the questions we address to it, the closer we must be getting to the truth. This dogged refusal to face up to our flawed methodology is based on the assertion that history, as a crossbred discipline, in fact blends the analytical features of a science (our critical procedures) with the imaginative and figurative qualities of an art.

This widespread view of history as both science and art is founded on several related assumptions. Not least the assumption that good historians, by definition, deploy a sophisticated constructionist (see CONSTRUCTIONIST HISTORY) methodology that grows organically out of the evidence. What this means is that evidence is never question-begged by our concepts (see CONCEPTS IN HISTORY). Even more significantly, however, is the implicit assumption that the scientific model that detaches being (see ONTOLOGY) from knowing (epistemology) produces factualism, referentiality, objectivity, and the disinterested separation of observer and observed (see MODERNISM; the ENLIGHTENMENT). The science model, with its corollaries, requires we believe the evidence is capable of supporting truthful interpretations. But, despite all the problems with evidence, and the epistemic uncertainty that surrounds it and all our work, it is claimed the smart historian, who knows his/her job, will probably succeed (against all the odds) in getting the story straight (see COLLIGATION; EMPLOTMENT).

If we unburden ourselves of this delusion, what does it mean for our use of evidence? Well, among other things, it means accepting the consequences that flow from the location of evidence within an imposed explanatory framework predicated on the historian's views on human behaviour – prefiguring the evidence of an event or process as part of a chosen pattern of historical change and explanation (see TELEOLOGY). Furthermore, as French historian Roger Chartier suggests, all cultural texts, literary or historical, ultimately result from the historian's composition process (Chartier 1988: 42). It is through the interpretative and imaginative mind of the historian that all history texts become *a* representation of the past (see HISTORICAL IMAGINATION; Hayden WHITE). How the historian organises or emplots the evidence creates the-past-as-history for his/her readers. Rather than the bond that cements the past to history through the referential narrative, this places evidence in a secondary position in the history production process (see FORM AND CONTENT).

The challenge mounted through **continental philosophy**, especially by Roland **Barthes**, Jacques **Derrida** and Michel de Certeau, to the straightforward referential bond of the world and its words is one of the main contemporary objections to the traditional understanding of how historians use evidence. So, while no one today seriously advances the idea that we can reconstruct the past by the close scrutiny of evidence viewed as scattered bits of past reality, most historians still maintain the only avenue to the past is through its traces (see RECONSTRUCTIONIST HISTORY). The contention is now regularly put, however, that at best all historical methodology can do (through its treatment of the evidence – inference to the best explanation) is help us create a preferred, socially useful and ideologically plausible reality effect (see REALITY/REALISTIC EFFECT).

The weaknesses of the historical method means historians are being forced to consider what is, in effect, a frontal attack on the notion of historical truth and objectivity. It suggests we can not discover the intentionality of the author of the evidence, it means working on the principle of chains of interpretative signification rather than discoverable primal meaning, it disposes with the correspondence theory of knowledge, and it rejects the idea of the objective historian being able to weave the analytical and the imaginative as two separate strands to create a pattern of truth. Despite this critique the majority of historians still endorse the idea that historical truth corresponds to past reality by means of referentiality and induction. This requires historians to seek out *the* story that represents *the* truth to be found in *the* past through the factual detail of past events. While most historians accept narrative as the vehicle for the empiricist reconstruction of the past, its essential fictive power is assumed to work in the service of the evidence under all circumstances. It is this foundational belief that is now under its severest test.

Further reading

Achinstein, P. (1983)
Bloch, M. (1954)
Chartier, R. (1988)
Collingwood, R.G. (1994 [1946])
Donagan, A. (1961 [1952])
Dowe, P. (1992)
Hoffer, P.C. and Stueck, W.W. (1994)
McCullagh, C.B. (1998)
Mandelbaum, M. (1977)
Sosa, E. (1988)
Stanford, M. (1986)
Tosh, J. (1991)

F

FACTS

The concept of the historical fact is a complex and contentious one among historians. Even more annoyingly what constitutes the historian's facts, and how they are derived and used, also seems to change between generations of historians. For early twentieth-century French historians Charles Seignobos and Charles Victor Langlois following in the steps of Leopold von Ranke, because history was scientific, empiricist and therefore objective, facts were akin to atoms of information that once collected and collated would definitively reveal the **truth** of the past (see EMPIRICISM; EVIDENCE; OBJECTIVITY). They assumed the empirical method, rather than the testing of hypotheses, reveals the truth of the past. Subsequent generations of historians have always been in a dialogue with this foundationalist position.

At its most basic for historical fact(s) to exist there must be a consensus among historians that a particular statement about a historical **event** is true. Facts are taken to be true statements about the past. So how is it possible to achieve this consensus about what is truthful in what we say about the past? Unfortunately, while there may be consensus about a single event having occurred, there is often no consensus about what it may mean. But at a more basic level increasingly historians are asking if it is even possible to get at the truth of the past. To establish the truth of historical descriptions demands the assumption that the world of the past is an extension, as philosopher of history C. Behan McCullagh argues, 'of the present everyday world and conceived of in the same terms' (McCullagh 1984: 4–5). Most historians would regard this assumption as unproblematic. But does accepting that the past once existed mean it is possible to have direct access to the discoverable truthfulness of past reality? A growing number of historians no longer regard either our methods or our language as having the power to represent the past accurately. The notion of truthful interpretation is increasingly contested.

Conventionally, historians believe that historical truth is a matter of the correspondence between description and discoverable and verifiable facts, with a fact defined as an event, or a process, or a piece of social action upon the occurrence of which historians undisputedly agree, and which, by that token as much as any other, convincingly demonstrates the correspondence of reality and description (the Battle of Waterloo occurred in 1815 – all of the historians and sources agree). A historical fact is, therefore, a referential single truth-conditional statement about the actuality of the real world that, by definition, remains unaffected by the act of its description. It is, moreover, usually assumed that the demarcation line between what is fact(ual) and the conceptual process of organising raw data so as to grasp its meaning does not ultimately affect what makes a fact true (see CONCEPTS IN HISTORY).

The historian most often associated with the accurate derivation of historical facts as the central feature of historical study is the German historian Leopold von Ranke (1795–1886), with his belief that history should hold up a mirror to nature recording how things really were. For Ranke, and generations of subsequent historians, this is enough to constitute history as a separate and independent **epistemology** or way of knowing. Translated as the classical position it holds that, like experienced craftsmen and women, the more accurate historians can become in the discovery of facts, then the closer we get to fulfilling Ranke's nineteenth-century dictum *wie es eigentlich gewesen* or knowing history as it actually happened. Deriving the truth is the same as deriving the facts. The central tenet of this, what would now be regarded as an extremist form of empiricism, is an antipathy to the testing of preconceived theories of explanation.

Extreme empiricists claim to verify their knowledge of the past by insisting their experience of the real world must be as unaffected by their perception of it as possible – hence they remain objective (see ONTOLOGY). We can gain a useful insight into this position, the conservative heart of empiricism, by reading G.R. **Elton**'s aptly entitled 1991 book, *Return to Essentials*. Elton insists the most valuable aspect of the historian's work is the 'rational, independent and impartial investigation' of the documents of the past (Elton 1991: 6, 77–98). Arguing that this reliance on common-sense empiricism does not constitute a theory of knowledge, but is history as it should be properly understood, he goes on to dismiss '[i]deological theories imposed upon the reconstruction of the past rather than derived from it' (Elton 1991: 3–26) (see HISTORICAL EXPLANATION; HISTORICISM; INFERENCE; INTENTIONALITY; POSITIVISM; POSTMODERNISM).

Elton believes that historians must, by definition, pursue the empiricist ideal of passionless disinterest. In rejecting hypothesis-testing we become objective and not judgemental. The way to ensure this is through the usually bone-wearying critical study of the archive (see HERMENEUTICS). Know the archive, know the past. Do away with all social theory and philosophy in favour of the forensic treatment of the evidence. However, beyond the immediate level of the factual statement of verifiable relationships, historians enter the realm of interpretation. What do we do with the fact(s) when discovered or derived from the evidence? How do we sequence and explain them? In practice this is the same as saying how do we colligate or emplot/narrate them (see COLLIGATION; EMPLOTMENT; NARRATIVE)? Beyond the usual problems with evidence – that it may be of doubtful authenticity, or unreliable (lies), or simply absent – historians have many other difficulties in constituting facts. What criteria should be used by the impositionalist historian to winnow out that evidence that he/she judges to be irrelevant to the constitution of a fact?; how reliable is inference as a method for establishing facts?; should historians all become constructionists 'testing' evidence against a hypothesis to establish a fact?; what of the unreliable nature of the signifier–signified–sign equation (see CONSTRUCTIONIST HISTORY)? What of the continuing debate on the linguistic and/or social construction of reality (see LINGUISTIC TURN)?

Today there are a number of different ways to conceive of the origin, nature and functioning of fact(s). The role of language in the construction of reality and facts is important. The American Renaissance historian and philosopher of history Hayden **White** claims when historians attempt to explain the facts of the French Revolution or decline of the Roman Empire:

> What is at issue ... is not What are the facts? but rather, How are the facts to be described in order to sanction one mode of explaining them rather than another? Some historians will insist that history cannot become a science until it finds the technical terminology. ... Such is the recommendation of Marxists, Positivists, Cliometricians, and so on. Others will continue to insist that the integrity of historiography depends on the use of ordinary language. ... These latter suppose that ordinary language is a safeguard against ideological deformations of the *facts*. What they fail to recognise is that ordinary language itself has its own forms of terminological determinism, represented by the figures of speech without which discourse itself is impossible.
>
> (White 1978: 134)

White is making the post-empiricist point that facts are far more complex than is usually imagined by the hard-line empiricist. Faced with the tangle of historical fact(ual) data the historian must unravel them, then re-weave them into a narrative in order to explain their meaning. It is the view of White that historical facts are always constituted a second time as constituents of a rhetorical or narrative structure that is invariably written for a particular purpose. Historical facts are, therefore, always the constructions of historians. For White, as we invent an emplotment to transform events into historical facts, in its turn the emplotment becomes more than the sum of its parts. As both White and F.R. Ankersmit argue, it is the prefigured emplotment in the mind of the historian that initially defines the selection of evidence as well as its description and interpretation. If it is the writing of history that creates understanding, a reality effect may thus be generated as we emplot the past (see Roland BARTHES; REALITY/REALISTIC EFFECT). No matter how pure is our technical recovery/discovery of the past in the contextualising and creation of historical facts, it may be argued that its meaning is always going to be imposed by an ideologically aligned and rhetorically constructionist historian (see DISCOURSE).

This point is well made by the French philosopher Michel **Foucault** in his argument that the language of the document(s) (constituted as a particular discourse) precedes truth, fact creation, and interpretation. When we historians interpret the evidence, so he argues, we contribute to a presumed centre of 'truth' by adding our interpretation to the weight of existing interpretations. The meaning of historical facts so created, in effect, mutate as historical interpretations are continually revisited and the meaninglessness of the past has a fresh order imposed upon it through the constant revisioning process of the discipline of history. At the end of the day, perhaps, all the creation of historical fact(s) demonstrates is the complex and unresolvable nature of the relationship between epistemology and interpretation.

Further reading

Ankersmit, F.R. (1994)
Elton, G. (1991 [1955])
McCullagh, C.B. (1998)
Munslow, A. (1997a)
Ranke, L. von (1867–90)
Searle, J.R. (1995)
Stanford, M. (1994)
Stevenson, C.L. (1963)
Taylor, B. (1985)
Tosh, J. (1991)
White, H. (1978)

FORM AND CONTENT

The term is used to designate the connection between the structural design of the history text (form), and the exterior real-world events, actions and processes to which reference is made (content). How the connection is made, whether it be equality between the two terms or dominance/subordinance determines how we perceive the character of history as an **epistemology**, as a way of knowing. It is inevitable, perhaps, that the relationship of form and content is not an unchanging or immutable one but is, to a greater or lesser degree, constituted by the historian. The individual historian's ontological position on how they connect form and content is determined by how he/she sees the extent to which changes in one determine changes in the other (see Immanuel KANT; Friedrich NIETZSCHE; ONTOLOGY).

The reconstructionist historian (see RECONSTRUCTIONIST HISTORY) views the connection as invariably one of the priority of content over form because this allows him/her to endorse the objectivist position that form is strictly about the 'writing up' of the content. The question resolves itself into a matter of format rather than form. What this means is that for such historians form and content are indistinguishable in practice. Such a conflation is required because the whole point of reconstructionist history is to objectively report discoveries made in the archive. From this perspective, history as a form serves the **evidence** as the material reality of the past. History, as an inductive interpretative **narrative** is, therefore, always dominated by its content through the mechanism of **inference**. Historical knowledge derives from the historian's forensic empirical methodology that is then offered as a truthful narrative (see EMPIRICISM; TRUTH). Without this commitment to the content of the past as the determinant of form, so the argument runs, we can have no proper history and we shall slide toward epistemological **relativism**, ontological uncertainty and eventually be able only to write fiction.

The constructionist historian (see CONSTRUCTIONIST HISTORY) is less empirically deterministic given his/her practical realist investment in the constructed nature of his/her a priori (see A PRIORI/A POSTERIORI) categories through which he/she views the material content of the past. Constructionist history, as a theoretically informed and empiricist practice, is like reconstructionist history also ultimately committed to an inferential and empirical methodology, and as such demands the historian must, like his/her more empirically conservative reconstructionist colleague, place content prior to form. Most historians accept that their findings, when narrated, do not simply chronicle events. The narrative is the interpretative vehicle. Constructionists and reconstructionists alike know neither of their discourses simply report on the unalloyed state of reality. Moreover, both kinds have to connect with the reader. They have to tap into his/her culture and expectations (see TELEOLOGY). Arguments, it is understood, can not rely on **facts** standing alone. Hence all history texts, in order to be cognitive, are dependent as much on their narrative composition as they are on their sources (see EMPLOTMENT; TROPE/FIGURATION). All historical interpretations are narrated so as to influence, be convincing, and ultimately persuade the reader that they are truthful accounts. Indeed, it may be that storytelling with tropes is mandatory in every account of the past (Reedy 1994: 19).

The historian Peter Gay certainly recognises this when he comments that it is the historian's style that allows him/her to map the content of past. But Gay views style in history to be 'of a very special kind. A few flourishes apart, it must not interfere with the historian's science' (Gay 1988 [1974]: 216). So, even though he argues that form and content are united by style, Gay rejects what he assumes is E.H. **Carr**'s argument that to understand history one begins with the historian not the facts (Gay 1988 [1974]: 3, 17). Gay clearly leans toward the reconstructionist orientation with his conclusion that history is 'not a construction but a discovery. The order, the period, are there' (Gay 1988 [1974]: 217). Form is still secondary to content in Gay's vision of history.

The deconstructionist historian (see DECONSTRUCTIONIST HISTORY), however, questions the very idea that content and form are naturally polarised. What is there in the nature of **historical explanation** that demands such a dualism? It is, presumably, the empiricist belief in referentiality and factualism, the idea of a knowable and readily translatable material world. This means the reconstructionist and constructionist historian does not have to invent a narrative form because the events, actions and processes themselves generate the facts that produce the story form of history – this happened, and then that. If, however, the basic assumption of a knowable and representable past reality is disputed, the polarity and priority of content before form come into question. The obvious question then is what happens to history when we reverse the polarity, with form placed before content? What might be the metaphysical consequences of such an idealist or postmodern (see POSTMODERNISM) reversal? An absolutist placing of form as epistemically prior to content leads to a formalist history whereby historical understanding is known and understood through the cultivation of artistic and stylistic technique rather than through its subject matter. This procedure could so redefine history that epistemologically (as a way of knowing) it eventually metamorphoses into fiction. But this is likely to be the extreme consequence of a narrativist position that maintains a genuine knowledge of past reality is unobtainable so that which we call history is only ever a composed narrative written for someone and for some purpose: the-past-as-history.

The extent to which history may claim to represent the content of the past through its narrative form is dependent, therefore, on the degree to which narrative is viewed as an adequate vehicle for historical explanation. Several questions about what constitutes history proceed from the belief that history as it is written is structured as much by its form as its content. Not only are we forced to ask if empiricism can constitute history as a separate epistemology, but several other questions arise, such as what subordinate function does evidence perform, what is the functioning of social theory in the construction of explanatory frameworks, and just what is the role of the historian?

Historians and philosophers as diverse as Allan Megill, David Harlan, Dominic LaCapra, Frank Ankersmit, Hayden **White**, Iain Chambers, Joan W. Scott, Julia Kristeva, Keith Jenkins and Paul Ricoeur all, at some point, place 'conventional empiricism' and 'social science theorising' in quotation marks emphasising instead the importance to historical understanding of the structure of language and the relationship of form and content both in history's sources and its interpretations. Such critics argue that history's content effectively only exists when it is described by the historian. History is a stock of literary goods the significations or meanings of which emerge through (and from?) the narrative structures that are themselves in turn influenced by many social and ideological forces.

Roland **Barthes** and Michel **Foucault**, in particular, suggest that reconstructionist and constructionist historical explanations are inadequate. They argue that if we do not have as a primary consideration how we use language, how language uses us and, for that matter, language's inadequacy, we will inevitably neglect the manner in which figuration directly determines the power of the narrative to explain. In our naïveté we will continue to believe that history, through its representational authority, must correspond to reality. We will forget that historical truth is often little more than a plausible perspective that appeals to a particular readership because, as the cultural critic Paul de Man pointed out, historical knowledge moves within societal power structures (de Man 1983: 165). For the American philosopher-historian Hayden White history is primarily a literary endeavour inflected with ideology. What we know about the past emerges as much through the architecture of its narrative as from its content. Like Frank Ankersmit, White views language as an active medium that requires historians to resist any pretence to an unmediated knowable past reality. In *Metahistory* (1973) White claimed all history-writing is a poetic act. Facts are not discovered but are constituted out of sources according to literary as much as to empirical criteria. So far as White is concerned the historian has to shape *a* story so as to give *a* meaning to events (see EVENT), actions and processes that do not intrinsically possess one. These events, actions and processes do not in and of themselves have a story to tell. It is provided by the historian. The past becomes history through the form imposed upon it by the interventionist historian. The only truth in history is that it is the result of a fictive process.

White argues that historians utilise the formal structures of narrative used by writers of realist literature. These are rooted in the tropes. Historians create explanatory narratives through **emplotment** and argument, and their ideological implications. Working from the principle that historical writing is primarily a process of intellectual production, White's thinking about the nature of history begins with its end product – the written artefact – and then working backward infers the nature of the mechanism that gives the historical text its particular form. Because this form is literary historians are advised by White to extend their methodology to include the examination of literary theory. It is largely because of the influence of White that Carl Schorske has argued the toolbox of the historian today carries literary theory as well as tools borrowed from anthropology, psychology, sociology, gender studies, etc., etc. (Schorske 1998: 230–2).

In White's **historical imagination** the deep well of consciousness (at the level of the tropes) generates the strategies of explanation that determine how historians choose to interpret the content of their narratives. Emplotment, argument and ideology produce what White famously called the content of the form. As White readily admits, events happen, as do actions and processes. They all occurred in the past. But to make sense of them, to 'know about them', historians have to configure them, give them a particular form, by selectively constructing them. So it is that we periodise events, actions, processes, highlight their main features, and bring forth a meaning from the chaos of the past. The historian thereby constitutes the content of the past as an object of inquiry (Jenkins 1998a: 70). Prioritising form over content thus directly confronts the empiricist philosophical position by suggesting history is not a common-sensical craft and certainly not a scientific undertaking. This means neither expression of history – craft or science – can be redeemed by giving it a practical realist spin. History is, instead, a **discourse**, a manufactured cultural practice. As White suggests, the historical narrative always carries the imprint in its form and, therefore, in its content, of the influence of language and cultural self-interest. History can never escape into disinterestedness.

The implications of rethinking the relationship of form and content are highly significant, therefore, for our understanding of the nature of history. Take the use we put to evidence. The reversal that prioritises form over content reminds us that it is we who use the evidence; it does not dictate to us. Historians constantly re-work its meanings like the potter shaping a bowl on the wheel. The clay remains what it is and, in a literal sense, the 'fact of the matter' does not change. But what does alter is the shape we give to the clay as culture makes its demands upon the potter-historian. The central lesson for Foucault is that we can, if we wish, take possession of a new conception of history when we accept it is informed by the cognitive sway of its narrative form, itself fashioned by linguistic and social perspectives (see Friedrich NIETZSCHE).

It is often pointed out by empiricists like Perez Zagorin, Mark Bevir and C. Behan McCullagh that there is a problem in the extent to which White's tropes control the past through its form as history. Surely it must be the historian who control the tropes? If this is not so, then what we believe about the past is not determined by the traces of the real world. From the post-empiricist perspective it may well be that the past is governed by the dominant tropic influences at work in both the evidence as well as in the constitution of their own world-views. Following Louis Althusser, White argues such a self-reflexive process should inform the nature of how historians see the ideological relationship between form and content. In other words, writers of history should review the character of troping *in and of* history (see EPISTEME). It is possible that history may become a much more interesting and livelier project as a result of this extension of the historical enterprise beyond the confines of the supposedly value-free correspondence theory of knowledge.

In the 1990s **deconstructionist history** has attempted to make historians self-conscious (as many as will listen anyway) about how they metaphorically prefigure, construct, emplot, explain and make ethical or political judgements about the past. As the American pragmatic philosopher Richard **Rorty** has regularly argued, knowledge comes through some form of representation. This may help us answer the question as to why do the histories written by the many different kinds of historians – Marxist, subaltern, gendered, feminist, post-colonial, liberal, conservative – convince only their own readership constituencies? It may come down to the fact that if the tropic conventions used by the historian are shared with the reader and agreed by them, then the narrative will appear plausible, cognitive and truthful – whether it be of the genus reconstructionist (the third-person and realist narrative where the past comes alive), constructionist (the third-person and realist narrative is a truthful creation) or deconstructionist (the third-person and realist narrative is primarily an invention and not necessarily the way to represent the past at all).

Because language is neither transparent nor innocent, as Foucault and White have tried to demonstrate, the linguistic form of the narrative is implicated in how we understand historical content. But can history be understood in forms other than that of the narrative? By this I do not mean the modernist disruption of the narrative shape that deploys problem or themed history – chapters or titled sections that break up the chronology by dealing with topics taken out of their time-sequence. Nor do I refer to a number of historical objects, concepts and ideas arranged alphabetically (like this book). Such ways of doing the work of historical explanation are still representations as opposed to what I shall call performances (i.e. presentations). Once we start to rethink form and content it should be possible to produce various radical conceptions of history. Is there anything intrinsically 'wrong' or 'unnatural' about refusing the omniscient narrator-historian in favour of exploring the implications of the historian-as-**author**? Is there an embargo on experiments with stream-of-consciousness history?

But the big question remains. In any experiment with form is the final objective still to seek order in the past, whether it be *the* story or *a* story? The idea of a narrative story suggests an ordered structure (regardless of whether it is claimed to be found or imposed). Empiricists will ask if we abandon the pursuit of the formal, the orderly, the classified, the categorised and the organised, will we not lose the ability or (worse still?) the desire to judge the significant from the insignificant? In such a situation can we still claim to be 'doing history' and how can we possibly tell good from bad history? In this welter of foundationalist worries we should not forget we historians may rethink our explanatory structures, but we still have to communicate through the some kind of prose(aic) narrative – literally transforming ideas into language. Empiricists would say this process is not, of course, reliant solely on the correspondence theory of knowledge but is, additionally, dependent on inductive and (its specific form of) abductive **inference**. When we ascribe **intentionality** or agency to people in the past we are only inferring meanings and there are always immense unmapped tracts of uncertainty and indeterminacy. It is at this point, perhaps, that we can most fruitfully exercise our historical imagination. Once we are freed from the boundaries erected by the placing of content before form we are at liberty to challenge every position regularly deployed as collateral support for empiricism. We can confront inference, **causation**, progress, disinterestedness, narrative accuracy, referentiality, realism, truth and **objectivity**.

What makes prioritising form over content even more dangerous is that the choice of emplotment and accompanying argument of explanation imply the forefronting of a possible philosophical position on the part of the historian. It seems placing form over content must lead to relativism and a history doomed to collapse into **historicism** (writing history from the perspective of the present) and ideology. What White is saying, in fact, is that whether we like it or not we do not have much choice in the matter: the reality that exists in the past can only be knowable through the shape we give to it in the here and now. The question is, as Hayden White asks, why assume history has to be narrativised or story-shaped? Why not try to make history a performance? This might be through a resurgence in experiments with an authorial and interventionist historian, or it may take the form of a non-written narrative, perhaps cinema, television or a computer construction? If prose is chosen why not history as collage, pastiche, and/or fiction? History today does not always have to take the form of the empiricist's *trompe l'œil* representation.

Further reading

Ankersmit, F.R. (1994)
Ankersmit, F.R. and Kellner, H. (1995)
Bann, S. (1984)
Berkhofer, R.F. (1995)
Bevir, M. (1994)
Carr, D. (1986a)
Danto, A. (1985)
Gay, P. (1988 [1974])
Harlan, D. (1989)
Jenkins, K. (1998a)
—— (1995)
LaCapra, D. and Kaplan, S.L. (1982)
Lemon, M.C. (1995)
McCullagh, C.B. (1998)
Mink, L. (1978)
Munslow, A. (1997a)
Norman, A.P. (1991)
Reedy, W.J. (1994)
Rosenstone R.A. (1995)
Schorske, C.E. (1998)
Scott, J.W. (1989)
Walsh, W.H. (1981)
White, H. (1996)
—— (1992)
—— (1987)
—— (1973b)
Zagorin, P. (1999)

FOUCAULT, MICHEL (1926–84)

Michel Foucault was the leading philosopher of history to have emerged from the structuralist (see STRUCTURALISM) and **continental philosophy** revolution of the twentieth century. But, because of his trajectory out of the postmodern (see POSTMODERNISM), his influence within history has been disputed by many conventional or practical realist historians (see CULTURAL HISTORY). Foucault's contribution to the study of the past is to be found in the way he has confronted the Western philosophical and metaphysical (see METAPHYSICS) tradition that assumes our concepts (see CONCEPTS IN HISTORY) are extra-cultural and extra-linguistic representations of reality – the belief that the word represents the world transparently and largely without deforming it. Equally, he criticises the **Enlightenment** idea that the knowing subject (thinker, historian, intellectual, philosopher), by rationally deploying concepts, can stand above and beyond the material world of social institutions, customs and power relations (see LIBERAL HUMANISM; MODERNISM). Foucault, in his histories of madness, deviant behaviour and sexuality demonstrated how modernist thought is moulded by Western patriarchal culture to create the 'other' and how history is complicit in the linkage of knowledge and power (see EPISTEMOLOGY; WOMEN'S HISTORY). Both lived experience and history are, for Foucault, best viewed by reference, therefore, to the conventions, practices and discourses (see DISCOURSE) of social behaviour rather than a given or natural reality that the historian neutrally comes 'to know about'. To replace the notion of representation through conceptualisation Foucault offered, as we shall see, his own epistemological inventions: archaeology and genealogy.

Foucault was born in Poitiers in 1926 and was a schoolboy friend of Jean-Paul Sartre and Maurice Merleau-Ponty. Foucault immersed himself in Marx, Freud and Friedrich **Nietzsche** while he attended the École Normale Supérieure (1946–50). It was at this time, when he was in his twenties, that he acknowledged his homosexuality and the idea that biological boundaries, like discipline boundaries, are conventional rather than natural. Disobeying and violating cultural and disciplinary boundaries, in effect, became the motif of his life and work. In 1950 he became a communist, prompted in part by the social conflict in France in the late 1940s, but also as a result of the encouragement of his teacher, the French cultural critic Louis Althusser. This was also the period of the high tide of phenomenology in France (introduced by Edmund Husserl in the late 1920s). Under the influence of the philosopher Georges Dumézil, Foucault came to believe that the norms and practices of society are produced according to the internal economy of discourse. He said 'It was he [Dumézil] who taught me how to describe the transformations of a discourse and its relations to an institution' (Foucault 1972: 98). At this time in his life Foucault lived in the maelstrom of French intellectual life, being further influenced by university teachers and philosophers like Gaston Bachelard, Emile Benveniste, Georges Bataille, Pierre Klossowski and Maurice Blanchot.

Foucault learned from his reading of these intellectuals, as well as Nietzsche, that life has a strong tendency to disrupt the Enlightenment subject as a subject, in fact to tear the subject from itself and so become something 'other' than a unified self. It becomes dis-associated from itself, decentred. This decentring process emerged especially in his critique of the historian as a knowing subject. Such a traumatic deformation of the subject led him into the study of psychology in the early to mid-1950s and his working briefly with patients in the Hospital of Saint Anne. Recognising the homophobic boundaries within the French Communist Party, Foucault resigned in 1953. Between 1955 and 1959 he taught at the Universities of Uppsala, Warsaw and Hamburg, moving back to France to teach at the University of Clermont-Ferrand in 1960.

Four books in the 1960s established his professional reputation. His 1961 doctoral dissertation became his first major published work, *Madness and Civilization*, which was followed by *The Birth of the Clinic* (1963), *The Order of Things* (1966) and *The Archaeology of Knowledge* (1969). It is within these texts Foucault conceived and applied his archaeological-genealogical epistemology, producing ideas on the connections between discourses, customary practices, disciplines, historical period (see EPISTEME), power, and knowledge. In the politically climactic year of 1968, after two years in Tunis, Foucault returned to France and took up a philosophy position at the University of Vincennes. Disclaiming by then to be a Marxist, structuralist, phenomenologist, or even a philosopher, the following year Foucault was awarded a personal chair in the History of Systems of Thought at the Collège de France. His 1970 inaugural lecture, *The Discourse on Language*, was another milestone. His next project was his study of the will to knowledge and the nature of the control exercised in prisons over those individuals and groups society assumes to be abnormal or deviant. His study of this in nineteenth-century France was eventually published as *Discipline and Punish* (1975). His final major area of work was within the field of sexuality with the publication of Volume One of his *History of Sexuality* in 1976. The second and third volumes appeared in the year of his death in 1984 from AIDS-related complications (published in English in 1985 and 1986).

In this corpus of work we find Foucault translate his archaeological-genealogical epistemology into a method that is both synchronic (structural) and diachronic (historical). His archaeological method is a synchronic analysis of the statements or principles within any discourse that unconsciously influence what can and can not be articulated within it. His archaeology can be seen in his use of the **episteme** or slice of history that characterises the construction of its discourses, cultural practices, knowledges, and power arrangements. Genealogy is a diachronic method that reconstructs the origins and evolution of discourses within the flux of *present* experience. Genealogy (after the genealogy of Nietzsche) denies there are foundational origins for anything in the past. Meaning is never foundational but exists only in relationships as we perceive them from the standpoint and needs of today. There is never an absolutist meaning to be derived from either a transcendental metaphysical fact or principle, or from rational discourse. So, the **evidence** appealed to by the traditional historian for access to the **truth** is perceived as polluted because it is always subject to a contemporary methodology or a formative set of rules that deforms the object or referent of the evidence (see HISTORICISM; OBJECTIVITY). For Foucault the conventional historian's disinterested truth-conditional narrative description, which emerges after much labouring in the archive and the strict application of empiricist **inference**, is not a neutral or natural process at all.

What is wrong with this process? First of all Foucault rejects the conventional historical practice of smoothing the past into a seamless narrative that is then taken to constitute an adequate *and* truthful representation of the past. The modernist process of writing a problem-solving history requires, so Foucault suggests, a contrived bridging of the inherent discontinuities in the past, it demands planing its jagged edges and irregularities, and it results in an act of closure that can only claim to explain the inexplicabilities of the past. There is also a deceitful drive in modernist history to discover *the* essential meaning of events, practices and processes. Not least there is a will to discover *the* pattern to the past in order to own it (as history and) for what are patently ideological purposes. All this is achieved because the historian is assumed to be *the* knowing subject. Foucault rejects all this. The only order to be found in the content of the past is that provided by the form of the history we write (see FORM AND CONTENT).

History is not the end result of a neutral process of disinterested exploration in the archive by a knowing subject who exists outside time and place. Rather, when we write the past we are doing so as part of a writer–text–reader interactive situation – within the perimeter of what Foucault calls a discursive formation. It is this discursive formation that shapes the meaning we take from the past, not the reverse. History, therefore, has no intrinsicality beyond the historian. Indeed all we have is the-past-as-history. In thinking widely over the nature of modernist history, Foucault questioned, for example, whether there are essential themes in the-past-as-history – or are the historian's topics merely the interests of the present projected onto the screen of the past? But Foucault's most basic charge against conventional history remains, however, the dependence of its practitioners on its empiricist inferential foundations (see EMPIRICISM). The fixation of modernist history with the mechanism of empirically based inference obscures history's true character as a narrative construction shaped by the culturally situated and discursively constituted historian. Once this is recognised, then there is nothing in the past that we must address, and there is nothing we must know that is not dictated by our present needs. The text you are reading probably illustrates that process.

But, if the-past-as-history is always in the present, then it must constantly be being rethought and re-visioned (revisioned). History's revisionism is not just the re-interpretation of its events and processes, but its rethinking by historians acknowledging the changing conditions under which it is written and researched. Historical revisionism is the product of the epistemological conditions within the episteme. The-past-as-history is always about how we can achieve our future ends by changing the way we create the-past-as-history now (see TELEOLOGY). History is written as a part of that business of desiring what we want for the future from the past. To borrow and redefine the French philosopher Gilles Deleuze and Félix Guattari's term, history is a future-orientated desiring-machine. It is a mechanism by which historians give concrete form to their wants and dreams.

The-past-as-history is, consequently, a relativistic enterprise (see RELATIVISM). This problematises the idea of CAUSATION. There can be no straightforward causal connections discovered in the past and, perhaps, even less between the past and the present. In its turn this suggests the past can not be understood in its own terms because to understand causes we must start with what you want the effect to be in the future. To summarise: history is unavoidably relativist, presentist and teleological, and the reason is because it is an engagement between the historian (as writer/**author**), their text (the written past-as-history), and the reader (as a consumer who wishes to 'know' the past in their own way) (Barthes 1974, 1975).

This interactivity of subject positions – writer and reader via the text (in the past as evidence and now as history) – creates meanings. Such interactivity does not permit the discovery of *the* meaning. The historian as author may still try to manipulate the reader by concealing their existence, as in the liberal humanist empiricist and objectivist written act we call the-past-as-history (letting the text speak for itself in relating *the* meaning) or, alternatively, he/she may choose instead to acknowledge his/her situatedness as the historian-as-author. So, here I am, Alun Munslow, the historian-as-author speaking. What is my being and my agenda and, dear reader, what is yours (see ONTOLOGY)? What does this text tell you about my a priori (see A PRIORI/A POSTERIORI), for example, or tell you about the epistemological decisions I have made about the history production process and, withal, the nature of the episteme in which we both exist but that we mediate and understand differently?

What makes Foucault such a significant historian is his commitment to rethinking but not demeaning or undervaluing the-past-as-history. Everything has its past as well as a history – every action, person, thought, event, place, process, idea, and text. But the-past-as-history for each is plastic, unfixed, not immutable. History is never given, once and for all, or permanent. It is always in flux, always subject to perspective and, occasionally therefore, to parody. Lest there be any doubt, I make the assumption that the traces of the once real past remain available, but the past and its referents are only accessible as a text, set in a discourse, within an episteme, and understood by an implicated historian who writes it up for an engaged reader/author. It is this judgement, as an engaged reader/author, that I wish to take from Foucault's work. The past counts but, like Nietzsche, Foucault accepts that all history's claims must be, to a greater rather than lesser extent, counterfeit. In his 1971 essay, 'Nietzsche, genealogy, history', he is scornful of the empiricist's attempt to locate the historical truth, arguing instead that because history is formally contrived we are wrong to persist with the fiction that we can stand outside history or our texts. What is worse, this lie is determinedly hidden from history. Foucault agrees with Nietzsche (Nietzsche's genealogy) that history should be 'explicit in its perspective' and should acknowledge that its 'perception is slanted, being a deliberate appraisal, affirmation, or negation', and history (which he recasts as 'effective history') should not efface itself 'before the objects it observes' (Bouchard 1977: 157). This is a postmodern history that rejects the correspondence theory that the 'truth' is 'out there' and dismisses the coarse myths that flood from the conventional model of history: factualism, detached historians, transparent representation, objectivity, and the clear distinction between history, ideology and fiction. Perhaps history is the 'other' of the present?

Further reading

Barthes, R. (1975)
—— (1974)
Bernauer, J. and Keenan, T. (1988)
Dean, M. (1994)
Deleuze, G. and Guattari, F. (1984 [1972])
Dreyfus, H.L. and Rabinow, P. (1983)
Foucault, M. (1985, 1986)
—— (1980)
—— (1979 [1976])
—— (1977 [1975])
—— (1977)
—— (1975)
—— (1973a)
—— (1973b)
—— (1972)
—— (1970)
Gutting, G. (1994)
Megill, A. (1985)
Munslow, A. (1997a)
Noiriel, G. (1994)
Poster, M. (1984)
Rabinow, P. (1999)

H

HEGEL, G.W.F. (1770–1831)

History is central to the German **Enlightenment**-inspired and anti-positivist philosopher G.W.F. Hegel (Beiser 1993: 270). Rather than viewing philosophy as the universal master discipline with history its hand-maiden, Hegel turns to history as the only genuine basis for knowledge of reality. The irony is all the stronger, therefore, that Hegel has never been attractive to English-speaking empiricist (see EMPIRICISM) or reconstructionist historians (see RECONSTRUCTIONIST HISTORY). In part this is because of his idealist conviction that empiricism alone can not find **truth**, that concepts (see CONCEPTS IN HISTORY) have priority over objects, and his belief that the historian is the key to the study and writing of the-past-as-history. In addition, Hegel also fails to appeal to constructionist historians (see CONSTRUCTIONIST HISTORY) because there are now so few large-scale system-building members in that guild to find his totalising and deterministic pattern-seeking history plausible. In sum, although Hegel turned to history as the only true foundation for knowledge, he has been largely rejected by historians. In fact his influence has been limited to the minority of idealist historians who placed empathy and thought at the centre of the historical undertaking like R.G. **Collingwood** and Benedetto **Croce**, the former largely pro-Hegel, the latter anti-Hegel. Furthermore, because there is seemingly little in his contribution to the study of the past, it is difficult to offset some of his more outlandish notions concerning non-historical peoples, his praise for the Great Man theory of history and his unreserved reverence for the state find little appeal in a postmodern (see POSTMODERNISM) world that has little time for such intellectual grand-standing.

The fundamental problem with Hegel is that his theory of historical knowledge (his **epistemology**), which is that the reality of the past is to be found through the mind of the collective subject, which he refers to as the logic of the 'spirit' (*Geist* in German), not only sounds far-fetched today, but what is worse it is founded upon the notion that the spirit must ultimately unify subject with object. Hegel apparently diminishes the importance of the empirical in favour of jacking up history to the level of a philosophy, that is, understanding the big mechanism of ideas or concepts rather than being satisfied with discovering the meaning of **facts**. Most empiricists are worried by R.G. Collingwood's commentary on Hegel that 'all history is the history of thought' (Collingwood 1994 [1946]: 115). To empiricists conflating history with philosophy is not a good idea at the best of times, but it becomes just plain silly when the aim is to suggest that the end of history can be reached in the blending of subject with object.

The independently derived, yet collective or organic, gift of self-knowledge that leads to the realisation of the 'World' or 'Absolute Spirit' demonstrates to Hegel our human progress toward a rationalist (and nationalist) community of belief (which Hegel believed happened to exist in the Prussian state in which he lived). For Hegel human activities and events have a design *because* of their spiritual direction. While mainstream historians today view this sort of mystical thinking as of archaic interest at best, deconstructionist historians (see DECONSTRUCTIONIST HISTORY) regard it as nonsense given their antipathy not so much to the unity of subject and object (which is not really a problem), but to grand explanatory or teleological (goal-orientated) narratives translated as (knowable) history. Through his idealism Hegel believed he knew the reality of history. Empiricists are more at ease with his conclusion if not his method, deconstructionists the method but not the conclusion.

Although most historians today thus reject Hegel's notion of the Absolute Spirit and historical determination through ideas, a good many nevertheless still find his basic method whereby ideas come into conflict – the dialectic – as attractive. Its allure is due to two factors: the notion of it as a kind of scientific procedure, and the often quite un-self-conscious assumption that the dialectic exists as a 'natural' feature of humanity, namely, it is the destiny of human beings to struggle and overcome opposing forces in order to achieve. This double potential in the dialectic for objective history and/or emplotting history as the overcoming of tragedy by beating life's obstacles has a potent charm (see EMPLOTMENT; Hayden WHITE).

For Hegel, however, the dialectic only has one purpose, to demonstrate the progressive conflict of opposing ideas revealed as the steps toward the highest stage of historical development. Hegel thus found history littered with examples of strife and conflict as he pursued his big idea of the fulfilment of the human spirit. Nevertheless, when shorn of its Hegelian spiritual aim this dialectical principle retains a strong law-like epistemological elegance – the notion that each step, phase or epoch in history contains within itself the source(s) of its own dissolution (see Michel FOUCAULT; EPISTEME). The essence of Hegelianism, the determinism of ideas in progressively creating *the* pattern of real historical change, is dumped in order to retain the dialectic as a neutral mechanism of historical explanation (see HISTORICISM).

What makes Hegel unfashionable is not just his spiritual determinism (his idealist dialectic), but in addition what he sees as the necessity for an activist historian in the constitution of the-past-as-history. Like everyone else in the early years of the nineteenth century Hegel was in a dialogue with Immanuel **Kant**'s theory of knowledge. Both philosophers wanted to know what it is that drives history along. According to Kant it was nature. Nature, defined as things-in-themselves, can be known but only through the screen of the concept. Hence knowledge comes from sense-experience as it is shaped by human, or in our case the historian's, categories of thought. This is the so-called epistemological basis of knowledge – that reason can discover both its foundations in the knowing subject and its limits in the categories the human mind deploys to carve up reality (hence the description of Kant's thinking as non-empirical transcendental idealism). Hegel's response was to extend Kant's limits of (rational) knowledge beyond that of the conceptual. Hegel deployed reason differently. He chose to believe we can know things-in-themselves because rational thought can give access to the world beyond the appearance. Because things-in-themselves do exist so our concept of existence must make things knowable.

If Hegel had ended at this point he might well have kept an irresistible appeal for empiricists everywhere – the greater our knowledge of reality through sense-experience the closer we shall get to the **truth** of reality. But he did not end there; instead he pushed his line of thinking toward absolute idealism. The logical conclusion of his premises is if the real is open to rational conceptualisation then everything must be ultimately knowable *through* the thought of the historian. It is this extraordinary universalism that destroys the Kantian distinctions of subject and object, **form and content** and **a priori/a posteriori** whereby the (a priori) form provided by the mind is given its (a posteriori) content by historical experience. For Hegel our knowledge *is* reality because concepts (like those used in history) represent the rational mind at work. So history becomes knowable through the unfolding of the logic of conceptualisation (as Hegel liked to argue what is rational is real and what is real is rational); indeed history *is* the unfolding logic of conceptualisation via the dialectic (concepts in conflict). R.G. Collingwood concluded Hegel was right that 'there is no history except the history of human life, and that, not merely as life, but as rational life, the life of thinking beings' (Collingwood 1994 [1946]: 115).

Like many of the other major historical thinkers of the Enlightenment, Hegel also considered the connections between epistemology (knowledge) and aesthetics (art). Along with **Vico**, **Nietzsche** and Croce, Hegel philosophised about history as revealed as a form of writing cast in the historian's preferred figurative style. As Hayden White describes Hegel's vision of history it is written in the form of a tragic drama unfolding into comedy (White 1973b: 81–131). Hegel's views on language are, therefore, instructive in the context of today's postmodern (see POSTMODERNISM) reversal of content and form in history. Hegel argues that no matter how much the historian strives to reproduce actual historical facts (and he/she must attempt to do this), he/she has to infuse them with his/her own creativity in order to make the content of the past vivid as history. Language, as used by the historian, mediates between consciousness and reality and, it follows, history must be close companion to poetry and, specifically, to drama. The function of the historian's language is to seek out the inherent idealism in the prosaic or literalist world (see TROPE/FIGURATION).

Hegel thus offered a grand metaphysical (see METAPHYSICS) and deterministic framework for the understanding of the-past-as-history that has been rejected by almost every historian of whatever stripe. He is rejected because of the 'corruption' of his esoteric idealism (his over-emphasis on knowledge through rational thought), because of his unwarranted teleological assumptions, and, while there is still a residual appeal for his dialectical mechanism for constructionists, the resolution of opposites in the pursuit of closure is abandoned by deconstructionists (D.D. Roberts 1995: 87). The Hegelian appeal to the totalising or grand narrative to which the idealistic dialectic leads is cast out in favour of accepting otherness, alternatives, and constantly deferred meaning (there are no ultimates whether in meaning or as the Absolute Spirit). The realist philosopher of history Michael Stanford claims that today 'hardly any historian is a Hegelian' (Stanford 1998: 197). However, although speculative history of the Hegelian kind may be out of fashion, it should not obscure the fact that it was Hegel who, almost on his own, made history an occupation worth undertaking.

Further reading

Adorno, T. (1983 [1966])
Beiser, F.C. (1993)
Collingwood, R.G. (1994 [1946])
Hegel, G.W.F. (1975 [1821])
Knox, T.M. (1975)
O'Brien, G.D. (1975)
Popper, K. (1962 [1945])
Roberts, D.D. (1995)
Stanford, M. (1998)
White, H. (1973b)

HERMENEUTICS

Originally a post-Reformation practice of Biblical textual explanation (exegesis), developments in the nineteenth and twentieth centuries re-defined hermeneutics as the theory (or philosophy) of interpretation rather than as an interpretative textual practice (a methodology). Although it was recognised in the nineteenth century that the rupture between the reader and the **author** can create a cloudy, if not at times an impenetrable, barrier to meaning/understanding, that did not stem the desire to recover the text's 'real' meaning. In the twentieth century, however, the relativism immanent in the author–reader relationship has been generally viewed as inevitable, suggesting that meaning is probably a cultural variable rather than a discoverable given. Historians, as interpreters of the textual **evidence** of the past, live in this uncomfortable situation of knowing it is impossible to recover *the* meaning of the past, yet being pushed constantly in that direction by the professional culture of getting the story straight.

Most (practical realist) historians today are still wedded to a crude kind of **Enlightenment** hermeneutics. There is a strong urge to believe there is probably an original meaning in the evidence, but the circumstances under which they labour to reconstruct the past will never permit that original meaning to emerge – and even if it did they would not be able to recognise it (see RECONSTRUCTIONIST HISTORY). Nevertheless, the aim remains to objectively serve the evidence within our historical **narrative** (see OBJECTIVITY). Serving the evidence entails an engagement by the historian but one that is rigorously controlled by **truth**-conditional statements, propositional logic, strict rules of **inference**, referentiality, the contextualisation of evidence, the deployment of a limited range of explanatory theory and **concepts in history**, and keeping one's distance from the object of study (separation of knower and known). The most that can be said is that historians today are only just starting to engage with the broader issues of how we understand – in philosophical terms (see EPISTEMOLOGY). The shift away from being solely concerned with the impossible dream of *the* truthful interpretation, recovering through various kinds of **empiricism** and varieties of sophisticated constructionist methodologies, the givenness of the past, is an immense step for today's historians (see MODERNISM). It is a move that radically changes the conception and character of the discipline by injecting into it a fundamental ontological aspect to the historian's work – that there is a case to be made for the fruitful collapse of subject and object (see FORM AND CONTENT; ONTOLOGY).

Recognition (by post-Hegelian (see G.W.F. HEGEL) **continental philosophy**) that language can not fix meaning, that in practice power and perspective do replace objectivity and rationality, that truth is situational and culturally and epistemologically relative, suggests not merely that texts have multiple meanings, but that the big issue is the nature of our being-in-the-world. How we think about that question as historians infuses the history we write with our individual and collective senses of what we want out of the future (see TELEOLOGY). While it is still a minority pursuit, more and more historians are displaying an interest in teleology, replacing the profession's traditional preoccupation with the discovery of original meaning with a re-casting of the discipline.

This potential reorientation of history is indebted for its philosophical foundations to the German phenomenologists and hermeneuticists Martin Heidegger (1889–1976) and Hans-Georg Gadamer (1900–). Heidegger suggests we all possess a foresight, a pre-critical understanding that makes all our acts of interpretation also acts of inquiry about our own existence. From Gadamer historians observe that our prejudices and pre-judgements are not capable of suspension, but are an integral part of what we do. What Gadamer calls the 'effective-historical consciousness' is the recognition, as we interpret the documents of the past, of the 'horizon' of our cultural situatedness. History is about our own existence as much as about the past. Historical interpretation – hermeneutics – is not just about practice (empiricist methodology) or epistemology (knowledge), it is about ontology (existence).

This divorce of truth and method (truth from method?) does not yet convince many practical realist historians. It has not, for example, convinced the likes of E.D. Hirsch or Jürgen Habermas, the major critics of Heidegger and Gadamer. Habermas insists there is room for, indeed it is vital that there be, a *rapprochement*, within the field of hermeneutics, of methodology and epistemology. As Hirsch argues, without this – established through the correspondence (theory of knowledge/interpretation) of meaning and **author intentionality** – we are rudderless in a sea of ideology and cultural relativism. Paul Ricoeur's contribution to hermeneutics is also important in his work on the nature of the **historical imagination**, especially the functioning of memory and symbolism. Because historians rarely read any philosophy of history, the philosophical thinking and debates about hermeneutics of Heidegger, Gadamer, Hirsch, Habermas and Ricoeur has tended not to make it into the mainstream of the profession's consciousness. This can be rectified by reference to the Further reading below.

Further reading

Gadamer, H.-G. (1998)
Heidegger, M. (1962)
Hirsch, E.D. (1976)
Müller-Vollmer, K. (1986)
Palmer, R.E. (1969)
Pickering, M. (1999)
Ricoeur, P. (1981)
Thompson, J.B. (1981)

HISTORICAL EXPLANATION

Historians tend to ask three questions about the events, processes and people of the past. These are: what happened (discovering the **facts**)?, how did it happen (historical interpretation)?, and why did it happen in the way the **evidence** suggests it did (see CAUSATION)? Historical explanation requires addressing and answering all three: what, how and why in the-past-as-history? The kind of explanation any individual historian appeals to in answering these questions informs their perception of history as well as their cache of historical knowledge, and determines the kind of historian they are. The complementarity of the entries in this book should give some sense of the interconnected nature of historical explanations, involving as they do a great many of the key features of the historical project (see CONSTRUCTIONIST HISTORY; DECONSTRUCTIONIST HISTORY; EMPIRICISM; EPISTEMOLOGY; HISTORICAL IMAGINATION; HISTORICISM; INFERENCE; NARRATIVE; OBJECTIVITY; ONTOLOGY; POSITIVISM; RECONSTRUCTIONIST HISTORY; STRUCTURALISM).

Before getting to historical explanation, however, a brief preliminary word about explanation in general terms, and then scientific explanation in particular. To explain something is to describe it (to act epistemologically by creating knowledge), and to justify its existence (its ontology) at a certain time and place (to be in touch with reality – the metaphysical) (see METAPHYSICS). Explanation at a general everyday level is, therefore, a fearsomely complex thing, but in order to get on with life we assume explanation simply means that events and occurrences follow on from other events (see EVENT) and occurrences (which we might call preconditions or antecedents) in a sequential order, and that we describe such occurrences to each other in the shape of a narrative: 'this happened, then that, because . . . '. This explains why, for most historians, the narrative is the peculiar form of explanation: to explain historically is to discover *the* story (Gallie 1964) or, more radically, to impose one that is invented as much as found (White 1973b) (see FORM AND CONTENT).

How does this shape up to so-called scientific explanation? Thanks to the work of Karl Popper and Carl Hempel the dominant view of scientific explanation holds, although it has been increasingly challenged in the 1980s and 1990s, that a scientific explanation means subsuming an explanation under a law of nature. Water freezes and bursts central heating pipes when, in an empty house, the temperature falls to a certain level. This hypothesis is testable empirically and accountable for by an appeal to a universal law of nature. The premises, which are known in philosophy as the *explanans* (that which does the explaining – the temperature level) predicate a certain known outcome (based on previous empirical experience), which is called the *explanandum* (that which is to be explained – burst pipes). The *explanans* contains a universal or covering law (see COVERING LAWS) to which appeal is made for the purpose of demonstrating that the *explanandum* had to happen. This kind of explanation contains all the features we would expect of a conventional scientific explanation: it is subject–object in architecture, inferential – specifically hypothetico-deductive (or propositional-inferential) – referential, realist, foundational, capable of re-testing, empiricist, factual, rational, objective, has no room for interpretation, is cause–effect in character, endorses the correspondence theory of knowledge, and is, therefore, predictive. As Carl Hempel said, somewhat dismissively, if historians do not make an appeal to a general or covering law, they are just talking in metaphors. In a clean fight over **truth** a deductive empiricism will always beat imagination (see TROPE/FIGURATION).

But is Hempel correct? Is this hypothetico-deductive inferential model appropriate for the study of the-past-as-history? Can historians infer necessary consequences from the data? Although, while agreeing with Hempel to the extent that history is indeed an empirical project, is it also not about the one-off and the contingent rather than the universal? Doesn't history explain unique and differentiated events in a sequential order? Positivists counter, saying that every individual micro-level event in order to be explained must be subsumed, at some point, under a universal (at the macro-level). But, the humanist historian responds in turn, where there are no universal laws of nature involved, as in history and the rest of the humanities and social sciences, the deductive-nomological model (which is the philosophical description for Hempel's scientific model described above) surely must give way to another form of argument, a fuzzier, less deterministic model? Explaining why, for example, the process of capitalist industrialisation *tends* to occur uncertainly, presumably requires a different model of explanation from the scientific. At best we are looking here for a statement of statistical probability, rather than an immutable law of economic and/or human behaviour? Such a model would not be classically scientific, and certainly not predictive. It would be a model of explanation that is after-the-event and inductive meaning that, from a range of examples sharing a common feature, the historian generalises to further unobserved instances. As the historian might say 'from this evidence it seems likely that . . .'. This is much closer to the way historians explain things.

Given certain initial conditions of time and place, is it more or less likely capitalist industrialisation will occur? By examination of the evidence, did it occur? Were there discoverable patterns to it? Is there a universal law of capitalist industrialisation? Explanations suited to this kind of problem conform, then, more to the inductive-statistical model (as it is known) in which the *explanans* requires we inductively infer a high (or low) probability in the *explanandum*. The fewer the number of assumptions I have to make in order to arrive at my explanation, the more I can be justified in the veracity or truth of my explanation. The way to reduce the number of assumptions, and to offer a workable compromise with covering-law positivism (if a compromise is what I want), is for me to produce as wide a spread of contextualising evidence as possible so as to define and refine my hypothesis so I can draw reasonable inductive inferences and make justifiably true historical statements. This particular inductive inferential mechanism – evidence steered by a suitable social theory resulting in the truth-conditional statement – leads me to (one of the huge varieties of) constructionist history (see CONCEPTS IN HISTORY). My preference for one form of constructionist history over another usually depends on my own criteria as to what it is that constitutes genuine knowledge. That, of course, is likely to be influenced by my politics, my age, my gender, my professional training, my class affiliations, and my views on human nature (if I believe in such a thing).

The problem with covering laws in historical explanation (usually referenced as concepts, categories, or appeals to theory) seems to be that they are either so broad and plastic they become meaningless, or so narrow and rigid as to barely qualify for the title. Moreover, much of history is concerned with the actions of individual human beings (and their attendant hopes, desires, fears, intentions, and a whole variety of psychological states) to which proclaimed universal laws of behaviour do not regularly apply. So, what are the alternatives if history does not conform to a scientific model ofexplanation? It suggests the need for some more elastic kind of framework. William H. Dray has been influential in proposing that historians apply criteria of rational behaviour to people's actions in the past in order to provide solid criteria for historical judgements and interpretations (Dray 1957). Developed from R.G. **Collingwood**'s notion that historians can usefully re-enact the thoughts of historical agents, rational action theory helps account for agent **intentionality** and leads to a reconstructionist history that assumes historians can explain (given enough evidence and a degree of empathy) why something very probably happened, or why a historical agent took a certain course of action for explicable reasons. In practice, explaining the reasons for a historical agent's actions usually also means invoking some kind of judgement about the broad generalities of human behaviour. Thus we end up with the dominant form of history today – a hybrid: a sophisticated practical realism that carries within it appeals to various kinds of arguments that, based upon empirical research, purport to explain human behaviour from the level of the rational individual acting intentionally, up to that of major event, social structure, institution, process, nation or empire.

Given the fuzzy nature of historical explanation as I have described it so far, no historian claims to tell the absolute truth about the-past-as-history. Clearly this is not possible given its inferential and indirect evidence-based nature. The sensible and moderate aim of most historians is to establish a high degree of probability that things actually happened as we say they did in our narratives, and hence their meaning becomes demonstrable. We do this through the conjunction of our data with our sophisticated explanatory conceptual hypotheses. This conjunction is achieved by the referentiality demonstrated in the correspondence theory of knowledge – what we describe corresponds to the evidence and, ideally, through a statistical correlation in the case of numerical data. In practice historians seek to explain the past by discovering and narrating the real causes of the social institutions and structures inherent in society that influence events, people and processes. What do we mean by causation/causality? I take it to mean the understanding I have of the determining relations between events, processes and people's actions. Historians tend to talk of primary and secondary causes, and necessary and sufficient conditions for occurrences to take place. Necessary causes are found in the majority of cases generating a particular effect, whereas a sufficient cause alone can be taken to account for a particular event. Causation is complicated further in that it has to embrace explanation at different levels: that of the actions of individual people (invariably named), collectivities like classes or occupational groups, and also at the level of large-scale social, economic and political practices, processes and structures.

But regardless of the level of causal explanation, the past becomes history through the correspondence theory of knowledge: the empirical discovery of the real structures that are believed to have governed the choices of historical agents, and which in their turn were influenced by those choices. This methodology assumes a realist position on the epistemological problem of how accurately our categories and concepts can capture the real world (see G.W.F. HEGEL; Immanuel KANT). It assumes words, discourses and narratives can not change physical realities, actual events, social structures, so our representation is of secondary significance. The historical narrative (if written with due care and attention to the evidence and appropriate theory) is taken to be homologous to the actual narrative found in the structural and causal arrangement of the past. A mountain is still a mountain, and the independence and partition of India still occurred on 15 August 1947, even if I describe the first from several different physical locations, or the second from competing ideological perspectives.

The thrust of much postmodern (see POSTMODERNISM) argument is to problematise that thinking by offering an a priori (see A PRIORI/A POSTERIORI) challenge (to this practical realist foundationalism in explanation), by re-examining the nature of language, representation, the historical narrative and inference. All our knowledge in the humanities and social sciences comes to us in narratives composed from words, sentences, discourses (see DISCOURSE), emplotments (see EMPLOTMENT) and language. The historian's self-imposed dependence upon a sophisticated process of empiricism and conceptualisation can not alter the fact that he/she is directly implicated in the process of knowing through what is a description of a highly mediated experience of the past. For this reason it is held that objectivity-in-knowing is a position that must be surrendered. What this means for historical explanation is the rejection of the epistemological subject–object model in favour of (what is claimed to be) an unavoidable subject–subject relationship (see WOMEN'S HISTORY). It must also mean that in its creation of facts history is ultimately dependent upon a severely flawed methodology – inference to the best explanation – if the stated aim of history is to reproduce *the* meaning of the past.

Historians conventionally work, then, by drawing inferences. At its most straightforward this means interpretations and explanations are supposedly amended according to the latest available evidence, although in practice this often seems to be the result of the most plausible and popular current tweak to our theory. There are, in fact, three types of inference that historians deploy: two have already been mentioned, the deductive and inductive. The third is the abductive. Although induction, as I have noted, is generally regarded as the primary mechanism of historical explanation (along the lines of the statistical-inductive model), strictly speaking abductive inference is *the* characteristic feature of historical explanation and the historical imagination. Where a statistical correlation is inappropriate or undemonstrable it falls to the historian to generate a pattern of meaning (see COLLIGATION). It occurs to me that the present interest in narrative's role in historical explanation derives in part from the failings of abductive historical thinking defined as inference to the best explanation, in addition to the difficulties with the covering law. It also derives from the belief I noted at the start of this entry, that historical explanation is taken by most historians to be fully understood only through the narrative form.

If the historian presupposes an objectivist history then the explanation will take the form of a factual (proper historical) narrative. If he/she entertains a different pre-supposition, the form of his/her history will change, and the nature of explanation will also. Hayden **White**'s model of the historical imagination, for example, presupposes a prefiguration (tropes) and connected levels of historical explanation: emplotment, argument and ideological preference. It is White's (now famous) argument that the tropes anticipate and structure these other elements of the historical explanation. White thus denies that historical explanation emerges primarily from referential correspondence/inferential thinking, but instead arises through the process of prefiguring the data by the mental processes of analogue, similarity or difference (hence tropes = different types of metaphor). White is suggesting that although historical explanations may possess referentiality (in abundance), and reasonable inferences can be drawn, ultimately we cast it all into a narrative, and no individual emplotment, argument or ideological explanatory connection can be more truthfully described than any other. White is saying narratives can not be true or untrue just because they do or do not correspond with past realities. This rhetorical constructionism is certainly not a view shared by narrativist and realist philosophers like W.B. Gallie and C. Behan McCullagh, who between them defend narrative and historical explanation as capable of being either true or false (McCullagh 1998: 127–8). Perhaps all we can say is that historical explanation is not yet a settled matter. One reason for this is the fact that historians do not read much of what is written on the philosophy of history. A great deal of thinking about historical explanation tends, therefore, to be neglected. Historians might benefit by consulting the following key thinkers on how historical explanation could work.

Further reading

Achinstein, P. (1983)
Atkinson, R.F. (1978)
Collingwood, R.G. (1994 [1946])
Danto, A. (1968a)
Dray, W.H. (1957)
Gallie, W.B. (1964)
Gardiner, P. (1961 [1951])
—— (1959)
Graham, G. (1983)
Hempel, C.G. (1965)
Jenkins, K. (1999)
McCullagh, C.B. (1998)
Mandelbaum, M. (1977)
Oakeshott, M. (1933)

Popper, K. (1959)
Roberts, C.D. (1996)
Ruben, D.-H. (1993)
— (1990)
Snooks, G.D. (1998)
Topolski, J. (1991)
von Wright, G.H. (1971)
Walsh, W.H. (1984 [1967])
White, H. (1973b)

HISTORICAL IMAGINATION

The human mind has the capacity to bring forth things that are not directly accessed by the senses and to address that which is not real. That this power of imagination is particularly important to the process of historical interpretation is attested to by the number of philosophers and historians who have addressed its nature and functioning in the creation of historical meaning. Historians regularly exercise the mental power of rehearsing possible past cause and effect relationships, connections and situations.

I assume, therefore, the historical imagination to be the application of the general capacity of the human mind for comparison, connection, analogy and difference to the study of the past and its sources. This is, in effect, a metaphoric process that allows the historian to relate different domains of knowledge in many general and particular ways toward the aim of interpretation and understanding. As the philosopher Peter Strawson suggests, our perception of objects owes its character to the internal links that we bring into being through our preferred metaphorical descriptions (Strawson 1974: 53). What I am suggesting here is that the line between **inference** and imagination is normally and regularly crossed by the historian. The act of historical re-creation means picturing the linkage possibilities in the past. The peculiar form that this picturing of links takes is the figurative **narrative** (see TROPE/FIGURATION; Hayden WHITE; REALITY/REALISTIC EFFECT).

It follows that to gain some kind of understanding of the historical imagination we must examine the historian's narrative composition process and the manner in which historians deploy metaphor to 'fix' meaning. This directs me to the cognitive value of metaphor/trope and troping, and its potential for truth in historical knowledge. How does metaphor, trope and troping function within the historical imagination? Metaphor, along with its two main forms of metonymy and synecdoche, is the transference principle of all language use. It allows historians to re-describe patterns perceived between different domains of experience and evidence. The narrative, being the vehicle for this process of re-description, permits the historian to 'see' and compose/configure a set of relationships that did not previously exist between events.

The historian imagines a cognitive relation in a figurative sense between a new/borrowed word, and the proper meaning of the deliberately absented word. The meaning of this relationship is the 'reason' for the substitution. This 'reason' takes the form of a figurative substitution. In metaphor this has the form of a structure of resemblance. As the French narrativist philosopher Paul Ricoeur describes it, metaphor is representational in object-to-object terms, metonymy is reductive in part-to-part correspondence or contiguity terms, and synecdoche is integrative in a part-to-whole essentialist or connective way. Necessarily each of these is protean in the potential range of relationships they permit. Thus metonymy – the relationship of correspondence – allows historians to deploy cause to effect, propensity to action, sign to signifier. Synecdoche connects one to many, species to genus, or species to individual (Ricoeur 1994 [1978]: 56).

Now, the question here is that given this is just a substitution between terms and no new information is provided in the text, surely troping is just rhetoric and not cognitively useful to historians? Presumably it can not give access to the truth of history? It has been argued, however, that if truth is what you seek, figurative language need not stand as an obstacle because metaphor works at a secondary imaginative level consequent upon the initial reference. Truth can be obtained, therefore, via the metaphorical acts of the historical imagination. The issue, therefore, is not simply one of explanation through empirical correspondence but, as Paul Ricoeur argues, rather analogue, resemblance or substitution (Ricoeur 1984: 3). This would also seem to reinforce the point made by the philosopher of metaphor, Donald Davidson, that metaphor allows us to make new connections and create new theories that lead to knowledge, rather than being knowledge itself (Rorty 1991: 163).

Hayden White also argued the case for the historian's choice of figurative styles as rhetorical models of historical representation, implying that form is as significant a feature of historical study as content (White 1973b) (see FORM AND CONTENT). Metaphor, for White, is *the* means for explaining human intentions/actions, operating through the displacement of meaning as analogy, imitation, resemblance, essence, and/or contiguity at the level of words and sentences (the money to finance the Civil War came in at first like a trickle from a faulty tap ...), and again structurally at the level of the emplotment (the history of these events was a tragedy ...). How we tropically imagine the emplotment creates explanatory coherence out of the jumble of the past at the level of the chosen word or sentence, but it also organises such coherence in a particular way, with an end in mind that will result in a prefigured emplotment and/or argument and/or ideological position (see TELEOLOGY).

Realist philosophers of history, like C. Behan McCullagh, indict White's rhetorical constructionism on several counts: for what is claimed to be his failure to address content and for his failure to accept that truth derives from the contextualisation of sources, but mostly for his failure to accept that the truth-conditional statement makes historical descriptions reliable. McCullagh is happy to acknowledge that metaphor has a role to play in doing history. It is his argument that the metaphoric historical imagination can be truthful but only at the level of the singular descriptive statement. Truthful statements originating in the historical imagination can be established by substantiating truth-conditions and inference, leading to conclusions that are then translated into language both literal and/or metaphoric (McCullagh 1984: 4–44). This is done through the formation of an explanatory hypothesis – the singular descriptive statement – and the inference or deduction of testable consequences of that hypothesis according to the principles of fewest suppositions, probability, plausibility, contextualisation, etc. So it is that language can accurately represent past reality through either a literal or a metaphoric rendition.

McCullagh agrees that the historical imagination works through analogies that are helpful in establishing possible connections between things in the past. Among examples that McCullagh gives are the comparison, of the slave plantation and the Nazi concentration camp, made by American historian Stanley Elkins to explain the infantile nature of black slaves. Both sets of circumstances generated the same effect. Another example he offers would be to describe the debates in Parliament between Gladstone and Disraeli as a duel. Such a description is true if, in the context of the public mind at the time, their relationship manifested some of the salient characteristics of a duel. Equally, there is another context, that of a shared language and culture between the historian and the reader (see EPISTEME; Michel FOUCAULT). For a metaphoric statement to be metaphorically true, the reader must share in the meaning of the terms of the metaphor with the historian. So, historians can offer true and fair interpretations, according to McCullagh, by deploying metaphor when the metaphor displays an adequate resemblance or saliency between statements and objects, and such statements are adequately contextualised. Rejecting what he calls a naïve correspondence, McCullagh allows himself the argument that while metaphorical statements can not be literally true, they can be metaphorically true.

Historians know the narratives they write are not wholly accurate pictures of past reality, yet they write them on the assumption that the past is an object that is given and independent of the discourse through which it is appropriated. As Ricoeur dryly observed, 'If history is a construction, the historian instinctively would like his construction to be a reconstruction' (Ricoeur 1984: 26). Although the historian is implicated in the writing, he/she is not permitted by canonical law to intrude on the factualism of the real past. The important issue is the one that White alerted us to, namely the absenting of the figurative modes in which the historical imagination is framed. The result is the vain attempt, as Roland **Barthes** claims, of most historical narratives at degree zero writing: a style barren of figurative language that assumes the world can be represented accurately through the word.

In his evaluation of the historical imagination, R.G. **Collingwood** rejected any conception of history that depended on empiricism (the authority of the evidence) to the exclusion of the historian's imagination.

For Collingwood the idea of history was of an imaginary picture of the past in the form of a Kantian-type a priori (see A PRIORI/A POSTERIORI) that all humans possess (Collingwood 1994 [1946]: 248). No matter how fragmentary or faulty might be the results of the historian's work, for Collingwood the idea which governed its course was 'clear, rational and universal. It is the idea of the historical imagination as a self-dependent, self-determining, and self-justifying form of thought' (Collingwood 1994 [1946]: 249). However, in spite of this bold idealism, ultimately Collingwood also makes the representationalist choice (along lines similar to McCullagh and Ricoeur) endorsing the ultimately impermeable barrier between the linguistic world and the world of things and their perception – metaphoric truth is still truth.

Collingwood's endorsement of the absolute centrality of metaphor as a cognitive instrument for the characterisation of the historical narrative is not, in his lights, incompatible with referentiality and truth. Naturally (ironically?), Collingwood's thoughts about metaphor were cast figuratively. Employing the picture metaphor, he argued the historical narrative should construct a picture of things as they really were. In another metaphor he described the historian as a lawyer placing his/her evidence in the witness-box. If the evidence is unforthcoming or the source offers false witness, then the authority is rejected and the historian makes his/her own connections between the fixed points of the statements of the sources (Collingwood 1994 [1946]: 238–49). To do this Collingwood argues we deploy the human mind's universal faculty for imagining relationships between the selected fixed points (statements of the sources). So history, because it is in large part the product of the historical imagination, is constructive because it works by interpolating and inferring connections between the evidence of the sources, or the other thoughts and statements implied by them.

In another metaphor Collingwood describes this process as the creation of a 'web of imaginative construction' (Collingwood 1994 [1946]: 242). But he insists the historian him/herself fixes those points as he/she interrogates the sources through contextualisation and verification, and so he/she 'constructs an imaginary picture' that becomes coherent and continuous, and which eventually becomes its own touchstone and measure (Collingwood 1994 [1946]: 242–5). Not surprisingly perhaps, Collingwood argues at this point for the resemblance between the historian and the novelist. Both the novel and the history are self-explanatory, self-justifying, autonomous. The 'only' difference, but one that is crucial, of course, is the historical narrative's requirement to produce a picture 'of things as they really were and events as they really happened' – 'is like' rather than 'looks like' (Collingwood 1994 [1946]: 246). But this constraint must also exist in tandem with the fact that, as he says, every generation 'must re-write history in its own way' (Collingwood 1994 [1946]: 248) (see Geoffrey ELTON). So, what is there in the mechanisms of the historical narrative as the product of the historical imagination, that inclines us toward one reading rather than another to fix the statements in one way or another?

To illustrate how metaphor might drive the historical imagination I will take one of the most famous interpretations of American history, Frederick Jackson Turner's 'The significance of the frontier in American history' (1893)7. Turner was writing at a time – the 1890s – when America was undergoing a cultural crisis brought on by disruptive industrialisation, mass immigration, wholesale political corruption, metropolitanisation, the emergence of **class** conflict, and the 1890 Bureau of the Census declaration that the western movement was now over. This is the era of progressivism and the crusade for social justice. How did his historical imagination work at such a time?

At the level of the single historical descriptive statement Turner said 'The existence of an area of free land, its continuous recession and the advance of American settlement westward explain American development' (Turner 1961 [1893]: 1). You will recall metonymy and synecdoche shape our statements of relations of cause and effect and inference. In metonymy the name of an attribute is substituted for the thing itself – reductively the part stands in for the whole. Free land is presented here metonymically to stand in for the frontier, and eventually in Turner's imagination for the generic characteristics of American democracy. It is an association by contiguity.

But even the most strictly referential metonymic sentences are located within the larger literary artefact of the emplotted historical narrative. Reminder: the historical narrative reveals the historian's thinking about difference and resemblance. It is not, therefore, only a matter of the single statement that, in this instance, conveys metonymic meaning, but the epistemic and culturally disciplined intertextuality of the historical narrative itself. How does Turner compose his 1890s narrative during a time of cultural conflict and division? At this point, as a historian-**author**, I speculate that Turner's objective in his fixing of the role of free land in the pushing back of the frontier was to judge its significance in the subsequent creation of a unified American national identity. This, in turn, is likely to be dependent upon the epistemic character of the historical context in which both Turner and his reader existed – the episteme that embraced the 1890s. Turner's history was in harmony with a contemporary popular consensus on the unique character of American identity as demonstrated in the evidence of a substantial nationalist literature.

From the available evidence, for example, he chose to quote from Peck's *New Guide* to the west, where the wave metaphor is dominant. Turner evidences his argument with phrases like 'another wave rolls on. The men of capital and enterprise come. . . . Thus wave after wave is rolling westward' (Turner 1961 [1893]: 19–20). This selection of the evidence on Turner's part I take to be a demonstration of his imaginative creation of a narrative of inexorable and unstoppable nation-building, the tide of nationality as he says at one point. Before Turner the historical literature had not created the links that Turner's history did. This demonstrates, I think, that the fictional narrative can rarely construct a fiction so convincing as the historical narrative given the latter's presumed association with the referential.

In his search for a relevant past upon which to build a national popular culture Turner used a rhetoric that matched his own and his culture's prefigured vision of America as an exceptional historical creation. Turner's language evidences the existence of White's deep structural level to the historical narrative that is specifically linguistic in nature, and which serves as the pre-critically accepted model of what a distinctively 'historical' explanation should be.

America in the 1890s needed its own utilitarian history, an exceptional (i.e. a non-European) history. This was provided by Turner in his argument that America was a new frontier, 'free land' was its essence and, by inference, *the* causal factor in America's exceptionalism (see CAUSATION). Unlike metonymy, synecdoche operates integratively, suggesting a qualitative relationship among the elements of a totality. By injecting a class analysis at this point, I am suggesting the demands of the emergent and rapidly dominant industrial bourgeoisie necessitated Turner re-configure free land at the structural level of the narrative. The narrative is now re-cast, therefore, in the archetypal trope of synecdoche so as to meet contemporary cultural and epistemic demands for coherence, and class unity. At a second-order cultural or mythic level Turner's history, therefore, signifies America's exceptional historical creation through its classless frontier-inspired unity.

Having speculated on the nature of the historical imagination I do not know if Turner's history is generating the truth, either metaphorical or literal, at either the level of the single statement or the finished narrative. I have no measure except, perhaps, plausibility. I suspect his use of metaphor is cognitive, but whether or not it apprehends reality, I do not know. I do not know if this is *really* how the historian's imagination works. However, if we agree historical knowledge is primarily, or in substantial part, the metaphoric creation of the historical imagination, historians should reorientate themselves epistemologically, to consider form as anterior to content. If the historian's imagination is built upon his/her assumptions about life and how it worked in the past as well as now (assumptions Turner had), then the historical imagination allows us to create different pasts dependent on how we choose to relate the evidence not only within its historical context and upon what particular theory of human behaviour we invoke to connect action with structure, but also to broaden the forms through which we can create historical knowledge.

Further reading

Collingwood, R.G. (1994 [1946])
Curthoys, A. and Docker, J. (1997)
Davidson, D. (1984)
Fiumara, G.C. (1995)
Hesse, M. (1983)
Johnson. M. (1981)
McCullagh, C.B. (1998)
—— (1984)

Munslow, A. (1992)
Ricoeur, P. (1994 [1978])
—— (1984)
Rorty, R. (1991)
Sachs, S. (1979)
Strawson, P.F. (1974)
Turner, F.J. (1961 [1893])
White, H. (1973b)

HISTORICISM

Historicism is a troubling concept (see CONCEPTS IN HISTORY) because its definition is so fluid yet it is acknowledged to be central to how historians do history. Indeed historicism is taken by many to be the essence of historical method. To make matters worse historicism has been appropriated by other disciplines and this has further muddied the waters. For the sake of explanation, however, historicism seems to have three related meanings: for most historians it is the primary historical act of perceiving historical periods in their own terms rather than any imposed by the historian; second and relatedly, it means accepting that every historical period had its own standards through which it determined what was trustworthy knowledge and warranted **truth**; third, that there are inclusive, demonstrable and determining patterns in the process of historical change.

In its primary meaning historicism refers specifically to Friedrich Meinecke's judgement that historians should aim to understand the events (see EVENT), actions and thoughts of people at their own historical moment – the observation and report of the individual occurrence when and as it actually happened. This leads to understanding people as they understood themselves rather than through the imposition of present-day concepts and categories of analysis. By this argument historians empathise with the social conditions that gave rise to actions that occurred at a particular place in time. Historical understanding is thus entirely derived from within that place and time. It is, moreover, this process that reveals the nature of change and continuity, and allows us to rationally locate past things and put them in their proper (temporally sequential) order.

This is a contextualist or 'then and there' variety of historicism that can be traced back at least to Wilhelm Dilthey and R.G. **Collingwood** who, in their different ways, suggested that historians had to insert themselves into the lives and stories of people in the past, escape the present and restrain their own powers of **narrative**. Although they tend to dispute this empathic process, reconstructionist historians (see RECONSTRUCTIONIST HISTORY) find an appeal in what is a definition of historicism that rejects extra-historical (extra-historicist) **covering laws**, social theories, too many and complex concepts that beg questions and a role for language beyond that of simple referentialism. Such things, they believe, can only be alien impositions on past times and places (from present times and places). History thus serves the strata of chronologically laid down **evidence**.

A sceptical **empiricism** is the central feature of this view of how to do history, and its corollary is a suspicion of any history not done in this way, that is, done with the needs of the present or future in mind (see TELEOLOGY).

Historicism thus defined pushes historicism toward its second meaning, which takes on a more relativist hue (see RELATIVISM). In understanding the past on its own terms (the 'then and there' approach), historians quickly came to realise that each historical epoch possessed its own standards by which it judged what was reliable knowledge and verifiable truth. Each period was/is thus unique in the process of its generation of knowledge, that there are no universal extra-historical or transcendental standards by which we can judge the past, so every person, event and process was/is historically unique. What particularly distinguished historical periods was the manner in which each age symbolically and metaphorically expressed itself to itself (see EPISTEME; TROPE/FIGURATION). Of course, in reconstructing the past in its own terms the historian has again to be aware of, and be able to control, his/her own forms of expression. To be a historicist in this second meaning of the term means, therefore, also escaping from any kind of here and now linguistic determinism.

The nineteenth- and twentieth-century reaction against the then and there varieties of historicism came with positivist (see POSITIVISM), constructionist (see CONSTRUCTIONIST HISTORY) and structuralist (see STRUCTURALISM) thought. This reaction assumed science offered a transcendental method, which permitted the rational study of human behaviour by spectators standing apart from the object of observation, who could 'really see' what was going on. Positivism holds, for example, that it is feasible and proper to account for human activity in accordance with recurring covering laws of behaviour.

This logic, when viewed through the events of the twentieth century, persuaded the philosopher Karl Popper (1902–97) to radically re-define historicism (effectively giving it a personal definition) as a dangerous belief in historical determination and the existence of universal patterns in historical processes. Popper specifically had Marxism and fascism in mind as examples of this dubious universalising tendency in history. His book, *The Poverty of Historicism*, is, in fact, dedicated to the memory of all who 'fell victims to the fascist and communist belief in Inexorable Laws of Historical Destiny' (Popper 1957). Popper's personal re-definition of historicism suggests not just that the meaning of historicism is not fixed, but by implication neither is that which is conventionally to be history's proper methodology.

What is at issue with historicism is the question of epistemological relativism: how accurately can we represent the-past-as-history through our words and concepts in the here and now (see EPISTEMOLOGY)? The American pragmatic philosopher Richard **Rorty** has claimed it is no sort of answer to say that historical accuracy can be assured by the good historian who judiciously and fairly represents what they find in the archival record

(Rorty 1998: 73). That they do not misrepresent the record says nothing about the reality of past events, nor the truth-conditions of the statements they make, nor the **hermeneutics** or interpretational character of the discipline.

In spite of the claim that we can know the reality of the past above and beyond what we write about it, history's puzzle must lie in its intertextuality. At what point can/does the historian break into the seemingly eternal and closed loop of evidence and written interpretations – the hermeneutic intertextual circle? Is it possible that historians can distinguish the *real* meaning of the evidence from the meaning *it held for* people at the time, and then from the overlaid *interpretations of subsequent generations* of other historians? If historians can break the circle – escape from intertextuality – to achieve foundational truth (*the* meaning of the text) then the relativist implications of historicism can be avoided. If not, they can not. This position declares the epistemological bond between the past and its accurate representation to be an assumption. The language used by historians is epistemologically autonomous and can not accurately represent history's content (see FORM AND CONTENT). If this is a correct view, then any 'logic' to historical method is akin to literature's critical evaluation of a text rather than the discovery of objective reality, and the essence of history is hermeneutic not factual, linguistic not empirical, fictive not real.

From this perspective it is impossible to accurately recover the past, and all we have is the-past-as-history because historicism (if defined as the proper historical method of telling it as it really was) ignores its object's poetic, presentist and intertextual nature. History *is* conceived in the historian's mind, history *is* literature, and history *is* generated in the here and now. There is no reason, therefore, not to abandon historicist approaches to history defined in the three ways I have indicated. None of them carry any baggage that is significant to the-past-as-history. If we choose to abandon historicism – or do what Popper did and re-define it, but now in a postmodern or hermeneutic fashion by recognising that we 'style the-past-as-history' and use the present to understand it – we may become more open to the idea that referentiality, rather than determining our rhetoric, may be the result of it (form is prior to content). This does not, of course, mean we are destined to go off the rails or lose that sanity that can *only* be assured by empiricism.

Some historians experience further confusion with historicism since it has been appropriated by literature in the shape of the New Historicism. Just as history has made a **linguistic turn** so literature has made a historicist turn. This is literature's turn toward interpreting the literary text in its historical context (the world external to it) rather than evaluating it primarily as a text (its internal world). In certain respects this has a parallel with developments in history's 'old' historicism. While I may elect to re-define historicism (and therefore history) by accepting that history can not be hermetically sealed off from either its linguistic conventions in the here and now or the purposes for which it is written, New Historicism is characterised by the literary critic's awareness of the historical traditions of literary criticism and how changes in its methods have *in the past* served special interests: like those of white, middle-class males, or the forces of imperialism. These are sensitivities that, when directed at written history, are, of course, shared with many post-colonial and feminist historians (see WOMEN'S HISTORY). I could suggest there is now a post-empiricist historian's version of historicism that we might call history's New Historicism, and which effectively ceases to worry about historicism – but to have two New Historicisms would surely over-egg the pudding?

Further reading

Berlin, I. (1976)
Collingwood, R.G. (1994 [1946])
Dilthey, W. (1976)
Hamilton, P. (1996)
Meinecke, F. (1972)
Popper, K. (1957)
Rorty, R. (1998)
Veeser, A.A. (1989)
Worton, M. and Still, J. (1990)

HISTORIOGRAPHY

The term historiography is normally taken to refer to the act of the writing of history, the collective writings of history (or writings on the past if you prefer), and the history of such activities over the centuries. A recent definition of historiography by Keith Jenkins draws out the self-reflexive aspect of the activity with his distinction (which he makes regularly) between 'the past' and 'history'. Jenkins's use of the term directly addresses the philosophical problems that arise for history given its essential interpretative and written form. As he says, echoing Michel de Certeau, history is a **discourse** about, but different from, the past. Jenkins suggests 'It would be preferable, therefore, always to register this difference by using the term "the past" for all that has gone on before ... whilst using the word "historiography" for history' (Jenkins 1991: 6).

By this way of thinking history becomes merely an umbrella term for the whole enterprise of studying the past in all its facets, in other words, the past plus dedicated methods/concepts plus historiography equals history. For Jenkins the last two terms in the equation – historiography and history – are synonymous. If this is so, then the act of writing history produces many questions that focus upon the impositional role of the historian, the nature of the social construction of reality, the character of **historical explanation**, the art of interpretation and the constitution of the **historical imagination**, the relationship of **form and content** and the problems of representation and the **linguistic turn**. Questions are also raised about cultural and historical **relativism** and the cognitive links between history and literature, history and theory, and the philosophy of history more generally (see EPISTEMOLOGY; ONTOLOGY).

The centrality of historiography to the historical enterprise, which is made amply clear with Jenkins's claim, is confirmed by the editors of the *Blackwell Dictionary of Historians* who seem to be suggesting that it is so important it does not even require them to offer a generic defining entry. Because writing history is what historians do, it is enough to acknowledge the act by the many entries on national historiographies (from Australia and Austria through to Scandinavia), and also the historiography of themes/ periods (with entries on black historiography, classical historiography, Jewish historiography, and feminist historiography) (Cannon *et al.* 1988). This heavy emphasis on historiography ought not, however, be read as support for Jenkins's position that history consists in the works of interpretation of historians. The logic would seem to be that to know the past we should begin with what historians tell us about it – the discourse of historians – but I suspect it is meant to denote a body of interpretation rather than the act of interpretation.

This is an important point. It is one also made (I'm not sure whether wittingly or unwittingly) by Joyce Appleby, Lynn Hunt and Margaret Jacob in their book, *Telling the Truth About History* (1994), when they explicitly argue that proper history (that which for them seeks a necessarily pragmatic access to a knowable past reality) can be compatible with the creation of a national (which in the case of the USA is also a democratic, open and multi-cultural) identity. Telling the **truth** about history (a historiographical act to be sure, but one that gets the **facts** straight) in their case means having discovered and written down the truth of the events (see EVENT) of 200 years of American history, which point to the achievement of its multi-cultural democratic heritage. So history, historiography and now a moral positioning also conveniently coincide.

If history is historiography (defined as the act of writing the-past-as-history) then it is reasonable that we understand the material and/or ideological situatedness (translated as moral choices and/or attitudes) of the historian who writes (shapes, structures, emplots, forms, interprets?) the past (see EMPLOTMENT). But there is a big problem here. Not all historians accept the ultimate logic of the equation historiography equals history. E.H. **Carr** in *What is History?* (1987 [1961]) seemingly accepts that the historian 'is of his own age, and bound to it by the conditions of human existence' and that 'The very words he uses ... have current connotations' (Carr 1987 [1961]: 26). But he immediately goes on to deny any association with the result of an inevitable present-centred, pragmatic or relativist history that can have 'an infinity of meanings' as if it were 'spun out of the human brain' (Carr 1987 [1961]: 26). Like Appleby, Hunt and Jacob, Carr understands that history is written by historians, but this element does not mean that 'the facts of history are in principle not amenable to objective interpretation' (Carr 1987 [1961]: 27). Making sense of the facts remains the ordinance. Carr is trying here to square this modernist epistemological circle with an inevitable appeal to the legacy of **empiricism** (the existence of a real past that is factually knowable by objectively observing, by rational, non-future anticipating or teleological historians) (see the ENLIGHTENMENT; MODERNISM; TELEOLOGY).

The most recent substantial foray into the nature of historiography is Michael Bentley's edited *Companion to Historiography* (1997). Here again the issue of history as the discourse of historians is recognised with entries on the ancient, medieval, the early-modern, and modern styles of historical writing (historical periods!) sub-divided into national historiographies. There is also a substantial section on the writing of history with explorations of the connections between history and **narrative**, and related disciplines like archaeology, anthropology, philosophy and women's studies. The point is well-made in this collection that historiography is a contested terrain at many levels, not least that of competing interpretations, but also at the level of the assumptions historians make about what constitutes particular varieties, versions, visions, re-visions, and conceptions of history (see METANARRATIVE).

Further reading

American Historical Association (1995)
Ankersmit, F.R. (1994)
Breisach, E. (1983)
Cameron, A. (1989)
de Certeau, M. (1988 [1975])
Iggers, G. (1997)
Jenkins, K. (1997)
Momigliano, A. (1990)
—— (1985 [1966])
—— (1977)
Stanford, M. (1994)
Warren, J. (1998)

I

INFERENCE

Conventional historical understanding depends on the way in which historians choose to infer conclusions from the **evidence**. They try to provide the most likely explanation of an object of study (**event**, process, action or whatever) that is justified by the sources of information available to them about that object. Why is it important to historians, and to society more widely, that their conclusions are grounded in the sources? The argument is that to seek the **truth** in the past not only must we be justified in what we believe, we must know that other people (past and present) are justified in what they claim. The sources, it is assumed, provide the foundation for this justification. Axiomatically, therefore, historians are interested in the epistemological process of inference that, it is believed, has the power to distinguish assertion from historical knowledge thus providing access to the truth of the past (see EPISTEMOLOGY).

Modernist historians and realist philosophers argue that historical explanations and descriptions are true if they can be verified by other explanations that are themselves supported by sources (McCullagh 1998: 20–3) (see CONSTRUCTIONIST HISTORY; MODERNISM; RECONSTRUCTIONIST HISTORY). Hence the conclusions we infer from the evidence as to its meaning (in the shape of historical descriptions) can be true if they meet these conditions. Historians – even deconstructionist historians (see DECONSTRUCTIONIST HISTORY) – accept that much about the past, certainly at what I would call the almanac(ish) level, can be true. I can not think of any historian who would deny that, according to the evidence, on 13 April 1846 the Pennsylvania Railroad received a charter or that on 3 December 1947 Tennessee Williams's play, *A Streetcar Named Desire*, opened in the American city of New Orleans. These are simple descriptive statements amply supported by the evidence. For all intents and purposes they are truthful descriptions.

Historians usually work at a much higher level than this of course. We draw inferences so as to construct interpretative narratives but only initially by reference to the most recently available evidence. This constructionist history process is informed by a priori theorising (from premise to proposition) that eventually launches us into the realms of interpretation (see A PRIORI/A POSTERIORI). Inference is a form of logic, therefore, that consists of the connection between the premises and the conclusion of a logical argument. Put another way, it is the drawing of a conclusion from premises that support it either deductively or inductively.

Strictly speaking there are three types of inference we need to distinguish: the deductive, inductive and abductive. Deductive (or logical) inference is generally regarded as inappropriate for the study of the past. This is because such inferences are established without reference to the empirical to reach a truthful (or a false) conclusion (see EMPIRICISM). Deductive inferences follow on from premises that, if true, mean the conclusion reached is valid – if A, then B. Deduction, therefore, has two stages: initially we must understand the premises, and then we draw a conclusion. There is, however, a further optional stage whereby we are free to test the validity of our deductive conclusions empirically – the process of model-testing. Constructionist historians – those of a social scientific persuasion – often do indeed infer (i.e. set up) models to be tested. But the majority of historians believe history to be content-led, hence they operate primarily through some kind of induction. The evidence, they claim, guides their conclusions and their 'models' are really just the categories and concepts of analysis suggested by the evidence itself (see CONCEPTS IN HISTORY).

Inductive inferences are commonly drawn when a historian reads the available evidence to reach an interpretation about its intrinsic meaning. An inductive inference is at best only probably true. Unlike deductive inferences, inductive inferences offer conclusions that broaden and deepen knowledge beyond the simple level of the initial premises, but can not guarantee truth. With inductive inference we are not deriving logically true statements (all Xs are Ys, all Ys are Zs, therefore all Xs are Zs), but statements that may be truthful when judged empirically (by the nature of what X, Y and Z actually represent). The process of induction is fourfold: initially it requires the historian to discover and observe the event, process or action (the evidence as a text); next he/she sets up a hypothesis (an explanation) that tries to account for the data referring to the event, process or action within a wider circle of evidence (the context); then he/she is expected to recognise and explain how his/her conclusion/interpretation takes us beyond the available evidence and existing conclusion/interpretation; and, finally, evaluate that fresh conclusion/interpretation by reference once more to the evidence. Clearly, inductive inference exists within an empirical loop grounded in the material world. This becomes the ultimate guarantor of **objectivity** in the work of the historian. His/her interpretations serve the evidence. Although historians are increasingly loathe to deploy them, inductive inference is also the means for inferring **covering laws** or general statements of behaviour – inference from the particular to the general. Suspicion about covering laws derives precisely from the fact that unlike deduction, induction can not guarantee its conclusions. It can not certify laws of behaviour and/or theories, only suggest possible causes *post hoc* from events, imply meaningful analogies and propose the best (the most likely) explanation (see HISTORICAL EXPLANATION; HISTORICAL IMAGINATION).

The peculiar method of inductive inferential reasoning by which the historian speculates as to what constitutes the best explanation without generalising is abduction (see COLLIGATION). Abductive historical reasoning, unlike induction that leads to covering laws and general explanations, accepts conclusions/interpretations on the grounds that they explain the ***particular*** event that is to hand. Historians observe the evidence of the event and then set up a hypothesis to explain an apparent anomaly or surprising situation they believe they have 'found' therein, and then inductively test the explanation/supposition via further evidence. As the American pragmatic philosopher Charles S. Peirce described it, the abductive inferential process is characterised by the inductive mind-set of realism, discovery and anti-scepticism to arrive at the conclusions that best explain the available evidence (Peirce 1958: 89–164).

An example may be helpful. Historians find they are surprised that Terence V. Powderly, in the 1880s, became such a successful leader of the American trade union, the Knights of Labor, given that, in most respects he appeared unqualified and, therefore, unlikely to succeed. But we suppose (hypothesise?) that his actual success was perhaps because he had a long and varied career in local politics before he became a trade union leader. If we accept this was indeed a valuable training, then his success as a trade union leader is more explicable. So, by that union leadership success there is good reason to believe (*post hoc* or literally after the event) that his local-government career was a good training. Abduction, therefore, allows for imaginative if not indeed surprising conclusions about specific cases. In this example the historian (with surprise) notes Powderly's successful union leadership, then frames an explanation (after the event) from which a particular inference flows – most plausibly as no other hypothesis or supposition seemingly can explain Powderly's union success so well. It follows we are justified in believing that his local-government career is the correct explanation for his union leadership success.

A postmodern (see POSTMODERNISM) or deconstructive vision of inductive and abductive inferential historical explanation points out, of course, that as a foundationalist or realist-inspired reasoning process it must be subject to an infinite regress of justified beliefs. By following the logic of history's inductive-abductive inferential method the assumption can not be made that at some point the historian will discover the original source of meaning – the correct supposition – upon which all later justified explanation is built (e.g. Powderly's local-government career). Historians know they can not deduce or infer any original truths or explanations about past experience simply through the observation of the evidence. There is no empiricist originary point of knowing. So it is admitted that there is no absolute, truthful or given meaning to be discovered. It follows, because historical explanation is abductive, history's conclusions must be provisional no matter how extensive is the reservoir of either old or new evidence. It can not be other because there can be no bedrock of empirical knowledge that grounds all other historical knowledge. The post-structuralist critic points out this means all historical knowledge is propositional and incapable of ultimate justification. History is subject, at best, to only highly localised verification, and remains a petty narrative.

This critique is usually pushed further with the claim that, because historical explanation is inductive-abductive, history's interpretations are at best just sophisticated guess-work that only exists in a reality-effect (see REALITY/REALISTIC EFFECT) universe generated by forces other than merely the (intrinsically laden with meaning!) evidence, such as the historian's own ideological situatedness and the historian's preferred social theories (see Roland BARTHES). It follows that explanation (and meaning) in history is as much about form as content (see FORM AND CONTENT). It means in a non-justifiable universe of historical knowledge **facts** become beliefs that can only be 'justified' relative to the arbitrary preconceptions, prefigurations or desires of the historian and his/her culture (see TELEOLOGY). It also means historical explanation should primarily be construed as a **narrative**-fictive process that is concerned as much with the needs of the present or the future as with those of the past. It reveals the idea of a real and knowable past about which true or false statements can be made is, at best, just another in a long line of modernist suppositions about how we know things. Accepting this means not just no longer believing in the reliability of inferred historical descriptions, but that history is not a legitimate or privileged epistemology by virtue of its inferential methodology. It is only the extent to which we believe in the abductive form of inference that we believe in the truth of historical knowledge.

There are at least five criticisms now regularly offered against an inferentially based and truthful history. They are: that history can at best only represent the past through concepts that are primarily language-based and language is a notoriously poor conductor of meaning; that in his/her use of concepts the historian unavoidably imposes his/her present culture on the past and so can not understand the past in its own terms; that he/she imposes his/herself on the past through his/her individual ideological and moral perspective; that the writing of history has an epistemic (knowing) priority over the content of the past inasmuch as the historian must eventually compose the past as (an invented) narrative; and, finally, the modernist investment in the unified knowing subject can be demonstrated to be little more than a Western metaphysical (see METAPHYSICS) wish fulfilment (see the ENLIGHTENMENT). All we can know of the past are our present, cultural, linguistic and ideological descriptions of it. The drastic conclusion is that we can never know the past except in the ersatz version of it we choose to call the-past-as-history.

Further reading

Audi, R. (1998)
Hanson, N.R. (1958)
Josephson, J.R. and S.G. (1994)
McCullagh, C.B. (1998)
Peirce, C.S. (1958)
Rorty, R. (1998)
—— (1991)

INTENTIONALITY

Intentionality is the connection between a state of mind (a mental state), its expression or representation (signifier), and that to which it refers (referent). Historians regard intentionality as one of the central features of **historical explanation** and specifically of the study of **causation**. The British philosopher-historian R.G. **Collingwood**, for example, stressed that historians seek out the thought behind the action in order to get at the **truth** that lies in the past. While the second-hand nature of history means that observation of the **evidence** does not permit the *real* character of events or processes and individual actions to be known through the deployment of **inference**, historical explanation demands historians give a plausible and supported account of agent intentionality (and the extent of free will). To be truthful in history we are expected to seek the correspondence between the mind and the fact. This requires that we explain the reasons why, for example, Stalin wanted to put Leon Trotsky on trial, why Harry S. Truman in March 1947 promulgated the doctrine that bears his name, why Hitler invaded Poland, why the Nazis acted as they did toward Europe's Jewish population, and why the cold war occurred. Historians should, therefore, understand the motivation, purposes and intentions of individuals before adequate explanations of events (see EVENT) and processes can be made.

However, in pursuit of Collingwood's notion that to comprehend human actions we must understand the intentions they manifest, historians have to face the dilemma that to know intentions means having to infer mental states from the evidence of actions. Determining what certain actions or events signify (what they mean) in terms of the mental states that may have given rise to them is notoriously difficult. Working on the principle of purposive and rational action seems to most historians to be the only way to approach it: that is, by assuming people act in such a way as to achieve a specified objective (see TELEOLOGY).

For example, why did the American president Abraham Lincoln issue the Emancipation Proclamation (1 January 1863)? Was it because slave labour was useful to the Confederate cause? Or because low morale in the North necessitated an injection of high moral tone? Or Northern public opinion demanded it? Or ending slavery would preclude the support of Britain and France for the Confederacy? Or was it a strategic thing to do because General Lee had been expelled from the North after the battle of Antietam?

So, what was the objective in emancipating the slaves? Conventionally, historians are contextualists who, in this example, are likely to assume all these reasons/causes were intertwined, and all were related by an ultimate purpose or objective – which will, of course, constitute *the* explanation (see COLLIGATION). But is this a reasonable assumption? Can we really expect to 'discover' *the* explanation? Can we make our decision about what is *the* explanation only by forming yet further sets of assumptions, in this case about Lincoln's intentions, within the wider framework of events based on our personal selection from the available evidence? Each set of assumptions that conventionally is meant to bring us closer to the truth is, in fact, moving us further into speculation and supposition.

This seems fair enough, perhaps even unavoidable if, as a historian, you are predisposed toward believing that people's intentions are the central feature of historical explanation and that they can be knowable (see LIBERAL HUMANISM). It seems quite wrong if you do not make this assumption (i.e. you reject the idea of consciousness determining being), or if you believe it is ontologically (see ONTOLOGY) (as in the construction of reality) and epistemologically (see EPISTEMOLOGY) (as in the construction of knowledge) impossible to know how intentionality fits in with the context, or what the agent's motives were, or what *we think* their objective was. In fact, to explain the intentions of people in the past requires the presumption that they are the same as us and it can be demonstrated that they, like us, were capable of making explicable rational decisions (!) or, given their circumstances, they displayed behaviour that can be explained by their failure to be rational. And it also demands that the textual evidence can be deciphered so as to reveal all relevant hidden intentionality, their likely mental state, and consequent motive and purpose.

Of course, if we believe we can not recover the intentionality of the author of the evidence, it implies several significant things about doing (or not doing!) history: it suggests that we can not know the original or primal meaning of the evidence; it means rejecting the correspondence theory of knowledge; it casts doubt on the idea of **objectivity**; it challenges conventional notions of history as a legitimate empiricist undertaking; it questions the possibility of a knowable historical reality; and it means evidence (as texts) can only be studied for their multiple meanings or their **reality/realistic effect** (see COVERING LAWS; EMPIRICISM; Jacques DERRIDA). But all this may be the unavoidable price historians have to pay if they choose to invoke the *post hoc* argument that we know people in the past are likely to have thought in such and such a way because our world thinks the way it does.

'Discovering' agent intentionality depends, therefore, largely on how the historian conceptualises or represents the intentional act linguistically (see CONCEPTS IN HISTORY; LINGUISTIC TURN; Hayden WHITE). The thoughts that generated an action are states of mind presumably directed at things in the real world. But the historian can only explain them a posteriori (see A PRIORI/A POSTERIORI) through the evidence of the intention as ink stains on paper: the word that references the action. In practical terms agent intentionality presents itself to the historian as a function of language rather than a direct plug-in to the mind of the agent. Historians are, consequently, always subject to the intentional fallacy of assuming an access to the **author**'s real motives from which we can deduce the person's true intentions. This is especially so if the historian claims an authoritative piece of evidence when it is, in fact, only a trace of the author's act of self-reflection – just another text the meaning of which is forever deferred.

So, how should we deploy agent intentionality? It seems to depend on both the **form and content** choices made by the historian. Hayden White and Frank Ankersmit suggest that because history is essentially a literary commodity historians use the history story form prior to the 'discovery' of agent intentionality. For White what this means is that there is nothing in history's empiricist methodology that requires *or permits* historical narratives to relay the past realities of human intentions and beliefs. Our prefigured preferences will, in fact, largely determine how we trope or emplot the individual and his/her intentions even if, following Collingwood's advice, we have tried to rethink the thoughts of the historical agent and measured them referentially against the evidence (see EMPLOTMENT; TROPE/FIGURATION).

The philosopher Arthur Danto has also concluded that language, being opaque and cloudy, means that linking language to intention is usually a reduction too far. It would appear that the truth or plausibility value of the historian's written sentences about mental states can readily be altered if one replaces certain expressions or metaphors by others. We can only believe in knowable intentionality, therefore, if we accept there are real stories that were once lived, that they are available to be 'discovered' and now re-told accurately and so correspond to the **facts**. If, however, we choose to interpret mental states as what they manifestly are – representations – as in words, sentences, paintings and graphs, then we have the same problems of deciphering them as we do with any texts in history.

Further reading

Ankersmit, F.R. (1983)
Collingwood, R.G. (1994 [1946])
Danto, A. (1981)
Dray, W.H. (1957)
Olafson, F.A. (1979)
Roberts, G. (1997)
Searle, J.R. (1983)
Weber, M. (1957 [1947])
Wilson, G.M. (1989)

K

KANT, IMMANUEL (1724–1804)

Immanuel Kant was one of the key philosophers of the eighteenth-century **Enlightenment**. What makes Kant's **metaphysics** so important is his **epistemology**, namely the foundational belief that reason has the power to probe and establish its own boundaries (*Critique of Pure Reason*) (see G.W.F. HEGEL). Kant's contribution to the modernist (see MODERNISM) project lies in his assertion that knowledge is grounded in the knowing subject. Kant claimed such a knowing and rational subject can save us from the competing sways of illusion, scepticism and **relativism**. Kant's basic aim was to demonstrate that a reality exists (the world) independent of our representations of it (the word). In addition he thought at great length about ethics (*Critique of Practical Reason*), aesthetics (*Critique of Judgement*), politics (*Ideas on the Philosophy of the History of Mankind*), and history (*What Is Enlightenment?*, and *Idea for a Universal History with a Cosmopolitan Purpose*). Kant tried to overcome what he saw as the problems of David Hume's sceptical empiricism and G.W. Leibnitz's extreme rationalism by arguing, following Descartes, in favour of a transcendental idealism, that the mind has pre-programmed categories, intuitions and concepts that command, construct or order our understanding of the real world. This is undertaken by the unified self through the adding together (synthesis) of perception with perception according to given rules that determine in advance how the object will appear to us.

With this thinking Kant offers us the central modernist intellectual expression, that there are given and natural conditions through which we experience reality. Such categories (he proposed a four-fold division – Quantity, Quality, Modality and Relation – with three categories in each) are the filters of reason offering the synthetic a priori (see A PRIORI/ A POSTERIORI) foundation with which we make sense of experience. Through these filters we can know the reality behind our experiences. Under

Relation we have, for example, substance and accident, cause and effect, and reciprocity. The circularity in this lies in the fact that as we place this grid of categories on our lived experience, those features of existence that derive from the categories/intuitions must correspond to reality as we experience it because they are universally prior to it. Our minds are created in a certain way and we perceive the external world accordingly. Our reason creates the conditions for our experience – the epistemological paradigm. So, rather than believing our knowledge corresponds to the world of things, things conform to our means of knowing (time is conceived of as one-dimensional, space as three-dimensional, cause before effect, and so on). Our knowledge, therefore, is derived from sense-experience as formed and filtered through our categories.

Kant claimed in the opening to his *Critique of Pure Reason* that it was beyond a doubt that all knowledge begins *with* experience, but this does not mean it derives *from* experience. There is a component part of knowledge independent of experience that he terms a priori, which stands to be distinguished from empirical knowledge (from the senses) (see EMPIRICISM). How can we further distinguish what is pure a priori from what is empirical? Kant's fortification against Humean scepticism resided in the transcendental ego, which is the human mental source of this rationalist power. In following his stated objective to discover how it is we can objectively know, his route was to posit the two worlds of that which appears to us (phenomena), and that which undoubtedly exists, things-in-themselves (noumena) but that, while they are knowable, are not subject to reason. This means the human mind can discover the **truth** of the world only as it appears to us, not the world as it is in reality. We can not ever know for certain that the objects we perceive are organised by our categories, but we know the categories exist and we believe they organise our sensory input. We cannot escape this situation. We can not escape from the categorical form of our knowledge into the world or content of reality (empirical realism) (see FORM AND CONTENT).

This rejection of an empiricism that insists what we know can only be derived through unmediated experience is the basis of Kant's legacy for historians. Also clearly significant in that legacy is what is usually taken by historians to be Kant's assurance that while the mind is a processing mechanism that renders the stream of data intelligible (and making reason transcendent in the process), this does not mean our knowledge must be subjective or contingent. It is possible, therefore, for the historian to derive objective knowledge. While for Kant the form of our experience is what we know a priori (mental categories or forms independent of experience), the content is always derived a posteriori (according to the **evidence** of experience). It is only when we deploy both form and content that we can hope to derive objective knowledge of the real world. As rational creatures we know objects universally through these forms. Kant's transcendental idealism led him to the conclusion that all forms or ways of conceiving the historical process are, therefore, imposed by the rational mind in the shape of the preferred emplotments (see EMPLOTMENT) of historians.

But, and it is a big but, we can not know for sure that the content of the real world is organised according to our category forms of emplotment, because we only know content through the forms. All we can know is that the content of the world seems to conform to the forms. In the ironic Kantian universe we can not escape the form of our cognition to see if the emplotments do really apply. So, we are left with the ironic situation that there *must be* a correspondence of form and content, even if we can not be *really* sure about it. Whatever we think of this, it is the relationship of the form and the content of history that remains central to the connection between **narrative** and **objectivity**.

Experience (the-past-as-history?) taught Kant humanity had not, at least to his satisfaction, demonstrated historical change was necessarily smooth or continuous (our lives are subject to chaos, especially the dislocation of wars) but, nevertheless, the advance toward rationality is a moral demand all must obey. Kant believed history was an ethical imposition. Obeying this demand led him to the three rational conceptions of the historical process historians could choose to endorse – progress, degeneration and/or stasis – which match the emplotments of Comedy, Tragedy or Epic. For Kant history represented the human mind's capacity to impose different forms on the process of historical change. Any wish to secure the truth must, therefore, be understood through these aesthetic categories. This imposition raises all kinds of questions, not least whether the narrative form for producing a particular kind of history is a category that corresponds with reality because it *is* a condition of knowing? Some history *really* is Epic, other *really* is Tragic!

Kant was a product of his age (as, I assume, we all are) and one of his key assumptions, which was outlined in his short article, *What is Enlightenment?* (1784), written for the 'enlightened' emperor Frederick, was Kant's bourgeois celebration of individual freedom and his belief in the essential autonomy of the free agent. While the early 1780s in Europe were not an especially enlightened age, or so it seems to me, the way was opening for men (if not for women) to free themselves from what Kant called self-imposed tutelage. His ideological commitment to human (male) freedom influenced his vision of history, and unavoidably this inflected his message to later generations of historians. He rationalised his bourgeois ideological commitment arguing that since men have been endowed with the powers of reason, so history must demonstrate the development of mankind toward ever greater levels of intelligence. The ultimate success of rationality is defined in the *Idea for a Universal History with a Cosmopolitan Purpose* in the forms of a republican state, political liberalism, individual emancipation, equality, liberty, free will, the principles of right – what Lyotard would later describe as metanarratives (see METANARRATIVE) – the stories Enlightenment philosophers (like Kant) elected to tell about emergent-dominant bourgeois Western European culture.

Built on Kant's basic premise then – the match or correspondence between subjective categories/concepts and objects – is his contribution to the study of history and the work of historians. It resides in his combined belief in rationality, objectivity, a particular **teleology**, the form/content duality, an emergent bourgeois ideological positioning, the knowing subject, and that it is clearly not possible to accept a crude variety of empiricism. The circularity in his arguments (the ideological content of his logic) is the basis of much deconstructive debate. What happens if we place object before subject, or argue form always precedes content? So it is today that we can and do debate whether the historical narrative corresponds to *the* (real and genuine) story, or whether it merely reflects an emplotted invention of the historian (see Hayden WHITE).

Further reading

Beck, L.W. (1963)
Cassirer, E. (1981)
Fackenheim, E. (1956/57)
Guyer, P. (1992)
Kant, I. (1993 [1781])
O'Brien, K. (1997)
Reiss, H. (1991 [1970])
Yovel, Y. (1980)

L

LIBERAL HUMANISM

Although the Renaissance advanced respect for the individual and the decline of the feudal system assured it, it was not until René Descartes's insistence on the thinking self, and the **Enlightenment**'s progression toward the victory of **modernism**'s bourgeois industrial capitalism as a social and economic system, that the modernist conception of the human individual burgeoned. But it was not until liberalism emerged, as the political, economic and intellectual force most closely associated with the Enlightenment and nineteenth-century scientificism, that this individual was placed at the centre of everything. This revolutionary (literally in some cases) and all-powerful individual was cast in humanist fashion as the rational man. He was accompanied by popular sovereignty, equality of opportunity, the free market and, most importantly, the ability to control the creation of knowledge. Humanism as a philosophy developed, therefore, within the context of an emergent capitalism, new **class** relations, and a new human-centred framework for the comprehension of reality. This man was privileged because 'he' (the pronoun is apt given the patriarchal inclination of modernity) (see WOMEN'S HISTORY) was at once the median and high point of the historical process. In what was quickly appropriated as a bourgeois conception, man was regarded as a unified, coherent, stable, but above all an atomistic self-acting human agent. This subject at the heart of the Enlightenment project was supplied with the will, the ability, and the power (the freedom) to make rational social, political and economic choices about the real world out there (see Benedetto CROCE; G.W.F. HEGEL; Immanuel KANT; Friedrich NIETZSCHE).

This liberal humanism, as the bourgeois ideology of the age of capital may be called, found it (socially, culturally, politically, philosophically and economically) necessary to generate what soon found its shape in Enlightenment philosopher Immanuel Kant's rational autonomous subject (as opposed to one possessing a collectivist consciousness) who could carve his place in the universe through his capacity to know. In the 1890s the American historian of the frontier, Frederick Jackson Turner, supplied what is for me the definition of the modernist subject with his description of the early nineteenth-century American pioneer. The frontier pioneer, as a Modern Man, possessed 'acuteness and inquisitiveness; [and] that practical, inventive turn of mind, quick to find expedients; that masterful grasp of material things, lacking in the artistic but powerful to effect great ends; that restless, nervous energy; that dominant individualism, working for good and for evil, and withal that buoyancy and exuberance that comes with freedom' (Turner 1961 [1893]: 37). The dominant entrepreneurial and exploitative nature of the individual demanded that he be given – as a natural right – command over his environment, and that history should recognise and map his progress toward self-realisation.

Liberal humanism defined man as the engineer, the maker of history, the creator of empires, the founder of nations, the subduer of lesser peoples, the **author** and master of language, and his identity would not be fragmented or dissolved by forces greater than himself. The ideology of liberal humanism takes for granted a world in which conflict and dispute can be arbitrated by the knowing subject, nature can be chastened, knowledge can be compartmentalised but, above all else, man has dominion over language. The self, as the mainspring and origin of consciousness, understanding, meaning, knowledge and agency, can overcome all obstacles particularly when the knowing self is linked to science and technology (see INTENTIONALITY). Liberal humanism in the defence of its self, therefore, has a major stake in the philosophy of reason and science as it pursues knowledge and, equally, in denying the arbitrary social, cultural or linguistic construction of the individual, or that nature (the real world) will ultimately determine his actions. Liberal humanism has no time at all for the idea that knowledge of the real world may be unobtainable or inconsistent, or that the real world can not be discovered and represented as it actually is.

Historians within this liberal humanist tradition are locked into this image of the man in control: the man who can offer the **truth** of the past which his power over the sources and method has disclosed. This is achieved by the paradox of humanism, the exclusion of the historian, so 'history' may reveal its own truth through disembodied narration, displaying it rather than speaking it, as a report rather than a conversation (see Roland BARTHES; NARRATIVE; REALITY/REALISTIC EFFECT). The form of the liberal humanist-inspired history text is seen in its attempt to obliterate itself (see FORM AND CONTENT). The text tries to diminish its own existence to the point when it is not history that speaks, but the past. The historian remains there, of course, but as a pale if not shadowy facilitator in the background who invites the reader to accept the reality of his/her invisible text. That reality that the historian has mastered is offered clearly, transparently, and in an unmediated fashion to the reader as another way of extending the realm of the knowing subject. The reader of history is thus sucked into the ever-widening and 'self-perpetuating' world of the unified knowing subject. The assumptions of liberal humanism seem to present few problems to reconstructionist historians (see RECONSTRUCTIONIST HISTORY) and, for that matter, much conventional practical realist or **constructionist history** also fosters the liberal humanist ideological perspective that embraces **empiricism**, the methodological individualism of rational-action theory (the belief in agency/intentionality), **objectivity**, factualism, representation and truth-conditional narratives.

Further reading

Branstead, E.K. and Meluish, K.J. (1978)
Bullock, A. (1985)
Carroll, J. (1993)
Cox, C.B. (1963)
Davies, T. (1997)
Margolin, J.C. (1989)
Roberts, D.D. (1995)
Rockmore, T. (1995)
Sartre, J.-P. (1989)
Turner, F.J. (1961 [1893])
Williams, C.D. (1997)

LINGUISTIC TURN

The term 'the linguistic turn', which according to Richard **Rorty** was coined by the Austrian realist philosopher Gustav Bergmann, has been used by advocates and critics alike to describe the shift in **historical explanation** toward an emphasis on the role of language in creating historical meaning (Rorty 1992 [1967]). The debate over the linguistic turn hinges on the extent to which one believes **objectivity** and **truth** are possible in historical descriptions. As an **epistemology**, as a theory of knowing, defenders of the linguistic turn ask are there **facts** to be discovered and captured outside language and, moreover, can the historical **narrative** accurately represent this factualist reality as genuine knowledge? Because of its inherently figurative nature and the manner in which textual meaning is constantly deferred, is language destined to remain the ultimate barrier (through which we can not pass) to the discovery of reality (see EMPLOTMENT; Jacques DERRIDA; TROPE/FIGURATION)? Or can historians access the real by curing language of its figurativism so that it mirrors the reality beyond itself by means of the logical form of the propositional sentence? The alternative is to adopt Ludwig Wittgenstein's position that language is a set of games each possessing its own rules for constituting truth (see RELATIVISM).

In general, historians still tend to move in a particular epistemological direction regarding language as an adequate representational vehicle, and so the linguistic turn to an anti-realist orientation is not an option (see EPISTEMOLOGY). The American philosopher of history Hayden **White** is often regarded as the leading advocate of the linguistic turn in his comparison of the past to a text that needs interpretation (see HERMENEUTICS). Through his recognition of the power of language to create meaning he has described how the form of the language we use as historians has a determining effect on the meaning we 'extract' or, to be more accurate, we 'impose' on the-past-as-history (see FORM AND CONTENT). As the philosopher Frank Ankersmit describes it, the historian translates the text of the past into the narrative text of the historian, the-past-as-history, guided by the four major tropes (the figurative devices of metaphor, metonymy, synecdoche and irony (Ankersmit 1994: 64). In his book, *The Content of the Form* (1987), White argued that the choices the historian makes in organising the-past-as-history are less to do with the reality (see EVIDENCE) and more to do with the historian's own **ontology** (his/her understanding of the nature of being), ideology, epistemology, and emplotment choices. The narrative shape selected by the historian, therefore, carries within it its own prefigured agenda. As Hayden White describes it, the form provides for the content of the past.

The term has been notorious among reconstructionist (see RECONSTRUCTIONIST HISTORY) and mainstream constructionist (see CONSTRUCTIONIST HISTORY) historians since the early 1980s because of the widespread misunderstanding of Hayden White's position on what was taken to be his supposed turn to anti-realist linguistic relativism. Although he is still often accused of this by hard-hat reconstructionist historians like Arthur Marwick, what White is actually saying is that language operates within the framework of a **discourse** (the narrative beyond the level of the single sentence), which unavoidably influences how we create the-past-as-history (Marwick 1995; White 1995) (see Roland BARTHES; EPISTEME; Michel FOUCAULT; HISTORICISM; REALITY/REALISTIC EFFECT). The linguistic turn is not anti-realist but is post-empiricist in the sense that it questions the notion that social and material forces always have a primacy over cultural and linguistic structures. The linguistic turn offers up to historians several disquieting arguments – that the past consists of texts that are largely self-referential, that aesthetic decisions are as important as the evidence in generating a narrative, that the **intentionality** of the author can not be known with any certainty, that history beyond the sentence is all interpretation, and that the correspondence theory of knowledge is too frail to support all that is claimed for it. By not addressing these arguments history opens itself to the charge of endorsing a coarse **empiricism** that is, in practice, hard to combat as it is usually cast as a highly refined, sophisticated and suitably sceptical methodology. But at the end of the day history will seem to remain an epistemologically unreflective process of objective knowing and objectified meaning if it does not turn to the consideration of its own linguistic and philosophical features.

Further reading

Ankersmit, F.R. (1994)
Fay, B., Pomper, P. and Vann, R.T. (1998)
Harlan, D. (1989)
Hollinger, D.A. (1989)
Iggers, G. (1997)
Jenkins, K. (1997)
Joyce, P. (1991)
Kellner, H. (1980)
LaCapra, D. (1995)
Lorenz, C. (1994)
Marwick, A. (1995)
Mink, L. (1970)
Munslow, A. (1997a)
Rorty, R. (1992 [1967])
Toews, J.E. (1987)
Vann, R.T. (1987)
White, H. (1995)
—— (1987)
—— (1973b)

M

METANARRATIVE

Literally a **narrative** about narratives, the term was popularised by Jean-François Lyotard in his book, *The Postmodern Condition: A Report on Knowledge* (1979), in which he argued that metanarratives or master narratives, the stories told about how we gained and legitimated knowledge in the past, underpinned human progress and history. Such stories or narratives are various and broad, encompassing philosophical, political, economic and cultural processes like Hegelianism, Marxism, liberalism, **hermeneutics**, modern science/scientific knowledge, the **Enlightenment**, the free market, the power of language to represent accurately, even the very notion of transcendent legitimacy. According to Lyotard all have reached the end of their useful life in what is now the postmodern (see POSTMODERNISM) era. The fact we can no longer depend on such grand stories as universal benchmarks against which we can measure or ensure **truth** is what supposedly characterises our postmodern condition – there are no foundational truths, no epistemological givens (see EPISTEMOLOGY). What we are left with are numerous 'little narratives' or performances/practices that effectively become self-legitimating, and that by their nature can not offer our culture transcendent or unqualified access to the reality of the world as it actually is, or was. It follows these narratives about narratives cannot guarantee **objectivity** in the study of the past.

The effects of such a sweeping rejection of the master narratives have been nothing less than a total questioning of the conditions under which we generate knowledge and understand our situation in the world both present and past. This general anti-Cartesian or post-empiricist orientation has been explicit in all realms of study – from philosophy (Richard **Rorty**'s postmodern pragmatism) and feminism, to our construction of time, and the collapse of representation in written history, hence postmodernism's 'anti-historical' stance (see Roland BARTHES; Michel FOUCAULT; Hayden WHITE).

The challenge to the concept of the metanarrative prompts many questions for those who write history. Do we continue to narrate even if no one believes in narration or its use? Can we stop narrating? Do we narrate our lives to ourselves as we live them? Do historians re-tell *the* story of the past (according to the given metanarrative or canon of empiricism) or do historians tell *a* story about the past (invoking selected and even invented metanarratives thus ditching empiricism in favour of some other performance or individual practice(s))? Posing and answering these kinds of questions has produced an extensive literature on metanarratives since the mid-1980s.

Further reading

Ankersmit, F.R. (1994)
Ankersmit, F.R. and Kellner, H. (1995)
Berkhofer, R.F. (1995)
Bertens, H. (1995)
Carr. D. (1986a)
Ermarth, E.D. (1992)
Jenkins, K. (1991)
Lyotard, J.-F. (1979)
Norman, A.P. (1991)
Putnam, H. (1992)
Scott, J.W. (1996a)
White, H. (1987)

METAPHYSICS

In philosophy the term conventionally designates the broadest of inquiries into reality, being, what exists, and how we can classify or categorise it (see A PRIORI/A POSTERIORI; CAUSATION; EPISTEMOLOGY; EVENT; FACTS; OBJECTIVITY; ONTOLOGY). The metaphysician (the knowing subject, the 'I') asks the ontological question, 'What is there "out there" to be known?' Next, the metaphysician asks the epistemological question how can 'I' delineate those categories into which everything 'out there' can be divided? The answers to these two questions eventually translate into a methodological procedure. Unfortunately, given the highly abstract nature of metaphysics, there has never been any general agreement not only as to the nature of reality, but also as to what constitutes the categories of knowledge, how the categories are related, how useful they are as representations of reality and, in the late twentieth century, what is the point of it all when critics increasingly doubt the existence of the knowing subject? So, metaphysics push the questioner into ontology, epistemology and methodology. For example, explaining the causes of the American Civil War covers all three areas: the process of causation exists in the real world of ontology, and explaining its nature is an epistemological and methodological process of thinking about and organising that past reality. 'I' place it into categories and conceptual schemata to interpret and explain it (see CONCEPTS IN HISTORY).

As might be imagined, over 2,000 years of thinking about the nature and organisation of reality has generated a number of different conclusions about its nature and our categorial access to it. Aristotle initially defined metaphysics as the search for first causes aimed at proving the **truth** of the existence and nature of God (the Unmoved Mover). But for Aristotle metaphysics also sought out the meaning of those very general concepts or categories that are the foundations of all other disciplines. Enlightenment thinkers (rationalists like Descartes, Spinoza and Leibniz) vastly extended the realm of metaphysics to include a new range of issues prompted by developments in science (the mind–body duality), experimentation (empirical inquiry) (see EMPIRICISM), and mathematics (Cartesian geometry). The attempt was made to unify this new world of metaphysics as the study of the nature of 'being'. As one might anticipate, the centre did not hold and metaphysics collapsed into a new configuration of subject matters that eventually became the modernist (see MODERNISM) disciplines that, in their different ways, have assessed that nature of human being and existence.

The Enlightenment metaphysicians proved to be somewhat quarrelsome, taking up a number of separate positions on the character and knowability of reality. In opposition to the rationalist argument that the human mind can discover truths about itself and the real world by reason alone (and that the senses are not to be trusted), other metaphysicians argued that knowledge founded on sensory input and experience was superior to that obtained from reason. These empiricists (Locke, Berkeley, Hume) did not doubt that there must be some a priori (derived by reason) truths that are knowable independent of experience, but ultimately knowledge of the metaphysical (real) world must be empiricist because all our knowledge of reality has to be reducible to experience, that is, it must be a posteriori (derived from experience). For propositions and concepts to be truthful they must, therefore, be grounded in the actual world, in other words they must be factually based.

Immanuel **Kant** offered the insight that understanding in the metaphysical world requires a connection to be made between innate rational concepts *and* sensory input (producing a compromise or new synthesis of the rationalist and empiricist positions). The raw data, he argued, is processed by our concepts to generate an object of knowledge. That object is, therefore, only accessible to us through our cognitive faculties. So, in the Kantian metaphysical word, the empirical is organised rationally. Neither can act alone to create genuine knowledge of reality. Kant's reconciliation of the rationalist and empiricist minds lay in his argument that we can know about the real world a priori, even though such knowledge of the real world can not go beyond its appearance to us. We can have such knowledge thanks to our practical distinction of **form and content**. The form of our sensory input (data, **evidence**) is knowable a priori while the content is provided a posteriori. Only with form and content together can we make a reasonable stab at knowing reality. It is by this means that our knowledge transcends the merely sensory (hence the description of Kant's metaphysics as transcendental idealism).

Metaphysicians since Kant have not agreed on the meaning of his legacy. Some argue that the structure of our thought substantially reflects the world as it is: thought is the mirror of nature. This is the opinion of those we might call metaphysical realists. Other metaphysicians emphasise Kant's argument that all we know is what our concepts represent to us (or tell us): nature is the mirror of thought – a view held by those we might call metaphysical relativists. Your position on this debate, dear reader, depends on how you answer the following question: is what I discern as an object primarily the result of how I conceptualise and represent it to myself? The extreme version of this is, of course, idealism. This holds that all I can apprehend are my concepts and representations (of an assumed real world) and how I fit them into the pictures I have of reality, or the stories about reality I tell myself. Reality is, in effect, a string of statements put into a **narrative**. Truth is measured in the plausibility of the story. Of course, the question then becomes are we creatures that tell invented stories, or are we creatures that exist in real stories? Moreover, how do we re-tell them? Is this story, for example, just my story?

There is a weaker version of the idealist variant of metaphysical relativism. One does not have to be an extreme idealist to accept that reality is only ever viewed though the grid of our concepts. Through concepts we invoke Kant's Quantity, Quality, Relation and Modality, or we may deploy others, like the four primary tropes (see TROPE/FIGURATION). According to this weaker position we are to some extent always constructing reality. Accordingly, no one can provide undisputed, genuine and unmediated knowledge of the structure or nature of reality. Although time and circumstance have eroded their initial Enlightenment conservatism (so they are more amenable to this general neo-Kantian position), the response of rationalists and intractable reconstructionist (see RECONSTRUCTIONIST HISTORY) empiricists is to point out that this metaphysical constructionist (see CONSTRUCTIONIST HISTORY) position is built on a paradox (which is far worse for idealists). If we can not know reality except through what our concepts represent to us about reality, how can we know we are constructing adequate conceptual schemes? If concepts inevitably stand between us and the full representation of a real object, why should we accept the constructionist's request that we accept their conceptual representation? This is not, of course, just the response of the sceptical empiricist or rationalist, it is also the response of the postmodern (see POSTMODERNISM) deconstructionist (see DECONSTRUCTIONIST HISTORY).

But there is a meeting of reconstructionist and constructionist minds in their ultimate agreement on the big ontological and epistemological question of the essential objective knowability of past reality. The empiricist reconstructionist historian (the archetypal metaphysical realist) argues that proper history continues to speak reasonably about the metaphysical past, its events, people, processes, more or less as they happened, rather than just as they are worked out in our concepts and/or narratives. For the metaphysical constructionist also, the past remains finally knowable in a mind, culture and language-independent way. The concepts and social theory deployed by constructionists they claim are less an obstacle to knowledge than they are actually tools for breaking out of the prison-houses of mind, culture and language. Both metaphysical realists and constructionists agree, therefore, that while it may be difficult to discover the truth of the reality out there, in their different ways it should not be impossible. Reality can be described accurately.

The metaphysical debate continued with the two post-Kantian German philosophers Georg Wilhelm Friedrich **Hegel** and Friedrich **Nietzsche**. The metaphysical question was still the same: how can we know the nature of reality when all we have are its appearances? Which concepts are most realistic? Hegel argued that our concepts can be valid for both things-in-themselves (reality) and their (its) appearance. For Hegel there exists an absolute unity of intellect and reality, and this unity that transcends subject and object means our concepts are valid not just for appearances. In Hegel's metaphysics to know the concept is to know the reality, is to know the truth, and is to be objective. History is of prime importance in Hegel's metaphysical world because of his argument that to know the world (i.e. get at truth) we must begin with the act of rational knowing – cognition – and the historian is the cognitive knowing subject *par excellence*. Moreover, the prime vehicle for this knowledge is history through its prime mechanism the dialectic (thesis, antithesis, synthesis). Contrary to this Nietzsche maintained our concepts possess no universal validity and have no symmetry with reality. Concepts are all perspectives generated by our cultural situation. No conceptual schema can offer truth, and no such schema can be objective. The mind of the knowing subject can not unify or capture the reality of the world.

It should be starting to be clear by now how this short history of metaphysics translates into something that is important to historians. Metaphysics, like history, is about the study of reality. What has emerged from this history of metaphysics is a metaphysics of history that distinguishes three main orientations: metaphysical realism, metaphysical relativism and a form of idealism I call post-empiricism. At the risk of over-simplification there is a homology here with developments in what I have called reconstructionist history, constructionist history and deconstructionist history. Each poses the metaphysical question how can we know the reality of the past?

Metaphysical realist conceptions of the world tend toward the belief that reality is rather too complex for the conceptual constructionist's best efforts (see POSITIVISM), while deconstructionists are just off-the-wall idealists who have wrapped themselves in the fashionable cloak of postmodernism. When cast in the shape of a reconstructionist historian, the metaphysical realist tends to claim that particular things located in time and space (people, events, buildings) can be understood, and the true meaning of past experience can be inferred through their general attributes, made usually in a subject–predicate sentence (see INFERENCE). Take the sentence, 'Napoleon Bonaparte was misogynous'. The truth of that description inheres, for the reconstructionist historian, in the correspondence of the sentence's linguistic structure, to the way the world was. Both subject and predicate are referenced in the real world by their respective bodies of evidence – that Napoleon Bonaparte existed, and he hated women. The realist position would also hold for the sentence, 'Napoleon Bonaparte was fearless', because fearlessness is a universal that can be attributed to that particular historical figure. There is, therefore, everything a realist could want here: attribution (predicates express universals), correspondence, referentiality (evidence supported inference), truth, factuality, historical transcendence (Bonaparte hated women then, now and always until new evidence to the contrary comes along), and adequate representation and objectivity because the description is independent of the mind of the historian and his/her social situation.

The metaphysical realism that underpins reconstructionist history thus effectively divorces ontology from epistemology, detaches subject and object, and disconnects the knower from that which is known. Such history insists that its empirical inferential methodology permits the historian (as a knowing subject, the 'self', the 'I') to dispassionately detect the truthful interpretation located in the past's documentary evidence, and then relate it appropriately in a transparent narrative. What they do is also mind-, culture- and language-independent. For the reconstructionist historian metaphysical realism translates directly into objectivity. For the neo-Kantian constructionist, however, it is always more messy than this, knowing reality is a mix of relativism and realism. The 'practical realist' appellation coined in the mid-1990s to describe the sophisticated mainstream historian of today is a useful description of this individual (Appleby *et al.* 1994). The metaphysical realist middle position is well-described as practical realism or constructionism.

The metaphysical relativism that supports constructionist history assumes that the realist can not gain truthful insights into the experience of the past without the application of the right social theory (categories of analysis). All history, constructionists claim, is ineluctably theoretical and must be presentist inasmuch as the theory is constructed and applied in the here and now. Nevertheless, constructionist history can also be truthful because it endorses the epistemological position that facts can be derived through theory by the sophisticated neo-Kantian knowing subject (a.k.a. the practical realist historian). The empirical has to be organised in some way, and when the organisation is appropriately done through our concepts then we can truthfully represent the past. For the constructionist historian history is interpretation so, by definition, it can not be reconstruction. Historical knowledge emerges relative to both theory and evidence.

As soon as this position is reached the historian is immediately shifting into what is, to be fair, at least a situation of moderate anti-realism. Constructionist historians do not doubt the real past existed, just that it doe not exist now, hence the need for theory to help recapture it. None of this, however, invalidates the truthfulness of the interpretation for constructionists, nor does it cast doubt on our powers of historical representation; indeed hypothesis-testing makes it more likely to be truthful. So the constructionist is a hypothesis-tester, empiricist, a realist (his/her interpretations are mind-, culture- and language-independent), believes in referentiality, is objectivist, and some hardened social science historians will display their tendency toward positivism, statistics and **structuralism**. The slide into relativism is not unavoidable; it can be stopped at this point. It has to be stopped!

But once we break out from a metaphysical realist position where do we draw the line if we want to find the truth? Can we, in fact, find the truth anymore? How can we stop history collapsing into full-blown relativism? And if we can not is this actually a problem? The issue seems to be that historical interpretation, once we abandon an absolutist metaphysical realist position, becomes unavoidably mind-, culture- and language-dependent. This raises doubts about all the central features of the reconstructionist and constructionist positions. Once we challenge inductive inference, the correspondence theory of truth, objective knowing and representation, what happens to history? Can we still have truthful history without these realist attributes? If we assume a particularly sceptical, idealist, postmodern or deconstructionist position about the constructed social, cultural, political, gendered, racial and ideological nature of our categories for the organisation of past experience and assume there can be no adequate representation of reality as a result, then we simply can not do reconstructionist or constructionist history. In fact we are living in a world without modernist history (see MODERNISM).

The most significant attack on the Western metaphysical tradition after Nietzsche came in the twentieth century with the advent of **continental philosophy** and particularly French philosopher Jacques **Derrida**'s assault on the metaphysical notions of the unified knowing subject, knowable reality, and the adequacy of representation. Derrida is suspicious of the idea that words are stable in their reflectivity of original meaning and when we hear or write them an imposed meaning is already present in our minds. Instead of this 'metaphysics of presence' Derrida invites us to consider the cultural intertextuality of words and concepts as well as the slippery and fictive textuality of narratives. Derrida claims Western metaphysics is based on the fundamental illusion that there is a unified knowing subject and the 'I' has full control over language and original meaning. This critique applies to adherents of both realist and relativist metaphysics because, while they may argue like squabbling siblings, both assume they can (through their own individual epistemologies and methods) reach and represent the extra-discursive (non-linguistic) exterior world of reality (see DISCOURSE).

Doubting knowable reality, because we believe the categories are inadequate to the task of representation (metaphysical presence is an illusion), does not mean we can simply replace them with others that are better, because this swings us back on the route to realism, presence and just another interpretation of past reality. If sceptics do want to practice what they preach, then they have to radically change their notion of what is history. In a postist universe there are no empirical foundations for knowing, positivism is a deficient epistemology, and we can not know anything independently of our mind, language use or culture, and so we can not know the past, and all we have is the-past-as-history. With the collapse of the knowing subject (the conflation of subject and object, and form and content) we are no longer in history but only ever live on the outer edge of a wave of time.

Losing touch with the reality of the past is a grim vision for reconstructionist and constructionist historians. But whether we endorse this post-empiricist position or not, we can not escape the fact that history (not to be confused with the past) does not exist until the historian composes it as a narrative. In the narrative the historian chooses events and places them in a preferred order so as to tell a (or, if they prefer to see it this way, the) story. Regardless of the burden of empirical referentiality, range and sophistication of the concepts employed or the hypotheses tested, historical explanation exists only in the form of a narrative. In the wake of the **linguistic turn**, therefore, the reality of the past exists only in its story. And, as no story can be fully comprehensive, as the philosopher Arthur Danto points out, we can never hope to 'know' the past in the fullness of its meaning; at best all we can have is a highly selective, poorly represented, and ideologically influenced set of beliefs about the past. And anyway, history is still going on so we can never have a final truth of any event (Danto 1985). There is much for historians to debate here. Is the past knowable as history? Is history only about language as opposed to **class**, gender or race? Is history primarily a conceptualisation process that is then represented in language? It comes down to the question of whether there is a knowable meaning to be found in the reality of the past and how we can acquire it, and if there is not, how do we invent it and for what purposes?

Further reading

Bunzl, M. (1997)
Collingwood, R.G. (1940)
Danto, A. (1985)
Derrida, J. (1978)
—— (1976)
Loux, M.J. (1998)
Putnam, H. (1987)
Roberts, D.D. (1995)
Walsh, W.H. (1966)

MODERNISM

There is no single or easy definition of modernism. Usually the term is taken to refer to the aesthetic or cultural dimension of the historical period of modernity. Modernity is, unfortunately, almost impossible to date, but may be regarded as being constituted out of a series of events around the time of the **Enlightenment** and it has been regarded as continuing up to the present. This implies it is just a period of European historical change, but this would be an inadequate definition. It may be helpful to consider modernism more broadly as a **discourse**, a highly complex yet coherent **narrative** containing assumptions about how it is possible to represent the state of nature as supported by a new realist historical consciousness of change over time (see Michel FOUCAULT). This suggests modernism is a conception of a world continuously being brought into existence through a set of beliefs, significations, cultural practices, and spoken and unspoken 'rules' that themselves became its own essence. Modernism, therefore, signifies changes to the aesthetic practices of modernity. In fact modernism overpowered ancient ways of thinking, knowing and believing in all fields of human endeavour: in technology, science, the social sciences as well as philosophy, history, literature and the visual arts.

Perhaps the central feature of this widespread reorientation of mental life from the seventeenth century is modernism's self-reflexive nature that recognises the enormous complexity and paradoxes inherent in controlling technological, industrial and urban existence. Jürgen Habermas's definition of the Enlightenment serves as a useful commentary on the broad nature of modernism when he says its primary feature is the control exercised by human beings over both objective reality as well as human nature (see EPISTEMOLOGY; ONTOLOGY). This suggests all fields of knowledge (including history) are a construction that involve the exercise of a regulatory power. Indeed, Michel Foucault argues, in his linkage of power and knowledge, that viewing modernism as a discourse is the key to understanding its identity. For Foucault knowing how a discourse works, as a cultural regime for authenticating and controlling the process of knowledge creation, is essential to an understanding of modernism (see EPISTEME). From Foucault's perspective modernism is best summarised as the Enlightenment-inspired drive to **truth** through the domestication of the world out there by the (European and male) human mind. While modernists subsequently have debated if this meant representation (form) was secondary to reality (content), for Foucault the important point is that the will to truth (the will to know) is inextricably connected with the Will to Power.

Given its Enlightenment origins modernism possesses a long list of characteristics all based on the idea that solutions are always available to the rational, technologically educated, and realist human mind. As Immanuel **Kant** had pointed out, however, giving organisation to the world does not mean it is possible to know what its content really means or how it actually comes to be what it seems. Nevertheless, the characteristic features of modernism have proceeded from the principle that there is always a way of finding out the truth. Its principles include **empiricism** with its investment in the correspondence theory of knowledge, the verification of **evidence** through comparison, and the derivation of **causation** through **inference** to the best explanation. Other key modernist principles include the belief in human **intentionality** and agency, naturalism (science will explain), scepticism (translating eventually into pragmatism), secularism, progress and newness. Modernism (as the master narrative) also gave birth to other 'big' narratives such as **historicism** and liberalism, and eventually Western imperialism, fascism, Marxism, paternalism, and the global dominance of bourgeois capitalism. All these are modernist ways to acquire power and all have claimed to tell the truth.

Modernism was thus influenced by the challenge it offered to itself. This is illustrated by the problems associated today with the term postmodern (see POSTMODERNISM), as in 'postmodern history'. The term postmodern is regularly used to denote the succession of the postmodern over the modern. In the case of postmodern history it means the appearance of a variety of properties associated with historical study that have occurred subsequently (hyphenated post-modern) but this is not so. The origins of much that is described as postmodern already existed in nineteenth-century modernism's criticism of its own founding principles. For example, there is nothing postmodern in Friedrich **Nietzsche**'s deconstruction of causality, which is that the effect is primary in the search for cause. Modernism's auto-criticism means the features we associate with postmodern history tend to derive from modernism's self-reflexivity over content, form, **objectivity**, ambiguity in knowing and being, and that language constructs rather than reflects reality.

The contribution, for example, of much twentieth-century **continental philosophy** has been built on the work of Nietzsche confronting and criticising modernism as a description of Western **metaphysics**. The critique has concluded that modernism has outlasted its intellectual utility and that greater attention should now be paid to the final collapse of objectivity and the instability of representation through language (as the only access we have to constructed reality). Modernism has existed fitfully, therefore, in the midst of its own self-determined and self-imposed dialectical (opposing) directions: reason and unreason, concealment and disclosure, freedom and terror, **liberal humanism** and anti-humanism, reality and myth, certainty and mutability, history and fiction, past and present, object and subject.

This self-reflexivity of modernism so far as the discipline of history is concerned has, therefore, produced a super-modernist (though it is more often called a postmodernist) critique. This critique has had rather more impact in mainland Europe than in the United Kingdom or the USA where Anglo-American **hermeneutics** are entrenched. Enlightenment rationality has had a chequered career in Europe in the past 200 years, being more often turned to vicious de-humanisation than in either the USA (slavery and the native American genocide notwithstanding) or the UK. This may help explain why modernism is less intellectually secure in Europe. This is evidenced in the 1990s debates on how to represent European modernist events like its alarmingly regular holocausts. Modernism has been seen by many twentieth-century European thinkers, therefore, as a failed experiment in living and thinking.

In the UK and USA modernist history remains (for the majority) the means for continued intellectual advancement and square dealing with the past. Indeed, the argument runs that by relativising history we can no longer grasp the significance and meaning of the present. This is the claim usually made by the more militant reconstructionist historians (see RECONSTRUCTIONIST HISTORY). But modernism has produced at least two other main varieties of historian, each of whom remains in dialogue with their reconstructionist colleagues as well as each other. These are the twentieth-century positivist-inspired social theory devotees of **constructionist history**, which it may be useful to think of as 'late-modernist' historians; the third type are postmodernist or deconstructionist historians (see DECONSTRUCTIONIST HISTORY). This latter group are very much the product of the present generation who have taken their cues from post-structuralism and the works of F.R. Ankersmit, Roland **Barthes**, Jacques **Derrida**, Michel Foucault and Hayden **White**.

While accepting modernism's recognition that uncertainty exists in knowledge, not all historians slavishly followed the empiricist model. In the USA the historians Carl Becker and Charles Beard in the 1930s pointed out the cultural relativism inherent in writing history, as did R.G. **Collingwood** and Benedetto **Croce** in Europe. In its more recent self-reflexive state, modernism's realist constructionist historians like Appleby, Hunt and Jacob have acknowledged that there is an unavoidable perspective in writing about the past, that the historian's social theories are always compromised by the present, that inference does have severe failings, that the telling of a myth can possess a hard reality, and that the historian is an **author** as much as a disembodied observer. But, when push comes to shove, the argument is still made that empiricism remains the best way of objectively coming to terms with the past in the present.

None of this convinces the deconstructionist post-empiricist critics of modernist and late-modernist history. They maintain that no amount of experimentation with form avoids the fact that even the most sophisticated and self-reflexive of historians still pursue the epistemological model. That is, they seek adequacy in their representation, reject the **linguistic turn** against objectivity, proclaim knowability through referentiality, deny the rupture of the signifier–signified relationship, accept the need for truthful interpretations, regard **historiography** as secondary to methodology, deny that the **emplotment** of the narrative has primacy over factualism in generating historical knowledge and, withal, remain unwilling to accept there is no mind-independent reality.

Self-critical and self-reflexive modernism, especially in the literary and artistic worlds, has long generated experiments in, and outright rejections of, modernism: impressionism, futurism, cubism, Dadaism, and surrealism in art, movements in literature from naturalism to postmodernist subjectless fiction, and the development of absurdist drama. But not in history. Dadaist, pastiche, montage or absurdist history has yet to arrive even from the word-processors of the deconstructionists. While for the majority of historians history is still in the age of 'pointing' (a term I have borrowed from sculpture used to describe the long established method for mechanically transferring as exactly as possible the proportions of a three-dimensional model to another model), the experiments of the deconstructionists do not fully exemplify the anti-modernism that is the signature of a radically different approach to the past. No historian has yet produced an overtly anti-modernist work of history the equivalent of Marcel Duchamp's scandalously successful 1913 painting, *Nude Descending a Staircase*, nor Antonin Artaud's work in the theatre, nor the writer Alain Robbe-Grillet's highly self-conscious text, *In the Labyrinth*.

It seems unlikely there will be such an equivalent in history until historians embrace the idea that history can be freed from the restraints of maintaining the epistemological and ontological gap between process (form) and its product (content). Only once history's invention and theatricality is accepted and exploited, can history as process take over from history as product, and the anti-modernist historian will finally have the chance to reflect upon the infinite regress of meaning and the nature of history's existence. Anti-modernist experiments in historical process will, I suspect, only be prompted by the disquiet of historians about what can genuinely be known in a representational literary form. The ontological character of future anti-modernist history will be revealed not in asking how can we know about the past but, perhaps, how can we live without a modernist historical consciousness at all?

Postmodern history, so-called, often fails to deliver. Why? It seems to be because of the nature of the experiments with form that retain a referentialist connection. Experiments in postmodern history do, of course, acknowledge the aesthetic nature of historical writing in which the form of the statement is one of the prerequisites for the truth of the statement (Ankersmit 1994: 170–2). In postmodern historical writing form is increasingly recognised as just as important as content. It follows that postmodern historians often claim to be no longer primarily interested in the real story hidden in or between the lines of the evidence, but work instead on the principle that evidence signposts not the past, but other interpretations of the past. In pursuit of this claim the act of postmodern history sometimes begins with the historian's present construction of the evidence. He/she looks for its gaps and silences and injects his/her own needs as well as those of his/her present cultural, epistemic and teleological context. Such historians do not fill the gaps and silences exclusively with inference to the best explanation founded on an assumed knowable reality. Such history tends to be both historiographic and psychoanalytic and is far more complex than empiricism conceives it.

The ultimate denial of modernism may well be to move beyond the incipient deconstructionism of historians like Hans Ulrich Gumbrecht, Simon Schama, Natalie Zemon Davis, Mary Poovey, George Duby and Carlo Ginzburg, to take up a thorough anti-modernist stance that demands not only the disavowal of experiments with form, but also the denial of a history defined in any way as a referential text in favour of studying the absurd nature of the metaphorical relationship of the present to the past. Indeed, future history may require a wholly new non-written form and a content that is allusive and metaphorical, and which will expand our capacity to grasp meaning as well as make ethical decisions in the present.

This may be too heady a brew for some (or, depending on their opinion, just a pointless waste of time). Alternatively, and somewhat less radically, it might be that so-called postmodernist history, as a kind of metafictional historiography, will prevail. In this 'history' historians will reflect upon their own status as historians and authors, and they may choose to disrupt the flow of narrative in order to confront the constructed nature of what they write, yet all the while they still reference a generally recognisable and knowable real past. Disruption of form is not, of course, a disruption of the modernist historical consciousness; more often than not it merely illustrates its self-reflexivity. By exposing the fictive nature of history by closing the ontological and epistemological gap between process and product, deconstructive historians may more effectively dispute the sustainability of the modernist distinction between history and fiction, but in so doing they are not necessarily denying the historical consciousness that is the discourse of modernism's greatest legacy.

Further reading

Ankersmit, F.R. (1994)
Appleby, J. *et al.* (1994)
Danto, A. (1998)
—— (1997)
—— (1985)
Davis, N.Z. (1987)
Duby, G. (1993)
Ermarth, E.D. (1992)
Ginzburg, C. (1982)
Gumbrecht, H.U. (1997)
Habermas, J. (1987)
Jenkins, K. (1999)
Poovey, M. (1988)
Rosenstone, R.A. (1995)
Schama, S. (1991)

N

NARRATIVE

Narrative is central to **historical explanation** as the vehicle for the creation and representation of historical knowledge and historical explanation. What is narrative? For the historian it is the telling of an event or connected flow of events, by a narrator (the writer/historian) to a narratee (the actual/imagined reader) and rarely is it so abstruse (akin to a scientific narrative) that it is cast in other than a relatively jargon-free language (see EVENT). The historical narrative, because it is composed within the realist mode, is normally invested with a naturalism concerning **truth** that more obviously fictional narratives do not claim. Prior to the act of narration the given events and **facts** are arranged as an **emplotment** according to the understanding of their causal connections as held by the narrator (see CAUSATION; COLLIGATION). In the case of realist-inspired narratives like history it is assumed the causal connections parallel the actuality of the events and facts described, hence narrative usually takes the shape of 'this happened, then that, because ... '. Normally the narrator of historical narratives (the historian) is a voice cast in the third person. This is a conscious act intended to reference the **objectivity** of the undertaking, by confirming that the required distance exists between historian, real event and accurate description. So far as the historical narrative is concerned, the historian traditionally has only one position – that of the dispassionate observer and it is this position that ensures the truthfulness of that which is recounted/interpreted. In summary, the historian's narrative is the vehicle for plainly stated historical facts, and while the facts are arranged by the historian, the arrangement will, if done properly, uncover *the* real story (*the* real narrative) in, and according to, the **evidence**. This is the commonly accepted understanding of the nature of the historical narrative, one that is founded on a particular epistemological position, namely that **empiricism** has the power to reveal the past as it actually happened by getting the story straight (see EPISTEMOLOGY). This, indeed, is the cognitive or knowledge-making function of narrative. Narrative (form) effectively references and relates the past (content) as history (see FORM AND CONTENT). Narrative thereby provides the dedicated means for articulating the given nature of the past.

Why is narrative important to historians? The answer ought to be clear by now. It is accepted by most historians that narrative is important because it is through it that we establish the cognitive link between form and content, the word and the world. Narrative acts as the (aesthetic) expression of (in the case of history) an evidenced and, therefore, knowable past material reality. Through it we accurately interpret and relate the discoveries we have made in the archive. From this perspective the term 'narrative historian' really has no meaning because all historians tell stories about people in the past who themselves 'naturally' led narrativised lives. Adding the term narrative to historian is simply redundant. Life is narrative-shaped and so it can best be understood (and analysed) as a narrative.

Working within this logic, form must follow the historian's avowed function, which is to truthfully explain the content of the past. It follows that because life is narrativised narrative possesses the power to disclose *the* story of the past as history – always presupposing the proper methodological rules have been followed at the research and archival stage. Thus narrative does not present an obstacle, in the words of Peter Gay, to Ranke's 'celebrated wish to relate the past as it actually happened', neither will it permit Ranke's history to be 'a fantasy nor a concealed ideology' (Gay 1988 [1974]: 199). As Gay describes it in evidencing the case of Gibbon, his 'ironic vision equipped him to penetrate the fraudulent machinations of Roman politicians, and the all-too-human pettiness of the Church Fathers' (Gay 1988 [1974]: 199–200). If the intention of the historian is to get the story straight (as Ranke and Gibbon are presumed to have so wished), then narrative construction will not get in the way of accessing the truth of the past. Indeed, for Gay, what makes the task of the historian special is the precise fact that his/her science is, and can only be transcripted as, a narrative couched in an appropriate style of rhetoric. Style and truth are compatible because, as Gay concludes 'Style is the art of the historian's science' (Gay 1988 [1974]: 217). For Gay form does indeed follow function – getting at *the* story and getting it straight.

This is a position famously established by William B. Gallie, that historical narratives may be judged correct inasmuch as we believe them to be 'supported on every main point by evidence of some kind' (Gallie 1964: 21). Gallie insists there is only *one* true story to be discovered. By **inference** to the best explanation according to the evidence the historian can (if he/she does the job properly) reasonably expect to discover *the* particular story-shape pre-existing in the past: the one and true emplotment. For Gallie historical understanding rests on the reader being able to follow *the* story so carefully reconstructed through the hard work of the historian actively seeking the truth as he/she arranges the facts according to the available evidence (Gallie 1964: 105, 108) (see RECONSTRUCTIONIST HISTORY). The role of the historian as interpreter is, therefore, like that of the foreign-language translator (the past is a foreign language!), who renders the text as accurately as possible so its true meaning will emerge. All this adds up to the fact that the historian's narrative conveys knowledge – it does not constitute it.

What then is narrative's relationship to the **discourse** of the historian? From what I have said so far it would seem unproblematic. Put another way, we ought to know where exactly is the line between the discovery and constitution of knowledge in the historical narrative. Most historians, in accepting that history and narrative have much in common for the reason just noted, would also accept that because evidence is not a collection of building blocks past reality can not be reconstructed unproblematically. But they would not endorse the claim of American philosopher of history Hayden **White** that attention to the way in which a historical narrative is constructed may tell us rather more about the historian's emplotment choices than about the past. Because of this, much mainstream **constructionist history** is built on the argument that it is better to relate the past in a non-narrative form. This has led many such historians to write the past in ways they believe breaks with the above description of narrative, that is, by means of thematic or concept-led approaches (see CONCEPTS IN HISTORY).

Needless to say the truth-claims that 'non-narrative historians' make for their written history also remain intact. Indeed, some constructionist historians find it tempting to suggest an even higher level of truthfulness for their non-narrative historical analyses. Marxists, for example, tend to hold that the complexities of the model(s) they construct out of the evidence allow for a complex structural and functional cross-hatched historical explanation that is particularly faithful to the past as it actually happened. Marxist history, like virtually all other kinds of constructionist history, is thematic, topic and/or concept-based, and often non-chronological. Even in such histories, however, I would suggest there is an irreducible narrative dimension (see Roland BARTHES; EPISTEME; Michel FOUCAULT; TROPE/FIGURATION).

Like most aspects of what historians do, the role and functioning of narrative has been much discussed of late, especially Gay's insistence that style is not necessarily incompatible with *the* truth, as well as Gallie's notion that the historian's narrative is capable of rendering *the* true story. Leaving aside the general and detailed criticisms of the representational and referential character of language that have surfaced as part of postmodern (see POSTMODERNISM) developments, and that highlight, among many other things, the **reality/realistic effect** of history writing and the possible incommensurability of style and truth, the major concerns about narrative have centred on its supposed inherent capacity for objectivity and truthful interpretation. This focuses on the parallel that can be reasonably assumed to exist between lived experience and its accurate representation. The greater the parallel the more truthful the historical knowledge. So just how adequate is the historical narrative as a form of explanation? To what extent can the narrative itself determine its content? To what degree does the historian impose a narrative on the past through the process of his/her emplotment?

We already have Gallie's answer to the question of the adequacy of narrative as historical explanation – generally it is adequate because the narrative and what actually happened share the same story-shape. This assumes narrated conceptions of **intentionality** and **causation** operate in an isomorphic relationship (one-to-one correspondence of shape and structure) to their real counterparts. As already noted, it is a precondition of this view of historical narrative that the historian be omitted from the process except to acknowledge that it is he/she who is midwife to that culturally neutral isomorphic product called history. The fact that this is a rather difficult position to sustain has not deterred historians and philosophers of history from defending it. The question, of if viewing the historian as midwife undersells the extent of his/her interventionism in researching and then configuring the past, has engaged a good number of commentators ranging from those such as William B. Gallie, David Carr, Arthur Danto, William H. Dray, Andrew P. Norman, John E. Toews, Geoffrey Roberts, C. Behan McCullagh, M.C. Lemon, Dorothy Ross and Peter Munz who all, in varying ways, accept that history is story-shaped and is recoverable through narrative pretty much as it actually happened, to others less convinced like Paul Veyne, Hayden White, Keith Jenkins, Louis Mink, Paul Ricoeur, Frank Ankersmit and Hans Kellner, Michel Foucault and Jacques **Derrida**.

The two at the extreme in this debate are David Carr and Hayden White. Both, as narrativists, insist that narrative and explanation are coincident. For Carr it is because narrative and real life are co-terminous. For White this is because it is the preference of the historian to view them as such. Both agree with Peter Munz's position that the past was once real, but that the stories historians tell about it are constructions (Munz 1997: 851–72). Where they differ is over the truthfulness of those constructions. In Carr's words does the structure of narrative inhere 'in the events themselves' and far from being any kind of distortion a narrative account 'is an extension of one of their primary features' (D. Carr 1986a: 117). This is the isomorphic relationship – a community of form as Carr has it between action, event and the narrative constructed to explain them (D. Carr 1986a: 117).

In opposition to this view Hayden White maintains that the past does not *necessarily* conform to a given, and therefore, discoverable true kind of narrative. He claims we do not live stories, at best we give meaning to our lives by (retrospectively) casting them in the form of stories. It comes down to whether you believe the emplotment is discovered or imposed (or invented as White says) by the historian. In both cases the assumption is that the essence of the historical narrative is the historian's emplotment. Because the past for White is not shaped according to a given narrative that is discoverable through the evidence, then it is the historian who must provide it with the emplotment. Indeed, for White, the historian is more like an **author** and their emplotted historical narrative is, as a result, also an instrument of ideological construction. History is not only an emplotted narrative but, because it is the-past-as-history, it is also always a political text of dissent or affirmation even though its author may proclaim to be in pursuit of the truth. Historical narrative as it exists today is the result primarily of the bourgeois **Enlightenment** and its Marxist critique. White views both as efforts to control and domesticate the past either through the correspondence theory of knowledge (rather than aestheticism), or constructionism (rather than as an acknowledgement of the sublime and ineffable) (White 1987: 67–8). Neither view of history takes the cognitive nature of narrative adequately into their accounts.

Further reading

Ankersmit, F.R. (1994)
—— (1983)
Ankersmit, F.R. and Kellner, H. (1995)
Callinicos, A. (1995)
Canary, R. and Kozicki, H. (1978)
Carr, D. (1986a)
—— (1986b)
Curthoys, A. and Docker, J. (1997)
—— (1996)
Danto, A. (1985)
Derrida, J. (1979)
Dray, W.H. (1970)
Foucault, M. (1977)
Friedlander, S. (1992)
Gallie, W.B. (1964)
Gay, P. (1988 [1974])
Heise, U.K. (1997)
Jenkins, K. (1995)
Kellner, H. (1989)
Klein, K. (1995)
Lemon, M.C. (1995)
Lipton, P. (1993)
McCullagh, C.B. (1998)
—— (1984)
Maza, S. (1996)
Mink, L. (1978)
—— (1970)
Munslow, A. (1997a)
—— (1992)
Munz, P. (1997)
Norman, A.P. (1991)
Ricoeur, P. (1984, 1985)
Roberts, G. (1996)
Ross, D. (1995)
Stone, L. (1979)
Toews, J.E. (1987)
Veyne, P. (1984)
White, H. (1998)
—— (1987)
—— (1984)

— (1978)
— (1973b)
Zagorin, P. (1999)

NIETZSCHE, FRIEDRICH (1844–1900)

Some of the ideas of the German philosopher Friedrich Nietzsche (1844–1900) have been particularly important to historians in the late twentieth century. His interpretation of Immanuel **Kant** to argue in favour of perspectivism (*not* to be confused with **relativism**) is especially significant for a re-casting of the nature of history and what it is that historians do. Essentially Nietzsche suggests that our categories or forms of knowing have no transcendent or universal validity, and **concepts in history** are interpretations largely determined by our cultural situatedness, perspective, and/or bias. Nietzsche concluded there are no absolutes, no origins, no **facts**, no answers, no given meaning, all is fiction, all is false, and all attempts to organise and systematise knowledge are merely expressions of a will to control (which he described as the Will to Power). His famous claim that God is dead in *The Gay Science* (1882) refers to this belief that there is no longer any absolute authority for **truth** (faith in God equals truth). This constitutes a wholesale rejection of **modernism** and the **Enlightenment** project.

Nietzsche's approach to philosophy, history and life was one of irony and scepticism. In *On the Genealogy of Morality: A Polemic* (1887) he claims scepticism sprang up in his life 'so early, so unbidden, so unstoppably, and which was in such conflict with my surroundings, age, precedents and lineage that I would be almost be justified in calling it my "a priori" ' (Ansell-Pearson 1994a: 4–5) (see A PRIORI/A POSTERIORI). Such a comment served clear notice of his opinion of Kant, modernism and rationality. There is also a strong tongue-in-cheek sense, as the American philosopher of history Hayden **White** argues, of Nietzsche's self-awareness of the fictive nature of his ironic perceptions (White 1973b: 69), and how this translates into his belief in the fictive nature of the historical enterprise. In his second text *Unfashionable Observation* (1874), for example, Nietzsche questioned whether or not historical knowledge is in and of itself useful. He concluded it was, but only when it was pursued, not for its own sake, but as an art form that can allow us to forget! Such a position is profoundly antagonistic to the modernist conception of history as the way to the truth. Although Nietzsche continued to believe research in the archive could lead to the de-bunking of myths (i.e. religion) the general tenor of his unfashionable observations sets the stage for his career attitude toward history and historians.

Interestingly, given the emphasis Nietzsche always placed on language as an obstacle to knowledge, his written style is difficult (see LINGUISTIC TURN). His aphoristic style emerged first in *Human, All Too Human* (1878/79), which he later acknowledged ironically by claiming one needed 'to be a cow' rather than a 'modern man' to read him, by which he meant we have to acquire the power of 'rumination' (Ansell-Pearson 1994a: 10). Though difficult and idiosyncratic, his narrative style is the perfect vehicle for his philosophy of history. As he breaks the literary philosophical conventions Nietzsche's contribution to the study of history is revealed to be important because his written form reinforces notions that are a direct challenge to the very concepts and language in which Enlightenment or modernist (especially Kantian) philosophy poses its problems. Put straightforwardly, Nietzsche maintained that the rational analysis of the world – such as that claimed by Kant – can not resolve all problems of knowledge; indeed rationality and language soon reveal their severe limitations.

Most significantly for historians, Nietzsche argues that which we take as fact is actually nothing more than a layered earlier interpretation that has somehow managed to throw off its referent, be it empirical or interpretative. He was, of course, particularly scathing about the Christian religion in this respect, maintaining that Christian moral precepts were merely conveniences to make life more tolerable for the mass of people (which he metamorphosed as the herd, and for whose moral behaviour he coined the term the 'herd instinct'), or to constrain those who would otherwise rightly reject organised religion's proclaimed moral Christian universalism (the *Übermensch*).

So, the universal or transcendental categories that Kant proposed (like space, time, perception and causality), because they are valid for all rational people (subjects), are consequently objective, are rejected or literally deconstructed by Nietzsche. He claims that Kant's a priori categories have no foundation except in other than cultural convention. This means they are ultimately arbitrary. They are interpretations or value positions dependent upon personal perspective, psychological need, ideological orientation, desire for power, and/or cultural situation. What often confuses is the fact that, in addition, certain positions/interpretations become fixed over time. Particularly where certain key cultural texts are concerned they can become concretised as 'facts'. As already noted, they lose their interpretative anchorage. Nietzsche uses what he calls his genealogical method to demonstrate this process of how 'facts' are really unavowed interpretations (see Michel FOUCAULT). *The* facts can not exist, and no single interpretation can be definitive; hence there is no such thing as *the* text. For Nietzsche both **form and content** and, therefore, all meaning are aesthetic attempts to impose an order on our experience. In respect of history, Nietzsche was determined to view it as an act of tragic aestheticism, as in 'Use and abuse of history' (1874). Why? Because he conceived the **emplotment** of Tragedy as the best means available to demolish the idea of an objective stance from which historians can access truth.

We should be aware, therefore, that any methodology or **epistemology** is in practice *free to claim access* to the real world if it so wishes, and we should be wary of all that do, because there are no universally valid perspectives. We can not peer round our forms to see what is actually happening. We must, of need, treat all claims to *the* truth with scepticism. This means there are no disinterested historians, no historical concepts that can lay a claim to reconstructing the past as it actually was, and no historical method (construed literally as a metahistorical method) that can overcome this perspectival condition of knowledge (see CONSTRUCTIONIST HISTORY; DECONSTRUCTIONIST HISTORY; RECONSTRUCTIONIST HISTORY). The apparent success of **empiricism** (with its disinterested historians on a voyage of discovery in the archive) resides not in its access to *the* truth, but because it has successfully supported the modernist bourgeois power superstructure that has grown up in Western society. Indeed, it is because of empiricism's referential claims to a knowable independent reality and the common-sense correspondence of the word and the world that it has ensured the survival of that culture. This is why it remains so central to it. But, for proper historians, because Nietzsche casts his dismissal within his own peculiar history of morality (in *The Genealogy of Morals* (1887), in which he argued against a foundationalist goodness in humanity), his view of historical knowing seems to sanction (under the appeal to truth) any old nonsense cast as morality and history. Ironically, of course, this is probably the point Nietzsche is making.

The further response of proper historians is that even if we grant that truth (truthful historical interpretation) is indeed influenced by a Will to Power or by personal or ideological preference, this does not *necessarily* mean the correspondence theory is wrong. The existence of a particular **teleology** (history written with an end product in mind) does not mean we can not hold up a mirror to nature. Another flaw in Nietzsche's position is also fairly obvious. Every time we point out that there is no absolute truth because everything is perspectival, surely we have to do so from our own particular point of origin – the self-conscious, rational, knowing subject? So, as we claim there is no truth, we are making a claim that we believe to be truthful! In postmodern (see POSTMODERNISM) terms, of course, the decentred subject does not, *in fact*, exist. For Nietzsche the truthfulness of this resounds in the Will to Power, by which I think he means that no interpretation can be an impartial reflector of the facts – especially given they do not exist anyway. We get out of the text what we put into it. What we get out of the past is the history we put into it.

Nevertheless, Nietzsche's view that truth is perspectival resounds in a profoundly imaginative and interpretational discipline like history (see HISTORICAL IMAGINATION). In his rejection of the *error* of the 'old conceptual fairy-tale' (Ansell-Pearson 1994a: 92) of the rational knowing subject of knowledge in favour of the realm where reason is firmly excluded, it may become more difficult to sustain the idea of history as being merely the accurate and literal translation of the archive. For Nietzsche (as later for Jacques **Derrida**) the pursuit of knowledge is forever clouded by its embedded linguistic and specifically metaphoric structure. What we take to be our knowledge of the world (and the past), derived from the correlation of empiricism and conceptualisation, is merely the collected tropic conventions of representation (see TROPE/FIGURATION). To grasp what is the past, we have first to understand that history is merely an invented match between facsimile and concept. There is no extra-linguistic platform upon which we can stand in order to exert leverage on reality.

Nietzsche's attitude to language was that it seduced humanity into a dream-like state with which we cloak the horrors of everyday existence. We have art so as not to die of the truth, that is, knowing there is no truth. All forms of knowing are ultimately metaphoric, and phenomena simply exist as images possessing no referentiality beyond themselves. Debating the epistemological bases of history, as Nietzsche does, eventually means addressing – as many have done – the narrative form of historical writing and the **metanarrative** form of historical study. Practical realists accept the reconstructionist position of knowing the past as it actually was is not tenable. They tend to do so, however, on grounds that explicitly reject Nietzsche's sceptical arguments. Certainty, it is accepted, is not possible in history because it is always a second-hand and interpretative experience, and the historical narrative is never a perfectly reflective mirror. But **objectivity** is possible because of rational Kantian categories of knowing, which are themselves reflective of the reality out there. There is, consequently, a high correlation between form and content. While there may be something of a fissure between the word and the world, this does not mean, as Nietzsche seems to be saying, there must be ontological uncertainty (about our state of being) (see ONTOLOGY).

Apart from the rump of hard-hat reconstructionists, most historians accept that the notion of truthful interpretation reads somewhat more awkwardly these days than previously, when history was unembarrassingly in the grip of unreflective empiricism, covering laws, the social sciences, and cliometrics (see POSITIVISM). The Nietzschean world-view has had its impact – one where it is agreed that objective truth is impossible because no system or historical methodology can guarantee truth. While we may not exist in a constant flux of being, it follows that while historians generally still prefer to imagine history as rooted in the evidence of a knowable external reality, the line between fact and interpretation is often too fine to draw with certainty.

The point at issue is not just that everything is interpretation. It is that some interpretations and meanings, under the hand of historians and because of the way we use language (subject–predicate, correspondence of sign and signifier), take on the appearance of facts. Interpretations like the cold war, the Industrial Revolution and the Monroe Doctrine – but much worse, interpretative concepts like **class**, **intentionality** and **evidence** – have become facts. The **discourse** of constructionist history in particular is prone to confusing facts with concepts. The metaphoric nature of language means reality and, therefore, truth is not directly or objectively accessible. As Nietzsche claims, truth is a 'mobile marching army of metaphors, metonymies and anthropomorphisms' (Norris 1982: 58). Because of this the story offered about the past by the historian is imposed by the historian as he/she looks at his/her own life, and the ideology he/he serves. **Historiography** becomes history. History, as the ultimate form of knowing and sense of what we want from the future, is thus imposed on an unknowable past. The irony is that because the past becomes the subject of history, so it can be emplotted however the historian chooses, with whatever ending he/she has in mind (see EMPLOTMENT).

Further reading

Ansell-Pearson, K. (1994a)
—— (1994b)
Danto, A. (1965)
Derrida, J. (1979)
Magnus, B. (1993)
Magnus, B. and Higgins, K.M. (1996)
Megill, A. (1985)
Nehamas, A. (1985)
Norris, C. (1982)
Rabinow, P. (1999)
White, H. (1973b)

O

OBJECTIVITY

In 1972 the Belgian literary critic and philosopher Paul de Man argued that the bases for historical knowledge are not **facts** but written texts, even if they masquerade as wars or revolutions (de Man 1972). Within a year of that bald deconstructionist (see DECONSTRUCTIONIST HISTORY) pronouncement Hayden **White**'s book, *Metahistory*, appeared with its now famous message that writing history is about configuring stories as we order the events (see EVENT) of the past, not about objectively discovering *the* given **truth** that is presumed to exist in the past (White 1973b). This judgement is central to deconstructionist history and the **linguistic turn**, being not just another theory or conceptualisation about how we do history but is commentary on the present conditions in which we generate historical knowledge.

White's argument would not persuade all historians, largely because the concept of objectivity is not regarded as a disputable concept in history (see CONCEPTS IN HISTORY). However, I would suggest it has several different meanings. At the naïve extreme of **reconstructionist history** it means the pursuit of genuine knowledge of the past thing-in-itself, and the translation of this knowledge (of the past as it actually happened) into an accurate and unbiased historical **narrative** based on the sources (see EMPIRICISM). At this extreme, objectivity and historical truth are synonymous. This is revealed in the effacement of the historian from the written text. Objectivity is thereby regarded as a function of proper historical thinking. The realist philosopher of history C. Behan McCullagh offers us a clear summary of how to achieve a state of reconstructionist history objectivity when he says 'Most historians see themselves as trying to discover what actually happened in the past' and why historians 'pay such attention to the accuracy of their observations of evidence and to the adequacy of their inferences from it, and why they refuse to put forward any descriptions of the past for which there is not good evidence' (McCullagh 1984: 2) (see INFERENCE).

Most constructionist historians (see CONSTRUCTIONIST HISTORY) (those within the practical realist mainstream) view objectivity as somewhat less cut and dried than McCullagh seems to think it is, but still have an investment in conceiving objectivity as the opposite of **relativism**, which is viewed as an attack on truthful knowing. This is the vision of E.H. **Carr** and the American social and cultural historians Joyce Appleby, Lynn Hunt and Margaret Jacob (Appleby *et al.* 1994: 241–70). Appleby, Hunt and Jacob elect to defend what they maintain is the sensible constructionist middle-ground, warning against the 'fluid scepticism' that now appears to cover 'the intellectual landscape' (Appleby *et al.* 1994: 243) and that denies the goals of truth-seeking and objectivity. The roots of this are supposed to be those disillusioned social and historical constructionists and deconstructionists who recklessly doubt that a knowable reality exists, and/or that the world can indeed be mind-independent. While acknowledging the subjectivity of much historical interpretation Appleby *et al.* maintain a core belief in the referentiality of the historical narrative (the accuracy and completeness of the observations rather than the perspective of the historian) that ultimately guarantees its veracity, accuracy and objectivity. While a gap undoubtedly exists between the record and the interpretation, this does not cast us into a state of ontological relativism with an inability to judge reality from fiction, or mean no knowable referential correspondence exists between the word and the world (see ONTOLOGY).

Upon what basis do naïve and/or practical realists still claim genuine historical knowledge (see EPISTEMOLOGY)? There are three epistemological principles of standard history: namely, the belief that the past once really existed; that which constitutes historical truth is found in the correspondence of the historians' facts to that reality through the empirical reconstruction of agent **intentionality**; and the facts precede interpretation confirming the process of inference as central to historical interpretation (except when social theory constructionists argue inductive and deductive reasoning can not operate independently). The four corollaries to these three principles are that there is a clear division between fact and value; that history and fiction are not the same; that there is a clear separation between the knower and the known; and truth is not perspectival. The adherence to these principles with their corollaries determines the understanding of objectivity in historical practice, and together are taken to constitute the objectivisation of the-past-as-history.

Having said that, the post-empiricist challenge's success is evidenced by the fact that very few historians today accept these principles and corollaries at face value. To do so would be to endorse a naïve, if not a brutalist, realism that ill fits the sophisticated levels of analysis to which most historians aspire. The majority of historians are empiricist (rather than epistemological) sceptics. As the philosopher of history Mark Bevir has suggested, historians know they make observations under the influence of their current opinions, and that the facts of history are ultimately squeezed out through the mental filter of categories of analysis and a priori (see A PRIORI/A POSTERIORI) theories (Bevir 1994). The realist-inspired philosopher David Cockburn endorses this view, arguing in favour of a qualified realism, promoting a historian's emotional sensitivity that does not preclude a rendering of the past faithfully (Cockburn 1997). Cockburn's position is that of most constructionist historians. It is predicated on a perception of **evidence** not as statements of reality, but as collectivities of sources from which we can infer their true meaning by verification and comparison within a known context and through the use of appropriate social theory. Our knowledge may not be direct, but it can be truthful (Cockburn 1997: 247–8).

Historians may, therefore, distinguish factual from normative (assumptive) statements in their work, that is, recognise the two planes of the historical enterprise: research and the narrative explanation of what it means. However, as we know, facts alone can not determine historical understanding. As a hermeneutic process (an act of textual interpretation) history is subject to the ontological beliefs held about society by historians, and to the ideologies to which they subscribe, and what they anticipate their audience will wish to hear and/or read (see HERMENEUTICS). These expectations usually translate into beliefs about the nature of **causation** and of the character of temporal change. It is at this second level of interpretative statement that the conflict of objectivism couched as realism and relativism arise.

It seems clear that, while historical understanding is viewed not as a brutalist empirical enterprise, most historians still follow E.H. Carr and Appleby, Hunt and Jacob in drawing back from the logic of their thinking. As practical realists most historians argue the reality of the past is prefigured by reference to the evidence and not by the fictive narrative inventions of historians as Hayden White would have us believe. History is generated by *the* narratives inherent in the evidence of the past, what the American historian Sarah Maza has called 'stories in history' (Maza 1996: 1493). The historian-observer relates *the* story he/she has sensitively witnessed in the evidence rather than authored and on which he/she has placed no prior value (see AUTHOR). This echoes British historian Geoffrey Roberts's argument that there are 'real stories in the past to which historical narratives can correspond, and the narrative structures . . . of historians . . . mimic or resemble the action/story/narrative of past happenings' (G. Roberts 1997: 257).

Ultimately then, the purpose remains the same even if the standard model has been modified. History remains about discovering, as the philosopher William Gallie insists, *the* real story that is then re-told *accurately* (Gallie 1964: 105; Mink 1978: 129–49; Carr 1986a: 117–31). The narrative is discovered by the historian in the events themselves and is objective and realistic because, as realist philosopher of history George Iggers confirms, it possesses referentiality (Iggers 1997: 12). The American philosopher of history David Carr summarises this view with his conviction that there is a correspondence between history as it is lived (*the* past) and history as it is written (*the* narrative). Narrative and history are homologous.

But as the philosopher Martin Bunzl asks, can we leave 'the status of facts undisturbed' when we turn to the consideration of writing history (Bunzl 1997: 27)? How reasonable is it to expect that narrative historical interpretations are likely to be correct, not because we have generated factual accuracy, but because our lives are narrativised and the past itself conforms to the discoverable structure of narrative? Are past lives story-shaped? It is an important question if you choose to believe that historians impose stories rather than 'discover' stories that have hitherto lain hidden from history, but which nevertheless pre-exist as cultural narratives, either as Maza's stories in history, or White's figuratively determined emplotted historian's narratives (see EMPLOTMENT; TROPE/FIGURATION).

White reverses the Maza position, arguing *the* narrative does not pre-exist but *a* narrative is invented and provided by the historian. Of course the situation is complicated by the fact that the historian's narrative may itself be culturally provided because it presently exists intertextually as a cultural **discourse** (see EPISTEME; Michel FOUCAULT). Consequently, for White, there are many different yet equally legitimate stories to be told about the same facts, the same events, the same past. While still constrained by what actually happened, as the French historian Paul Veyne suggests, the meaning of history as a story comes from *a* plot, which is imposed, or as Hayden White insists invented, as much as found by the historian (Veyne 1984; White 1978: 82).

Hayden White's point, which he made almost thirty years ago, has now become a commonplace assumption for many historians, that when we attempt to explain the facts of the French Revolution or decline of the Roman Empire: 'What is at issue ... is not What are the facts? but rather, How are the facts to be described in order to sanction one mode of explaining them rather than another?' (White 1978: 134). White is suggesting here that facts are far more complex than McCullagh, for example, imagines. In the view of White historical facts are always constituted a second time in the form of a rhetorical or narrative structure that is invariably written for a particular purpose – hence his well-known emphasis on the content of the form (see FORM AND CONTENT).

Such a prefigured emplotment may well be the wish to 'discover' the 'real' cultural narratives that existed in the past. Arguably this has been the agenda of cultural historians like Judith Walkowitz with her narratives of sexual danger (Walkowitz 1992), Elizabeth Deeds Ermarth and her disquisitions on time (Ermarth 1992), Natalie Zemon Davis's pardon tales from sixteenth-century France (Davis 1987), or Mary Poovey's deconstructive feminism (Poovey 1988), while even more open to the sublime and self-reflexive nature of the historical enterprise is Robert Rosenstone's multi-voiced study of cultural engagement between the United States and Meiji Japan (Rosenstone 1988).

If it is as much at the level of writing as well as research that understanding and meaning are created, a **reality/realistic effect** may thus be generated as we emplot the past (see Roland BARTHES). No matter how well done is our technical recovery/discovery of the past in the verification and authentication of sources, in the contextualising process, or in the accurate rendition of the meaning of individual texts or, for that matter, the recovery of author intentionality and/or agent action in our creation of historical facts, it may be that unless we accept that the realist narrative conception – that *the* story pre-exists in *the* action – *a* meaning is always going to be imposed by an ideologically aligned and rhetorically and/or socially theoreticised constructionist historian.

Where then is the objectivity and guarantee of truth in this? I submit that any truth we can find is at best an epistemological truth. Any corroborated evidence-based historical narrative on the political career of 1930s and 1940s would-be US president, Thomas E. Dewey, has referentiality and is cognitively authentificatory – in one sense objectively true. But it is only an epistemic truth. If we pose questions of meaning – what is the meaning of Dewey's career? – then such a question still has referentiality but can not be answered cognitively. When we put real events into an interpretative narrative we shift on to another plane of knowledge creation because we are creating meaning within a larger cultural and intellectual discourse.

If we reject the correspondence theory with its assumption that our forensic scrutiny of the evidence somehow ensures our descriptions refer accurately to their presumed inherent narrative shape, then our image of the historian as the impartial observer ultimately unmoved by his/her situatedness and who simply relates the facts, requires me to ask how many of us do believe we are writing *the* story, whether it be national? feminist? gay? subaltern? class?, rather than *a* story?

The debate on objectivity and the written historical narrative resolves no questions. It does not invalidate the pursuit of objectivity, truth and the self-effacement of the historian – if that is what you want. It merely exposes the limits of these aims. Whether an event was real or not is no longer relevant when it is placed in a narrative, unless one believes the past possesses, or is shaped according to, one particular story. All historical narratives in that sense are fictional artifice, quite unverifiable at the ontological level for their objectivity or their truthfulness. From this perspective, I submit, the principles and corollaries of standard history start to look even more precarious than before.

Further reading

Ankersmit, F.R. (1994)
Bevir, M. (1994)
Bunzl, M. (1997)
Burke, P. (1997)
Callinicos, A. (1995)
Carr, D. (1986a)
Cockburn, D. (1997)
Davis, N.Z. (1987)
de Man, P. (1972)

Ermarth, E.D. (1992)
Evans, R.J. (1997a)
Forum (1991)
Gallie, W.B. (1964)
Iggers, G. (1997)
Lorenz, C. (1994)
McCullagh, C.B. (1991)
—— (1984)
Maza, S. (1996)
Mink, L. (1978)
Munslow, A. (1997a)
—— (1992)
Novick, P. (1988)
Poovey, M. (1988)
Popper, K. (1979)
Roberts, G. (1997)
Rorty, R. (1991)
Rosenstone, R.A. (1996)
—— (1988)
Sellars, W. (1997 [1956])
Veyne, P. (1984)
Walkowitz, J. (1992)
White, H. (1978)
—— (1973b)

ONTOLOGY

Rather too many historians, while they may be methodologically sophisticated, still tend to share the naïve empiricist (see EMPIRICISM) reconstructionist (see RECONSTRUCTIONIST HISTORY) suspicion of philosophy fostered by colleagues such as Geoffrey **Elton**, Keith Windschuttle, Jack Hexter, Gertrude Himmelfarb, Arthur Marwick and Richard Evans. Many among the profession endorse their collective misgivings about what Elton has called the dangerous cocktail of German philosophy and French *esprit*, by which he means idealism and twentieth-century **continental philosophy**. In addition to doubtful thinkers like Martin Heidegger, Theodor Adorno, Hans-Georg Gadamer, Roland **Barthes**, Jacques **Derrida**, Hayden **White** and Michel **Foucault** the naïve empiricists have also named and shamed Benedetto **Croce**, R.G. **Collingwood**, E.H. **Carr** and Keith Jenkins. Elton *et al.* reject critical theory, **hermeneutics**, **structuralism** and deconstructionism (see DECONSTRUCTIONIST HISTORY), maintaining that **truth** in history is discoverable in the **event**. While most historians might not accept their hard-hat reconstructionism, they would agree with them that history is about serving the **evidence**. What most would agree is that history is not a philosophical disputation on the ontological condition of either the mind of the historian or his/her construction of past relationships of being, space and time. The historian is dedicated to discovering the reality of the past rather than debate **metaphysics**, that is, dispute the nature and construction of reality and being.

Ontology is that branch of metaphysics that addresses the general state of being, the nature of existence, and how the human mind apprehends, comprehends, judges, categorises, makes assumptions about and constructs reality. For the historian ontological questions arise when we address how to create historical **facts** within the larger ontology of our own existence, that is, the condition(s) of being under which we create or construct the-past-as-(the discipline of)-history. While the historian is necessarily an ontological creature who has prejudices, preconceptions and beliefs about the nature of existence (past, present and future) for Elton *et al.* this does not mean he/she can not escape them when researching and writing history. Such an escape from ontology is warranted for Elton, by our being constrained by the authority of the evidence (Elton 1991: 43, 49).

This empiricist-objectivist perspective views history as primarily concerned with those practice(s) dealing with the evidence that permit us to acquire genuine and, therefore, mind- and **discourse**-independent knowledge about the past: history is perceived exclusively as a methodology that allows escape into the past. The issue of **epistemology** (the nature, theory, foundations, conditions, limits and possibilities of knowing), if raised at all, rarely gets further than formally re-stating the assumption that historical knowledge is discovered through evidence-based **inference** and the delineation and specific application of social theories/categories of analysis that 'naturally' emerge from the evidence. Ontological questions are largely ignored. The reason according to conventional wisdom is because historians are insulated from their present conditions of existence by their skills/inferential methodology (see EMPIRICISM).

It is quite possible, therefore, to have truthful historical knowledge. The routes to 'ontology-free' justified historical knowledge can and have taken many forms. Examples of such routes might include **covering laws** (the positivist (see POSITIVISM) 'social science' route), service before the evidence (the 'empiricist-objectivist epistemological' route), practical realism (the 'lots of things in history are relative' route), truth-conditions (the 'induction does work' route), or the gendered re-casting of time (the 're-gendering time can produce a new and really proper history' route), etc., etc. The upshot, anyway, is that the reality of the past is accessible.

However, the ontological conditions of historical inquiry are presently more fiercely debated than ever before. Historians are asking and answering questions about the bases of their theories of explanation that form the a priori (see A PRIORI/A POSTERIORI) grounds or ontological presuppositions of the discipline. Having said this, most historians still find it hard to imagine a history other than the 'normal' one. What would a history written by reversing the being and knowing or content and form polarity look like (see FORM AND CONTENT)? Indeed, can history be history if it is viewed as a series of ontological rather than resolvable methodological (or occasionally epistemological) problems? The most obvious example is probably the **linguistic turn** that, in reversing content and form, makes history more than a little like literature, that is, it denies the knowable reality of the past.

Such a radical construal of history – reversing the polarity – means our knowledge is not necessarily discovered in the real past. While historians are happy to endorse Immanuel **Kant**'s view that philosophy can not grasp reality, fortunately history can – it has the methodology. Consequently, most historians are still not prepared to accept that any form of genuine, useful or plausible historical understanding may be achieved without benefit of an objective evidence-based (science-like) methodology. Of course, as sceptical empiricists they all know of the perennial and substantial problems that are part and parcel of the inferential method. Although our knowledge is, therefore, indirect and evidence-dependent, the hypothesis-induction-deduction, truth-conditional mechanism is rigorous and sophisticated (see CAUSATION; COLLIGATION)

This conception of what are the proper means for acquiring historical knowledge deliberately brackets off the ontology of history. Denying the need to philosophise on the status of history permits the comforting notion that history is a truth-acquiring discipline. It invariably also leads to an uncritical acceptance of referentiality, factualism and the correspondence theory of knowledge, as well as the belief that a history that prioritises being is certain to degenerate into a dangerous subjective anti-history idealism that might fool the unwary into believing it could still be history.

Once we doubt that useful knowledge can only emerge from rational explanation and knowable objects, then we are admitting that knowledge must, to some extent, be subjective and perspectival – and here historians enter the murky world of Friedrich **Nietzsche** and a kind of history that is no longer an independent reconstruction, but is historian- or observer-relative (see AUTHOR). Reversing the polarity also means losing faith in the accuracy of our representation of the past, for how can we write about the real past when we do not 'know' that our language is an adequate vehicle for relaying the truth that, we assume, is out there? In practice it may be we do not really have a choice, for the notion that language constitutes both ontological and epistemological states has already destabilised our priority of knowing over being. The reversal means that ontology, whether it is called our present condition, our ideology, **historicism**, **reality/realistic effect**, the constant deferral of meaning, will always get in the way of knowing the past.

Further reading

Elton, G. (1991)
Evans, R.J. (1997a)
Grossmann, R. (1992)
Hexter, J.H. (1972)
Himmelfarb, G. (1994)
Marwick, A. (1989 [1970])
Mensch, J.R. (1996)
Windschuttle, K. (1995)

P

POSITIVISM

An **epistemology** or theory of knowledge developed by the nineteenth-century French sociologist Auguste Comte as part of his grand three-stage theory of progressive historical evolution (theological, metaphysical and the scientific or positive stage). The final stage (which Comte saw himself as ushering in) is characterised by the verifiable or empirical measurement and predictability of the relationship between discrete phenomena. As an extension of established notions of **empiricism**, positivism insists on no speculation about natural phenomena. Because positivism assumes a uniformity in scientific method it allows for the analytical study of human behaviour – a science of society – by observers who stand outside that which is being observed. In terms of the study of the past, positivism assumes it is possible to characterise human experience according to discoverable and repeatable laws, namely, **covering laws** of human activity that allow for the creation of categories of both people and analysis, the functions and structures of which are determined by such laws (for example gender-, class- and race-determined behaviour). This is the essence of the inductive empirical method whereby observation of repeated occurrence suggests patterns of human behaviour (see INFERENCE). This observation and measurement requires no impositionalism by the historian.

Among the practical consequences of positivism is the belief in the facticity of the past: historical **evidence** can be discovered, evaluated and objectively constituted as **facts**. Beyond the simple level of events (see EVENT), positivism spurs some historians to seek out the infrastructural laws that guide, constrain and/or determine human society and its progress (see CONSTRUCTIONIST HISTORY). This means understanding the motors of history prior to a close scrutiny of its content. This may involve hypothesis-testing whereby the historian seeks to test an explanation in the crucible of the evidence. Or it may, more likely, mean offering an interpretation already brought to a corpus of evidence by the examination of other evidence, and/ or by a pre-existing mental state or set of beliefs (interpretation preceding evidence) (see ONTOLOGY; TELEOLOGY).

Further reading

Berkhofer, R.F. (1995)
Braudel, F. (1980)
Burke, P. (1993)
—— (1992)
Forum (1991)
Gardiner, P. (1959)
Hempel, C.G. (1942)
Kolakowski, L. (1972)
Lloyd, C. (1993)
Lorenz, C. (1998)
Novick, P. (1988)
Roberts, D.D. (1995)
Snooks, G. (1998)
Tosh, J. (1991)

POSTMODERNISM

Postmodernism is a general description for the conditions of our present existence – what might better be called postmodernity. According to the French cultural critic Jean-François Lyotard (1924–) postmodernism is distinguished by its denial of grand or meta- narratives (see METANARRATIVE) as deployed since the **Enlightenment** to explain and justify the Western conception of human progress. Our postmodern age is characterised generally by a self-conscious reaction against the vehicle for the Enlightenment's notion of progress, its cultural product, **modernism**. But the act of rejection is only found in certain spheres of intellectual activity. In others it is manifest, as the philosopher Michael Stanford has pointed out, as modernism's self-reflexion, or a case of modernism turning to challenge its own shortcomings (Stanford 1998: 246–63).

Such a situation has generated a number of claims and counter-claims about what this means for the discipline of history. These arguments are, as one would expect given the above definition of our postmodern condition, couched in terms of rejection and/or self-reflexion. Our postmodern condition, because it has destabilised the foundations of understanding, meaning and existence, has spawned, in the view of 'proper' or 'normal' historians, a series of anti-history developments. These include the rejection of representationalism in favour of the **linguistic turn** whereby the written form of history is as important as the past's content in creating meaning (see FORM AND CONTENT); the acceptance of **relativism** rather than **objectivity**; and the willing loss of the knowing subject resulting in the destruction of a sense of reality and referentiality because of the disruption of the signifier–signified relationship (see DECONSTRUCTIONIST HISTORY; REA-

LITY/REALISTIC EFFECT). The result is that postmodern history is no longer an empirical enterprise but simply a variety of fiction that is wholly dependent upon self-referentiality for its meaning (see EMPIRICISM). Hence postmodern historians argue we must defer interpretational closure because we are all cut adrift by the inadequacy of language and **narrative**. So it is that such historians are predisposed to prioritise historiography over the past through the arrangement, configuration and **emplotment** of the data (form rather than content as the source of meaning) (see TROPE/FIGURATION; Hayden WHITE).

In the literature-based humanities postmodernism is characterised, however, less by these rejections than by a modernist self-reflexiveness, the kind of modernism that makes its methods and the nature of its perceptions an object of study. This has been most apparent in developments generally in **continental philosophy**, and especially in the challenges to the Enlightenment realist assumption of, among other things, universal and fixed meanings (hence the challenge to representation), the correspondence theory of knowledge (the challenge to empiricism), truth-conditions (the challenge to analytical philosophy), the priority of knowing over being (the challenge to **epistemology**), and that the stories we tell can not capture the reality of the past or present (the challenge to narrative). It also disputes several realist epistemological (knowing) and ontological (being) dualisms: the separations of knower and known, observer and observed, subject and object, form and content, and fact (see FACTS) and value (see ONTOLOGY). Postmodernity, as our condition of not knowing the true origins or foundation of knowledge or its trajectory, has produced (whether we like it or not) a state of ontological drift, epistemological uncertainty, and the ungluing of methodological confidence.

Even though I have my doubts about modernist conceptions of objectivity, **inference**, **truth**, representation and finding firm foundations to knowledge in the humanities, I still agree with my realist colleagues that there remains a strong need in our Western culture to come to terms with the past by understanding it. But what I am saying is that this is no longer (if it ever was) an option. Postmodern history is not just a negative anti-realist 'anti-the past club' that we can join if we want. Rather we are being forced by our present conditions of existence to rethink how we construct the-past-as-history. Postmodern history is a history effectively liberated from what Keith Jenkins and Robert A. Rosenstone have called History (upper-case H) and history (lower-case h) (Jenkins 1991; Rosenstone 1996).

History (upper-case) is the central Western cultural metanarrative, a modernist speculation that we traditionally assign to chance events (see EVENT), a trajectory and significance determined by the bigger programmes of historical development and progress – Marxism, liberalism, capitalism, socialism, nationalism or whatever. Upper-case History, in order to be plausible, has had to annex lower-case or university-level professional history's features: its investment in **positivism**, reason, rationality, inference, probability and truth-conditional descriptions, reality, objectivity, explanatory closure, and common-sense factualism. But this is no longer the only way to study the past. H/history in our postmodern era is now being placed in inverted commas. 'History' eschews H/history in favour of problematising the whole idea of historical knowledge by placing ontology before epistemology, and studying the past without the urge to write the indescribable or reconstruct the inaccessible.

For me postmodern 'history' is no longer about domesticating or controlling the past without acknowledging why you are doing it, why you choose to deploy one ontology, epistemology or methodology over another, or what you hope to get out of it. It does not bother me at all if my realist colleagues choose to work on the assumption that their methods permit a match between **concepts in history** and events in the past. After all, they can believe that particular fiction if they want. I only get uneasy when they tell me it is through their methods *alone* that we can *properly* understand the past (i.e. match history with *the* past). From my position I question the assumptions that underpin that view, usually beginning by pointing out the substantial epistemological failings of the inferential method that is H/history's foundation (and that most historians tacitly admit anyway). It is not, as my realist friends still sometimes claim, a matter of me not recognising the existence of the material world but is rather a recognition on my part that the connection between the real and its representation in **discourse** and language is not fixed by a privileged method (their method). As an act of faith I choose to believe in the reality of the past. I do not believe the past has no substance other than being just another text or linguistic entity. But understanding the meaning of history, like all the literature-based humanities, is a figurative/linguistic activity (see Roland BARTHES; Jacques DERRIDA; HISTORICAL IMAGINATION; Giambattista VICO). It is not, as many proper historians claim, a matter of postmodernist historians trashing the past (defined, as I have suggested, as the-past-as-history) and then not being able to offer a better historical practice. The point is that under our postmodern conditions there is no practice or set of rules of the kind normal historians insist upon (i.e. extra-historical) that can *exclusively* reveal the truth(s) of the past.

Further reading

Ankersmit, F.R. (1994)
—— (1989)
Appleby J., *et al.* (1996)
Attridge, D. *et al.* (1987)
Bann, S. (1984)
Bauman, Z. (1998)
—— (1997)
Belchem, J. and Kirk, N. (1997)
Bertens, H. (1995)
Connor, S. (1989)
Domanska, E. (1998a)
Ermarth, E.D. (1992)

Harvey, D. (1989)
Heise, U.K. (1997)
Hollinger, D.A. (1991)
Hutcheon, L. (1988)
Jenkins, K. (1999)
—— (1997)
—— (1995)
—— (1991)
Klein, K. (1995)
Lechte, J. (1994)
Luntley, M. (1995)
Lyotard, J.-F. (1979)
Marshall, B.K. (1992)
Marwick, A. (1995)
Mensch, J.R. (1997)
Munslow, A. (1997c)
Norris, C. (1990)
Poster, M. (1997)
Roberts, G. (1997)
Rosenstone, R.A. (1996)
Southgate, B. (1996)
Stanford, M. (1998)
Zagorin, P. (1990)
Zammito, J.H. (1998)

R

REALITY/REALISTIC EFFECT

A concept explored at some length by Roland **Barthes** in his essay, 'The discourse of history' (1967), it is his argument that the connection between language and history does not rely on any genuine conformity between **evidence** and its constitution as historical fact (see FACTS). This means that what historians take for the actual past is only a reality-effect generated by our assumption that the correspondence theory of **truth** allows us to adequately reconstruct the past (see RECONSTRUCTIONIST HISTORY). In this essay Barthes claims written history is only one **narrative** among many, and is in no way epistemologically privileged (see EPISTEMOLOGY). As Barthes's interpreter Stephen Bann comments, the 'rhetorical analysis of historical narrative ... cannot grant to history, a priori, the mythic status which differentiates it from fiction' (Bann 1984: 5).

In 'The discourse' Barthes begins by stating the issue that strikes at the very existence of history as an epistemology. History, he notes, is usually legitimised by the principles of 'rational' exposition but, he asks, does this type of narration really differ in some distinctive way from imaginary narration, as found in the novel or drama? He goes on to challenge the authority of the historian based not only on his/her access to the sources, but more importantly their translation into historical knowledge and meaning as a narrative of historical interpretation – the translation of the object into a subject of study. Barthes's challenge takes the shape of a critique of the structure of the historian's **discourse**. The examples he offers include the deployment of lots of the minutiae of events (see EVENT), what in the history of art is called the *trompe l'œil* principle whereby such detail aims to give the sense of reality. Barthes further probes the collateral process whereby the historian absents his self/her self from their discourse to create the impression of realism through direct access to the referent from:

> where there is in consequence a systematic deficiency of any form of sign referring to the sender of the historical message. The history seems to be telling itself all on its own. This feature . . . corresponds in effect to the type of historical discourse labelled as 'objective' (in which the historian never intervenes). . . . On the level of discourse, objectivity – or the deficiency of signs of the utterer – thus appears as a particular form of imaginary projection, the product of what might be called the referential illusion, since in this case the historian is claiming to allow the referent to speak all on its own.
>
> (Barthes 1967: 65–75; trans. Bann 1981: 11)

The epistemological status of historical discourse is thus asserted. The historical fact is privileged by being placed in the specially reserved position of a superior claim to truthfulness as warranted by both a plain language and an independent research methodology as supported in the references – the scaffolding of proper historical methodology. Barthes is suggesting history is performing an epistemological trick through which the referent is placed in a privileged world of the real beyond arbitrary signification. As he says, in classically structuralist terms, 'The historian is not so much a collector of facts as a collector and relator of signifiers; that is to say, he organises them with the purpose of establishing positive meaning' (Barthes 1967: 65–75; trans. Bann 1981: 16). Following Barthes we may also acknowledge the issue of representation and the troping of the real as central to creating historical meaning (see DECONSTRUCTIONIST HISTORY; TROPE/FIGURATION; Hayden WHITE).

Further reading

Bann, S. (1984)
Berlin, I. (1997)
Bunzl, M. (1997)
Carr, D. (1986a)
Iggers, G. (1997)
Lorenz, C. (1994)
Putnam, H. (1988)
—— (1983)
Ricoeur, P. (1984)
Sahlins, M. (1981)
Searle, J. (1995)
Tallis, R. (1998)
White, H. (1998)

RECONSTRUCTIONIST HISTORY

Reconstructionist history describes the self-proclaimed metaphysical (see METAPHYSICS) realist, common-sense, empiricist, referential, truth-conditional, objectivised, inferential, non-theory, and non-ideological professional history produced in the wake of the **Enlightenment** in the mid- to late-nineteenth century after the advent and rejection of **positivism** (see Geoffrey ELTON; EMPIRICISM; EVIDENCE; FACTS; HISTORICAL EXPLANATION; INFERENCE; OBJECTIVITY; TRUTH). This modernist-inspired (see MODERNISM) scientific model for the study of the past resulted directly from the severing of **ontology** from **epistemology**, a move that demanded the separation of subject and object, and the observer from that which is observed. Reconstructionist history insists that its methodology (underpinned as it is by this philosophical position) allows the historian to disinterestedly discover the most probably truthful (and also, therefore, morally certain) interpretation inherent in the documents of the past, and write it up in a monograph. It is claimed that the true intentions and voices of people in the past will speak to, and through, the reconstructionist historian (see INTENTIONALITY).

The success of this kind of history has been such that by the end of the nineteenth century it had become culturally embedded as the proper way to re-animate the past. The present generation of historians have, however, experienced a challenge to that model. This has taken shape as a postmodern (see POSTMODERNISM) rethinking of history's literary form as a cognitive (knowing) instrument and consequently raised questions about history's legitimacy as an independent epistemology. Baldly stated, this challenge has confronted history as an inferential procedure through the **linguistic turn**, which is itself underpinned by developments in **continental philosophy**, critical theory, and post-structuralism. That challenge emerged in the last thirty years as a part of our postmodern conditions of knowledge creation. The habit of history-writing in the West was fixed originally and firmly in the correspondence theory of knowledge (common-sense empiricism). It has become so entrenched that any questioning of it generates reconstructionist claims of, at the very least, moral degeneracy in the questioner. The anticipated truthfulness in its accounts (reconstructing the past as it actually was, or to use Ranke's dictum of *wie es eigentlich gewesen*) emerges because it was/is built upon the primary sources and, so the reconstructionist argument runs, we are capable of writing truth-conditional descriptions in everyday language. History has a formal and generally accepted assortment of operations and practices that permit genuine knowledge about the past.

Empiricism, as the methodology of reconstructionist history, assumes its mode of explanation springs from the skills of the historian in addressing the **evidence**. Reconstructionist historians substantiate their factual knowledge of the past, in large part, because they claim they can remain unmoved by their perception of it; what the most vociferous of reconstructionists, G.R. **Elton**, described as the 'rational, independent and impartial investigation' of the evidence (Elton 1991 [1955]: 6). The reconstructionist methodology of interrogating the evidence through comparison, verification, contextualisation and authentication entails rejecting both R.G. **Collingwood**'s idea that writing history can involve an intellectual re-enactment in the historian's mind (producing the danger of **relativism**), and the misplaced idea that we can never have a genuine knowledge of the real past because of the instability of language and its fabricated **narrative** form (see FORM AND CONTENT).

The greatest mistake historians can make, so Elton and more recent reconstructionists like Richard Evans and John Warren argue, is to deny the possibility of objectivity because of the unavoidable imposition of the voice of the **author** (Evans 1997a; Warren 1998). Placing his defence within his rejection of the positivist wing of reconstructionism (an important border skirmish on the road to reconstructionism's purist empiricism) Elton offers the example of how objectivity disappears when social science theories are imported into history. He argues such imports arrive at their dubious results by setting up a theoretical model that their makers then claim to either validate or disprove by an 'experimental' application of factual detail, a process Elton believes to be honoured more in the breach than the observance (Elton 1991 [1955]: 10). When probed, Elton's careful attention to the archive that reconstructionists insist upon, rests on several related beliefs: that the past is real, that it is knowable because truth corresponds to that reality through the unearthing of the facts in the evidence, that there is an unambiguous distinction of fact and fiction, that truth to be truth must be derived independently of the historian and, consequently, truth is not perspectival. Elton summarises the reconstructionist view of knowledge creation when he says 'We are looking for a way to ground historical reconstruction in something that offers a measure of independent security – independent of the historian, independent of the concerns of his day, independent of the social and political conditions imposed on him. And the obvious answer to this quest, as it has always been and must continue to be, lies in the sources he has at his disposal' (Elton 1991 [1955]: 52).

In the last two decades a practical realist consensus has developed in response to the postmodernist attack on reconstructionist history. This new consensus has, by and large, not been raised in defence of Eltonian reconstructionism, but rather to modify the crudities of naïve empiricism – to also tactfully and tactically point out the straw-man nature of the object of the postmodernist attack. This consensus of constructionist historians (see CONSTRUCTIONIST HISTORY) of various stripes (sociological, anthropological, conceptual) claims to inject into the debate a more sophisticated and sensible appreciation of the difficulties of researching and writing history. After all, so the new consenting realists argue, no one these days really practises the absolutist kind of history that old-fashioned reconstructionism represents. This reasonable (in tone) and rationalist new practical realist or constructionist voice stresses the complexity of the relationship between facts and interpretation. It acknowledges the central problem of written history's poor fit with the realities of the past. The precursors to this new practical realism emerged in the United States in the 1930s with the first (pre-Eltonian) reaction against nineteenth-century positivism led by the two American historians Carl Becker and Charles Beard. Influenced by the Italian historian Benedetto **Croce**, Becker and Beard contested the possibility of an objectivist history that claimed to be above and beyond present cultural concerns. Becker summarised his idea of **relativism** by arguing that historical thinking 'is a social instrument, helpful in getting the world's work more effectively done' (Becker quoted in Novick 1988: 98).

In a suitably sceptical new practical realist fashion the American intellectual historian David Hollinger has argued that the historian's personal leanings are less a constraint, but more an imperative that makes historical interpretation possible (Hollinger 1989: 613). Historians, but not of a crude reconstructionist kind (the straw-man hypothesis holding that there are none around anymore), are now fully aware of the hermeneutic (see HERMENEUTICS) circle. This is a situation that, so Hollinger claims, critics like Joan Scott and David Harlan seem not to be aware of. In other words, the historian today knows how tricky hermeneutics is, and that we can never encounter an Archimedian point of a grounded or true historical object, and can not, therefore, reconstruct the past as it actually happened. Hollinger accepts the difficulties historians have translating the documents into facts and generating an appropriate interpretation of events (see EVENT). Along with all new practical realists (i.e. simply all historians), Hollinger claims to recognise that the historian can not be insulated from the construction(ist history) process as reconstructionists like Elton once naïvely believed. Hollinger insists, speaking for practical realists and, by implication, also for reconstructionists, our theories about the past must be tested in the crucible of the evidence, and while our measures of agent intentionality are not absolute, the voice of the past remains in the documents. Postmodern concerns about our ability to know and to represent what we believe we know are not convincing enough to cast genuine doubts about proper history for the reconstructionist historian. As Hollinger concludes, 'I do not understand the mystery of knowing, but I believe this mystery has survived the return of literature' (Hollinger 1989: 621). Or, as another reconstructionist historian is quoted as saying recently, try punching a postmodernist in the face and see if he could explain why it hurts (Colin Richmond quoted in Warren 1998: 191).

Further reading

Appleby, J. *et al.* (1994)
Beard, C. (1935)
—— (1933)
Becker, C. (1931)
Berkhofer, R.F. (1995)
Bunzl, M. (1997)
Carrard, P. (1992)
Collingwood, R.G. (1994 [1946])
Croce, B. (1970 [1927])
Domanska, E. (1998a)
Elton, G. (1991 [1955])
Evans, R.J. (1997a)
—— (1997b)
Harlan, D. (1997)

—— (1989)
Hexter, J.H. (1991)
Hollinger, D.A. (1991)
—— (1989)
Hunt, L. (1989)
Jenkins, K. (1999)
—— (1997)
—— (1995)
—— (1991)
Kellner, H. (1989)
Lorenz, C. (1994)
McCullagh, C.B. (1991)
Mink, L. (1978)
Munslow, A. (1997a)
Norman, A.P. (1991)
Poster, M. (1997)
Roberts, G. (1998)
—— (1997)
Scott, J.W. (1996a)
Topolski, J. (1991)
Warren, J. (1998)

RELATIVISM

Adherents of **postmodernism** tend to hold that conventional history can no longer be regarded as an objective method for the discovery of the **truth** of the past (see EMPIRICISM; OBJECTIVITY). Postmodern thinking certainly maintains that we can no longer be assured a posteriori (see A PRIORI/A POSTERIORI) that correspondence or representational theories of knowledge work despite the claims of practitioners of **reconstructionist history** to the contrary. This means there are no solid meanings, no certain **facts**, no foundational knowing subject, and we are witness to the collapse of various dubious binomials: knower and known, subject and object, fact and fiction, **form and content**, etc. The representational connection between the word and the world is rejected as a naïve assumption. So, the grandest modernist **narrative**, history is revealed to be a hollow and illicit **epistemology**: the last refuge of **modernism**'s empiricist delusion. Such anti-historical opinions, according to the empiricist response, open the floodgates of moral relativism because they indicate a failure to ground truth as conforming to reality and, what is worse, permit the anti-representationalist argument, for example, that the Nazi Holocaust or the ethnic cleansing of Kosovan Albanians by the Yugoslav Serbs can only be understood as a text and as such trivialises genocide. Fortunately, so the reconstructionist argument runs, relativism can be easily diagnosed and, if proper action is taken early enough, it can be cured.

Relativism comes in two varieties: metaphysical (see METAPHYSICS) and epistemological. Metaphysical relativism doubts there is a reality 'out there' independent of our minds. For such a full-blooded relativist it is not a matter of the adequacy of our concepts in history to grasp reality, but that our concepts actually create reality for us. Metaphysical relativists believe that what we call reality is only an appearance in our mind's eye. All objects are mental fabrications, representations, semblances, linguistic constructs. Reality can not be known (if it exists) independently of our minds and those inventions we call our organising concepts.

Epistemological relativism falls somewhat short of the fully matured metaphysical variety, suggesting that our knowledge of the real world has to be assisted by our mental constructs. But our situation in the world and, therefore, our conceptualisation and representation is affected by many forces beyond our control: how old we are, our race, the class we think we belong to, our gender, our ideological preferences, and the historical time and place in which we live. To argue these constraints have at least some effect on how and what we think is hard to dispute. They are bound to affect how we think about the past and influence how we write history. But most epistemological relativists, in acknowledging such constraints, stop well short of denying there is no approximate truth in history. They are content to distance themselves from the metaphysical relativism found in much postmodernist thinking (Appleby *et al.* 1994).

The roots of postmodernist relativism are to be found in the **historicism** of Friedrich **Hegel** and Karl Marx, and in the inspiration of Friedrich **Nietzsche** as digested by Ludwig Wittgenstein and more recently Jean Baudrillard, Richard **Rorty**, Keith Jenkins, Hayden **White** and Jacques **Derrida**. Historicism, as understood by Hegel, assumes that truth is relative to time and place. Marx took up a similar relativist position in his base–superstructure metaphor through which he imagined truth to be contingent on economic structures via false consciousness. But the likes of Hegel and Marx apart, historians have tended to express their faith in their craft by investing in the certainty of representation while being judicious about the stories it tells of the past.

However, no amount of judicial circumspection about historical narratives or, for that matter, feelings of moral superiority can deny the nature of linguistic and cultural relativism. Linguistic relativists maintain that what counts as truth is at best the product of grammatical rules and structures. Ludwig Wittgenstein famously argued from this perspective that language creates our apprehension of reality. Just as air is the medium in which birds fly, so language conditions how we exist. Wittgenstein called the codes structuring a language a 'game' that we all must play when we express ourselves through a language. Playing the 'language game' means we are participating in a particular life. So, when we write history – as a conditioning part of our life – it too is formed by our language use. As the French cultural critic Jean Baudrillard has suggested, the sign according to modernist thinking has been taken (by representationalists) to be capable of being exchanged for true meaning (history is thus seen as an exchange for the past). That exchange has conventionally been guaranteed by the referential power of representation, which permits historians to know through **inference** the **intentionality** in the mind of the historical agent.

But what if we call the bluff of representation? If we do, then surely is not historical representation, by definition, a constant simulation? In Baudrillard's terms history is nothing more than a gigantic simulacrum. This does not make the past unreal but it does make the-past-as-history a simulacrum, a simulation exercise, a pretence, a hyper-real version. So, although it can never actually exchange itself for what was once real, the empiricist claim for such an exchange continues to be made with its charge of moral relativism if it can not (see Roland BARTHES; REALITY/REALISTIC EFFECT). What reconstructionist empiricists and even more sophisticated constructionist historians (see CONSTRUCTIONIST HISTORY) have in common is their bedrock belief in knowable reality, so both reject the postmodern idea of history as an uninterrupted interpretative circuit, a fictive intellectual process ultimately without reference or boundary. Empiricism denies (by its definition) that we can only 'know' history through history, in other words, only through a perspective that is within history. Empiricists tend to regard as sinister the postmodern vision of the world 'back there' as just a jumble of signs and symbols, the meanings of which are constantly deferred and self-referential, with signifiers signifying only themselves.

Based on the thinking of Baudrillard, for example, I can imagine several stages (of representation) through which history passes in its descent into simulacra. History begins by being conceived as the mirror image of the reality that exists in the archive; next history dissembles and corrupts past reality as the historian domesticates, prefigures, configures, plans and organises it; next it necessarily (and cunningly?) disguises its growing lack of contact with past reality through the device of referentiality; finally, with its bluff called, it is shown to have lost all connection to past reality. It has become a simulacrum. History has achieved its ultimate state of relativism when it can only be judged by itself as when historians judge each other, and the past becomes forever unknowable. At this postmodern *ultima Thule* (farthest unknown region or point) there is no longer a foundational standard by which we can judge the-past-as-history.

In his book, *Philosophy and the Mirror of Nature*, the American philosopher Richard Rorty declared dead modernist (i.e. foundationalist, representationalist, grand narrative) philosophy. In applying Rorty's thinking to history, Keith Jenkins makes the point that Rorty (who, like Baudrillard, is starting from a Nietzschean position that doubts the knowability of the real world) is saying to historians we have to come to terms with a compromised correspondence theory of truth, and that the past can only be usefully understood as **historiography**. This means any claims history makes to an epistemological hold on the past should be seen at best as spurious, and at worst as dangerous, repressive nonsense. How many times has the phrase empirical reality been used to defend the morally indefensible?

After Baudrillard and Rorty (and Jenkins, White and Derrida) it is reasonable to ask if in our postmodern age, with its demise of the knowing subject, can we ever again claim to experience the unalloyed joy of empiricist and meaningful history? Most historians argue we can overcome this lurch into relativism by maintaining a 'bystander' theory of historical knowledge. They believe they can avoid (both varieties of) relativism by endorsing the 'common-sense' or 'natural' empirical wish to give credence to a knowable and real past 'by standing' outside the language and belief game. This is then reinforced by their regular empirical drills of **evidence** verification and comparison, contextualisation, **colligation**, establishing **causation** and intentionality (rational-action theory) and the argument that relativists try to retain to themselves what they deny to everyone else with relativism proposed as the true way of seeing reality(!). In being self-referential deconstructionist (see DECONSTRUCTIONIST HISTORY) historians are being inconsistent – to be relativist you have to accept the relativism of your relativist position. Mainstream sophisticated, if sceptical, representational empiricist historians accept a degree of perspectivism in their work, but as a group they do not give up on the idea of deriving meaning through representation and, therefore, objectively discovering the truth of the past. Historians, in spite of all the pitfalls of relativism, can still, so the majority believe, produce truth-conditional sentences. When the evidence is adequately supported by appropriate social theory historians can escape from the relativism of beliefs, language and simulacra.

Further reading

Baudrillard, J. (1983)
—— (1976)
Bernstein, R. (1983)
Davidson, D. (1984)
Finney, P. (1998)
Harris, J.F. (1992)
Jameson, F. (1976)
Krausz, M. (1989)
Putnam, H. (1981)
Quine, W.V. (1969)
—— (1960)
Rorty, R. (1991)
—— (1982)
Sellars, W. (1997 [1956])
Warren, J. (1998)
Wittgenstein, L. (1995 [1921])

RORTY, RICHARD (1931–)

Although originally an analytical philosopher trained to pursue the **truth**-conditions of propositions and the logical structure of thought, in the second half of his career from the late 1970s, Richard Rorty began to question the conventional categories of analytical philosophy – knowable reality, **objectivity**, truth, and **epistemology** (theory of knowledge). He replaced these interests with a postmodernist rendering of pragmatism in the tradition of the **continental philosophy** of Hans-Georg Gadamer, Martin Heidegger, Jürgen Habermas, Jacques **Derrida** and Michel **Foucault** as well as his own rendition of the work of the American pragmatist John Dewey (see HERMENEUTICS). Rorty's philosophical ideas are important to the humanities in general but especially to literary theory and history. His significance as a key thinker in postmodern (see POSTMODERNISM) philosophy lies in his rejection of reasonless foundationalism in all its disguises: as grand theories, as notions of truth and meaning, as the autonomous knowing subject, **empiricism**, limpid representation leading to unclouded or mirror-like referentiality, distanced objectivity, the correspondence theory of knowledge, and knowable reality.

Instead Rorty favours the sceptical acceptance of contingency and uncertainty, the necessity for perpetual dialogue rather than truthful or absolute answers, the parochial rather than universal nature of truth (localised truth-effects), situational ethics, the unresolvable polarity of appearance and reality, and the **relativism** associated with the inability of the human mind to stand outside its own terms of reference (in order to mirror reality). But Rorty rejects as a misunderstanding of his position (associated with critics like Christopher Norris) the idea that he is either sceptical or relativist, arguing instead that he is merely pointing out the anti-representational/description-dependent, gendered, ethno-cultural and historical situatedness of knowledge. Rorty's argument is that just because our beliefs are constituted within our situation, this does not mean we can not rationally justify our views. Moral truths may not be objectively derived but we can still tell the fascists from the good guys and that holocausts occurred in the past and are occurring in the present. What Rorty is saying is that how we narrate such events (see EVENT) influences the meaning we derive from them (see DISCOURSE; NARRATIVE).

Analytical philosophy, as the central twentieth-century tradition of Western **metaphysics** tried, in the work of Bertrand Russell and the younger Wittgenstein, to expose reality's logical form – attempting to demonstrate that language is essentially representational and transparent. Through language, specifically the grammatical sentence, analytical philosophers told us we could access the real world of our present and past existence. In later years Wittgenstein rebelled against this, taking up what has been called ordinary-language philosophy and in the process stimulated a fresh interpretation of the connections between language, philosophy and knowledge. Rorty's post-epistemological radicalism (that is, a state wherein knowledge can not precisely represent reality) is derived from the anti-representationalist view he has of language. This view is derived from the pre-postmodern and pre-post-structuralist critique of the representational language of Friedrich **Nietzsche**, Ferdinand de Saussure, John Dewey, Wittgenstein (later in life), Donald Davidson and W.V. Quine. During his own working career Rorty has been influenced by the deconstructionism of Derrida, Foucault and Roland **Barthes**. The point here is the simple one that once we move from the single statement of fact (the factual sentence) to the level of discourse (the interpretation), that which we believe we know, and that which we metaphorically create, are no longer completely separate entities and, significantly, the subject–object binary effectively disappears (see HISTORICAL IMAGINATION; TROPE/FIGURATION).

Rorty's most influential book is *Philosophy and the Mirror of Nature* (1979) in which he argues against essentialist and representationalist thinking in philosophy. For historians Rorty's message is that **empiricism**, the correspondence theory of truth, and **inference** to the best explanation are not universally valid methods because they are constantly jeopardised by the historicist nature of language (see HISTORICISM). In his book, *Consequences of Pragmatism* (1982), he rejects the description of him as a relativist in favour of that of pragmatist, arguing that the search for absolutist methodologies that will deliver *the* truth is a fruitless exercise and should be abandoned. Instead he favours the pragmatic pursuit of the useful and prods us toward accepting that knowledge is subject to the context of its production/construction. In his book, *Contingency, Irony and Solidarity* (1989), Rorty turns to face the issue of the intellectual's private imaginative construction of knowledge, the sharp edges of which are publicly held in check by the political ethics he associates with liberalism.

Language is no longer the vehicle to deliver truth. Instead it is an elastic medium for self-realisation and for the creation of new kinds of expression. Conventionally language is used by historians as a largely unproblematic way of organising our perceptions of the content of the past, the organisation of which permits the use of the logic of inference. But Rorty argues that perception and inference are the somewhat limited consequences of viewing language as the medium for expressing the inexpressible. Instead Rorty suggests that by a recognition of the power of language to turn meaning – through the power of the metaphor – we can rethink language as a mechanism that can re-form our historical truths by the translation of the metaphoric into the literal (see LINGUISTIC TURN). In this way the American historian of the frontier experience Frederick Jackson Turner's waves of western pioneers expressed the inexorable movement of American nationalism, and the American race leader and social historian William E.B. Du Bois's key metaphor of the veil of race served to describe a whole culture's historical experience. Neither use of language is 'wrong' because they serve liberating purposes in writing history.

While it is possible to remain relaxed about the fact that such descriptive language is a form of knowing, the historian becomes what Rorty calls an 'ironist' only when he/she faces up to his/her doubts about language and the influences exerted over him/her by being born at a certain time in a certain place (Rorty 1998: 307). Rorty's 'liberal ironist' thus speaks of 'truths' ill-recognised and constantly doubted rather than merely stretching the expressive powers of language. In the postist world the 'real', as Hayden **White** suggests, is always cast in a self-consciously sceptical tone, the intention of which is to constantly bring forth the relativism of the 'real' (White 1973b: 37). Irony is, therefore, the intellectual form of postmodernism: that phase of consciousness in which the cloudy nature of language has been finally grasped and in which reality can only be expressed through the negation of the literal (see EPISTEME). Irony should not, after all, upset the already sceptical empiricist as it often seems to, rather it should assist them in taking that extra step that will extend their scepticism to the language they use.

The fact that universal truth is thus replaced by a continuing ironic narrative ought to strengthen the historical consciousness, because the historian can now only touch base with the past once he/she has realised that language no longer faithfully represents transcendentant or universal truths. However, it is not all good news for historians – especially reconstructionist historians (see RECONSTRUCTIONIST HISTORY). By accepting a Rortyan post-epistemological position it becomes increasingly difficult to sustain the notion of reaching not just final, but any genuinely truthful, conclusions about what actually happened in the past. The aim in a Rortyan world is to acknowledge and welcome, even celebrate, the indeterminate and interpretational nature of history as a linguistic dialogue about the past, rather than try to empirically domesticate it by trying to find out what really happened (hence the oxymoron of the definitive interpretation!). In this way post-epistemological historians are allowed to see themselves as authors (see AUTHOR) who intervene and recreate the connection between reality and writing. They no longer *have to* see themselves as objective explorers who can only infer and theorise according to the **evidence**.

Experimentation rather than definitive truth-seeking is now the keystone of this new version of (Rortyan) or postmodern history. The fact that the methodological rituals of traditional modernist history are imposed in the public sphere is a bad habit we should try to break, if only in private (see the ENLIGHTENMENT; MODERNISM). Forcing our views on others through the public sphere would be, after all, an unwelcome form of intellectual coercion ill-befitting an ironic and laid-back Rortyan historian. So, it's live and let live among historians of every stripe – reconstructionist, constructionist (see CONSTRUCTIONIST HISTORY) and deconstructionist (see DECONSTRUCTIONIST HISTORY). If some historians wish to claim their own particular method delivers truth through their arrangement of **form and content** then so be it – but let others do it differently if they so wish. While Rorty's position has been variously described (and usually unfairly) as linguistic reductionism, or as being out of touch with reality, or profligate in its incapacity to tell right from wrong, doing history differently does not necessarily equate with social irresponsibility. Indeed, might it not be more irresponsible to beat the past to death with the blunt instrument of a doubtful empiricism in the belief that eventually it will be forced to yield 'the truth'?

Further reading

Bhaskar, R. (1991)
Davidson, D. (1984)

Norris, C. (1992)
Quine, W.V. (1990)
—— (1969)
Rorty, R. (1998)
—— (1992 [1967])
—— (1992)
—— (1991)
—— (1989)
—— (1982)
—— (1979)
Sellars, W. (1997 [1956])
White, H. (1973b)

S

STRUCTURALISM

The modern (see MODERNISM) or post-**Enlightenment** historian engages with the past by demonstrating its possible meanings, by re-animating its inhabitants as they live out their lives over time. The nature of this engagement is determined by the inescapable fact that we can not experience the lives of people in the past as they did. The past is only alive in the eye and **historical imagination** of the historian as he/she looks at the **evidence** and scours the archive. But, rather than simply accept the harsh epistemological (see EPISTEMOLOGY) limitations of this situation, a peculiar double consciousness has developed in the modernist historian's thinking. The modernist post-Cartesian, post-Enlightenment, liberal humanist (see LIBERAL HUMANISM) historical mind requires the imposition of a methodology and a structure on the past that permits and quickly demands to know its **truth**. The double consciousness that characterises the modernist historian's mind necessarily regards history on the one hand as a privileged, truth-conditional and truth-transmitting discourse, while at the same time acknowledging the nineteenth-century legacies of **empiricism** and **positivism** are actually inappropriate methodologies through which to (scientifically?) grasp the truth of the past. The emergence of another way of thinking about the past, shorn of those crudities – structuralism – has promoted a highly successful third road to historical understanding.

The historian's double consciousness – he/she knows he/she can only construct the past (see **constructionist history**) while longing to reconstruct it (see **reconstructionist history**) – has been the site of much postmodern (see POSTMODERNISM), deconstructionist (see DECONSTRUCTIONIST HISTORY), and post-empiricist critique. That critique has proven useful insofar as it placed the double consciousness in a context of scepticism about our ability to know things and offer that knowledge within the form of **narrative** (see **form and content**). Such sceptical post-realist perspectives have assisted in puncturing the historian's modernist dogma about the absolute need, as well as his/her ability to know the truth of the past. However, the practical realist part of the historian's double consciousness prompts the response that such puncturing has gone beyond the salutary, and has reached the level of absurdity. It is one thing to recognise the limitations of history's empiricist, indirect, inferential (see INFERENCE) and over-ambitious positivist methodology, but it is another to argue historians are, as a result, intellectually incapable of telling fact from fiction, reality from invention, truth from lies, or that meaning is always arbitrary. How did this war over the truthfulness of the **discourse** of history arise? In one sense it started with Western philosophy itself and its in-built scepticism about how we can know and then represent reality. If our present postmodern condition is indeed marked by a loss of belief in the power of language to accurately reflect human experience (the death of representation), its most recent manifestation began with an anti-foundationalism that rejected the basic tenets of what was the early twentieth-century high-tide of modernist thought, structuralism.

A movement called structuralism first emerged with the argument of the Swiss linguist Ferdinand de Saussure (1857–1913) that language is based on a knowable (if highly complex) set of rules (Saussure 1959 [1916]). The key idea of structuralism is that language works according to its own internal regulations, and is not directly connected to external reality. Saussure explains how this works through the dominant *langue* (language's foundational or deep structure) and its subordinate, the *parole* (examples of the deep structure in operation as a statement). To know how language operates we must first know the system that undergirds any word or statement. According to Saussure, words do not gain their meaning as reflections of their objects in the real world. The word and the world exist in a (strong and) conventional relationship, not a naturalistic referential one. By making the point of analysis the system itself – a synchronic examination that assumes structures are timeless – structuralism effectively cancels out history – the diachronic mode of knowing. This insight has been variously applied to other text-based epistemologies, but most notably within the field of literary criticism.

The logic of Saussure's structuralism suggests that words are signs defined by their difference from other words and signs. Language is, therefore, constructed as a series of signs produced by the culturally determined signifier (word)–signified (concept) connection. Although the sign–signifier–signified link is arbitrary, and although, as Saussure suggested, language does not reflect nature (because it is a culturally constituted medium) the modernist historian insists there is, in practice, a relatively stable connection between word and world. The modernist historian chooses to believe this union allows for the writing of truthful narrative interpretations based on his/her depth of both contemporary cultural knowledge and historical context. However, from a structuralist perspective, language is about the structure of the arbitrary connections between signifiers, and does not look beyond the language system at the historically determined signified – the empirical. Structuralists do not search for changes in language or word meanings as being constituted by external change over time, instead they seek out meaning in structural relationships. Because the meaning of the sign results from the arbitrary link between signifier and signified, language is a poor conductor for historical truth (or any other kind of truth). Language is always going to be polluted with social meaning and, as Michel **Foucault** suggests, homologous to the power and ideological relationships that exist within the social structure. The historian's language is, therefore, unavoidably presentist and ideological.

Structuralism, as originally formulated by Saussure, though having pretensions to scientificism, did not prove to be the model for the study of the past – it was sweepingly anti-empirical, anti-evolutionary and anti-representational. Other, yet more amenable social science constructionist history approaches to historical understanding, themselves occasionally and confusingly also called structuralist, were derived from, or were clear rejections of, the nineteenth-century empiricist and/or positivist scientific model. According to the nomenclature devised by Christopher Lloyd there are at least five distinguishable structural or structuralist history approaches – empiricist, systemic-functionalist, interpretist, relational-structurist, and structuralist/post-structuralist, with only the latter being derived from Saussure's model (Lloyd 1993).

Each approach is an orientation that regularly encompasses several different methodologies. Under empiricism, for example, Lloyd includes a range that covers biography, empiricist historical sociology, empirical social history, cliometrics, and behaviourist individualism. The dominant methodology here is inductivist and inferential. Rather more positivist in inspiration, the systemic-functionalist approaches adopt a deductivist methodology. Interpretist approaches reject all pretensions to scientific explanation of human action and encompass traditional historical interpretationism (what I have called **reconstructionist history**) as well as a variety of sociological and anthropological interpretisms (to include the *Annalistes*). Relational-structurist approaches include those formulated by the sociologist Anthony Giddens among others. The fifth group noted by Lloyd are structuralist/post-structuralist approaches (Lloyd 1993: 66–88). In the twentieth century, therefore, several structural history approaches to the study of the past have opened up, including the Saussurean structuralist approach. However, because this latter approach emerged in a French historical culture, it was regarded with suspicion by the Francophobic Anglo-American hermeneutic (see HERMENEUTICS) tradition.

As Lloyd points out, with the work of Lévi-Strauss, Roland **Barthes**, Michel Foucault, Louis Althusser and Immanuel Wallerstein we had an (often Marxist-orientated) attempt within history-writing to designate the structures of dominance and subordinance in evolving Western industrial and post-industrial society. With Lucien Febvre structuralism was transmuted into an interest in *mentalités*, and with Marc Bloch and Fernand Braudel the *long durée* (with events (see EVENT) only serving to evidence the enduring power of structures). Inevitably the French *Annalistes* came to terms with empiricism and positivism, claiming to successfully account for historical change and representation in their history. Where they did achieve a certain plausibility (like Febvre and Le Roy Ladurie) their work seeped into the Anglo-American bedrock, but where they didn't, as with Foucault's eruptive epistemes (see EPISTEME), they were far less successful.

Today social science structuralist history continues to flourish in a number of manifestations – demography, economic history, health, migration studies, quantitative studies, technology, social inequality, social mobility studies, political studies, and in theory and **historiography** – though only in rare instances has it prolonged the shelf-life of the covering law (see COVERING LAWS). By the same token, there are few historians today who are attracted by any constructionist or Saussurean structuralist mind-set that views the past as a fantastically complex series of transhistorical language, behaviour and thought codes that can be cracked given enough hard work in the archive. By the 1960s, when the high tide of social science history had been reached, the post-structuralist reaction had set in, rejecting structuralism's aspirations to timeless scientific explanation. The nature of the signifier–signified relationship – with its disruptive nature and endless intertextual deferral of signifier meanings as Roland Barthes and Jacques **Derrida** pointed out – placed bigger question marks over truth, reality, meaning and representation than ever before. The history text could no longer be regarded as providing *the* meaning of the past through the study of textualised evidence.

The importance of both Saussurean and social science structuralism, and their post-structuralist rejection, lies in the way it is forcing the modern liberal-humanist historian to ask basic epistemological questions about what they do as historians (see LIBERAL HUMANISM). Is there a past real world that we can grasp rationally, empirically, and can we adequately track institutional and structural changes over time? Can language (more or less) accurately reflect that reality? Is language the servant of the knowing subject? Does our language create history, thus pushing the historian, the historical agent, and the evidence to the margins of the process? How readily do we confuse **concepts in history** with events and **facts**?

Further reading

Caws, P. (1997)
Dant, T. (1991)
Dosse, F. (1997)
Hawkes, T. (1977)
Lechte, J. (1994)
Lloyd, C. (1993)
Saussure, F. (1959 [1916])
Snooks, G. (1998)
Sturrock, J. (1979)
Tallis, R. (1998)
Williams, R. (1983)

T

TELEOLOGY

In philosophy teleology refers to the doctrine that all agents that act with **intentionality** are goal-directed. Such thinking is characteristic of Aristotle. In history it means the belief that there is in the past a manifest destiny: history possesses a discernible end-directedness. Although it is usually claimed that the only way to determine if this is so is by a careful examination of the **evidence**; those who endorse teleological explanations always seem to find them in the evidence. However, for the reconstructionist historian (see RECONSTRUCTIONIST HISTORY) such totalising explanations are of doubtful value, being largely speculative rather than analytic. First of all, if there is actually a direction and, therefore, an end in history how can we yet know it as we have not, presumably, any evidence that we have reached the end of history? But rather more important is the consideration that large-scale teleological explanations are fundamentally anti-historical in that they assume the past *as a whole* can be accounted for by reference to the consequences of events, actions and processes, rather than their immediate (and often largely random) **causation**. Such criticism has been regularly levelled at those historians whose histories appear to be directed by an inner design as, for example, in the work of Giambattista **Vico**, Friedrich **Hegel** and Karl Marx.

One of the most famous of recent teleological explanations is that of the American Francis Fukuyama in his book, *The End of History and the Last Man*, in which he claims that the end of history had been reached by 1991 with the victory of liberalism over communism. For Fukuyama the collapse of Soviet communism evidenced the progression of history toward this final cause. Teleology, as used by Fukuyama, suggests there was a governing and universal power in history that drove it to its unavoidable conclusion. This grand-**narrative** philosophising is usually regarded as a form of doctrinal conviction that has rather lost touch with reality. This criticism is, of course, usually made by those empiricists who claim their methodology has pushed them to an alternative (and more truthful rather than grandiose) explanation (see TRUTH). The place for teleology in history is, therefore, strictly limited: to helping explain empirically verified and individual purposive human activity directed towards a known 'end' (see EMPIRICISM).

Such a definition of teleological explanation is founded on the assumption that only individual biological creatures are actually capable of directed action determined by subjective choices and wishes, intentions and designs, desires and wants. By this definition neither Fukuyama's all-conquering liberalism nor Marx's triumphant proletariat can be said to possess purposive intention. An ultimate purpose can only be ascribed to people. Hence, while individuals may indeed have acted according to some inner intentional drive, the question of whether this applies to social institutions, or mass movements, or ideologies is impossible to demonstrate beyond the level of stating what might be possible.

The mechanism historians use to constrain the dangerous impulse toward large-scale teleological explanation is the surgical application of the **colligation** process whereby the connections between events, actions and processes are established and contextualised. However, when colligating, historians quickly become aware that events, actions and processes that occur later in the cause and effect chain were most likely anticipated by earlier purposive action and intentionality. This means, because the thinking of people in the past was anticipatory of desired outcomes, the past and historical explanation are unavoidably teleological – teleology is already embedded in the past itself. It means the historian, in interrogating the past, has to understand the end to which the object, text or action was directed by its **author**. As to whether this can be legitimately inflated by the historian sufficiently to sustain a philosophical belief in a manifest destiny depends on several factors: the prejudices of the reader to accept such a claim, the manner in which the sources are disposed of, and the plausibility of the composed historical narrative that is built on individual action (see CONSTRUCTIONIST HISTORY).

The philosopher of history Clayton Roberts tries to sustain an anti-teleological position by suggesting large-scale teleological problems arise only if we confuse colligation with **emplotment**. Roberts defines emplotment as the configuring of events according to their known ultimate goal. Colligation on the other hand means tracing the causation of an event – via a suitable theory – in order to explain it. The former tactic reveals what may be illegitimate patterns in history, the latter discovers true causes. Emplotted (i.e. teleological) explanations imply a desire on the part of the historian to imagine or prefigure an explanatory outcome: and this is not proper **historical explanation** (C. Roberts 1996).

But is this strictly accurate? To emplot the past is to compose a narrative the aim of which is to explain events (see **event**) by either discovering *the* real story in the past or by imposing a meaning believed to be derived from the evidence – colligation is not, as Roberts implies, solely the preserve of non-narrative historians. Emplotment, in fact, almost always includes recourse to some kind of colligatory causal explanation. The fact that aesthetic choices are not regarded as necessarily secondary to the empiricist research enterprise does not mean emplotment is teleological and colligation is not (see TROPE/FIGURATION). The important point is the subtlety and plausibility with which teleological explanations are made about the purposive action of individual agents and how convincing is their extension to the philosophical level.

Teleological explanations have, therefore, had a bad press among reconstructionist historians because of their assumption that history is almost exclusively a process of discovering individual agent intentionality. From this perspective the historian who believes they *know* the outcome of history exists in a pernicious and confused state of ideological wish-fulfilment. The objective and distanced analysis of the evidence has clearly been sacrificed to a totalising explanation (an extrapolation too far). While this charge is probably unfair as few, if any, historians ignore individual human actions, such claims actually serve to disguise the fundamental significance of teleological explanations.

Both Western **metaphysics** and its offspring history are teleological in character. Modernist (see MODERNISM) historians view history and explanation as linear and, therefore, temporally directional. We seek to answer the question of what we are and what we may become. To do this we must heed the warnings and lessons of history. We try to find out why something happened in the past the way it did because we think we have alternatives in the future. It follows history is full of options. There is no givenness about it. As people in the past had choices so do historians in interpreting those choices. This relationship between cause and explanation, as Friedrich **Nietzsche** argued, is often one of the effect directing the search for cause. It is this that makes history unavoidably teleological at both the level of the philosophy of history and in the pursuit of agent intentionality. It means teleology confounds the wish to construe history as objective at all but the most basic level of the truth-conditional sentence (see OBJECTIVITY). Once the historian moves to interpretation he/she is making choices about preferred ends, and teleology can not be avoided.

Further reading

Barnard, F.M. (1981)
Carr, E.H. (1987 [1961])
Collingwood, R.G. (1994 [1946])
Donagan, A. (1959)
Dummett, M. (1978)
Fukuyama, F. (1993 [1991])
Gardiner, P. (1961 [1951])
—— (1959)
Hassing, R.F. (1997)

Nagel, E. (1979)
Roberts, C. (1996)

TROPE/FIGURATION

Tropes are figures of speech, primarily metaphor, metonymy, synecdoche and irony, but we could also include the variants simile, litotes, periphrasis and hyperbole. Figures of speech deploy words in such a way as to change, turn or translate meaning. Operating at the deep level of human thought, the early twentieth-century Swiss linguist Ferdinand de Saussure argued meaning emerges in language through binary opposition and, as employed by Michel **Foucault**, the sense of otherness or difference thus generated can, in any historical period, surface as a dominant cultural trope (see EPISTEME; STRUCTURALISM). Hence, in his book, *Metahistory* (1973), the American philosopher of history Hayden **White** examines the theory of tropes and troping as the means to distinguish the dominant modes of **historical imagination** in nineteenth-century Europe and thus identify their deep and surface structures. The troping process may be extended to include the creation of large-scale metaphors like the base–superstructure metaphor of Karl Marx as the basis of a total explanation of historical change, or create other models of historical change that rely upon the basic relationships of part-whole/whole-part. The tropes may thus reside, as the eighteenth-century Neapolitan philosopher of history Giambattista **Vico** suggested, at the heart of every historical period (defined by Foucault as the episteme) *and* in its description.

Because written history is a literary artefact White claims historians share the same formal **narrative** structures used by writers of realist literature that are based on the tropes as the main categories of figurative language. White uses something like a base–superstructure metaphor himself to explain how this works. Historians construct narratives (stories) to produce explanations employing three superstructural strategies of explanation, namely, explanation by **emplotment**, explanation by formal argument and explanation by ideological implication. These strategies of explanation are the surface features of the narrative, with White suggesting a deep or infra- structure of consciousness operating at the level of the tropes that ultimately determines how historians elect to explain the facts explored in their narratives. This is, in effect, a reversal of the conventional priority of content over form as the proper way to approach the discovery of historical knowledge (see FORM AND CONTENT).

Hayden White, as the leading theoretician of the narrativist revival in historical writing, is insistent that recognition of troping as the cognitive process of transition or transfer does not mean accepting textual determinism. Language and its figurative element do not determine what we can say, but they are constraints on how we create meaning (see AUTHOR;

DISCOURSE). It is important to understand that language is the medium, not the model of perception.

Further reading

Ankersmit, F.R. (1994)
Ankersmit, F.R. and Kellner, H. (1995)
Chartier, R. (1997)
Domanska, E. (1998b)
Jenkins, K. (1995)
Kansteiner, W. (1993)
Kellner, H. (1980)
Lemon, M.C. (1995)
McLennan, G. (1984)
Munslow, A. (1992)
Roth, P.A. (1992)
White, H. (1998)
—— (1987)
—— (1978)
—— (1973b)

TRUTH

Conventionally, in philosophy, truth is taken as a property of sentences, statements and propositions or beliefs. The sentence is a particular arrangement of words, the statement is the use put by a writer/speaker to the sentence, and the proposition or belief is the content of the statement. In a sentence then, we state as a proposition or a belief that something 'is true'. This can lead to at least two views about truth, either that it is primarily the property of a linguistic *representation* in that our propositions or beliefs are the result of language, or the other way around, that truth resides *propositionally* whereby propositional truth is expressed in our sentences and statements. This latter view assumes and requires a match between proposition and reality. **Historical explanation** is beset by the tension between these two perceptions of truth. Today most historians would probably accept that because the past is organised through the exercise of their **historical imagination** this means rejecting any absolutist notion of historical truth (see E.H. CARR; R.G. COLLINGWOOD; Benedetto CROCE; Giambattista VICO; HERMENEUTICS). Historical interpretations may be better regarded as likely to be true corresponding to the verified **evidence** and the coherence of the statement as judged by other historians, and the demands of their own culture.

The two theories of truth that most affect the work of the historian are the correspondence and coherence/consensus theories. Historians conventionally prioritise the correspondence theory, which holds that historical truth exists in the correspondence of historical descriptions to the **facts** – we discover facts by drawing inferences (see INFERENCE) from the evidence that leads to a correspondence between, as Michael Stanford says, 'fact and mind'

(Stanford 1998: 66). The argument runs that the more thoughtful and careful our inferences, the closer we are likely to get to the truth. To the extent such descriptions mirror past reality and are mind-independent they may be regarded as more or less possessing **objectivity**. The debate about truth in history hinges, therefore, on the extent to which historical descriptions can be regarded as truthful. Now, although historical descriptions are never or very rarely couched baldly in terms of 'it is a fact that . . . ' the implication is often exactly that. To illustrate this, take the statement 'the cotton industry was the key feature of the Industrial Revolution'. It intentionally comes across as a statement of a past reality because the historian believes it to be so. What it is actually is a propositional statement, or a series of events (see EVENT) under a description based on the evidence.

Now, the sceptical or practical realist historian accepts that historical practice means having to live with an absence of proof. As Appleby, Hunt and Jacob argue, at best 'the past only dimly corresponds to what the historians say about it [and] practical realists accept the tentativeness and imperfections of the historians' accounts' (Appleby *et al.* 1994: 248). Such historians willingly admit the problems of squeezing the truth out of the past and translating it as history. They know there are no transcultural or transhistorical iron laws of human behaviour to assist explanation, and that **empiricism** is a poor vehicle for studying the past because they can not stand apart from their object of study and their **evidence** is indirect. This is compounded because they can only understand and explain the past through **concepts in history** that are mediated by language (did '**class**' exist in the past or is it a concept they have imposed on it?). But this does not mean, as Appleby, Hunt and Jacob maintain, denying the existence of a past reality, or if the past did actually exist that it is unknowable, and it certainly does not mean swallowing the whole postmodern (see **postmodernism**) and relativist argument of unfixed and constantly deferred meanings, ending up with no anchors for objective knowledge (see RELATIVISM).

The reason for maintaining a belief in the truth of historical descriptions lies in the continuing power of the principle of correspondence between the word and the world. Historians who believe in the truth-conditions of historical descriptions do so because language is never so vague as to be wholly unreferential (plus the fact that historical method ensures truth through exhaustive study in the archive and solid inference). Consequently, historical descriptions can still be reasonably defended as being referential and representational even though our eventual written construction of the past is a linguistic creative act of the historian – and here I appropriate Aristotle's term, mimesis. Historians, I suggest, work by endorsing a weak version of the correspondence theory – call it a mimetic version – that allows for the existence of reality, a knowledge of it, and its adequate representation. This is usually summarised by the claim that historical descriptions are true if they are well-supported by the evidence. The problem with a representational or mimetic version of truth is how do we define the fact upon which we base our later interpretational descriptions? Do all our facts have to, at some point, fulfil an absolutist version of the correspondence test?

This unavoidable tension has led historians to seek collateral support in the coherence/consensus theory of truth. I define this as the accord that exists among well-informed and skilled historians. Such harmony is expressed through the range of other justified descriptions and propositions they make – in my example it means contextualising and verificatory statements being made and agreed about the growing numbers of cotton-spinning mills or cotton operatives employed between certain periods, or the swelling volume of profits from cotton manufacture as compared to, say, wool worsted. So, a descriptive historical statement may be regarded as very likely to be true if it coheres with other descriptive statements about the past world and a descriptive consensus is reached. It is probably false if it does not. That 'the cotton industry was the key feature of the Industrial Revolution' is a true statement according to a coherence/consensus theory of truth, so long as the bulk of historians agree with that description based on their knowledge of the evidence. Our prior belief in the correspondence theory allows us to assume, therefore, that the statement must be founded on an earlier correspondence to the facts. Hence, if the evidence changes so do the facts and their interpretation, and a new phase of revisionism is launched and a new consensus may emerge – a continuous process of evolving arguments to the best explanation. But, as we know, it does not always work that way – the same evidence is often used to infer quite different meanings.

As is well-known, the eighteenth-century German philosopher Immanuel **Kant**, inspired by the **Enlightenment** and the rationalist ideas of **modernism**, argued in favour of truth but admitted in doing so that our knowledge is only of the appearance of things rather than knowledge of things-in-themselves (see EMPIRICISM; EPISTEMOLOGY; G.W.F. HEGEL). His nineteenth-century critic Friedrich **Nietzsche** took up this point, maintaining that if knowledge of things-in-themselves is impossible then truth must be equally unrealisable in respect of correspondence. Nietzsche also rejected Kant's universal a priori (see A PRIORI/A POSTERIORI) cognitive principles in favour of individual perspective, and emphasised the role of language, specifically noting its metaphoric character, in shaping our beliefs and concepts (see TROPE/FIGURATION). It follows that if language is metaphorical, so is truth. In effect what is agreed in society to be truthful *is* truthful or, as Nietzsche puts it, the 'sum of human relations which have been poetically and rhetorically intensified, transferred, and embellished, and which, after long usage, seem to a people to be fixed, canonical, and binding' concluding that truths are 'illusions which we have forgotten are illusions; they are metaphors that have become worn out and have been drained of sensuous force, coins which have lost their embossing and are now considered as metal and no longer as coins' (Nietzsche quoted in

Cooper 1999: 186). Nietzsche is thus effectively endorsing the coherence/consensus theory of truth as a poor substitute for correspondence.

While having accepted, along with such as Appleby, Hunt and Jacob, the ultimate epistemological inadequacy of history's mimetic methodology (that makes correspondence between description and reality impossible), the deep desire for matching the word with the world, as pragmatic philosophers such as Richard **Rorty** has noted, nevertheless still remains potent (Rorty 1991: 32–3). Moreover, the mimetic or weak process of representational correspondence demands a number of associated beliefs that, paradoxically, tend to be cast as absolutes. Flowing from its realist inspiration and its particular belief in the status of facts, professional mimetic history tends to manifest its truth-claiming status in the deliberate avoidance of trope/figuration in favour of an ethnographic or referential style of **narrative**. Ironically empiricists incline to a neo-Nietzschean position here, not that truth is metaphor, but that too many metaphors must be injurious to truth, hence the necessity for referential transparency in language. Another disciplinary consequence is the denial of the anarchic, unfixed and unfixable nature of reality – the sublime – in favour of the 'common-sense' need to control the past, which is achievable by the accurate representation of *the* reality of the event. This realist inclination is summarised in the profession's insistence on the priority of content over form (see FORM AND CONTENT). Various other separations like those of fact and fiction, history and the present, and observer and observed, are also strenuously asserted. The **linguistic turn** is denied because it challenges all these principles. As the postmodern historian might say, recognising its metal as conventional history's unembossed coinage.

In summary, the acknowledged failings of history as a truth-establishing discipline are balanced by invoking the falsifiability principle, whereby historical interpretations are asserted as provisional propositions (hypotheses) to be falsified in the light of the evidence. When we judge we have reached a point of maximum falsifiability, we are left with a residue that is a description that we believe comes closest to the historical truth. The gap between fact and mind is then at its narrowest. The doubts concerning the possibility of historical truth derive ultimately, of course, from the pervasive condition of Nietzschean-inspired postmodern epistemological scepticism. Doubts exist not only concerning history's mimetic method, but also the adequacy of representational language. The mediatory role of the historical imagination through which the historian chooses to emplot the past as history is also claimed to be a major obstacle to objective knowing and truth (see EMPLOTMENT; Hayden WHITE). This is compounded by cultural relativism because historians can not escape their epistemic or cultural preferences. At present there seems little likelihood of a *rapprochement* between the sceptics (and relativists) and the supporters of weak correspondence.

Further reading

Alcoff, L.M. (1998)
Allen, B. (1998)
—— (1993)
Appleby, J. *et al.* (1994)
Audi, R. (1998)
Carr. D. (1986a)
Carr. E.H. (1987 [1961])
Cooper, D.E. (1999)
Davidson, D. (1984)
Dummett, M. (1978)
Evans, R.J. (1997a)
—— (1997b)
Horwich, P. (1990)
Jenkins, K. (1991)
Kirkham, R. (1995)
Luntley, M. (1995)
McCullagh, C.B. (1998)
—— (1984)
Putnam, H. (1981)
Quine, W.V. (1990)
Rabinow, P. (1999)
Rorty, R. (1998)
—— (1991)
Stanford, M. (1998)
White, H. (1998)
—— (1992)

V

VICO, GIAMBATTISTA (1668–1744)

Giambattista Vico, now widely regarded as the first of the truly self-reflexive modernist (see MODERNISM) philosophers of history, was for much of his career employed as a teacher of rhetoric at the University of Naples. His principal work was the *New Science*, first published in 1725 and then, after a 1730 edition, emerging in its final form in 1744. Vico is a significant historical thinker primarily because of two key ideas: his anti-Cartesian, anti-**Enlightenment** and, as it turned out, anti-positivist (see EMPIRICISM) principle of *verum ipsum factum* – that which is true is that which is made (as opposed to discovered in nature), and his translation of this metahistorical principle that, when modelled on the life-cycle of human beings, was turned into a stage theory of history (see CONSTRUCTIONIST HISTORY). His core notion that confidence in what we know can ultimately only be derived from what we ourselves create means that historians are also a part of history when we write the-past-as-history (see R.G. COLLINGWOOD; Benedetto CROCE; EPISTEMOLOGY; G.W.F. HEGEL; Friedrich NIETZSCHE; Hayden WHITE). As the first modernist philosopher of history Vico anticipated at least one strand of **historicism**, that to understand the past the historian has to get inside the minds and linguistic customs of people in the past. The Vichian paradox in this is that to empathise with the past how can we escape from the concepts (see CONCEPTS IN HISTORY) of the present? Whatever answer we have for that conundrum, empathy for Vico is at least as important in creating historical knowledge as either Enlightenment rational deduction or inductive **inference**.

With his new philosophical method (his empathic new science) Vico tried to answer a basic question that still preoccupies historians: how can we be certain about **truth**? For Vico the closest we get to certainty about the truth of our lives is through the interpretation of our decisions and what we do as human beings (see HERMENEUTICS). Vico claimed such interpretation was possible only through the (empathic historical) study of social customs, events (see EVENT) and, above all, language. This method would allow historians to locate examples of the universal law that governed particular instances or, as he said in his autobiography, to give certainty to the history of languages by reference to the history of things. This Vichian theory of knowledge obliges the historian to understand past cultures in their own terms, and his examination of the history of nations 'proved', at least to Vico's satisfaction, what became his universally applicable stage theory of history.

He reached the conclusion that all nations follow three recurring stages of development, the foundation for which lies in the shared human capacity for the metaphoric construction of reality. This was the universal Vico found and which could lead to the certain understanding by humans of their activities: the power of the human imagination. Hayden White described this special metaphoric apprehension of the world as containing within itself the potential for generating the tropes – metaphor, metonymy, synecdoche – and in Vico's model of history this is the case (White 1973b: 86) (see TROPE/FIGURATION). In the first or metaphoric stage all humans create fantastic myths and gods (*fantasia*). In the second stage human beings exercise our metonymically inspired poetic imaginations creating social institutions based on the concept of the heroic individual. After the age of gods and heroes comes the final epoch of what Vico dismissively calls the barbarity of reflection (rational conceptualisation) by humans as we imagine the world synecdochically. It is this poetically inspired rhythm of gods, heroes and humanity that creates nations and distinctive historical periods (see EPISTEME; Michel FOUCAULT). In the Vichian philosophy of history there is, therefore, no gap between the word (language) and the world (the real). The text and the context are indissoluble and the a priori (see A PRIORI/A POSTERIORI) of the metaphor and the a posteriori of its effects in the real world create the feedback loop that is the-past-as-history.

The universal truth Vico discovered – that of the primitive human aesthetic – is reflected in the story-telling power of **narrative**. A mythic or Homeric wisdom precedes all thought and it is this that constitutes our only avenue to truth. In respect of historical explanation this means a convergence with literary interpretation. This is demanded by what is the historicist idea of examining societies through their own linguistic and cultural expressions, rather than any imposed by the historian. This procedure – viewed as either a historical necessity or an impossibility depending on your point of view – has since been addressed by a variety of thinkers including Johann Herder, Jules Michelet, G.W.F. Hegel, Samuel Taylor Coleridge, Karl Marx, Friedrich Nietzsche, Wilhelm Dilthey, James Joyce, Benedetto Croce, R.G. Collingwood, Michel Foucault and Hayden White. The **historical imagination** itself is the most obvious agency of this human aesthetic power, inasmuch as the factually empirical can only be accessed by the imaginatively inferential (see EMPIRICISM). Re-creating the-past-as-history necessitates imagining the potential connections that are available when writing the historical narrative (see CAUSATION). To see how the historical imagination works requires dissecting the historian's narrative organisation in order to determine how he/she musters his/her metaphors and tropes so as to assign meaning. In so doing we should note Vico's and later Nietzsche's strong insistence that all our concepts are metaphoric (or the other forms of poetic figures) because they are echoes of our primordial imagination.

The influence of Vico has thus been substantial in the thinking of both modern(ist) and postmodern (see POSTMODERNISM) historians. Michel Foucault, for example, assumed in Vichian fashion that historical knowledge issues not just from the philological study and criticism of the **evidence**, but also from our own imaginative creations/social constructions. Foucault's own construction of the epistemic/figurative basis of historical experience is clearly derived from Vico. Foucault took Vico's belief that narrative and trope represent both the sources as well as the connections we imagine between them. The legacy of the Enlightenment, Foucault claims, has been to obscure this reality of the power of the imagination and the cognitive ascendancy of language. The result as Hayden White said was to make unclear 'to science itself an awareness of its own "poetic" nature' (White 1978: 254).

In his search for the correspondence between truth and certainty Vico deserted the Enlightenment in favour of the socially designed nature of knowledge. The un-reflexive and quite un-Vichian modernist (see MODERNISM) judgement that history can be secure because its truths derive from a knowable real world through inductive inference based on the evidence fails, as Vico and later Nietzsche and Foucault argued, to grasp both the frailty of the written form of the-past-as-history-as-text as well as the power of the aboriginal imagination. For historians of a relativist inclination the legacy of Vico is a break with the belief in distanced empiricism (see RELATIVISM). Writing the-past-as-history they take as an opportunity, therefore, to explore the tropic foundation to our understanding of the-past-as-history-as-text. Along with Foucault, Hayden White took up this idea suggesting that the mechanism of writing history operates at the subterranean level of language and human consciousness – the prefigurative act being divined in and through 'the dominant tropological mode in which it is cast' (White 1978: 197). Even if the stated aim for conventional reconstructionist (see RECONSTRUCTIONIST HISTORY) and constructionist (see CONSTRUCTIONIST HISTORY) historians remains the discovery of what actually happened in the past, even then they must first 'prefigure as a possible object of knowledge the whole series of events reported in the documents' (White 1978: 30).

Although followed by such as Wilhelm Dilthey, R.G. Collingwood, Michel Foucault and Hayden White, Vico was the first philosopher of history to accept the sway of the human imagination and its translation into figurative language: the-past-as-history-as-text(ual) product. No amount of hypothesis-testing and being fair and just to the evidence can avoid the fact that our primary tool to negotiate the past is language. The historical narrative is not pure representation; it is not even poor representation. It is instead a whole series of personal deals struck by the historian between his/her powers of expression and imagination and the evidence. Although Vico sought truth in history – a knowable past because we created it – he also understood that historians are not distanced observers (no matter how much they may desire such Olympian objectivity). Although for Vico the aim is still to approach as closely as possible the truth of the past, he reminds us that the historical imagination can not re-make the past with each new imaginative insight. But, as the first of the self-reflexive modernist philosophers of history, the legacy of Vico lies, at least in part, in his understanding that historical analysis should be focused as much on the fabulous, the poetic, the imaginative and the cultural, as it is on the sensible, the referential, the empirical and the factual (see CULTURAL HISTORY). While history may not be the same as poetry it is always the historian's imagination that has primacy in its command and composition of the empirical.

Further reading

Auxier, R.E. (1997)
Berlin, I. (1976)
Collingwood, R.G. (1994 [1946])
Croce, B. (1964 [1913])
Haddock, B.A. (1980)
Mazzotta, G. (1998)
Mooney, M. (1985)
Munslow, A. (1992)
Pompa, L. (1975)
Tagliacozzo, G. and Verene, D.P. (1976)
Tagliacozzo, G. and White, H. (1969)
Vico, G. (1968)
—— (1963)
White, H. (1978)
—— (1973b)

W

WHITE, HAYDEN (1928–)

Hayden White's major contributions to the study of history are to be found in *Metahistory* (1973), and two collections, *Tropics of Discourse* (1978) and *The Content of the Form* (1987). In these texts White addresses the relationship between the **historical imagination**, the historical **narrative** and past lived experience (see EPISTEMOLOGY; ONTOLOGY). White maintains history is as much the product of the historical imagination as discovery in the archive, and it follows history does not correspond to a pre-existing, or given, narrative/story. There is no intrinsic meaning to the past; this is provided by the historian who is him/herself the subject of a variety of cultural, professional and ideological discourses (see DISCOURSE). White is not anti-referentialist, but he does argue that we impose our stories on the past teleologically for a variety of reasons. Among these reasons are, of course, the reconstructionist historian's (see RECONSTRUCTIONIST HISTORY) claim to explain or to understand agent **intentionality** through **inference** from the **evidence**, and the constructionist historian's belief that all history is deeply conceptual and/or theoretical (see CONCEPTS IN HISTORY; COVERING LAWS; CULTURAL HISTORY; POSITIVISM; STRUCTURALISM). But for White there is nothing in the nature of historical study or its empirical (see EMPIRICISM) methodological underpinnings that permits historical narratives to relay *the* past realities of human intentions and beliefs.

For White history is the act of imposing a narrative or **emplotment** of a particular kind on the past. In effect this means our knowledge of the past is derived through an essentially poetic act. Reliant variously on Giambattista **Vico**, Kenneth Burke, Michel **Foucault**, Northrop Frye and Roman Jakobson, as well as a vast body of work on metaphor and **trope/figuration**, White characterises the deep structures of the historical imagination as conforming to the operation of the four major figures of speech: metaphor, metonymy, synecdoche and irony (all different ways whereby our minds make the connections we 'see' between parts and wholes). It is through this capacity, rather than the evidence (for this capacity determines our selection of evidence), that history is ultimately made. So the history we end up with, in all its varieties and revisions (strictly speaking we should talk of its re-visions), is the result of the aesthetic choices and prefigurations of the historian as well as his/her readership. In White's vision of history the four tropic orientations both determine and emerge in a complex superstructure of strategies of explanation that take the form of four emplotment types (Tragedy, Comedy, Romance and Satire), four modes of argument (Formist, Mechanist, Organicist and Contextualist), and their four respective ideological implications. (Anarchist, Radical, Conservative and Liberal).

Given this model and the logic behind it, White insists history can never provide *the* story, rather it is *a* narrative designed by the historian as he/she organises the contents in the form of a narrative of what he/she believes the past was about (see FORM AND CONTENT). As White says:

> Historical situations are not *inherently* tragic, comic, or romantic. . . . All the historian needs to do to transform a tragic into a comic situation is to shift his point of view or change the scope of his perceptions. Anyway, we only think of situations as tragic or comic because these concepts are part of our generally cultural and specifically literary heritage. *How* a given historical situation is to be configured depends on the historian's subtlety in matching up a specific plot structure with the set of historical events that he wishes to endow with a meaning of a particular kind.
>
> (White 1978: 85)

This vision of how the historical mind works rethinks many of history's traditional dualities. White is effectively reversing the relationships of content and form, ideology and trope, and empiricism and figurative style, while problematising the connections between the world and the word, the knower and the known, fact (see FACTS) and fiction, past and present, **truth** and interpretation, and history and narrative. The upshot is that White is concerned less with the reality of the past characterised and accessed primarily as an empirical undertaking, but instead as the composed narrative of the historian – creating what French cultural critic Roland **Barthes** calls the effect of reality (see REALITY/REALISTIC EFFECT). Although White's model does not, of course, disavow the study of the content of the past, it does require us to think about history not only for what it most patently is, a pre-configured narrative, but also consider the broader epistemological and ontological implications this has for our definition of what history is, and what it is that historians do.

Further reading

(1980) 'Metahistory: Six critiques', *History and Theory* (themed issue) 19
Ankersmit, F.R. (1994)

Carroll, D. (1976)
Chartier, R. (1997)
Fay, B., Pomper, P. and Vann, R.T. (1998)
Jameson, F. (1976)
Jenkins, K. (1998a)
—— (1995)
Kansteiner, W. (1993)
Munslow, A. (1992)
Roth, M.S. (1995)
Roth, P.A. (1992)
Vann, R.T. (1998)
White, H. (1998)
—— (1996)
—— (1995)
—— (1992)
—— (1987)
—— (1984)
—— (1978)
—— (1974)
—— (1973a)
—— (1973b)

WOMEN'S HISTORY

According to the postmodern (see POSTMODERNISM) women's history historian Joan Wallach Scott, writing in the late 1980s, women's history was then on the brink of producing a thoroughgoing reconceptualisation of historical practice (Scott 1988: 4) (see STRUCTURALISM). Scott's post-structuralist position is that language is the medium for the establishment of gender relationships and knowledge about women in the past and the present. For her at that time the direction of women's history was going to make it the vanguard of, although she does not use the description, a new kind of postmodernist history. Almost a decade later Scott had quite clearly shifted her emphasis to the problematic nature of women's history, which had become ever more sophisticated, theoreticised and complex (Scott 1996b). In 1991 she published a brief analysis of how women's history had developed up to then and, as an 'interim report', it reveals her moving away from her earlier claims for a new historical **epistemology** (in the wake of the work of Judith Butler), toward a toned-down and rather more restrained emphasis on the socially constituted nature of gender. This shift back in the direction of knowledge from knowable experience may also be taken as something of a commentary on the failure of postmodern (specifically post-structuralist) developments to penetrate historical criticism more generally.

In her 1991 interim survey Scott described what she took to be the conventional narrative of women's history. This held that the political dissent of the 1960s (initially in the USA) generated a desire for the recovery of women from history (creating 'herstory'). Feminism needed to provide role models or heroines for the purposes of post-1968 politics. Then, sometime in the 1970s, the link between academic 'herstory' and political radicalism was almost severed as a new field emerged within the academy – women's history. In the 1980s women's history transmuted again with a turn toward gender. At this point the academic and political worlds finally broke contact. The term gender seemed to suggest a new horizon of neutral and non-political history dealing with broad issues of the history of sexuality. So we have an evolution in three decades from political feminism, to women's history, to gender and, regrettably in Scott's opinion, a congruent de-politicisation of the academic study of the feminine (Scott 1991: 42–3).

However, Scott argues this narrative of women's history is too simplistic. The real history of women's history can only be understood as a much more complex series of parallel developments involving feminist political radicalism, women's history as a historical field, but most importantly in the growing epistemological challenges over those three decades to the discipline of history itself. Scott claimed many who were researching and writing gender history in 1991 overtly acknowledged an intellectual (theoretical) as well as an ideological (political) allegiance to feminism of some sort or another. The type of feminism endorsed carried with it theoretical and political baggage. This meant history, more broadly construed, did also. For her, Scott's feminism required a postmodernist theoretical orientation derived from Jacques **Derrida**'s deconstructionist notion of the disruptive sign. There are some words/concepts that defy signification because they carry culturally contradictory meanings. The idea of women as a 'supplement' to history falls into this category of contradictory signifiers – the idea of a supplement means both an addition to and, as Scott pointed out, a substitute for what pre-exists. Scott maintained this led to an irresolvable tension in women's history and it might suggest a devastating effect on the nature of history itself.

No doubt including women in history forced historians to confront not just what has hitherto been missing in history by adding women and women's experience, but this move must entail the second meaning of supplement, a substitution for what presently exists. The question has become, therefore, what is there in women's history and the rethinking behind it that carries with it the power to replace 'proper' history? Proper history is at one level, obviously, history without women, but what does women's history bring to the discipline in epistemological terms? Does it entail a new way of historical knowing? Is there something in conventional Western reasoning that makes it a male sort of thinking? If there is, how can we reconfigure it? What are those special structuring principles in women's history that are presently missing from history ('his-story')? It was (is?) clear to Scott that you can't have the first kind of supplement without the second. Bringing women (defined implicitly as the other) into history involves rethinking a discipline founded on a binarism that implicitly defines itself as a male **discourse** – the historian's Self as Male defined as such because it is in opposition to the other, which is Female (or a whole string of possible others: non-white, proletarian, non-Western, etc.).

The exclusion of women was an essential move because they clearly represented the other – the absence of which confirmed Man's own peculiar sense of himself (defined in his difference to the other). If women were to be embraced(!) in these male-dominant discourses the price would be a literal assimilation. Women would be necessarily and henceforth judged in male terms. They might become equal but they would be surrogate men. The **modernism** that ushered in the **Enlightenment** had at its centre a white, Western European, bourgeois, educated, property-owning, heterosexual male knowing subject (see LIBERAL HUMANISM). The double-bind that emerged subsequently in the nineteenth century was that if women were to be incorporated they must become white, Western European, bourgeois, educated, property-owning, heterosexual females. The sense of gender difference (like that of **class**) would disappear only through the process of assimilation.

While eventually rejecting much in his theory of language, the basis of post-structuralist history is Ferdinand de Saussure's structuralist notion that all meaning carried by language is derived instrumentally through arbitrary binary opposition. Exploring this logic Michel **Foucault** and Jacques Derrida argued that knowledge is created and constituted through our human understanding of difference and similarity within a power-laden cultural context. Central to their position is the way in which meanings are derived through the human sense of differentiation and contrast as translated culturally into institutions, theories, epistemologies and practices of opposition, dominance, subordinance and hierarchy. If traditional history was male-dominant (translated as a form of history that demanded polarities built on the master binary of subject–object, like truth–falsity, subjectivity–objectivity, imagination–reality and fiction–truth-conditional representation) then, presumably, through the introduction of woman as both the historian and subject matter (the content of the past), we might reasonably expect history would confront its traditional empiricist-based construction (see EMPIRICISM; FORM AND CONTENT). Furthermore, ought we not expect this to be achieved by post-structuralist feminists/women's history historians not only as they addressed the language of male dominance, but more significantly as they problematised the very notion of a knowable women's historical experience?

The heart of the epistemological challenge to proper history posed by women's history converges, therefore, on the conceptualisation of difference construed and constituted through the cultural construction of meaning and knowledge, and the power of language (see CULTURAL HISTORY; ONTOLOGY). Can knowledge and its creation be distinguished by means of a male/female duality? Exploring this difference has become the focal point of women's history. It follows we must ask if there a sexualised epistemology. So-called post-structuralist feminism argues the pursuit of equality is a modernist dead-end unless women want to be like men. If not, women should establish a peculiarly feminine way of looking at, and dealing with, the world in linguistic and epistemological terms.

In claiming equality, by dint of being a rational Enlightenment animal, liberal feminists since Mary Wollstonecraft have, in effect, argued in favour of the proposition that men and women are intellectually undifferentiated – for historians this translates (axiomatically?) into the foundational and working principle that there is only one way to create historical knowledge and that means a non-gendered way of thinking about history. But is this not just a cover for a male way of doing history? Recent adherents of a radical feminism, like Toril Moi, have argued against this universalising tendency of Western philosophy, arguing specifically against its dualistic mode of thought, specifically of binary oppositions that not only formed the basis of structuralism but all Western philosophy. The argument is put that women are marginalised precisely because of the binary form of such philosophy that requires one term to be always dominant (male, bourgeois, white, metropolitan, colonial) and the other subordinate (female, non-white, parochial, colonised). Reversing the hierarchy is necessary (in ideological, political and ethical terms) but is usually far from sufficient to correct the situation. So a feminist epistemology or, what has become increasingly popular, a deconstructionist (feminist) history (see DECONSTRUCTIONIST HISTORY) was conjured. This was an intellectual act that politics demanded of the academy.

Unavoidably, so the post-structuralist feminist argument runs, through convention the sexual hierarchy has become associated with male dominance. In philosophical terms this becomes the dominance and superiority of **objectivity** (male) over subjectivity (female), and reason (male) over emotion (female). This is important because maleness associated with reason is reified by social and cultural institutions, and becomes dominant, as Luce Irigaray claims, by a language that is masculinised. So it is that traditional (i.e. male) epistemology conspires to sustain a gendered framework of inequality by its dualistic nature. The debate over a feminist epistemology is thus an integral part of the debate over the nature of epistemology and, it follows, history as an epistemology.

Women's history (along with race and class histories) has posed the epistemological question for whom, from what perspective, and for what purposes do we write and constitute the practices and methods of history? Our answer to that question quite evidently generates particular epistemological expectations. If I assume the thinking historian normally occupies a disinterested position outside history, an epistemologist seeking the truth about people in the past as they made rational decisions as free agents, I end up with an idealised objectivist and empiricist epistemology (see INTENTIONALITY; FACTS). Feminist epistemologists of a practical realist or **constructionist history** persuasion, however, do not accept that picture. They assume that the historian is not value-neutral and can not produce an objective history. Rather, it is awash with unstated masculine bias. But, through a better informed feminist empiricist perspective (empiricism is, for them, still the only game in town), historians can yield ever more truthful (through a necessarily feminised) knowledge. Their informed empiricism will correct history's patriarchal squint.

The British feminist empiricist historian Catherine Hall exemplifies this position. As a sophisticated constructionist history realist she acknowledges that historians construct stories (feminist historians by their personal inclination will create feminist stories), but such story-writing does not take her into agreement with the post-structuralist position that all history must be essentially fictive (Hall 1992: 1). Hall argues that the dynamic of her feminist history consists of constructed stories, but her stories are grounded in the **evidence** as found through laborious archival work, and which are guided by appropriate conceptual frameworks. Writing at the same time that Scott wrote her interim report, Hall offered her own narrative of the development of women's history. She described British feminist history as profoundly empiricist in methodology and cross-hatched theoretically by Marxism. Hall accepts that postmodern (specifically post-structuralist) approaches have tested this gender–class theoretical framework, not least through the argument that the meaning of gender is socially constructed. This, Hall claims, required exploring the different class (and in post-colonial Britain race) experiences of women. The upshot has been her recognition that the 'differences between men and women' are established by 'discursively constructing "the other" ' (Hall 1992: 13) – but still ultimately grounded in women's experience of the real world, which is then translated faithfully by the historian (Burkitt 1998).

Feminist empiricists, like sophisticated empiricists everywhere, believe in access to knowable truths. Post-empiricist feminists such as Scott, Judith Butler and Elizabeth Deeds Ermarth argue that empiricism – even feminist empiricism – is no guarantor of truthful interpretations. Scott's position seems to be that past experience must be understood primarily through (and thereby defined by) language, and agency has a very limited compass because women are determined by social situation and male dominance, and such residual agency that exists is derived through discourse. Hence experience is discursively constructed. Postmodern women's history historians, especially those inspired by Derrida like Scott, can apparently find no anchor in knowable realism that permits circumvention of our categories, theories or discourses. Equally, there can not be any while the gold standard for historical knowledge is founded on the Western philosophical male/female binary. But the problem for feminist historians like Scott is how to generate a feminist epistemology that is not grounded or fixed in women's historical and material circumstances or, if like Hall their preference takes them in the opposite direction, one that is. While Scott is keen to argue that the very concept of experience has been rendered problematic, she nevertheless (by the mid-1990s) has fallen back to the (untenable?) idea that a sophisticated postmodern theorising can make the reality of social structures accessible. While she makes room for non-essentialised meanings and tries to incorporate the feminine unconscious and welcomes recognition of the partiality of the subject–subject relationship, she draws back from the abyss that history can not know reality, and all we have is that surrogate for the past we call history.

What the practitioners of women's history have done in the past thirty years, however, is to raise within the mainstream of historical thinking the 'problem of history', namely, is historical knowing of one kind or one piece? Can we view historians as disembodied and disinterested people who simply convert information into truthful interpretations through the discovery of facts? Women's history has confronted (and replaced?) the historian-as-observer with the historian-as-player, the historian as an **author** caught in a variety of competing discourses. Is it now always a matter of 'whose history' are we writing? Presumably, once knowledge production is situated within a gendered framework, objectivity also has to be acknowledged as being socially constructed?

The enhanced constructionist sophistication that women's history has brought to the profession has not changed the fact that the majority of feminists and women's history practitioners have, as I have already suggested, stayed loyal to their materialist or other culturalist ideological preferences. They were (and remain) unconvinced that any kind of deconstructionist history offers either a better way to study women and gender, or that there is a need to fundamentally alter the conventional reconstructionist, or (their preferred) constructionist, variety of history. For many leftist feminists postmodernism is a non-empirical distraction from the harsh realities of women's changing historical experience, the evidence of which provides the bedrock of facts upon which presentist political manifestos can be built and action taken.

What this indicates to me is that neither feminist empiricists nor some post-structuralists have come to terms with the fact that history is not a truth-acquiring discipline. Both groups accept that it is important to recognise that categories like women and gender are socially constituted and are not reliable transcriptions of past reality. This undoubtedly empowers women's history historians to offer a feminist critique of much social science theory that fails to recognise the polyvalent nature of the meanings of their categories. This allows both groups to reflect upon the gendered representation of women in historical evidence and the situated knowledge that derives therefrom. To explore if there is a different feminist epistemology is also important, but it often resolves itself into a debate over which kinds of historian have the truest experiential insight. In spite of these insights, to fall back on the foundationalism of an ultimately knowable experience is, I suggest, to make the assumption that gender is a social construction that must and will ultimately be decoded through **inference** from the evidence of experience. The aim of much women's history, even from Scott's post-structuralist perspective, still seems to be to control and domesticate the sublime.

Anti-foundational post-empiricism, cast as a feminist epistemology, is not pursued by Scott and it is not accepted by feminist historians of a more conventional historiographical and epistemological orientation. Some hardened empiricists writing in the late 1990s like Jean Curthoys reject the very notion that the problem inheres in the binarism of Western philosophy, while others like Penelope J. Corfield who, like Hall, continues to acknowledge the richness of the gender history produced by the postmodern discussion of difference, denies that the intellectual landscape of the discipline has been transformed or, indeed, rethought (Corfield 1997: 244–5). For Corfield postmodernism is unlikely to effect a radical change in historical methodology because, as she puts it, not everyone accepts the postmodern neo-idealist notion that reality can not exist outside the text, and just as importantly debates over the existence of a genuine feminist epistemology remain inconclusive (Corfield 1997: 253).

Further reading

Alcoff, L.M. (1998)
Alcoff, L.M. and Potter, E. (1993)
Antony, L.M. and Witt, C. (1993)
Baker, M. (1998)
Bock, G. (1991)
—— (1989)
Bordo, S. (1987)
Burkitt, I. (1998)
Butler, J. (1990)
Carroll, B.A. (1976)
Code, L. (1991)
Corfield, P.J. (1997)
Curthoys, J. (1997)
Davis, N.Z. (1976)
Degler, C.N. (1975)
Duran, J. (1997)
Ermarth, E.D. (1992)
Haraway, D. (1991)
—— (1988)
Hoff-Wilson, J. and Farnham, C. (1990)
Irigaray, L. (1992)
Kerber, L.K. (1988)
Laslett, B. *et al.* (1997)
Le Doeuff, M. (1989)
Lloyd, G. (1984)
Longino, H.E. (1990)
Moi, T. (1988)
Nelson, L.H. (1990)
NeSmith, G. (website: n.d.)
Offen, K. *et al.* (1991)
Perrot, M. (1992)
Poovey, M. (1988)
Rendall, J. (1991)
Riley, D. (1989)
Rothenburg, P.S. (1998)
Rowbotham, S. (1974)
Schmitt F. (1994)
Scott, J.W. (1996a)
—— (1996b)

—— (1991)
—— (1989)
—— (1988)
—— (1986)
—— (1983)
Shoemaker, R. and Vincent, M. (1998)
Smith-Rosenberg, C. (1985)
Williams, C.D. (1997)

BIBLIOGRAPHY

(1980) 'Metahistory: Six critiques', *History and Theory* (themed issue) 19.

Achinstein, P. (1983) *The Nature of Explanation*, New York: Oxford University Press.

Adorno, Theodor (1983 [1966]) *Negative Dialectics*, New York: Continuum.

Alcoff, Linda Martin (ed.) (1998) *Epistemology: The Big Questions*, Oxford: Basil Blackwell.

Alcoff, Linda Martin and Potter, Elizabeth (eds) (1993) *Feminist Epistemologies*, New York: Routledge.

Allen, Barry (1998) 'Truthfulness', *Common Knowledge* 7: 19–26.

—— (1993) *Truth in Philosophy*, Cambridge, MA: Harvard University Press.

Althusser, Louis (1971) *Lenin and Philosophy and Other Essays*, trans. Ben Brewster, London: New Left Books.

American Historical Association (1995) *Guide to Historical Literature*, New York: Oxford University Press.

Ankersmit, F.R. (1994) *History and Tropology: The Rise and Fall of Metaphor*, Berkeley: University of California Press.

—— (1989) 'Historiography and postmodernism', *History and Theory* 28: 137–53.

—— (1983) *Narrative Logic: A Semantic Analysis of the Historian's Language*, Martinus Nijhoff: The Hague.

Ankersmit, F.R. and Kellner, Hans (eds) (1995) *A New Philosophy of History*, Chicago: University of Chicago Press.

Ansell-Pearson, Keith (1994a) *Nietzsche and Modern German Thought*, London: Routledge.

—— (ed.) (1994b) *Nietzsche: On the Genealogy of Morality*, Cambridge: Cambridge University Press.

Antony, Louise, M. and Witt, Charlotte (eds) (1993) *A Mind of One's*

Own: Feminist Essays on Reason and Objectivity, Boulder, CO: Westview Press.

Appleby, Joyce, *et al.* (eds) (1996) *Knowledge and Postmodernism in Historical Perspective*, London: Routledge.

Appleby, Joyce, Hunt, Lynn and Jacob, Margaret (1994) *Telling the Truth About History*, New York: Norton.

Atkinson, R.F. (1978) *Knowledge and Explanation in History*, London: Macmillan.

Attridge, Derek, Bennington, Geoffrey and Young, Robert (eds) (1987) *Post-Structuralism and the Question of History*, Cambridge: Cambridge University Press.

Audi, Robert (1998) *Epistemology: A Contemporary Introduction to the Theory of Knowledge*, New York: Routledge.

Auxier, Randall E. (1997) 'Imagination and historical knowledge in Vico: A critique of Leon Pompa's recent work', *Humanitas* X.

Baker, Mary (1998) 'Feminist post-structuralist engagements with history', *Rethinking History: The Journal of Theory and Practice* 2: 371–8.

Bann, Stephen (1984) *The Clothing of Clio: A Study of the Representation of History in Nineteenth Century Britain and France*, Cambridge: Cambridge University Press.

—— (1983) 'Analysing the discourse of history', *Renaissance and Modern Studies* 27: 61–84.

—— (1981) *Comparative Criticism – A Yearbook*, vol. 3, University Park, PA: The Pennsylvania University Press.

Barnard, F.M. (1981) 'Accounting for actions: Causality and teleology', *History and Theory* 20: 291–312.

Barthes, Roland (1988) *The Semiotic Challenge*, New York: Hill & Wang.

—— (1986) *The Rustle of Language*, Oxford: Basil Blackwell.

—— (1984 [1967]) *Elements of Semiology*, London: Jonathan Cape.

—— (1983) *Empire of Signs*, trans. Richard Howard, London: Jonathan Cape.

—— (1981 [1967]) 'Le Discours de l'histoire', *Information sur les Sciences Sociales* 6: 65–75; trans. with an introduction by Stephen Bann (1981) *Comparative Criticism – A Yearbook.*

—— (1977) *Image-Music-Text*, trans. Stephen Heath, London: Fontana.

—— (1975) *The Pleasure of the Text*, trans. Richard Miller, London: Jonathan Cape.

—— (1974) *S/Z*, trans. Richard Miller, New York: Hill & Wang.

—— (1972) *Critical Essays*, trans. Richard Howard, Illinois: Northwestern University Press.

—— (1967) *Writing Degree Zero*, trans. Annette Lavers and Colin Smith, London: Jonathan Cape.

—— (1957) *Mythologies*, London: Pan Books.

Baudrillard, Jean (1983) *Simulations*, trans. Paul Fosse, Paul Patton and Philip Beitchman, New York: Semiotext(e).

—— (1976) *Symbolic Exchange and Death*, Paris: Gallimard.

Bauman, Zygmunt (1998) *Globalisation: The Human Consequences*, New York: New York University Press.

—— (1997) *Postmodernity and its Discontents*, New York: New York University Press.

Baynes, K., Bohman, J. and McCarthy, T. (eds) (1987) *After Philosophy: End or Transformation*, Cambridge, MA: MIT Press.

Beard, Charles (1935) 'That noble dream', *American Historical Review* 41: 74–87.

—— (1933) 'Written history as an act of faith', *American Historical Review* 39: 219–31.

Beck, Lewis White (ed.) (1963) *Immanuel Kant: On History*, Indianapolis: Bobbs-Merrill Co.

Becker, Carl (1931) 'Everyman his own historian', *American Historical Review* 37: 221–36.

Beiser, Frederick C. (ed.) (1993) *The Cambridge Companion to Hegel*, Cambridge: Cambridge University Press.

Belchem, John and Kirk, Neville (eds) (1997) *Languages of Labour*, Aldershot: Ashgate Publishing.

Bennett, Tony (1990) *Outside Literature*, London: Routledge.

Bennington, G. (1993) *Jacques Derrida*, Chicago: University of Chicago Press.

Bentley, Michael (ed.) (1997) *Companion to Historiography*, London: Routledge.

Benveniste, Emile (1971) *Problems in General Linguistics*, Miami: Miami University Press.

Berkhofer, Robert F. (1995) *Beyond the Great Story: History as Text and Discourse*, Princeton: Princeton University Press.

Berlin, Isaiah (1997) *The Sense of Reality*, New York: Farrar, Straus & Giroux.

—— (1976) *Vico and Herder: Two Studies in the History of Ideas*, London: Hogarth Press.

Bernauer, James and Keenan, Thomas (1988) 'The works of Michel Foucault, 1954–1984', in James Bernauer and David Rasmussen (eds) *The Final Foucault*, Cambridge, MA: MIT Press.

Bernstein, R. (1983) *Beyond Objectivism and Relativism*, Philadelphia, PA: The University of Pennsylvania Press.

Bertens, Hans (1995) *The Idea of the Postmodern: A History*, London: Routledge.

Bevir, Mark (1994) 'Objectivity in history', *History and Theory* 33: 328–44.

Bhaskar, R. (1991) *Philosophy and the Idea of Freedom*, Oxford: Basil Blackwell.

Bloch, Marc (1954) *The Historian's Craft*, Manchester: Manchester University Press.

Bloomfield, M.W. (ed.) (1972) *In Search of Literary Theory*, Ithaca: Cornell University Press.

Boch, Gisela (1991) 'Challenging dichotomies: Perspectives on women's history', in Karin Offen, Ruth Roach Pierson and Jane Rendall (eds) *Writing Women's History: International Perspectives*, pp. 45–58.

—— (1989) 'Women's history and gender history: Aspects of an international debate', *Gender and History* 1: 7–30.

Bonjour, L. (1985) *The Structure of Empirical Knowledge*, Cambridge, MA: Harvard University Press.

Bordo, Susan (1987) *The Flight to Objectivity: The Cartesian Masculinization of Culture*, Albany, NY: State University of New York Press.

Bouchard, Donald F. (ed.) (1977) *Language, Counter Memory, Practice: Selected Essays and Interviews*, trans. Donald F. Bouchard and Sherry Simon, Ithaca: Cornell University Press.

Branstead, E.K. and Meluish, K.J. (eds) (1978) *Western Liberalism: A History in Documents: From Locke to Croce*, London: Longman.

Braudel, Fernand (1980) *On History*, London: Weidenfeld & Nicolson.

Breisach, Ernst (1983) *Historiography: Ancient, Medieval and Modern*, Chicago: University of Chicago Press.

Brody, David (1979) 'The old labor history and the new: In search of an American working class', *Labor History* 20: 111–26.

Brown, Merle Elliott (1966) *Neo-Idealistic Aesthetics: Croce, Gentile, Collingwood*, Detroit: Wayne State University Press.

Bullock, Alan (1985) *The Humanist Tradition in the West*, London: Thames & Hudson.

Bunzl, Martin (1997) *Real History*, London: Routledge.

Burckhardt, Jacob (1990 [1860]) *The Civilization of the Renaissance in Italy*, ed. Peter Burke, London: Penguin.

Burke, Peter (1997) *Varieties of Cultural History*, Oxford: Polity Press.

—— (1993) *History and Social Theory*, Ithaca: Cornell University Press.

—— (ed.) (1991) *New Perspectives on Historical Writing*, University Park, PA: The Pennsylvania University Press.

—— (1989) 'History as social memory', in Thomas Butler (ed.) *Memory, History, Culture and the Mind*, pp. 97–113.

Burke, Sean (1992) *The Death and Return of the Author: Criticism and Subjectivity in Barthes, Foucault and Derrida*, Edinburgh: Edinburgh University Press.

Burkitt, Ian (1998) 'Sexuality and gender identity: From a discursive to a relational analysis', *The Sociological Review* 46: 483–504.

Butler, Judith (1990) *Gender Trouble: Feminism and the Subversion of Identity*, London: Routledge.

Butler, Thomas (ed.) (1989) *Memory, History, Culture and the Mind*, Oxford: Basil Blackwell.

Callinicos, Alex (1995) *Theories and Narratives: Reflections on the Philosophy of History*, Cambridge: Polity Press.

Calvet, Louis-Jean (1994) *Roland Barthes: A Biography*, trans. Sarah Wykes, Cambridge: Polity Press.

Cameron, Averil (1989) *History as Text: The Writing of Ancient History*, London: Duckworth.

Canary, R. and Kozicki, H. (eds) (1978) *The Writing of History: Literary Form and Historical Understanding*, Madison: University of Wisconsin Press.

Cannon, John, Davies, R.H.C., Doyle, William and Greene, Jack P. (eds) (1988) *The Blackwell Dictionary of Historians*, Oxford: Basil Blackwell.

Caputo, John D. (1997) *Deconstruction in a Nutshell*, New York: Fordham University Press.

Carr, D. (1986a) 'Narrative and the real world: An argument for continuity', *History and Theory* 25: 117–31.

—— (1986b) *Time, Narrative and History*, Bloomington, IN: Indiana University Press.

Carr, E.H. (1987 [1961]) *What is History?*, London: Penguin.

—— (1958–64) *Socialism in One Country, 1924–1926*, Harmondsworth: Penguin.

—— (1950–3) *The Bolshevik Revolution, 1917–1923*, 3 vols, London: Macmillan.

Carrard, Philippe (1992) *Poetics of the New History*, Baltimore: The Johns Hopkins University Press.

Carrier, M. and Machamer, P. (eds) (1997) *Mindscapes: Philosophy, Science, and the Mind*, Pittsburgh: Pittsburgh University Press.

Carroll, Berenice A. (ed.) (1976) *Liberating Women's History: Theoretical And Critical Essays*, Urbana, IL: University of Illinois Press.

Carroll, David (1976) 'On tropology: The forms of history', *Diacritics* 6: 58–64.

Carroll, John (1993) *Humanism*, London: Fontana.

Cassirer, E. (1981) *Kant's Life and Thought*, New Haven, CT: Yale University Press.

Caws, Peter (1997) *Structuralism: A Philosophy for the Human Sciences*, Contemporary Studies in Philosophy and the Human Sciences, Atlantic Highlands, NJ: Humanities Press.

Chartier, Roger (1997) *On the Edge of the Cliff: History, Language and Practice*, Baltimore: The Johns Hopkins University Press.

—— (1988) *Cultural History: Between Practices and Representations*, Cambridge: Cambridge University Press.

—— (1987) *The Cultural Uses of Print in Early Modern France*, trans. Lydia G. Cochrane, Princeton: Princeton University Press.

Cockburn, David (1997) *Other Times: Philosophical Perspectives on Past, Present and Future*, Cambridge: Cambridge University Press.

Code, L. (1991) *What Can She Know? Feminist Theory and the Construction of Knowledge*, Ithaca: Cornell University Press.

Collingwood, R.G. (1994 [1946]) *The Idea of History*, rev. edn, ed. Jan van der Dussen, Oxford: Oxford University Press.

—— (1940) *An Essay on Metaphysics*, Oxford: Clarendon Press.

Connor, Steven (1989) *Postmodernist Culture: An Introduction to Theories of the Postmodern*, Oxford: Basil Blackwell.

Cooper, David. E. (ed.) (1999) *Epistemology: The Classic Readings*, Oxford: Basil Blackwell.

Corfield, Penelope J. (1997) 'History and the challenge of gender history', *Rethinking History: The Journal of Theory and Practice* 1: 241–58.

Cox, C.B. (1963) *The Free Spirit: A Study of Liberal Humanism in the Novels of George Eliot, Henry James, E.M. Forster, Virginia Woolf, Angus Wilson*, Oxford: Oxford University Press.

Critchley, Simon (1996) 'Deconstruction and pragmatism – Is Derrida a private ironist or a public liberal?', in C. Mouffe (ed.) *Deconstruction and Pragmatism*, pp. 19–40.

Croce, Benedetto (1970 [1927]) *An Autobiography*, Freeport, NY: Books for Libraries Press.

—— (1968 [1917]) *The Theory and History of Historiography*, Geneva: Droz.

—— (1964 [1913]) *The Philosophy of Giambattista Vico*, trans. R.G. Collingwood, New York: Russell & Russell.

—— (1923) *History: Its Theory and Practice*, trans. Douglas Ainslie, New York: Harcourt & Brace.

Culler, Jonathan (1983) *Barthes*, London: Fontana.

—— (1982) *On Deconstruction: Theory and Criticism after Structuralism*, Ithaca: Cornell University Press.

Curthoys, Ann and Docker, John (1997) 'The two histories: Metaphor in English historiographical writing', *Rethinking History: The Journal of Theory and Practice* 1: 259–74.

Curthoys, Jean (1997) *Feminist Amnesia: The Wake of Women's Liberation*, London: Routledge.

—— (1996) 'Is history fiction?', *The UTS Review* 2: 12–37.

Dant, Tim (1991) *Knowledge, Ideology and Discourse*, London: Routledge.

Danto, Arthur (1998) 'Danto and his critics: Art history, historiography and after the end of art', *History and Theory* (themed issue) 37: 1–143.

—— (1997) *After the End of Art: Contemporary Art and the Pale of History*, Princeton: Princeton University Press.

—— (1985) *Narration and Knowledge*, New York: Columbia University Press.

—— (1981) *The Transfiguration of the Commonplace*, Cambridge, MA: Harvard University Press.

—— (1968a) *Analytical Philosophy of Knowledge*, Cambridge: Cambridge University Press.

—— (1968b) *Analytical Philosophy of History*, Cambridge: Cambridge University Press.

—— (1965) *Nietzsche as Philosopher*, New York: Macmillan.

Darnton, Robert (1986) *Mesmerism and the End of the Enlightenment in France*, Cambridge, MA: Harvard University Press.

—— (1980) 'Intellectual and cultural history', in Michael Kammen (ed.) *The Past before Us: Contemporary Historical Writing in the United States*, pp. 327–54.

Davidson, Donald (1984) *Inquiries into Truth and Interpretation*, Oxford: Oxford University Press.

—— (1980) *Essays on Actions and Events*, Oxford: Oxford University Press.

Davies, Tony (1997) *Humanism*, London: Routledge.

Davis, Natalie Zemon (1987) *Fiction in the Archives: Pardon Tales and Their Tellers in Sixteenth Century France*, Stanford: University of California Press.

—— (1976) ' "Women's history" in transition: The European case', *Feminist Studies* 3: 83–103.

de Man, Paul (1983) *Blindness and Insight*, Minneapolis: University of Minnesota Press.

—— (1972) 'Literary history and literary modernity', in M.W. Bloomfield (ed.) *In Search of Literary Theory.*

Dean, Mitchell (1994) *Critical and Effective Histories: Foucault's Methods and Historical Sociology*, London: Routledge.

de Certeau, Michel (1988 [1975]) *The Writing of History*, trans. Tom Conley, New York: Columbia University Press.

Degler, Carl N. (1975) *Is There A History Of Women?*, Oxford: Clarendon Press.

Deleuze, Gilles and Guattari, Félix (1984 [1972]) *Capitalism and Schizophrenia: Anti-Oedipus*, trans. Robert Hurley, Mark Seem and Helen Lane, London: The Athlone Press.

de Man, Paul (1983) *Blindness and Insight*, Minneapolis: University of Minnesota Press.

—— (1972) 'Literary history and literary modernity', in M.W. Bloomfield (ed.) *In Search of Literary Theory.*

Derrida, Jacques (1982) *Margins of Philosophy*, trans. Alan Bass, Chicago: University of Chicago Press.

—— (1979) *Nietzsche's Styles*, trans. Barbara Harlow, Chicago: University of Chicago Press.

—— (1978) *Writing and Difference*, trans. Alan Bass, Chicago: University of Chicago Press.

—— (1976) *Of Grammatology*, trans. G.C. Spivak, Baltimore: The Johns Hopkins University Press.

Dictionary of Philosophy of Mind, http://www.artsci.wustl.edu/~philos/MindDict/index.html.

Dilthey, Wilhelm (1976) *Selected Writings*, ed. and trans. H.P. Rickman with a Foreword by Isaiah Berlin, Cambridge: Cambridge University Press.

Domanska, Ewa (1998a) *Encounters: Philosophy of History After Postmodernism*, Charlottesville: University Press of Virginia.

—— (1998b) 'Hayden White: Beyond irony', *History and Theory* 37: 173–82.

Donagan, Alan (1962) *The Later Philosophy of R.G. Collingwood*, Oxford: Clarendon Press.

—— (1961 [1952]) 'Explanation in history', in Patrick Gardiner (ed.) *The Nature of Historical Explanation.*

—— (1959) 'Explanation in history', in Patrick Gardiner (ed.) *Theories of History*, pp. 427–43.

Dosse, François (1997) *History of Structuralism*, 2 vols, trans. Deborah Glassman, Minneapolis: University of Minnesota Press.

Dowe, P. (1992) 'An empiricist defence of the causal account of explanation', *International Studies in the Philosophy of Science* 6: 123–8.

Dray, W.H. (1995) *History as Re-Enactment: R.G. Collingwood's Idea of History*, Oxford: Oxford University Press.

—— (1989) *On History and Philosophers of History*, New York: Brill.

—— (1986) Review of *Justifying Historical Descriptions* (1984) by C. Behan McCullagh, in *History and Theory* 25: 331–6.

—— (1980) *Perspectives on History*, Cambridge: Routledge.

—— (1970) 'On the nature and role of narrative in historiography', *History and Theory* 10: 153–71.

—— (ed.) (1966) *Philosophical Analysis and History*, New York: Harper & Row.

—— (1957) *Laws and Explanation in History*, Oxford: Oxford University Press.

Dreyfus, Hubert L. and Rabinow, Paul (1983) *Michel Foucault: Beyond Structuralism and Hermeneutics*, second edn, Brighton: Harvester Press.

Duby, Georges (1993) *The Knight, the Lady, and the Priest*, Chicago: University of Chicago Press.

Dummett, Michael (1978) *Truth and Other Enigmas*, Cambridge, MA: Harvard University Press.

Duran, J. (1997) *Toward A Feminist Epistemology*, Savage, MD: Rowman & Littlefield.

Eagleton, Terry (1983) *Literary Theory*, Oxford: Basil Blackwell.

Ellis, John M. (1989) *Against Deconstruction*, Princeton: Princeton University Press.

Elton, Geoffrey (1991 Routledge edn [1955]) *England Under the Tudors*, London: Methuen.

—— (1991) *Return to Essentials: Some Reflections on the Present State of Historical Study*, Cambridge: Cambridge University Press.

—— (ed.) (1990 [1958]) *The New Cambridge Modern History II: The Reformation, 1520–1559*, Cambridge: Cambridge University Press.

—— (1986) *The Parliament of England, 1559–1581*, Cambridge: Cambridge University Press.

—— (1983) *Which Road to the Past?*, New Haven: Yale University Press.

—— (1973) *Reform and Renewal*, Cambridge: Cambridge University Press.

—— (1972) *Policy and Police*, Cambridge: Cambridge University Press.

—— (1970) *Modern Historians on British History, 1485–1945*, London: Methuen.

—— (1968) *The Future of the Past*, Cambridge: Cambridge University Press.

—— (1967) *The Practice of History*, London: Methuen.

—— (1966) *Reformation Europe, 1517–1559*, New York: Harper & Row.

—— (1960) *The Tudor Constitution: Documents and Commentary*, Cambridge: Cambridge University Press.

—— (1953) *The Tudor Revolution*, Cambridge: Cambridge University Press.

Ermarth, Elizabeth Deeds (1992) *Sequel to History: Postmodernism and the Crisis of Historical Time*, Princeton: Princeton University Press.

Evans, Richard J. (1997a) *In Defence of History*, London: Granta.

—— (1997b) 'Truth lost in vain views', *Times Higher*, 12 September, p. 18,

Fackenheim, Emil (1956/57) 'Kant's concept of history', *Kant Studien* XLVIII: 381–98.

Fay, Brian, Pomper, Philip and Vann, Richard T. (eds) (1998) *History and Theory: Contemporary Readings*, Oxford: Basil Blackwell.

Ferguson, Adam (1998 [1780]) 'History', *Encyclopaedia Britannica*, MultiMedia CD 1999 edn.

Finney, Patrick (1998) 'Ethics, historical relativism and Holocaust denial', *Rethinking History: The Journal of Theory and Practice* 2: 359–70.

Fiumara, Gemma C. (1995) *The Metaphoric Process: Connections Between Language and Life*, London: Routledge.

Forum (1993) *American Historical Review* 98: 338–81.

—— (1991) 'The objectivity question and the future of the historical profession', *American Historical Review* 96: 675–708.

—— (1989) 'Intellectual history and the return of literature', *American Historical Review* 94: 581–69.

Foucault, Michel (1985, 1986) *History of Sexuality*, vols 2 and 3, New York: Pantheon.

—— (1980) *Power/Knowledge: Selected Interviews and Other Writings*, Brighton: Harvester Press.

—— (1979 [1976]) *History of Sexuality*, vol. 1, London: Allen Lane.

—— (1977 [1975]) *Discipline and Punish*, New York: Pantheon.

—— (1977) 'Nietzsche, genealogy, history', in *Language, Counter Memory, Practice: Selected Essays and Interviews*, ed. Donald F. Bouchard, trans. by Donald F. Bouchard and Sherry Simon, Ithaca: Cornell University Press, pp. 139–64.

—— (1975) *The Birth of the Clinic*, New York: Vintage Books.

—— (1973a) *Madness and Civilization: A History of Insanity in the Age of Reason*, London: Tavistock.

—— (1973b) *The Order of Things: An Archaeology of the Human Sciences*, New York: Random House.

—— (1972) *The Archaeology of Knowledge*, New York: Harper & Row.

—— (1970) 'The order of discourse', Inaugural Lecture at the College de France, 2 December.

Friedlander, Saul (ed.) (1992) *Probing the Limits of Representation: Nazism and the 'Final Solution'*, Cambridge, MA: Harvard University Press.

Frye, Northrop (1957) *Anatomy of Criticism*, Princeton: Princeton University Press.

Fukuyama, Francis (1993 [1991]) *The End of History and the Last Man*, New York: Avon Books.

Gadamer, Hans-Georg (1998) *Praise of Theory: Speeches and Essays*, trans. Chris Dawson, New Haven: Yale University Press.

Gallie, William B. (1964) *Philosophy and the Historical Understanding*, London: Chatto & Windus.

Gardenfors, P. (1997) 'Meanings as conceptual structures', in M. Carrier and P. Machamer (eds) *Mindscapes: Philosophy, Science, and the Mind.*

Gardiner, Jane (ed.) (1988) *What is History Today?*, London: Humanities Press International.

Gardiner, Patrick (ed.) (1961 [1951]) *The Nature of Historical Explanation*, Oxford: Oxford University Press.

—— (ed.) (1959) *Theories of History*, Glencoe, IL: The Free Press.

Gasché, Rodolphe (1986) *The Tain of the Mirror: Derrida and the Philosophy of Reflection*, Cambridge, MA: Harvard University Press.

Gay, Peter (1988 [1974]) *Style in History: Gibbon, Ranke, Macaulay, Burckhardt*, New York: Basic Books.

—— (1966–9) *The Enlightenment*, New York: Knopf.

Geertz, Clifford (1983) *Local Knowledge: Further Essays in Interpretative Anthropology*, New York: Basic Books.

—— (1973) 'Thick description: Toward an interpretive theory of culture', and 'Deep play: Notes on the Balinese cockfight', in *The Interpretation of Cultures*, New York: Basic Books, pp. 3–31, 412–54.

Giddens, Antony (1976) *New Rules of Sociological Method: A Positive Critique of Interpretative Sociologies*, New York: Basic Books.

Ginzburg, Carlo (1982) *The Cheese and the Worms: The Cosmos of a Sixteenth Century Miller*, Harmondsworth: Penguin.

Goldstein, Jan (1994) *Foucault and the Writing of History*, Oxford: Basil Blackwell.

Goldstein, Leon (1976) *Historical Knowing*, Austin: University of Texas Press.

Goodman, Jordan (1997) 'History and anthropology', in Michael Bentley (ed.) *Companion to Historiography*, pp. 783–804.

Graham, G. (1983) *Historical Explanation Reconsidered*, Aberdeen: Aberdeen University Press.

Green, William A. (1993) *History, Historians, and the Dynamics of Change*, Westport, CT: Praeger.

Grossmann, Reinhardt (1992) *The Existence of the World: An Introduction to Ontology*, London: Routledge.

Gumbrecht, Hans Ulrich (1997) *In 1926: Living at the Edge of Time*, Cambridge, MA: Harvard University Press.

Gutting, Gary (1994) *The Cambridge Companion to Foucault*, Cambridge: Cambridge University Press.

Guyer, P. (ed.) (1992) *The Cambridge Companion to Kant*, Cambridge, Cambridge University Press.

Habermas, Jürgen (1987) *The Philosophical Discourse of Modernity*, trans. Frederick Lawrence, Cambridge: Cambridge University Press.

Hackett Fischer, David (1970) *Historian's Fallacies*, New York: Harper & Row.

Haddock, B.A. (1980) *An Introduction to Historical Thought*, London: Edward Arnold.

Hall, Catherine (1992) *White, Male and Middle Class: Explorations in Feminism and History*, Cambridge: Polity Press.

Hamilton, Paul (1996) *Historicism*, London: Routledge.

Hansen, Peter H. (1996) 'The dancing lamas of Everest: Cinema, orientalism, and Anglo-Tibetan Relations in the 1920s', *American Historical Review* 101: 712–47.

Hanson, N.R. (1958) *Patterns of Discovery*, Cambridge: Cambridge University Press.

Haraway, Donna (1991) *Simians, Cyborgs and Women*, London: Free Association Books.

—— (1988) 'Situated knowledges: The science question in feminism and the privilege of partial perspective', *Feminist Studies* 14: 575–99.

Harlan, David (1997) *The Degradation of American History*, Chicago: Chicago University Press.

—— (1989) 'Intellectual history and the return of literature', *American Historical Review* 94: 581–609.

Harris, James F. (1992) *Against Relativism: A Philosophical Defence of Method*, La Salle, IL: Open Court.

Harvey, David (1989) *The Condition of Postmodernity: An Enquiry into the Origins of Cultural Change*, Oxford: Basil Blackwell.

Hassing, Richard F. (1997) *Final Causality in Nature and Human Affairs*, Washington: Catholic University of America Press.

Hawkes, Terence (1977) *Structuralism and Semiotics*, London: Fontana.

Hegel, G.W.F. (1975 [1821]) *Lectures on the Philosophy of World History*, Cambridge: Cambridge University Press.

Heidegger, Martin (1962) *Being and Time*, trans. J. Macquarrie and E. Robinson, Oxford: Basil Blackwell.

Heise, U.K. (1997) *Chronoschisms: Time, Narrative and Postmodernism*, Cambridge: Cambridge University Press.

Hempel, Carl G. (1965) *Aspects of Scientific Explanation*, New York: The Free Press.

—— (1942) 'The function of general laws in history', *The Journal of Philosophy* 34: reprinted in Patrick Gardiner (ed.) (1959) *Theories of History*.

Hesse, Mary (1983) 'The cognitive claims of metaphor', in J.P. van Noppen *Metaphor and Religion*.

Hexter, J.H. (1991) 'Carl Becker, Professor Novick, and Me: or, Cheer Up, Professor N.!' *American Historical Review* 96: 675–82.

—— (1972) *The History Primer*, London: Allan Lane.

—— (1961) *Re-Appraisals in History*, Evanston: Northwestern University.

Himmelfarb, Gertrude (1994) *On Looking into the Abyss: Untimely Thoughts on Culture and Society*, New York: Knopf.

—— (1989) 'Some reflections on the new history', *American Historical Review* 94: 661–70.

Hirsch, Eric D. (1976) *The Aims of Interpretation*, Chicago: University of Chicago Press.

Hobsbawm, E. (1980) 'Some comments', *Past and Present* 86: 3–8.

Hoff-Wilson, Joan and Farnham, Christine (1990) 'Theories about the end of everything (editors' note)', *Journal of Women's History* 1: 6–11.

Hoffer, Peter Charles and Stueck, William W. (1994) *Reading and Writing American History: An Introduction to the Historian's Craft*, 2 vols, Lexington: D.C. Heath.

Hollinger, David A. (1991) 'Postmodernist theory and *Wissenschaftliche* practice', *American Historical Review* 96: 688–92.

—— (1989) 'The return of the prodigal: The persistence of historical knowing', *American Historical Review* 94: 610–21.

Horwich, Paul (1990) *Truth*, Oxford: Oxford University Press.

Hunt, Lynn (1998) 'Does history need defending?', *History Workshop Journal* 46: 241–9.

—— (1989) *The New Cultural History*, Berkeley: University of California Press.

Hutcheon, Linda (1988) *A Poetics of Postmodernism: History, Theory, Fiction*, New York: Routledge.

Iggers, George (1997) *Historiography in the Twentieth Century*, Middletown, CT: Wesleyan University Press.

Irigaray, Luce (1992) *Culture of Difference*, New York: Routledge.

Jameson, Fredric (1984) *Sartre: The Origins of a Style*, New York: Columbia University Press.

—— (1976) 'Figural relativism, or the poetics of historiography', *Diacritics* 6: 2–9.

Jenkins, Keith (1999) *Why History? Reflections on the Possible End of History and Ethics under the Impact of the Postmodern*, London: Routledge.

—— (1998a) 'A conversation with Hayden White', *Literature and History* 7: 68–82.

—— (1998b) 'Review of *The Degradation of American History* by David Harlan (1997), in *Rethinking History: The Journal of Theory and Practice* 2: 409–12.

—— (1997) *Postmodern History Reader*, London: Routledge.

—— (1995) *On 'What is History?'*, London: Routledge.

—— (1991) *Rethinking History*, London: Routledge.

Johnson, Marc (ed.) (1981) *Philosophical Perspectives on Metaphor*, Minneapolis: University of Minnesota Press.

Jones, Charles (1998) *E.H. Carr and International Relations*, Cambridge, Cambridge University Press.

Jones, Gareth, Stedman (1983) *Languages of Class: Studies in English Working Class History, 1832–1982*, Cambridge: Cambridge University Press.

Josephson, John R. and Susan G. (1994) *Abductive Inference*, Cambridge: Cambridge University Press.

Joyce, Patrick (1995) *Class*, Oxford: Oxford University.

—— (1994) *Democratic Subjects: The Self and the Social in Nineteenth Century England*, New York: Cambridge University Press.

—— (1991) 'History and post-modernism', *Past and Present* 133: 204–9.

Kammen, Michael (ed.) (1980) *The Past before Us: Contemporary Historical Writing in the United States*, Ithaca: Cornell University Press.

Kansteiner, Wulf (1993) 'Hayden White's critique of the writing of history', *History and Theory* 32: 273–95.

Kant, I. (1993 [1786]) 'Conjectures on the beginning of human history', in Hans Reiss (ed.) *Kant: Political Writings*, pp. 221–34.

—— (1933 [1781]) *Critique of Pure Reason*, trans. N. Kemp Smith, London: Macmillan.

Kaye, Harvey J. (1996) *Why do Ruling Classes Fear History?*, New York: St Martin's Press.

—— (1995) *The British Marxist Historians*, New York: St Martin's Press.

Kearney, Richard and Rainwater, Mara (eds) (1996) *The Continental Philosophy Reader*, London: Routledge.

Kellner, Hans (1989) *Language and Historical Representation: Getting the Story Crooked*, Madison: University of Wisconsin Press.

—— (1980) 'White's linguistic humanism', *History and Theory* (themed issue) 19: 1–29.

Kenyon, J. (1983) *The History Men*, London: Weidenfeld & Nicolson.

Kerber, Linda K. (1988) 'Separate spheres, female worlds, woman's place: The rhetoric of women's history', *Journal of American History* 75: 9–39.

Kiernan, V.G. (1988) *History, Classes, and Nation-States*, Cambridge: Polity Press.

Kirk, Neville (1995) 'The continuing relevance and engagement of class', *Labour History Review* 60: 2–15.

—— (1987) 'In defence of class', *International Review of Social History* 32: 2–47.

Kirkham, R. (1995) *Theories of Truth*, Cambridge: Bradford Books.

Klein, K (1995) 'In search of narrative mastery: Postmodernism and the people without history', *History and Theory* 34: 275–98.

Kloppenberg, James T. (1989) 'Objectivity and historicism: A century of American historical writing', *American Historical Review* 94: 1011–30.

Knight, Alan (1997) 'Latin America', in M. Bentley (ed.) *Companion to Historiography*, pp. 728–58.

Knox, T.M. (1975) *Hegel's Aesthetics*, Oxford: Clarendon Press.

Kolakowski, L. (1972) *Positivist Philosophy*, London: Harmondsworth.

Kozicki, H. (ed.) (1993) *Developments in Modern Historiography*, New York: St Martins Press.

Kramnick, Isaac (ed.) (1995) *The Portable Enlightenment Reader*, New York: Penguin.

Krausz, Michael (ed.) (1989) *Relativism: Interpretation and Confrontation*, Notre Dame, IN: Notre Dame University Press.

LaCapra, Dominick (1995) 'History, language and reading: Waiting for Crillon', *American Historical Review* 100: 799–828.

LaCapra, Dominick and Kaplan, Steven L. (eds) (1982) *Modern*

European Intellectual History: Reappraisals and New Perspectives, Ithaca: Cornell University Press.

Lamont, William (1998) *Historical Controversies and Historians*, London: UCL Press.

Laslett, Barbara *et al.* (1997) *History and Theory: Feminist Research, Debates, Contestations*, Chicago: University of Chicago Press.

Lechte, John (1994) *Fifty Key Contemporary Thinkers: From Structuralism to Postmodernity*, London: Routledge.

Le Doeuff, Michèle (1989) *Hipparchia's Choice: An Essay Concerning Women, Philosophy, Etc.*, trans. Trista Selous, Oxford: Oxford University Press.

Lemon, M.C. (1995) *The Discipline of History and the History of Thought*, London: Routledge.

Lipton, Peter (1993) *Inference to the Best Explanation*, London, Routledge.

Lloyd, Christopher (1993) *The Structures of History*, Oxford: Basil Blackwell.

Lloyd, Genevieve (1984) *The Man of Reason: 'Male' and 'Female' in Western Philosophy*, Minneapolis: University of Minnesota Press.

Longino, Helen E. (1990) *Science as Social Knowledge*, Princeton: Princeton University Press.

Lorenz, Chris (1998) 'Can histories be true? Narrativism, Positivism, and the "Metaphorical Turn"', *History and Theory* 37: 309–29.

—— (1994) 'Historical knowledge and historical reality: A plea for "historical realism"', *History and Theory* 33: 297–327.

Loux, Michael J. (1998) *Metaphysics: A Contemporary Introduction*, London: Routledge.

Luntley, Michael (1995) *Reason, Truth and Self: The Postmodern Reconditioned*, London: Routledge.

Lyotard, Jean-François (1979) *The Postmodern Condition: A Report on Knowledge*, Paris: Minuit.

McCullagh, C. Behan (1998) *The Truth of History*, London: Routledge.

—— (1991) 'Can our understanding of old texts be objective?', *History and Theory* 30: 302–23.

—— (1984) *Justifying Historical Descriptions*, Cambridge: Cambridge University Press.

McLennan, Gregor (1984) 'History and theory: Contemporary debates and directions', *Literature and History* 10: 139–64.

Magnus, Bernd (1993) *Nietzsche's Case*, New York: Routledge.

Magnus, Bernd and Higgins, Kathleen M. (eds) (1996) *The Cambridge Companion to Nietzsche*, Cambridge: Cambridge University Press.

Mandelbaum, Maurice (1977) *The Anatomy of Historical Knowledge*, Baltimore: The Johns Hopkins University Press.

Marable, Manning (1995) *Beyond Black and White*, London: Verso.

Margolin, Jean Claude (1989) *Humanism in Europe at the Time of the Renaissance*, Durham, NC: Labyrinth Press.

Marshall, Brenda K. (1992) *Teaching the Postmodern: Fiction and Theory*, New York: Routledge.

Marwick, Arthur (1995) 'Two approaches to historical study: The metaphysical (including postmodernism) and the historical', *Journal of Contemporary History* 30: 5–36.

—— (1989 [1970]) *The Nature of History*, third edn, London: Macmillan.

Maza, Sarah (1996) 'Stories in history: Cultural narratives in recent works in European history', *American Historical Review* 101: 1493–1515.

Mazzotta, Giuseppe (1998) *The New Map of the World: Giambattista Vico's Poetic Philosophy*, Princeton: Princeton University Press.

Megill, Alan (1985) *Prophets of Extremity: Nietzsche, Heidegger, Foucault, Derrida*, Berkeley: University of California Press.

Meinecke, Friedrich (1972) *Historism: The Rise of a New Historical Outlook*, trans. J.E. Anderson, London: Routledge & Kegan Paul.

Mensch, James Richard (1997) *Knowing and Being: A Postmodern Reversal*, University Park, PA: The Pennsylvania University Press.

—— (1996) *Knowing and Being: A Postmodern Reversal*, University Park, PA: The Pennsylvania University Press.

Merquior, J.M. (1985) *Foucault*, London: Fontana.

Mills, Sarah (1997) *Discourse*, London: Routledge.

Mink, Louis (1978) 'Narrative form as a cognitive instrument', in R.R. Canary, and H. Kozicki (eds) *The Writing of History: Literary Form and Historical Understanding*, pp. 129–49.

—— (1970) 'History and fiction as modes of comprehension', *New Literary History* 1: 541–58.

—— (1969) *The Philosophy of R.G. Collingwood*, Bloomington, IN: University of Indiana Press.

Moi, Toril (ed.) (1988) *French Feminist Thought: A Reader*, Oxford: Oxford University Press.

Momigliano, Arnaldo (1990) *The Classical Foundations of Modern Historiography*, Berkeley: University of California Press.

—— (1985 [1966]) *Studies in Historiography*, New York: Garland.

—— (1977) *Essays in Ancient and Modern Historiography*, Oxford: Basil Blackwell.

Mooney, Michael (1985) *Vico in the Tradition of Rhetoric*, Princeton: Princeton University Press.
Moser P.K. (ed.) (1987) *A Priori Knowledge*, Oxford: Oxford University Press.
Moss, M.E. (1987) *Benedetto Croce Reconsidered*, Hanover: University Press of New England.
Mouffe, Chantal (ed.) (1996) *Deconstruction and Pragmatism*, London: Routledge.
Müller-Vollmer, Kurt (ed.) (1986) *The Hermeneutics Reader*, Oxford: Oxford University Press.
Munslow, Alun (1997a) *Deconstructing History*, London: Routledge.
—— (1997b) Editorial, *Rethinking History: The Journal of Theory and Practice* 1(1): 1–20.
—— (1997c) Editorial, *Rethinking History: The Journal of Theory and Practice* 1(2): 111–23.
—— (1992) *Discourse and Culture: The Creation of America, 1870–1920*, London: Routledge.
Munz, Peter (1997) 'The historical narrative', in M. Bentley (ed.) *Companion to Historiography*, pp. 857–72.
Murphey, Murray G. (1986) 'Explanation, causes, and covering laws', *History and Theory* (themed issue) 25: 43–57.
Nagel, Ernest (1979) *Teleology Revisited*, New York: Columbia University Press.
—— (1961) *The Structure of Science: Problems in the Logic of Scientific Explanation*, New York: Harcourt Brace.
Nehamas, Alexander (1985) *Nietzsche, Life as Literature*, Cambridge, MA: Harvard University Press.
Neisser, U. (ed.) (1981) *Concepts and Conceptual Development*, Cambridge: Cambridge University Press.
Nelson, L.H. (1990) *Who Knows: From Quine to a Feminist Empiricism*, Philadelphia: Temple University Press.
NeSmith, Georgia (n.d.) *Feminist Historiography 1968–1993*, http://www.inform.umd.edu/EdRes/Topic/WomensStudies/Bibliographies/feminist-historiography.
Noiriel, Gerard (1994) 'Foucault and history: The lessons of a disillusion', *Journal of Modern History* 66: 547–68.
Norman, Andrew P. (1991) 'Telling it like it was: Historical narratives on their own terms', *History and Theory* 30: 119–35.
Norris, Christopher (1992) *Uncritical Theory: Postmodernism, Intellectuals and the Gulf War*, London: Lawrence & Wishart.
—— (1990) *What's Wrong with Postmodernism?*, Hemel Hempstead: Harvester-Wheatsheaf.

—— (1987) *Derrida*, London: Fontana.

—— (1982) *Deconstruction: Theory and Practice*, London: Methuen.

Novick, Peter (1988) *That Noble Dream: The 'Objectivity Question' and the American Historical Profession*, Cambridge: Cambridge University Press.

Nye, Andrea (ed.) (1998) *Philosophy of Language: The Big Questions*, Oxford: Basil Blackwell.

Oakeshott, Michael (1983) *On History and Other Essays*, Oxford: Basil Blackwell.

—— (1933) *Experience and Its Modes*, Cambridge: Cambridge University Press.

O'Brien, G.D. (1975) *Hegel on Reason in History: A Contemporary Interpretation*, Chicago: University of Chicago Press.

O'Brien, Karen (1997) *Narratives of Enlightenment: Cosmopolitan History from Voltaire to Gibbon*, Cambridge: Cambridge University Press.

Offen, Karin, Pierson, Ruth Roach and Rendall, Jane (eds) (1991) *Writing Women's History: International Perspectives*, Bloomington, IN: Indiana University Press.

Olafson, Frederick A. (1979) *The Dialectic of Action*, Chicago: University of Chicago Press.

Palmer, Richard E. (1969) *Hermeneutics: Interpretation Theory in Schleiermacher, Dilthey, Heidegger and Gadamer*, Evanston, IL: Northwestern University Press.

Payne, Michael (1997) *Reading Knowledge: An Introduction to Barthes, Foucault and Althusser*, Oxford: Basil Blackwell.

Peacocke, C. (1992) *A Study of Concepts*, Cambridge, MA: MIT Press.

Pecheux, Michel (1982) *Language, Semantics and Ideology*, Basingstoke: Macmillan.

Peirce, Charles S. (1958) *Collected Papers*, vol. VII, ed. A. Burks, Cambridge, MA: Harvard University Press.

Perrot, Michelle (ed.) (1992) *Writing Women's History*, Oxford: Basil Blackwell.

Pickering, Michael (1999) 'History as horizon: Gadamer, tradition and critique', *Rethinking History: The Journal of Theory and Practice* 3: 177–95.

Pittock, Jean H. and Wear, Andrew (eds) (1991) *Interpretation and Cultural History*, Basingstoke: Macmillan.

Pompa, Leon (1975) *Vico: A Study of the New Science*, Cambridge: Cambridge University Press.

Poovey, Mary (1988) *Uneven Developments: The Ideological Work of*

Gender in Mid-Victorian England, Chicago: University of Chicago Press.

Popper, Karl (1979) *Objective Knowledge: An Evolutionary Approach*, rev. edn, Oxford: Clarendon Press.

—— (1962 [1945]) *The Open Society and Its Enemies*, London: Routledge.

—— (1959) *The Logic of Scientific Discovery*, New York: Basic Books.

—— (1957) *The Poverty of Historicism*, London: Routledge.

Porter, Roy (ed.) (1997) *Rewriting the Self: Histories from the Renaissance to the Present*, London: Routledge.

Poster, Mark (1997) *Cultural History and Postmodernity: Disciplinary Readings and Challenges*, New York: Columbia University Press.

—— (1987) 'The reception of Foucault by historians', *Journal of the History of Ideas* 48: 117–41.

—— (1984) *Foucault, Marxism and History*, London: Polity Press.

Priest, Stephen (1990) *The British Empiricists*, London: Penguin.

Putnam, Hilary (1992) *Renewing Philosophy*, Cambridge, MA: Harvard University Press.

—— (1988) *Reality and Representation*, Cambridge, MA: MIT Press.

—— (1987) *The Many Faces of Realism*, La Salle, IL: Open Court Publishers.

—— (1983) *Realism and Reason*, vol. 3, Cambridge: Cambridge University Press.

—— (1981) *Reason, Truth and History*, Cambridge: Cambridge University Press.

Quine, W.V. (1990) *Pursuit of Truth*, Cambridge, MA: Harvard University Press.

—— (1969) *Ontological Relativity and Other Essays*, New York: Columbia University Press.

—— (1963) *From a Logical Point of View*, New York: Harper & Row.

—— (1960) *Word and Object*, Cambridge, MA: Harvard University Press.

Rabinow, Paul (1999) *Ethics, Subjectivity and Truth: The Essential Works of Michel Foucault, 1954–84*, London: Penguin.

Ranke, Leopold von (1867–90) *Sämmtliche Werke* (Collected Works), vols 33 and 34, Leipzig: Dunker & Humblot.

Reedy, W.J. (1994) 'The historical imaginary of social science in post-revolutionary France: Bonald, Saint-Simon, Comte', *History of the Human Sciences* 7: 1–26.

Reiss, Hans (ed.) (1993) *Kant: Political Writings*, Cambridge: Cambridge University Press.

—— (1991 [1970]) *Kant: Political Writings*, Cambridge: Cambridge University Press.

Rendall, Jane (1991) 'Uneven developments: Women's history, feminist history, and gender history in Great Britain', in Karin Offen, Ruth Roach Pierson and Jane Rendall (eds) *Writing Women's History: International Perspectives*, pp. 1–24.

Rethinking History: The Journal of Theory and Practice (1988), Special Issue, 2(3).

Ricoeur, Paul (1994 [1978]) *The Rule of Metaphor: Multi-disciplinary Studies of the Creation of Meaning in Language*, trans. Robert Czerny, London: Routledge.

—— (1984) *The Reality of the Historical Past*, Marquette University: Wisconsin-Alpha Chapter of Phi Sigma Tau.

—— (1984, 1985) *Time and Narrative*, 3 vols, Chicago: University of Chicago Press.

—— (1981) *Hermeneutics and the Human Sciences*, Cambridge: Cambridge University Press.

Riley, Denise (1989) *Am I That Name? Feminism and the Category of 'Women' in History*, Basingstoke: Macmillan.

Roberts, Clayton (1996) *The Logic of Historical Explanation*, University Park, PA: The Pennsylvania University Press.

Roberts, David D. (1995) *Nothing But History: Reconstruction and Extremity after Metaphysics*, Berkeley: University of California Press.

—— (1987) *Benedetto Croce and the Uses of Historicism*, Berkeley: University of California Press.

Roberts, Geoffrey (1998) 'Geoffrey Elton and the philosophy of history', *The Historian* 57: 29–31.

—— (1997) 'Postmodernism versus the standpoint of action', review of *On 'What is History?'* by Keith Jenkins, *History and Theory* 36: 249–60.

—— (1996) 'Narrative history as a way of life', *Journal of Contemporary History* 31: 221–8.

Rockmore, Tom (1995) *Heidegger and French Philosophy: Humanism, Antihumanism and Being*, London: Routledge.

Rorty, Richard (1998) *Truth and Progress: Philosophical Papers Vol. 3*, Cambridge: Cambridge University Press.

—— (ed.) (1992 [1967]) *The Linguistic Turn: Recent Essays in Philosophical Method*, Chicago: University of Chicago Press.

—— (1992) 'Trotsky and the wild orchids', *Common Knowledge*, winter: 140–53.

—— (1991) *Objectivity, Relativism and Truth: Philosophical Papers Vol. 1*, Cambridge: Cambridge University Press.

—— (1989) *Contingency, Irony and Solidarity*, Cambridge: Cambridge University Press.

—— (1982) *Consequences of Pragmatism*, Minneapolis: University of Minnesota Press.

—— (1979) *Philosophy and the Mirror of Nature*, Princeton: Princeton University Press.

Rosenstone, Robert A. (1996) 'The future of the past: Film and the beginnings of postmodern history', in Vivian Sobchack (ed.) *The Persistence of History: Cinema, Television and the Modern Event*, pp. 201–18.

—— (1995) *Visions of the Past: The Challenge of Film to Our Idea of History*, Cambridge, MA: Harvard University Press.

—— (1988) *Mirror in the Shrine: American Encounters with Meiji Japan*, Cambridge, MA: Harvard University Press.

Ross, Dorothy (1995) 'Grand narrative in American historical writing: From romance to uncertainty', *American Historical Review* 100: 651–77.

Roth, Michael S. (1995) *The Ironist's Cage: Memory, Trauma, and the Construction of History*, New York: Columbia University Press.

Roth, Paul A. (1992) 'Hayden White and the aesthetics of historiography', *History of the Human Sciences* 5: 17–35.

Rothenburg, Paula S. (ed.) (1998) *Race, Class, and Gender in the United States: An Integrated Study*, fourth edn, New York: St Martin's Press.

Rowbotham, Sheila (1974) *Hidden from History: Rediscovering Women in History from the 17th Century to the Present*, New York: Pantheon Books.

Ruben, David-Hillel (ed.) (1993) *Explanation*, Oxford: Oxford University Press.

—— (1990) *Explaining Explanation*, London: Routledge.

Sachs, Sheldon (ed.) (1979) *On Metaphor*, Chicago: University of Chicago Press.

Sahlins, Marshal (1989) *Boundaries: The Making of France and Spain in the Pyrenees*, Berkeley: University of California Press.

—— (1985) *Islands of History*, Chicago: University of Chicago Press.

—— (1981) *Historical Metaphors and Mythical Realities*, Ann Arbor: University of Michigan Press.

Sallis, John (ed.) (1987) *Deconstruction and Philosophy: The Texts of Jacques Derrida*, Chicago: University of Chicago Press.

Sartre, Jean-Paul (1989) *Existensionalism and Humanism*, trans. Philip Mairet, London: Eyre Methuen.

Saussure, Ferdinand de (1959) [1916] *Course de Linguistic Générale*, trans. Wade Baskin, London: Fontana.

Schama, Simon (1991) *Dead Certainties (Unwarranted Speculations)*, New York: Knopf.

Schmitt, Frederick (ed.) (1994) *Socialising Epistemology: The Social Dimensions of Knowledge*, Boston, MA: Rowman & Littlefield.

Schorske, Carl E. (1998) *Thinking with History: Explorations in the Passage to Modernism*, Princeton: Princeton University Press.

Scott, Joan W. (1996a) 'After history', *Common Knowledge* 5: 9–26.

—— (1996b) *Feminism and History*, Oxford: Oxford University Press.

—— (1991) 'Women's history', in P. Burke (ed.) *New Perspectives on Historical Writing*, pp. 42–66.

—— (1989) 'History in crisis? The others' side of the story', *American Historical Review* 94: 680–92.

—— (1988) *Gender and The Politics of History*, New York: Columbia University Press.

—— (1986) 'Gender: A useful category of analysis', *American Historical Review* 91: 1053–75.

—— (1983) 'Women in history: The modern period', *Past and Present* 191: 125–57.

Searle, John R. (1995) *The Construction of Social Reality*, London: Allan Lane.

—— (1983) *Intentionality*, Cambridge: Cambridge University Press.

Sellars, Wilfred (1997 [1956]) *Empiricism and the Philosophy of the Mind*, Cambridge, MA: Harvard University Press.

Sheridan, Alan (1994) *Michel Foucault, The Will to Truth*, London: Routledge.

Shoemaker, Robert and Vincent, Mary (1998) *Gender and History in Western Europe*, London: Arnold.

Smith, E.E. and Medin, D.L. (1981) *Categories and Concepts*, Cambridge, MA: Harvard University Press.

Smith, Paul (1988) *Discerning the Subject*, Minneapolis: University of Minnesota Press.

Smith-Rosenberg, Carroll (1985) *Disorderly Conduct: Visions of Gender in Victorian America*, New York: Oxford University Press.

Snooks, Graham D. (1998) *The Laws of History*, London: Routledge.

Sobchack, Vivian (ed.) (1996) *The Persistence of History: Cinema, Television and the Modern Event*, London: Routledge.

Sontag, Susan (ed.) (1982) *A Barthes Reader*, London: Fontana/Collins.

Sosa, E. (1988) 'Beyond scepticism, to the best of our knowledge', *Mind* 97: 153–88.

Southgate, Beverley (1996) *History: What and Why*, London: Routledge.

Spiegel, Gabrielle M. (1992) 'History and post-modernism', *Past and Present* 135: 197–8.

Stanford, Michael (1998) *An Introduction to the Philosophy of History*, Oxford: Basil Blackwell.

—— (1994) *A Companion to the Study of History*, Oxford: Basil Blackwell.

—— (1986) *The Nature of Historical Knowledge*, Oxford: Basil Blackwell.

Stevenson, C.L. (1963) *Facts and Values*, New Haven: Yale University Press.

Stone, Lawrence (1992) 'History and post-modernism', *Past and Present* 135: 187–94.

—— (1991) 'History and post-modernism', *Past and Present* 131: 217–18.

—— (1979) 'The revival of narrative', *Past and Present* 85: 3–24.

Strawson, Peter F. (1974) *Freedom and Resentment and Other Essays*, London: Methuen.

Stromberg, Roland N. (1994) *European Intellectual History Since 1789*, Englewood Cliffs, NJ: Prentice Hall.

Struckmeyer, Otto Keith (1978) *Croce and Literary Criticism*, Norwood, PA: Norwood Editions.

Sturrock, John (ed.) (1979) *Structuralism and Since: From Levi-Strauss to Derrida*, Oxford: Oxford University Press.

Tagliacozzo, Giorgio and Verene, Donald Phillip (eds) (1976) *Giambattista Vico's Science of Humanity*, Baltimore: The Johns Hopkins University Press.

Tagliacozzo, Giorgio and White, Hayden (eds) (1969) *Giambattista Vico: An International Symposium*, Baltimore: The Johns Hopkins University Press.

Tallis, Raymond (1998) *In Defence of Realism*, Lincoln: University of Nebraska Press.

Taylor, B. (1985) *Modes of Occurrence*, Oxford: Oxford University Press.

Thomas, Keith (1978) *Religion and the Decline of Magic: Studies in Popular Beliefs in Sixteenth and Seventeenth Century England*, Harmondsworth: Penguin.

Thompson, E.P. (1978) *The Poverty of Theory and Other Essays*, London: Merlin Press.

—— (1963) *The Making of the English Working Class*, Harmondsworth: Penguin.

Thompson, John B. (1981) *Critical Hermeneutics*, Cambridge: Cambridge University Press.

Toews, John E. (1987) 'Intellectual history after the linguistic turn: The autonomy of meaning and the irreducibility of experience', *American Historical Review* 92: 879–907.

Topolski, Jerzy (1991) 'Towards an integrated model of historical explanation', *History and Theory* 30: 324–38.

Tosh, John (1991) *The Pursuit of History*, second edn, London: Longman.

Turner, F.J. (1961 [1893]) *The Frontier in American History*, reprinted in R.A. Billington (ed.) *Frontier and Section*, Englewood Cliffs, NJ: Prentice Hall, pp. 38–60.

Van Noppen, J.P. (ed.) (1983) *Metaphor and Religion*, Brussels: The Free Press.

Vann, Richard T. (1998) 'The reception of Hayden White', *History and Theory* 37: 143–61.

—— (1987) 'Louis Mink's linguistic turn', *History and Theory* 26: 1–14.

Veeser, A. Aram (ed.) (1989) *The New Historicism*, New York: Routledge.

Veyne, Paul (1984) *Writing History, Essays on Epistemology*, Middletown: Wesleyan University Press.

Vico, Giambattista (1968) *The New Science of Giambattista Vico*, trans. Thomas G. Bergin and Max H. Fisch, Ithaca: Cornell University Press.

—— (1963) *The Autobiography of Giambattista Vico*, trans. Thomas G. Bergin and Max H. Fisch, Ithaca: Cornell University Press.

von Wright, Georg Henrik (1971) *Explanation and Understanding*, London: Routledge.

Walkowitz, Judith (1992) *City of Dreadful Delights: Narratives of Sexual Danger in Late Victorian London*, Chicago: University of Chicago Press.

Walsh, W.H. (1984 [1967]) *An Introduction to Philosophy of History*, Westport, CT: Greenwood Press.

—— (1981) *Substance and Form in History*, Edinburgh: Edinburgh University Press.

—— (1966) *Metaphysics*, New York: Harcourt Brace.

Warren, John (1998) *The Past and its Presenters: An Introduction to Issues in Historiography*, London: Hodder & Stoughton.

Weber, Max (1957 [1947]) *The Theory of Social and Economic Organisation*, trans. A.M. Henderson and Talcott Parsons, ed. and Introduction by Talcott Parsons, Glencoe, IL: The Free Press.

Weitz, M. (1988) *Theories of Concepts: A History of the Major Philosophical Traditions*, London: Routledge.

Wellek, Rene (1981) *Four Critics*, Seattle: University of Washington Press.

Whewell, William (1967 [3 vols 1837]) *History of the Inductive Sciences*, London: Cass.

—— (1967 [2 vols 1840]) *The Philosophy of the Inductive Sciences*, London: Cass.

White, Hayden (1998) *Figural Realism: Studies in the Mimesis Effect*, Baltimore: The Johns Hopkins University Press.

—— (1996) 'The modernist event', in Vivian Sobchack (ed.) *The Persistence of History: Cinema, Television and the Modern Event*, pp. 17–38.

—— (1995) 'Response to Arthur Marwick', *Journal of Contemporary History* 30: 233–46.

—— (1992) 'Historical emplotment and the problem of truth', in Saul Friedlander (ed.) *Probing the Limits of Representation*, pp. 37–53.

—— (1987) *The Content of the Form: Narrative Discourse and Historical Representation*, Baltimore: The Johns Hopkins University Press.

—— (1984) 'The question of narrative in contemporary historical theory', *History and Theory* 23: 1–33.

—— (1978) *Tropics of Discourse: Essays in Cultural Criticism*, Baltimore: The Johns Hopkins University Press.

—— (1974) 'Structuralism and popular culture', *Journal of Popular Culture* 7: 759–75.

—— (1973a) 'Foucault decoded: Notes from underground', *History and Theory* 12: 23–54.

—— (1973b) *Metahistory: The Historical Imagination in Nineteenth Century Europe*, Baltimore: The Johns Hopkins University Press.

Williams, Carolyn D. (1997) ' "Another self in the case": Gender, marriage and the individual in Augustan literature', in Roy Porter (ed.) *Rewriting the Self: Histories from the Renaissance to the Present*, pp. 97–118.

Williams, Raymond (1983) *Keywords*, Oxford: Oxford University Press.

Wilson, George M. (1989) *The Intentionality of Human Action*, Stanford, CA: Stanford University Press.

Windschuttle, Keith (1995) *The Killing of History: How Literary Critics and Social Theorists are Murdering Our Past*, New York: The Free Press.

Wiseman, Mary B. (1989) *The Ecstasies of Roland Barthes*, London: Routledge.

Wittgenstein, Ludwig (1995 [1921]) *Tractatus Logico-Philosophicus*, London: Routledge.

Worton, Michael and Still, Judith (eds) (1990) *Intertextuality: Theories and Practices*, New York: Manchester University Press.

Young, Robert (1990) *White Mythologies*, London: Routledge.

—— (ed.) (1981) *Untying the Text: A Poststructuralist Reader*, London: Routledge.

Yovel, Yirmiahiu (1980) *Kant and the Philosophy of History*, Princeton: University of Princeton Press.

Zagorin, Perez (1999) 'History, the referent, and narrative: Reflections on postmodernism now', *History and Theory* 38: 1–24.

—— (1990) 'Historiography and postmodernism: Reconsiderations', *History and Theory* 29: 263–74.

Zammito, John. H. (1998) 'Ankersmit's postmodernist historiography: The hyperbole of "opacity" ', *History and Theory* 37: 330–46.

INDEX

Main entries in **bold**

a priori/a posteriori 5, **21–4**, 38, 47, 51, 57, 62, 70, 79, 81, 88, 91, 101, 110, 115, 122, 127, 138, 142, 145–6, 156–8, 174, 180, 185, 193, 198, 217, 222
abduction (abductive) 4, 5, 6, 21–2, 105, 122–3, 138–40; *see also* **inference**
Absolute Spirit, the 114; *see also* **Hegel, G.W.F.**
Achinstein, P. 95, 123, 235
action (theory) 5, 7, 15, 22–3, 48, 60, 103, 110, 120–1, 125, 141, 150–1, 181, 183, 201, 209, 211–13; *see also* **intentionality**
Adorno, T. 57, 116, 184, 233
Ainslie, D. 240
Alcoff, L.M. 218, 233, 235
Allen, B. 219, 235
alterior, the 15
Althusser, L. 7, 28, 30, 57, 104, 107, 209, 235
American Historical Association 135, 235
anarchist 226; *see also* conservative; ideological implication; liberalism; radical; **White, Hayden**
Anderson, J.E. 251
Ankersmit, F.R. 9, 14, 49, 59, 60, 69–70, 73, 82, 89, 91, 99, 100, 102, 103, 106, 135, 143, 152, 153, 156, 165, 166, 167, 172, 173, 183, 190, 215, 226, 235
Annales 54, 65, 210
Ansell-Pearson, K. 174, 175, 176, 178, 235
anthropology 9, 15, 66, 103
anti-modernism 166, 167
anti-realism 50, 52, 59, 88, 151–2, 161, 189
anti-referentialism 225
anti-representationalism 8, 12, 50, 58, 198, 201–4, 209; *see also* **Rorty, Richard**
Antony, L.M. 233, 235
Appleby, J. 7, 58, 82, 86, 134, 160, 165, 167, 180, 181, 190, 197, 199, 214, 216, 217, 235, 236
archaeology 107–8; *see also* **Foucault, Michel**; genealogy
argument 83, 103, 123, 214, 226; *see also* contextualist; formist; mechanist; organicist; **White, Hayden**
Aristotle 157, 211, 216
Artaud, A. 166
Atkinson, R.F. 89, 123, 236
Attridge, D. 190, 234
Audi, R. 89, 141, 219, 236
author 9, 15, 19, **24–30**, 32, 58, 74, 76–7, 89, 105–6, 110, 116, 118, 128, 143, 150, 165, 167, 172, 181, 183, 186, 196, 212, 214, 232
autobiography 25
Auxier, R.E. 224, 236

Bachelard, G. 107
Bacon, F. 84
Baker, M. 233, 236
Bann, S. 14, 31, 55, 77, 106, 190, 193–4, 236
Barnard, F.M. 213, 236
Barthes, Roland 14–15, 26, 27, 30, **31–3**, 57, 72, 77, 89, 94, 100, 103, 110, 111, 126, 140, 150, 152, 156, 165, 171, 182, 184, 190, 193–5, 200, 202, 209, 226, 236
Baskin, W. 242
Bass, A. 242
Bataille, G. 107
Baudrillard, J. 199–200, 201, 237
Bauman, Z. 190, 237
Baynes, K. 58, 237
Beard, C. 165, 196, 197, 237
Beck, L.W. 148, 237
Becker, C. 165, 196, 197, 237
being 3, 117
Beiser, F.C. 113, 116, 237
Beitchman, P. 237
Belchem, J. 45, 190, 237
Bennett, T. 237
Bennington, G. 75, 190, 236, 237
Bentley, M. 135, 237
Benveniste, E. 76, 107, 237
Bergmann, G. 151
Berkeley, G. 81, 157
Berkhofer, R.F. 77, 84, 106, 156, 188, 197, 237
Berlin, I. 82, 133, 194, 224, 237, 242
Bernauer, J. 87, 111, 237
Bernstein, R. 58, 201, 238
Bertens, H. 156, 190, 238
Bevir, M. 89, 104, 106, 180, 181, 183, 238
Bhasker, R. 204, 238
biography 25, 65, 209
Black, C.E. 54
Blackwell Dictionary of Historians 134
Blanchot, M. 107
Bloch, M. 95, 209, 238
Bloomfield, M.W. 238, 242

Boch, G. 233, 238
Bohman, J. 58, 237
Bonjour, L. 24, 82, 238
Bordo, S. 233, 238
Bouchard, D.F. 111, 238, 244
Branstead, E.K. 151, 238
Braudel, F. 188, 209, 238
Breisach, E. 135, 238
Brewster, B. 235
Brody, D. 45, 238
Bross, J. 22
Brown, M.E. 63, 238
Bullock, A. 151, 238
Bunzl, M. 7, 8, 55, 162, 182, 183, 194, 197, 238
Burckhardt, J. 64–7
Burke, K. 225
Burke, P. 30, 65, 66, 67, 183, 188, 238
Burke, S. 33, 75, 239
Burkitt, I. 229, 233, 239
Burks, A. 253
Butler, J. 227, 233, 239
Butler, T. 239
bystander theory (of historical knowledge) 201

Callinicos, A. 7, 52, 55, 84, 173, 183, 239
Calvet, L.-J. 33, 239
Cameron, A. 135, 239
Canary, R.R. 173, 239, 251
Cannon, J. 134, 239
Caputo, J.D. 73, 239
Carr, D. 84, 106, 156, 172, 173, 181, 183, 194, 219, 239
Carr, E.H. 7, **35–7**, 38, 43, 49, 79–80, 101–2, 134, 180, 181, 184, 213, 215, 219, 239
Carrard, P. 197, 239
Carrier, M. 239, 245
Carroll, B.A. 233, 239
Carroll, D. 227, 239
Carroll, J. 151, 240
Cassirer, E. 148, 240
causation 2, 4, 5, 22, 28, **37–43**, 46, 48, 49, 52, 58, 59, 62, 71, 76, 83, 88, 105, 110, 118, 121, 125, 129, 146, 156, 164, 169, 172, 181, 186, 201, 210–13, 222–3; *see also explanandum*; *explanans*; **historical explanation**; **narrative**
Caws, P. 210, 240
Chambers, I. 102
Chartier, R. 55, 66, 67, 94, 95, 215, 227, 240
class 13, 20, 22, 23, **43–6**, 50, 53, 56, 58, 64, 65, 70, 71, 87, 128, 129, 162, 177, 183, 187, 199, 216, 229, 230
Classical episteme 86–7
cliometrics 65, 99
Cochrane, L.G. 240
Cockburn, D. 181, 183, 240
Code, L. 89, 233, 240
coherence/consensus (theory of knowledge/truth) 215–18
Coleridge, S.T. 222
colligation 4, **46–7**, 53, 59, 62, 76, 83, 88, 90, 94, 99, 122, 139, 142, 169, 186, 201, 212–13
Collingwood, R.G. 7, 18, 36–7, 38, 43, **47–9**, 53, 54, 55, 59, 60, 61, 62, 63, 65, 80, 89, 95, 113, 114, 115, 116, 121, 123, 126–7, 129, 130, 133, 141, 143, 162, 165, 184, 195, 197, 213, 215, 221, 222, 224, 240
comedy 83, 115, 147, 226; *see also* **emplotment**; romance; satire; tragedy; **White, Hayden**
communism 211
comparison 1, 25, 164; *see also* **evidence**; sources; verification
Comte, A. 54, 187
concepts in history 2, 4, 8, 21–3, 43–6, **49–53**, 54, 56, 58, 60, 61–2, 64–5, 79, 84, 88, 90–1, 94, 97–100, 107, 113–15, 117, 120, 130, 138–40, 142, 147, 157–9, 171, 174, 176, 179, 190, 198–9, 210, 216, 217, 221, 225
Conley, T. 241
Connor, S. 190, 240
conservative 226; *see also* anarchist; ideological implication; liberalism; radical; **White, Hayden**
constructionist history 6–8, 10, 12, 13, 14, 16, 22, 39, 40–1, 43, 46, 50, **53–5**, 59, 62, 63, 66, 73, 81, 94, 99, 101–2, 105, 113, 119, 131, 137–8, 151, 152, 158–62, 165, 171, 173, 176, 180–1, 183, 187, 196, 200, 204, 207, 209, 212, 221–3, 230–2
context/ualisation 48, 56, 57, 60, 77, 117, 120, 125, 127, 129, 138, 142, 166, 201, 212, 217
contextualist 226; *see also* argument; formist; mechanist; organicist; **White, Hayden**
continental philosophy 10, 47, 54, **55–8**, 89, 94, 107, 117, 161, 164, 184, 189, 195, 202
Cooper, D.E. 89, 217, 219, 240
Corfield, P. 233, 240
correspondence (theory of knowledge/truth) 4, 7, 8, 10, 11, 12, 13, 15, 18, 19, 21, 27, 31–2, 39, 56, 57, 62, 70–1, 73, 74, 83, 88, 95, 98–100, 103, 104, 105, 111, 121–3, 126, 141, 148, 152, 160–1, 164, 172, 176, 180, 183, 186, 189, 193, 195, 200, 202, 203, 215–18
covering laws 5, 38–9, 47, **58–60**, 62, 88, 90, 119–20, 130, 131, 138–9, 142, 185, 187, 210, 225; *see also explanandum*; *explanans*; **historical explanation**
Cox, C.B. 151, 240
Critchley, S . 71, 240
Croce, Benedetto 7, 10, 38, 43, 47, **61–3**, 70, 90, 113, 115, 149, 165, 184, 196, 197, 215, 221, 222, 224, 240
critical theory 57, 66, 75, 195
Cuban Missile Crisis, the 89–90
Culler, J. 33, 73, 240, 241

cultural history 13, **65–7**, 107, 224, 225, 229
Curthoys, A. 129, 173, 241
Curthoys, J. 232–3, 241
Czerny, R. 255

Dadaism 85, 166
Dant, T. 77, 209, 241
Danto, A. 14, 24, 91, 106, 123, 143, 162, 167, 172, 173, 178, 241
Darnton, R. 54, 67, 241
dasein 57
Davidson, D. 12, 17, 91, 125, 129, 201, 202, 206, 219, 241
Davies, R.H.C. 239
Davies, T. 151, 241
Davis, N.Z. 66, 167, 182, 183, 233, 241
Dawson, C. 245
Dean, M. 111, 242
death of the author 26–7, 29
de Certeau, M. 28, 30, 76–7, 94, 133, 135, 241
deconstructionist history 6, 8, 10, 12, 13, 15, 16, 17, 19, 28, 45, 49, 50, 60, 66, **69–74**, 82, 86, 102, 104, 105, 114, 119, 137, 158–9, 165, 166, 176, 179, 184, 188, 194, 201, 204, 207, 230, 232
deductive-nomological 21, 59, 120
Degler, C.N. 233, 242
Deleuze, G. 110, 111, 242
de Man, P. 103, 179, 183, 242
demography 210
Derrida, Jacques 10, 11, 14, 24, 30, 57, 61, 69, 70, 72, 73, **74–5**, 94, 142, 151, 161, 162, 165, 172, 173, 176, 178, 184, 190, 199, 200, 202, 210, 228, 229, 231, 242
Descartes, R. 24, 37, 84, 145, 149, 155, 157, 207, 221
Dewey, John 12, 45, 202
diachronic, the 108, 206; *see also* the synchronic
dialectic, the 114–16
Dictionary of Philosophy of Mind 242
Diderot, D. 84
difference 72, 87, 124, 128, 229
Dilthey, W. 57, 130, 133, 223
discourse 2, 9, 11, 13, 15, 17, 18, 20, 28, 31, 37, 42, 44, 54, 56, 58, 70, **75–7**, 86, 100, 107, 109, 110, 122, 126, 134, 152, 161, 163, 167, 171, 177, 182, 183, 185, 190, 193, 202–3, 208, 214, 225, 227–9, 232
Docker, J. 129, 173
Domanska, E. 190, 197, 215, 242
Donagan, A. 38, 43, 49, 59, 60, 95, 213, 242
Dosse, F. 210, 242
Dowe, P. 43, 82, 95, 242
Doyle, W. 239
Dray, W.H. 38, 43, 49, 59, 60, 121, 123, 143, 172, 173, 243
Dreyfus, H.L. 30, 111, 243
Du Bois, W.E.B. 203
Duby, G. 167, 243
Duchamp, M. 166
Dumézil, G. 107
Dummett, D. 12, 213, 219, 243
Duran, J. 233, 243

Eagleton, T. 73, 243
economic history ix, 210
Elkins, S. 126
Ellis, J.M. 73, 75, 243
Elton, Geoffrey 6, 59, 63, **79–80**, 82, 98, 100, 127, 184, 185, 186, 195–7, 243–4
empathy 48, 65, 80, 121, 130, 221–2
empiricism x, 1, 4–8, 10–12, 14, 15, 17, 18, 19, 21–5, 28, 29, 31, 36–9, 42, 45, 46–7, 48, 49, 50, 52, 53–4, 56, 58–9, 61, 64, 65, 71, 75, 76, 79–80, **80–2**, 86, 88, 92–5, 97–100, 101–2, 104, 105, 109, 113–15, 117, 119, 126, 131, 132, 135, 138–40, 142, 146, 148, 151, 152, 156, 157, 158, 162, 164–6, 169, 175–7, 179–83, 184–5, 187, 189, 194–7, 198–201, 202, 203, 207–9, 210, 211–13, 216, 217, 219, 222–4, 225–6, 229–32
emplotment 17, 18, 20, 28, 41, 50, 55, 58, 77, **82–4**, 86, 91, 94, 99, 101, 103, 104, 106, 114, 122, 125–9, 134, 143, 147–8, 151, 165, 169, 171–3, 175, 178, 182, 189, 212, 214, 218, 225–6; *see also* comedy; romance; satire; tragedy; **White, Hayden**
Encyclopaedia Britannica 1
Enlightenment, the ix, 1, 2, 21, 24, 26, 47, 56, 61, 64, 69, 73, 75, **84–5**, 88, 94, 107–8, 113, 115, 117, 135, 140, 145, 147, 149, 155, 157, 158, 163, 173, 174, 188–9, 194, 204, 207, 217, 221, 223, 229
episteme 16, 17, 18, 19, 20, 42, 50, 84, **86–7**, 104, 108–110, 114, 126, 128, 131, 152, 163, 171, 182, 204, 210, 214, 222
epistemology x, 3–6, 9, 11, 12, 14–17, 20, 21, 24, 26, 32, 35, 37, 41, 43–4, 47, 50, **53–5**, 58, 60, 61, 64, 67, 72–3, 75, 80, 81, 85, 86, **88–9**, 91, 92–5, 98–100, 100, 102, 107–11, 113–15, 117–18, 119, 122, 131–2, 134, 137–40, 142, 146, 151–2, 155, 156, 158, 160, 162, 163, 165, 167, 170, 175–6, 180, 185–6, 187, 189–90, 193–4, 195–7, 198–201, 201, 207–8, 210, 217–18, 225, 227–33
Ermarth, E.D. 89, 156, 167, 182, 184, 190, 233, 244
ethics 12, 13, 14, 15, 19, 23, 26, 40, 42, 58, 77, 91, 145, 147, 167, 176
Evans, R.J. 7, 184, 186, 196, 197, 219, 244
event 3–5, 8, 17, 26, 29, 36, 37–43, 44, 46, 48, 50, 58–60, 61–2, 76, 77, 80, 83, 84, 88, **89–91**, 92–5, 97–100, 103, 119, 121, 124, 130, 134, 137, 141, 156, 169, 179, 187, 189–90, 193, 197, 202, 210, 211, 212, 216, 218, 221
evidence x, 1–7, 9, 10, 11, 12, 14, 18, 19–20, 21, 23, 24, 26, 27, 36, 40, 44, 48, 49, 51–4, 56, 58, 59, 62, 66, 71, 76–7, 79–80, 81, 82, 87, 88, 91, **92–5**, 97–100, 102,

104, 109, 110, 117, 121, 122, 127, 130, 137–40, 141, 142, 143, 146, 152, 157, 164, 166, 169, 171, 177, 179, 181, 183, 184–6, 187–8, 193, 195–8, 201, 204, 207, 211, 215–18, 223, 224, 225–6, 231; *see also* comparison; sources; verification

explanandum 59, 119–20; *see also* **covering laws; historical explanation**

explanans 59, 119–20; *see also* **covering laws; historical explanation**

Fackenheim, E. 148, 244

facts 2–3, 12, 16, 18, 20, 25, 29, 31, 35, 36, 38–40, 46, 47, 48, 56, 58–60, 61, 75, 76, 77, 83, 88, 92–5, **97–100**, 101, 103, 114, 116, 118, 122–3, 134, 140, 143, 151, 156, 165, 169, 174–7, 179–83, 185–6, 187, 189–90, 193, 194–7, 198, 202–3, 208, 210, 217, 218, 224, 226, 230, 232

fantasia 222

Farnham, C. 233, 247

Fay, B. 55, 153, 227, 244

Febvre, L. 209–10

feminism 15, 50, 70, 80, 82, 104, 227

feminist epistemology 88, 228–33

Ferguson, A. 1–4, 14, 20, 244

fiction/fictive 2, 8, 14, 29, 31, 39, 56, 58, 76, 80, 92, 101, 103, 111, 128, 132, 140, 161, 164, 167, 174, 183, 190, 196, 200, 218, 226, 229, 231

Finney, P. 201, 244

first cause 62

Fiumara, G.C. 129, 244

Fogel, W. 79

footnotes 25

form and content 1, 8, 9, 10, 12, 14, 15, 20, 26, 31, 41, 43, 49, 50, 58, 60, 61, 64, 71, 73, 75, 76, 81, 82, 85, 89, 93–4, **100–6**, 109, 115, 117, 119, 125–9, 132, 133, 140, 146–8, 150, 152, 157–8, 163–7, 170, 172, 175, 177, 182, 185, 188–9, 196, 204, 207, 212, 218, 226, 229

formist 226; *see also* argument; mechanist; organicist; contextualist; **White, Hayden**

Forum 87, 184, 188, 244

Fosse, P. 237

Foucault, Michel 10, 11, 16, 17, 18, 26, 32, 42, 57, 66, 69, 70, 72, 73, 77, 86, 89, 100, 103, 105, **107–11**, 114, 126, 152, 156, 163, 165, 171–3, 175, 182, 184, 202, 209, 214, 223, 225, 229, 244–5; *see also* archaeology; genealogy

foundational(ist) thinking 6, 22, 45, 54, 56, 58, 69, 71–2, 95, 97, 105, 122, 139, 145, 155, 200, 202, 206, 230, 232

Frankfurt School 57

Friedlander, S. 91, 173, 245

Frye, N. 82, 84, 225, 245

Fukuyama, F. 211, 213, 245

Gadamer, H.G. 57, 61, 70, 117–18, 184, 202, 245

Gallie, W.B. 18, 41, 84, 119, 123, 170–3, 181, 184, 245

Gardenfors, P. 52, 245

Gardiner, J. 245

Gardiner, P. 38, 42, 43, 49, 59, 62, 63, 123, 188, 213, 245

Gasché, R. 75, 245

Gay, P. 86, 101, 106, 170, 171, 173, 245

Geertz, C. 54, 55, 66, 67, 245

gender 9, 11, 13, 15, 19, 22, 40, 50, 53, 56, 64, 65, 93, 103, 104, 162, 185, 187, 199, 227–33

genealogy 107–8, 111; *see also* archaeology; **Foucault, Michel**; **Nietzsche, Friedrich**

Genovese, E. 54

Gibbon, E. 170

Giddens, A. 54, 55, 209, 245

Ginzburg, C. 67, 167, 245

Goldstein, J. 245

Goldstein, L. 55, 245

Goodman, J. 67, 245

Graham, G. 123, 246

Gramsci, A. 44

Great Man theory of history 113

Green, W.A. 246

Greene, J.P. 239

Grossmann, R. 186, 246

Guattari, F. 110, 111, 242

Gumbrecht, H.U. 167, 246

Gutman, H. 54

Gutting, G. 111, 246

Guyer, P. 148, 246

Habermas, J. 57, 118, 163, 167, 202, 246

Hackett-Fisher, D. 246

Haddock, B.A. 224, 246

Hall, C. 231, 232, 246

Hamilton, P. 133, 246

Hansen, P.H. 246

Hanson, N.R. 141, 246

Haraway, D. 233, 246

Harlan, D. 102, 106, 153, 197, 246

Harlow, B. 242

Harris, J.F. 201, 246

Harvey, D. 191, 247

Hassing, R.F. 213, 246

Hawkes, T. 209, 246

Hegel, G.W.F. 10–11, 56, 57, 61, 63, **113–16**, 122, 145, 149, 155, 159, 199, 211, 217, 221, 222, 247; *see also* the Absolute Spirit

Heidegger, M. 11, 12, 57, 61, 70, 74, 117–18, 184, 202, 247

Heise, U.K. 173, 191, 247

Hempel, C. 38, 43, 58–9, 60, 119–20, 123, 188, 247

Herder, J. 222

hermeneutics 10, 13, 47, 55, 57, 59, 69, 72, 98, **116–18**, 132, 152, 155, 164, 181, 184, 197, 202, 209, 221

Hesse, M. 129, 247

Hexter, J. 6, 59, 184, 186, 198, 247

Higgins, K.M. 178, 250

Hill, C. 54
Himmelfarb, G. 6, 59, 184, 186, 247
Hirsch, E.D. 118, 247
historical agent(s) 48, 121, 143, 149, 183, 210, 211–13
historical explanation 3–5, 10, 25, 27, 38, 46, 54, 58, 59, 81, 82, 98, 102, 115, **118–24**, 133, 139, 141, 151, 169–74, 195–8, 212; *see also* **causation**; **covering laws**; *explanandum*; *explanans*; **narrative**
historical imagination 17, 23, 26, 41, 47, 49, 50, 53, 61–2, 91, 93–4, 103, 105, 118, 119, 122, **124–30**, 133, 139, 176, 190, 203, 207, 214, 215, 218, 222, 224, 225–6
historical materialism 8, 40; *see also* Marxist history
historicism 13, 16, 19, 43, 48, 50, 61, 98, 106, 109, 115, 119, **130–3**, 152, 186, 199, 203, 221
historiography 2, 5, 26, 44, 60, 76–7, **133–5**, 165, 200, 210, 232
Hobbes, T. 84
Hobsbawm, E. J. 54, 247
Hoffer, P.C. 95, 247
Hoff-Wilson, J. 231, 247
Hollinger, D.A. 153, 191, 197, 198, 247
Holocaust, the 12, 13, 16, 165, 198
Horkheimer, M. 57
Horwich, P. 219, 247
Howard, R. 236, 237
Huizinga, J. 65–7
Hume, D. 2, 38, 39, 70, 81, 145, 157
Hunt, L. 6, 7, 9, 66, 67, 82, 89, 134, 160, 165, 167, 180, 181, 197, 198, 199, 216, 218, 219, 236, 247
Hurley, R. 242
Husserl, E. 57, 74, 107
Hutcheon, L. 29, 30, 191, 247
hyperbole 213
hypothesis-testing 4, 22, 42, 81–2, 92, 93, 97, 98, 119, 121, 138, 161, 187, 223
hypothetico-deductive 119

idealism 48–9
ideology 8, 11, 18, 19, 20, 27, 28, 31, 40, 41, 42, 44, 50, 54, 55, 57, 58, 80, 83, 98, 100, 102–4, 109, 111, 122, 123, 125, 140, 147, 150, 152, 161, 173, 175–7, 186, 194, 198, 209, 225, 228–9, 232
ideological implication 212; *see also* anarchist; conservative; liberalism; radical; **White, Hayden**
Iggers, G. 7, 135, 153, 181, 184, 194, 248
inference 1, 3, 4–5, 6, 15, 18, 19, 20, 21–3, 24, 25, 26, 28, 36, 37, 39, 44–5, 46–7, 51, 53, 56, 58–60, 62, 76, 79–80, 88–9, 92–5, 98–100, 101, 105, 109, 117, 119–23, 124–9, **137–41**, 160, 164–5, 170, 179, 181, 185–6, 187, 189–90, 195–8, 199, 203, 208, 209, 215, 216, 221, 223, 225, 232; *see also* abduction (abductive)
intentionality 2, 4, 5, 6, 10, 19, 22, 38, 40, 41, 46, 47, 48, 49, 59–60, 74–5, 76, 79, 88, 93, 98, 105, 118, 121, **141–3**, 150–1, 152, 164, 172, 177, 183, 195, 199, 201, 211–12, 225, 230; *see also* action (theory)
interpellation 28
intertextuality 25, 89, 128, 132, 182, 210
Irigaray, L. 230, 233, 248
irony 203–4, 214, 225; *see also* metaphor; metonymy; synecdoche; **trope/figuration**; **White, Hayden**

Jacob, M. 7, 82, 134, 160, 165, 167, 180, 181, 197, 199, 216, 218, 219, 236
Jakobson, R. 225
Jameson, F. 91, 201, 227, 248
Jenkins, K. 9, 14, 35, 36, 37, 49, 69, 73, 80, 82, 89, 102, 104, 106, 123, 133, 134, 135, 153, 156, 167, 172, 173, 184, 189, 191, 198, 199, 200, 215, 219, 227, 248
Johnson, M. 129, 248
Jones, C. 37, 248
Jones, G.S. 44, 45, 46, 258
Josephson, J.R. 141, 248
Josephson, S.G. 141, 248
Joyce, J. 222
Joyce, P. 44, 45, 50, 52, 153, 248

Kammen, M. 241, 248
Kansteiner, W. 215, 227, 248
Kant, Immanuel 4–5, 10–11, 21–2, 24, 46, 50, 56, 61, 62, 70–2, 75, 82, 84, 100, 115, 122, 127, **145–8**, 149, 157–8, 160, 163, 174, 175, 177, 186, 217, 248
Kaplan, S.L. 55, 106, 249
Kaye, H.J. 45, 249
Kearney R. 58, 73, 249
Keenan, T. 87, 111, 237
Kellner, H. 106, 153, 156, 172, 173, 198, 215, 235, 249
Kemp Smith, N. 249
Kenyon, J. 80, 249
Kerber, L. 233, 249
Kiernan, V.G. 45, 249
Kirk, N. 7, 46, 190, 237, 249
Kirkham, R. 219, 249
Klein, K. 173, 191, 249
Kloppenberg, J.T. 249
Klossowski, P. 107
Knight, Alan 36, 249
knower and known 15, 23, 56, 57, 117, 160, 189, 198
Knox, T.M. 116, 249
Kolakowski, L. 188, 249
Kozicki, H. 173, 239, 249, 251
Kramnick, I. 86, 249
Krausz, M. 201, 249
Kristeva, J. 102

LaCapra, D. 55, 66, 102, 106, 153, 249
Le Roy Ladurie, E. 210
laminated text 77
Lamont, W. 249
Lane, H. 242
Langlois, C.V. 97

langue 208
Laslett, B. 233, 250
Lavers, A. 237
Lawrence, F. 246
Lechte, J. 58, 191, 210, 250
Le Doeuff, M. 233, 250
Leibnitz, G.W. 145, 157
Lemon, M. 106, 172, 173, 215, 250
Lessing, G.H. 84
Lévi-Strauss, C. 209
liberal 226; *see also* anarchist; conservative; ideological implication; radical; **White, Hayden**
liberal humanism/ist 2, 4, 5, 6, 7, 9, 19, 24, 27, 28, 84, 107, 110, 142, **149–51**, 164, 207, 210, 229
liberal ironist 203
liberalism 84–5, 155, 189, 203, 211–2
Lincoln, A. 39, 89, 141–2
linguistic turn ix–x, 8, 54, 60, 65, 69, 93, 99, 132, 133, 142, **151–3**, 162, 165, 174, 179, 185, 188, 195, 203, 218
Lipton, P. 173, 250
litotes 214
Lloyd, C. 42, 43, 188, 209, 210, 250
Lloyd, G. 233, 250
Lloyd, H.D. 22
Locke, J. 23, 84, 157
long durée 210
Longino, H.E. 233, 250
Lorenz, C. 59, 60, 153, 184, 188, 194, 198, 250
Loux, M.J. 162, 250
Luntley, M. 191, 219, 250
Lyotard, J.-F. 57, 155, 156, 188, 191, 250

McCarthy, T. 58, 237
Machamer, P. 239, 245
McCullagh, C.B. 7, 40, 43, 46, 47, 59, 90, 91, 95, 97–8, 100, 104, 106, 123, 125–7, 129, 137, 141, 172, 173, 179, 180, 182, 184, 198, 219, 250
McLennan, G. 215, 250
Magnus, B. 178, 250
Mandelbaum, M. 91, 95, 123, 250
Marable, M. 46, 250
Margolin, J.C. 151, 250
Marshall, B.K. 25, 30, 191, 251
Marwick, A. 6, 59, 63, 152, 153, 184, 186, 191, 251
Marx, K. 44, 54, 61, 85, 107, 199, 211–12, 214, 222
Marxist history 7, 8, 54, 54, 61, 73, 85, 99, 104, 131, 155, 173, 189, 211–12, 214, 222; *see also* historical materialism
Maza, S. 67, 173, 181, 182, 184, 251
Mazzota, G. 224, 251
meaning in history 6, 7, 9, 10, 18, 24, 26, 27, 40, 56, 64, 72, 75, 92–5, 104, 108, 110, 117, 122, 132, 140, 166, 208, 210, 216
mechanist 226; *see also* argument; contextualist; formist; organicist; **White, Hayden**
Medin, D.L. 53, 257
Megill, A. 73, 75, 102, 111, 178, 251
Meinecke, F. 130, 133, 251
Meluish, K.J. 151, 238
Mensch, J.R. 11, 14, 86, 186, 191, 251
mentalités 209
Merleau-Ponty, M. 107
Merquior, J.M. 251
'Metahistory: Six critiques' 226, 235
metanarrative 14, 85, 135, 147, **155–6**, 177, 188
metaphor 18, 23, 36, 61, 72–3, 77, 83, 87, 93, 104, 119, 123, 124–9, 167, 176–7, 203, 214, 217, 218, 222–3, 225–6; *see also* irony; metonymy; synecdoche; **trope/figuration**; **White, Hayden**
metaphysics 3–4, 12, 15, 19, 22, 37, 42, 53, 61, 63, 69, 75, 90, 107, 116, 119, 140, 145, **156–62**, 164, 184, 194, 198, 202, 212
metonymy 124–5, 128–9, 177, 214, 222, 225–6; *see also* irony; metaphor; synecdoche; **trope/figuration**; **White, Hayden**
Michelet, J. 222
Mill, J.S. 23
Mills, S. 75, 251
mimesis 216, 218
Mink, L. 14, 49, 84, 106, 153, 172, 173, 181, 184, 198, 251
Modern/Anthropological episteme 86–7
modernism x, 1, 3, 6–8, 11, 13, 15, 18, 19, 23, 24, 42, 50, 54, 64–5, 77, 79, 84–5, 91, 94, 105, 107, 117, 135, 137, 145, 149, 150, 157, 161, **163–7**, 174, 188, 195, 204, 207–8, 213, 217, 221–2, 229
modernist history 1, 4, 5, 15, 27, 29, 57, 109; *see also* proper history
Moi, T. 230, 232, 251
Momigliano, A. 135, 251
Mooney, M. 224, 251
Moser, P.K. 24, 251
Moss, M.E. 63, 251
Mouffe, C. 238, 252
Müller-Vollmer, K. 118, 252
Munslow, A. 6, 8, 17, 43, 55, 67, 74, 77, 84, 87, 100, 106, 110, 111, 130, 153, 173, 184, 191, 198, 215, 224, 227, 252
Munz, P. 172, 173, 252
Murphey, M.G. 60, 252

Nagel, E. 59, 60, 213, 252
narrative x, 1, 3, 8, 9, 11, 13, 14, 15, 16, 17, 18, 23, 26, 29, 31–2, 36, 39, 40–1, 45, 46, 49, 50, 54, 55, 58, 62, 70, 72–3, 75, 76–7, 82–4, 87, 89, 90, 93, 99–100, 101–2, 104, 105, 109, 117, 119, 121, 122–3, 124–9, 130, 135, 140, 147, 151–3, 155–6, 158–60, 162, 163, **169–74**, 175–6, 179–82, 193, 196, 198, 202–4, 207, 210–12, 214, 218, 222–24, 225–6; *see also* **historical explanation**
nationalism 22, 50, 53, 65, 85, 12
Nehamas, A. 178, 252
Neisser, U. 53, 252

Nelson, L.H. 82, 233, 252
NeSmith, G. 233, 252
New Cultural History 9
New Historicism 132–3
Nietzsche, Friedrich 10, 11, 14, 17, 22, 37, 39, 56, 57, 61, 70–2, 74, 85, 100, 104, 107–8, 110–11, 115, 149, 159, 161, 164, **174–8**, 199, 200, 202, 213, 217, 218, 221, 222, 223; *see also* genealogy
Noiriel, G. 87, 111, 252
Norman, A.P. 106, 156, 172, 173, 198, 252
Norris, C. 74, 75, 177, 178, 191, 202, 207, 252
Novick, P. 184, 188, 197, 252
Nye, A. 253

Oakeshott, M. 63, 91, 123, 253
objectivity x, 2–3, 5, 6, 8, 13, 15, 19, 21, 24, 25, 26, 29–30, 32, 37, 39, 40, 46, 47, 48, 52, 60, 65, 72, 75, 76–7, 79, 81, 88–9, 92, 95, 97–100, 105, 109, 111, 114, 117, 119, 122–3, 138, 142, 146–7, 151, 155, 156, 159, 160, 164, 169, 171, 177, **179–84**, 188–9, 194, 195–6, 198, 201, 213, 216, 224, 229, 230
O'Brien, G.D. 116, 251
O'Brien, K. 86, 148, 253
observer and observed 2, 56, 89, 94, 189, 195, 218
Offen, K. 233, 238, 253–4
Olafson, F.A. 143, 253
ontology 3, 5, 6, 9, 10, 11, 12, 15, 16, 19, 20, 25, 40, 43–4, 49–52, 56, 64, 81, 85, 86, 89, 90–1, 94, 98, 100, 110, 117–18, 119, 134, 142, 152, 156–8, 160, 163, 166, 167, 177, 180–1, 183, **184–6**, 188–90, 195, 225–6, 229
organicist 226; *see also* argument; contextualist; formist; mechanist; **White, Hayden**
other, the 2, 15, 77, 111, 116, 228, 231

Palmer, R.E. 118, 253
parole 206
past-as-history, the 2, 4, 9, 11, 12, 13, 14, 17–20, 24, 26–9, 43, 50, 60, 61–2, 102, 109–11, 113, 116, 118, 119, 121, 131, 132, 140, 147, 152, 162, 173, 180, 185, 189–90, 200, 223
Patton, P. 237
Payne, M. 33, 253
Peacocke, C. 53, 253
Pecheux, M. 77, 253
Peirce, C.S. 45, 139, 141, 253
perception 10, 20, 23, 38, 56, 62, 71, 74, 111, 145, 189, 195, 214
performance 24, 32, 76
periphrasis 214
Perrot, M. 233, 253
perspectivism 11, 70–3, 174–8, 180, 186, 201
phenomenology 56–7, 107, 117–18
phonocentrism 74
Pickering, M. 118, 253
Pierson, R.R. 233, 238, 253, 254
Pittock, J.H. 67, 253
pointing 166
politics 51
Pompa, L. 224, 253
Pomper, P. 55, 153, 227, 244
Poovey, M. 167, 182, 184, 233, 253–4
Popper, K. 59, 60, 116, 119, 123, 131, 132, 133, 184, 253
Porter, R. 30, 254
positivism ix, 1, 4, 5, 38, 47, 50, 59, 61, 84, 88, 90, 98, 99, 113, 119–20, 131, 159, 161, 165, 177, 185, **187–8**, 189, 195, 207, 209, 210, 225
post-empiricism ix–xi, 7, 9, 10, 12, 13, 14, 15, 16, 17, 18, 19, 29, 37, 50, 52, 53–4, 65, 87, 88, 99, 104, 133, 152, 155, 159, 162, 165, 231, 232
post-epistemology 202–4
Poster, M. 8, 67, 111, 191, 198, 254
postmodern history 29, 56–8, 111, 164–7, 189, 204, 227
postmodernism x, 1, 6, 9–20, 25, 28, 29, 35, 36, 47, 50, 54, 57–8, 65–6, 70, 85, 86, 93, 98, 102, 107, 111, 113, 115, 122, 139, 155–6, 158, 161, 164, 166, 171, 176, **188–91**, 195, 197, 198–201, 201–4, 207, 216, 218, 223, 227, 233
post-structuralism 9, 11, 13, 57, 140, 165, 195, 202, 209, 227, 229–31
Potter, E. 232, 235
Powderly, T.V. 139–40
practical realism/practical realist historians 6, 29, 53, 54, 88, 104, 121, 160, 180, 181, 185, 196–7, 208, 216, 230
presence 2, 10, 75, 161–2
Priest, S. 24, 82, 254
proper history 1, 4, 5, 6, 7, 19, 72, 188, 228; *see also* modernist history
proposition 21–2, 51, 56, 88, 117, 119, 138, 140, 151, 157, 201, 215–16, 230
Putnam, H. 24, 74, 156, 162, 194, 201, 219, 254

Quine, W.V. 12, 24, 45, 91, 201, 202, 207, 219, 254

Rabinow, P. 30, 111, 178, 219, 243, 254
race 11, 20, 22, 40, 50, 53, 56, 64, 65, 93, 162, 187, 230
radical 226; *see also* anarchist; conservative; ideological implication; liberalism; **White, Hayden**
Rainwater, M. 58, 73
Ranke, L. von 64, 97, 98, 100, 170, 195, 254
Rasmussen, D. 237
realist history 1–9, 14, 40, 44, 56, 58, 61–3, 69–73, 75, 105, 163, 204; *see also* **reality/realistic effect**
reality/realistic effect 14, 25, 31–2, 52, 56, 62, 77, 94, 100, 124, 140, 142, 150, 152, 171, 182, 186, 189, **193–4**, 200, 226; *see also* realist history
reconstructionist history 6–8, 12, 16, 22,

36, 39, 41, 43, 49, 50, 52, 53–4, 59, 63, 73, 79–80, 81, 85–6, 87, 92–5, 100–2, 113, 117, 119, 121, 130, 137, 151, 152, 158–62, 165, 170–1, 176–7, 179, 184, 193, **194–8**, 200, 204, 205, 207, 209, 211, 223, 225, 232
Reedy, W.J. 101, 106, 254
referentiality 4–7, 10, 14, 15, 16, 19, 20, 25, 26, 32, 36, 51, 56, 60, 62, 70, 75, 79–80, 83, 92–5, 98–100, 105, 110, 117, 119, 123, 128, 132, 138–40, 160–2, 175–6, 180, 183, 186, 188, 193, 194–7, 198–201, 208, 216–18, 224
Reform Bill, the (of 1832) 44
Reiss, H. 148, 249, 253, 254
relativism 3, 11, 13, 16, 36, 50, 62, 63, 65, 71, 76–7, 79, 81, 90, 101, 106, 110, 117, 131, 133, 145, 151, 152, 158–62, 165, 174, 180–1, 188, 195–7, **198–201**, 202–4, 216, 218, 223,
Renaissance, the 65, 86, 149
Rendall, J. 233, 238, 253, 254
representation x, 1–5, 7, 8, 9, 10, 12, 13, 18, 19, 20, 25, 26, 32, 36, 42, 44–5, 51, 55, 56, 57, 61, 62, 64, 66, 69–73, 74, 76, 80, 81, 82, 87, 89, 91, 97–100, 103, 105–6, 107, 111, 122, 127, 133, 140, 141, 143, 150–1, 155, 158, 161–2, 163–4, 166, 169, 171, 176–7, 186, 188, 190, 198–201, 202–4, 208, 209, 210, 215–18, 224, 229, 232
rhetoric 7, 13, 15, 31, 36, 54–5, 123, 125, 132, 170, 182, 193, 217
Richmond, C. 197
Rickman, H.P. 242
Ricoeur, P. 57, 70, 74, 102, 118, 125, 126, 127, 130, 172, 173, 194, 255
Riley, D. 233, 255
Robbe-Grillet, A. 166
Roberts, C. 38, 43, 47, 59, 60, 123, 212–13, 255
Roberts, D.D. 10, 14, 58, 63, 72, 74, 116, 151, 162, 188, 255
Roberts, G. 80, 143, 172, 173, 181, 184, 191, 198, 255
Rockmore, T. 151, 255
romance 83, 226; *see also* comedy; **emplotment**; satire; tragedy; **White, Hayden**
Rorty, Richard 8, 12, 13, 16, 17, 32, 45, 60, 61, 70, 104, 125, 130, 131–2, 133, 141, 151, 153, 155, 184, 199, 200, 201, **201–5**, 218, 219, 255; *see also* anti-representationalism
Rosenstone, R.A. 106, 167, 182, 184, 189, 191, 256
Ross, D. 172, 173, 256
Rostow, W.W. 54
Roth, M.S. 227, 256
Roth, P.A. 215, 227, 256
Rothenburg, P.S. 45, 233, 256
Rowbotham, S. 231, 254
Ruben, D.-H. 123, 256
Russell, B. 202

Sachs, S. 130, 256
Sahlins, M. 54, 55, 194, 256
Sallis, J. 75, 256
Sartre, J.-P. 57, 107, 151, 256
satire 83, 226; *see also* comedy; **emplotment**; romance; tragedy; **White, Hayden**
Saussure, F. de 70, 72, 202, 208–9, 210, 214, 229, 256
Schama, S. 167, 256
Schmitt, F. 233, 256
Schorske, C.E. 51, 53, 103, 106, 257
scissors-and-paste history 48, 53
Scott, J.W. 55, 89, 102, 106, 156, 197, 198, 227–8, 231, 232, 233, 257
Searle, J.R. 53, 100, 143, 194, 257
Seem, M. 242
Seignobos, C. 97
self-reflexive 23, 48, 57–8, 72, 163, 164–7, 188–9, 221
Sellars, W. 12, 45, 82, 184, 201, 207, 257
Selous, T. 250
semiotics 31, 36
Sheridan, A. 257
Shoemaker, R. 234, 257
sign 72, 74, 125, 177, 208, 228
signified 2, 10, 72, 74, 165, 208–10
signifier 2, 10, 12, 32, 72, 74, 125, 141, 165, 177, 194, 208–10
simile 214
Simon, S. 238, 244
simulacrum 200–1
Smith, C. 237
Smith, E.E. 53, 257
Smith, P. 30, 257
Smith-Rosenberg, C. 234, 257
Snooks, G.D. 7, 60, 123, 188, 210, 257
Sobchack, V. 91, 256, 257
social history ix, 65
social science ix, 42, 65, 196, 210
sociology 9, 15, 51, 57, 65, 75, 103
Sontag, S. 33, 257
Sosa, E. 95, 257
sources 7, 66, 92–5, 124, 137, 183; *see also* comparison; **evidence**; verification
Southgate, B. 191, 258
speech 74
Spiegel, G. 257
Spinoza, B. 157
Spivak, G.C. 242
stage theory of history 61, 86, 114, 187, 200, 222–3
Stanford, M. 35, 59, 60, 76, 95, 100, 116, 135, 188, 191, 215, 219, 257–8
statistical-inductive 122
Stevenson, C.L. 100, 258
Still, J. 133
Stone, L. 54, 55, 173, 258
Strawson, P. 124, 130, 258
Stromberg, R.N. 58, 258
Struckmeyer, O.K. 64, 258
Stueck, W.W. 95, 247

Sturrock, J. 75, 210, 258
structuralism 7, 24, 27, 31, 72, 75, 87, 107, 119, 131, 161, 184, **207–10**, 214, 225, 227
subject, the 2–4, 5, 6, 9, 10, 11, 12, 19, 24, 27, 28, 84, 108–9, 145, 148, 149–51, 156, 160–2, 175–6, 188, 200, 202, 210, 229
subject and object 6, 11, 25, 26, 74, 114, 117, 119, 122, 160, 162, 164, 195, 203, 229
sublime, the 14, 173, 182, 218, 232
synchronic, the 108, 206; *see also* the diachronic
synecdoche 124–5, 128–9, 214, 222, 225; *see also* irony; metaphor; metonymy; **trope/figuration**; **White, Hayden**

Tagliacozzo, G. 224, 258
Tallis, R. 194, 210, 258
Taylor, B. 100, 258
teleology 5, 11, 18–19, 39–40, 46, 48, 51, 58, 60, 84, 94, 101, 110, 114, 115, 117, 125, 131, 135, 140, 141, 148, 166, 176, 188, **211–13**, 225
textuality 7–8, 11, 13, 16, 18, 20, 25, 40, 43, 50, 73, 161
Thomas, K. 67, 258
Thompson, E.P. 7, 44, 54, 66, 258
Thompson, J.B. 118, 259
Toews, J.E. 153, 172, 173, 258
Topolski, J. 82, 123, 198, 258
Tosh, J. 7, 35, 41, 43, 95, 100, 188, 259
tragedy 83, 115, 147, 175, 226; *see also* comedy; **emplotment**; romance; satire; **White, Hayden**
transcendental idealism 115, 145–8, 158
transcendental signified/er 11, 24, 29, 57, 72, 74–5
trompe l'œil 193
trope/figuration 14, 16, 17, 18, 20, 23, 26, 28, 36, 41, 55, 72, 74, 82, 83, 86–7, 91, 93, 101, 103–5, 116, 119, 123, 124–9, 143, 151–3, 158, 171, 176, 182, 189, 194, 203, 213, **214–15**, 217–18, 222–23, 225–6; *see also* irony; metaphor; metonymy; synecdoche; **White, Hayden**
truth x, 2–5, 7, 8, 9, 10, 12, 13, 15, 16, 18, 20, 21–4, 25, 27, 32, 36, 37, 39, 45, 46, 50, 51, 53, 56–8, 60, 62–3, 65, 70–3, 74–5, 76–7, 79–80, 83, 88–9, 90–1, 92–5, 97–100, 101, 103, 105, 109, 111, 113, 115, 117, 119, 120, 123, 125–9, 130, 132, 134, 137–40, 141, 146, 150, 151, 155, 157, 158, 159–61, 164, 169, 171, 174–7, 179–83, 184–5, 189–90, 193, 194–7, 198–201, 201–4, 207–9, **215–19**, 221, 222, 226, 229–32
Turner, F.J. 128–9, 130, 150–1, 203, 259

Unmoved Mover, the 157
van der Dussen, J. 240
Van Noppen, J.P. 259
Vann, R.T. 55, 84, 153, 227, 244
Veeser, A.A. 133, 259
Verene, D.P. 222, 258
verification 1, 51, 99, 127, 137, 140, 183, 201, 217; *see also* comparison; **evidence**; sources
verstehen 48
Veyne, P. 89, 172, 173, 182, 184, 157
Vico, Giambattista 7, 17, 47, 61, 86, 115, 157, 190, 211, 214, 215, **221–4**, 225,
Vincent, M. 234, 257
Voltaire 84
von Wright, G.H. 59, 60, 123, 259

Walkowitz, J. 182, 184, 259
Wallerstein, I. 209
Walsh, W.H. 46, 47, 106, 123, 162, 259
Warren, J. 7, 13, 135, 196, 197, 198, 201, 259
Wear, A. 67, 253
Weber, M. 54, 143, 259–10
Weitz, M. 53, 260
Wellek, R. 64, 260
Whewell, W. 46, 47, 259
White, Hayden ix, 8, 13, 14, 16, 17, 18, 20, 33, 41, 42, 43, 47, 55, 60, 61, 66, 67, 69, 70, 73, 77, 82–4, 87, 94, 99, 100, 102–6, 114, 115, 116, 119, 123, 124–9, 130, 142, 143, 148, 151–3, 156, 165, 171–4, 178, 179, 182, 184, 189, 194, 195, 199, 200, 203, 205, 212, 213, 216, 217, 219, 223, 224, **225–7**, 260
Will to Power 174, 176
Williams, C.D. 151, 234, 260
Williams, R. 44, 210, 260
Wilson, G.M. 143, 260
Windschuttle, K. 7, 184, 186, 260
Wiseman, M.B. 33, 261
Witt, C. 233, 235
Wittgenstein, L. 12, 81, 151, 199, 201, 202, 261
Wollstonecraft, M. 229
women's history ix–x, 2, 13, 64, 107, 122, 133, 149, **227–34**
Worton, M. 133, 260
Wykes, S. 239

Young, R. 77, 190, 236, 260
Yovel, Y. 148, 260

Zagorin, P. 7, 13, 59, 60, 82, 89, 104, 106, 174, 191, 261
Zammito, J.H. 82, 191, 261